MW01039486

*The publisher gratefully acknowledges the generous support of the Jewish Studies Endowment Fund of the University of California Press Foundation, which was established by a major gift from the S. Mark Taper Foundation.*

The Invention of Judaism

THE TAUBMAN LECTURES IN JEWISH STUDIES

Daniel Boyarin, Series Editor

The Taubman Professorship and Lectures

The Herman P. and Sophia Taubman Visiting Professorship in
Jewish Studies was established at the University of California,
Berkeley, in 1975 by grants from Milton I. Taubman and the
Taubman Foundation; an equal sum was contributed by the
family of Maurice Amado, Walter A. Haas, Daniel E. Koshland,
Madeleine Haas Russell, and Benjamin H. Swig. Distinguished
scholars in the fields of Jewish studies are invited to teach at
Berkeley for the enrichment of students and to give open lectures
for the benefit of the public at large. Publication of the lectures is
made possible by a special gift of the Taubman Foundation.

# The Invention of Judaism

*Torah and Jewish Identity from
Deuteronomy to Paul*

John J. Collins

UNIVERSITY OF CALIFORNIA PRESS

University of California Press, one of the most
distinguished university presses in the United States,
enriches lives around the world by advancing scholarship
in the humanities, social sciences, and natural sciences. Its
activities are supported by the UC Press Foundation and
by philanthropic contributions from individuals and
institutions. For more information, visit www.ucpress.edu.

University of California Press
Oakland, California

Library of Congress Cataloging-in-Publication Data

Names: Collins, John J. (John Joseph), author.
Title: The invention of Judaism : Torah and Jewish
    identity from Deuteronomy to Paul / John J. Collins.
Other titles: Taubman lectures in Jewish studies ; 7.
Description: Oakland, California : University of
    California Press, [2017] | Series: The Taubman
    lectures in Jewish studies ; 7 | Includes bibliographical
    references and index.
Identifiers: LCCN 2016033502 (print) | LCCN 2016034742
    (ebook) | ISBN 9780520294110 (cloth : alk. paper) |
    ISBN 9780520294127 (pbk. : alk. paper) |
    ISBN 9780520967366 ()
Subjects: LCSH: Judaism—History—To 70 A.D. |
    Bible. Old Testament—Criticism, interpretation, etc.
Classification: LCC BM170 .C65 2017 (print) | LCC
    BM170 (ebook) | DDC 296.09/01—dc23
LC record available at https://lccn.loc.gov/2016033502

Manufactured in the United States of America

24  23  22  21  20  19  18  17  16
10  9  8  7  6  5  4  3  2  1

# CONTENTS

# PREFACE

Jewish identity is a controversial issue. Traditionally, anyone born of a Jewish mother is a Jew. Yet the rabbinate in Israel refuses to recognize marriages or conversions performed by conservative or reform rabbis. By some standards, genealogy is not enough. To be Jewish is to keep the Law of Moses, or even to keep it according to a particular interpretation.

The tension underlying these modern disputes is an old one. Judaism is an ethnicity, to which one may belong regardless of belief or religious practice, but it is also a religion, defined by adherence to the Law of Moses. The ethnicity can be traced back to the time of King David or beyond. The normative status of the Law is also ancient, but arose somewhat later. Contrary to popular belief, Judaism, in the sense defined by the Law, did not begin at Mount Sinai. The Torah, or Pentateuch (the five books of Moses), was formed over centuries, in a process that is still a matter of intense debate. Most scholars agree that it took its final shape either during or after the Babylonian exile, in the sixth century B.C.E. It was not immediately accepted as normative by everyone. This book is an attempt to trace the reception of the Torah in its first six hundred years or so, from the Babylonian exile to the end of the Second Temple period.

The discussion of this topic here is by no means exhaustive, but has rather the nature of a series of probes. Some significant corpora, such as the Deuteronomistic History and Chronicles are passed over, as are some related and relevant issues, such as the Samaritan adoption of the Torah. The revision of Jewish identity entailed by the development of early Christianity is represented only by the case of Saint Paul. The inquiry stops short of the rise of rabbinic Judaism. Nonetheless, I hope to have outlined the main contours of the history of the Torah in this period. These include the initial formulation of a way of life in the form of a law, in Deuteronomy; the official status granted to this Law in the Persian period; the *halakic turn* toward rigorous observance of the details of the Law, in the wake of the Maccabean revolt; the different ways in which the Law was construed in the diaspora and in sectarian Judaism; and the challenge posed to the normativity of the Law by the messianism of Paul.

Both nouns in the title of this book, *The Invention of Judaism,* are potentially controversial. To speak of "invention" is to accept a constructivist view of ethnic identity. Despite the undisputed givens of blood and land, Judaism was shaped by decisions and policies that were contested in their time. Some scholars nowadays deny that one can speak of "Judaism" in the ancient world at all. But, in fact, the people of Judea, both in the homeland and in the diaspora, had a distinctive way of life throughout the period under consideration. This way of life was constantly modified and contested, but we should miss the forest for the trees if we did not recognize it at all.

This book had its origin in the Taubman Lectures, delivered at Berkeley in September 2013. There were three lectures, roughly corresponding to the introduction (plus a summary of chapter 2) and chapters 3 and 6 of this book. The introduction and chapter 3 (with part of chapter 2) were delivered as the Birks Lectures at McGill University in October 2014, and the introduction and chapters 2 and 3 were given as the Haskell Lectures at Oberlin College in October 2015. The introduction was also given as the David S. Lobel Visiting Scholar Lecture at

Stanford University in May 2014. An abbreviated form of chapter 1 was presented both in Rome, at the Pontifical Biblical Institute, and at Oxford, in the Old Testament Seminar, in May 2016.

I would like to express my gratitude, first, to Daniel Boyarin, who invited me to give the Taubman Lectures and hosted me at Berkeley, and to his colleagues and others who hosted me, especially Robert Alter, Erich Gruen, and Ron Hendel. I am also grateful to Iain Henderson at McGill, Corey Barnes and Cindy Chapman at Oberlin, Steve Weitzman at Stanford (now at the University of Pennsylvania), Dominik Markl, SJ, at the Pontifical Biblical Institute, and Hindy Najman at Oxford.

I also wish to thank Adela Yarbro Collins, who read and commented on several chapters, including the concluding chapter on Paul. Others who read and commented on various chapters include Joel Baden, Rob Kashow, Mark Lester, Hindy Najman, and James Nati. To these colleagues, and to all who helped with the production of the manuscript, especially Eric Schmidt, Cindy Fulton, and Marian Rogers, I am grateful. I would also like to thank James Nati and Mark Lester for doing the indices.

John J. Collins
New Haven, June 2016

# Introduction

*Jews, Judeans, and the Maccabean Crisis*

In the reign of the Syrian king Antiochus Epiphanes, the inhabitants of Judea faced a crisis that would have far-reaching implications. Epiphanes had invaded Egypt for a second time, and unlike the first time, this invasion had not gone well. He had been forced to withdraw from Egypt in humiliating circumstances by the Roman legate Popilius Laenas.[1] A rumor spread in Judea that he had died in Egypt, and Jason the Oniad, who had briefly held the high priesthood but had been supplanted by Menelaus, seized the occasion to try to regain power. Civil war broke out in Jerusalem. According to 2 Maccabees, "When news of what had happened reached the king, he took it to mean that Judea was in revolt" (2 Macc 5:11). He proceeded to sack Jerusalem and pillage the temple.

But this was not all:

> Not long after this, the king sent an Athenian elder to compel the *Ioudaioi* to depart from their ancestral laws, and to pollute the temple in Jerusalem and name it for Zeus Olympios. The temple on Mt. Gerizim was to be named for Zeus Xenios, as those who inhabited that place requested.... It was impossible either to keep the Sabbath, to observe the ancestral festivals, or to openly confess oneself to be a *Ioudaios*. (2 Macc 6:1–2, 6)

The question I would like to pursue here is, what exactly could one not confess oneself to be? What did it mean to be a *Ioudaios* in the second

*contradiction,*
*with Judaisms?*

century B.C.E.? Was this a matter of consensus, or was it contested? And how did the understanding of Judean identity change in the course of the Second Temple period?

## JEW OR JUDEAN

For some time now a debate has raged as to whether *Ioudaios* should be translated as "Jew" or as "Judean."[2] Shaye Cohen distinguished three basic meanings of the term. A *Ioudaios* may be a Judean (a function of birth and/or geography) or a Jew (a function of religion and culture) or a citizen or ally of the Judean state (a function of politics).[3] The first and third of these senses are relatively uncontroversial. The main question at issue is whether and when we can speak of Jews who were *Ioudaioi* by religion and culture as distinct from being ethnically or politically Judean. For Cohen, a *Ioudaios* in the religious sense "is someone who believes (or is supposed to believe) certain distinctive tenets, and/or follows (or is supposed to follow) certain distinctive practices; in other words, a *Ioudaios* is someone who worships the God whose temple is in Jerusalem and who follows the way of life of the Jews."[4] Cohen argues that this sense of the word *Ioudaios* first appears in the second century B.C.E., and indeed is first exemplified in 2 Maccabees. It is this religious sense of the term that allows for the phenomenon of conversion to Judaism, which is reflected in the fantastic claim in 2 Macc 9:17 that Antiochus Epiphanes, on his death-bed, promised to become a *Ioudaios,* and in the forcible conversion of the Idumeans to the Judean way of life under John Hyrcanus. Before that point, wrote Cohen, the word *Ioudaios,* and its Hebrew and Aramaic equivalents, "always and everywhere mean 'Judaean,' and not 'Jew.'"[5] Thereafter, Judaism was an "ethno-religion:" "for most *Ioudaioi* in antiquity, the ethnic definition was supplemented, not replaced by the religious definition. Jewishness became an ethno-religious identity."[6]

*religion*
*+*
*culture*
*Can you*
*separate*

Cohen's proposal has been criticized from both sides. On the one hand, Joseph Blenkinsopp finds it "difficult to accept … that the geographical-ethnic connotation gave way to the religious cultural understanding of the term only in the Hasmonean period ... and that it was only at that time that Judaism began to accept proselytes."[7] There were, after all, foreigners who "joined themselves to the Lord" in the period of the restoration (Isa 56:3). In Blenkinsopp's view, this transition had already taken place in the Persian period. On the other hand, Steve Mason denies that there was any fundamental shift in the Hasmonean period or at any time before late antiquity. Mason argues that "there was no category of 'Judaism' in the Graeco-Roman World, no 'religion' too, and that the *Ioudaioi* were understood until late antiquity as an ethnic group comparable to other ethnic groups, with their distinctive laws, traditions, customs, and God. They were indeed Judaeans."[8] Conversion entailed "a decisive shift from one *ethnos* to another."[9] Mason translates *Ioudaioi* as "Judeans" by analogy with other ethnic groups in antiquity (Romans, Idumeans). What we might regard as religious observances were integral to ethnic identity.

Implicit in this discussion are distinct views of what it meant to be a *Ioudaios*. Mason's insistence on translating the term as "Judean" bespeaks a view that Judean identity is primarily determined by ancestral place of origin, and he argues that this is how it was perceived in the ancient world.[10] Those who prefer to translate the term as "Jew" see rather a way of life to which people can subscribe regardless of their ethnic origin. Whether the terms "Judean" and "Jew" can bear the weight of this distinction may be questioned. Danny Schwartz points out that the English word "Jew" entails descent as well as religion, in effect agreeing with Cohen that the word refers to an ethno-religion.[11] He also agrees with Cohen that *Ioudaioi* in the Hasmonean and Roman period could be defined by religion as well as by place and descent, notably in the case of conversion.[12] Nonetheless, he retains the distinction, which he reformulates in terms of "whether the *Ioudaioi* of whom we are speaking understood themselves more as residents of a country or as adherents of a religion."[13] So, he argues, *Ioudaioi* in 1 Maccabees should be translated as Judeans, while in 2 Maccabees, the same term is more appropriately rendered as "Jews."[14]

*Cut*

But on Mason's understanding, too, ethnicity entailed traditional cultic practices and beliefs about gods. His objection to the word "Jew" in the context of antiquity is that he takes it to refer to a religion in the modern sense of the term, as a privatized area of life that can be bracketed off from the rest of society. Indeed, in his view there was no "religion" in this sense in antiquity at all.[15] Neither Cohen nor Schwartz shares this restrictive understanding of the word "Jew," or of "religion."[16] Mason's insistence on referring to "Judeans" is helpful insofar as it defamiliarizes our understanding of the people in question, but the issue is not just a matter of terminology. The question is whether Judaism was ever conceived simply as a cult in antiquity, or whether Jewish identity could ever be formulated in terms that did not involve land and common descent, or conversely, whether it could be formulated as a way of life that was not necessarily tied to ancestral origin.

## ETHNICITY

In order to put this debate in perspective, it may be helpful to reflect on the category of ethnicity.[17] While the term *ethnicity* did not appear in the English language until the 1950s, the word from which it is derived, *ethnos,* goes back to Homer. In Greek, it can be used to refer to "a number of people or animals who share some cultural or biological characteristics and who live and act in concert."[18] (Homer uses it variously in reference to a people [the Lycians], to companions, and even to bees and birds.) The term is most often used for groups to which other peoples belong. The Septuagintal use of *ta ethnē* for the Gentiles is typical in this regard.

In popular perception, ethnicity is often bound up with a common homeland and common ancestry. It is difficult to distinguish between ethnicity and nationality.[19] I follow the view that nationalist identity involves an aspiration to political autonomy.[20] Such an aspiration becomes a factor in Judean identity beginning with the Maccabean revolt, although it may already be implicit in Deuteronomy.

*Ioudaioi* take their name from the province of Judah or Judea, which in turn is named for the putative common ancestor Judah. Josephus says that they have been called by that name from the time when they went up from Babylon (*Ant.* 11.173). People for whom ethnic identity is important generally accept the common homeland and ancestry as factual givens. This is known as the "primordialist" position.[21] The classic formulation of this view of ethnicity is provided by Clifford Geertz:

> By a primordial attachment is meant one that stems from the "givens"—or, more precisely, as culture is inevitably involved in such matters, the assumed givens—of social existence: immediate contiguity and kin connection mainly, but beyond them the givenness that stems from being born into a particular religious community, speaking a particular language, or even a dialect of a language, and following particular social practices. These congruities of blood, speech, custom, and so on, are seen to have an ineffable, and at times overpowering, coerciveness of themselves.[22]

In the words of Jonathan Hall,

> Put briefly, the primordialists consider ethnicity (along with religion, race and territory) to be a basic and natural unit of history and humanity. Ethnicity is merely an extension of kinship and the normal vehicle through which common goals might be pursued.[23]

Modern study of ethnicity, however, has generally rejected "primordialism," and denied that ethnic groups are determined by blood and land or other primordial factors.[24] Rather, it emphasizes the malleability of communal identity, and the role of discourse in shaping it. As Denise Buell puts it, race and ethnicity are "concepts to which fixity is attributed but that are nevertheless malleable."[25] Ethnic groups, like nations, are *imagined communities,* in the phrase of Benedict Anderson.[26] (There is an old European joke that "a nation is a group of people united by a common error about their ancestry and a common dislike of their neighbors."[27]) Fredrik Barth famously argued that it is "the ethnic boundary that defines the group, not the cultural stuff that it encloses."[28] Groups are identified by the things that differentiate them from their

e = a tool

neighbors, and these may change over time. Barth made a valuable point that culture and ethnic identity are not coterminous. "Most of the cultural matter that at any time is associated with a human population is not constrained by this [ethnic] boundary; it can vary, be learnt, and change without any critical relation to the boundary maintenance of the ethnic group."[29] Some cultural features or practices are assigned higher symbolic and diagnostic value than others, and these may vary over time, as they serve to distinguish an ethnic group from its neighbors.[30] This general approach to ethnicity is variously called "constructivist," "subjectivist," or even "instrumentalist."[31] A properly instrumentalist approach holds that ethnicity is a tool that can be manipulated for specific goals, whereby "some interest groups exploit parts of their traditional culture in order to articulate informal organizational functions that are used in the struggle of these groups for power."[32]

The "instrumental" manipulation of ethnic symbols is undoubtedly a fact of history, and it will concern us again, notably in connection with Ezra but to some degree in all attempts to shape ethnic identity in a particular way. But ethnic symbols cannot be conjured out of thin air. Abner Cohen, a leading "instrumentalist" theorist, also notes that "culture is not the sum total of the strategies adopted by independent individuals. Norms and beliefs and values are effective only because they are the collective representations of a group and are backed by the pressure of that group."[33] As Carly Crouch puts it, "The development of an ethnic identity is based in and draws power from a group's historical and cultural roots."[34]

Most anthropologists, while granting the importance of boundary issues, still feel that "the cultural stuff" is important in understanding ethnicity. Hutchinson and Smith list six features that ethnic groups habitually exhibit, albeit in varying degrees: a common proper name; a myth (rather than fact) of common ancestry; shared memories of a common past; one or more elements of common culture, normally including religion, customs, or language; a link with a homeland, or in the case of diasporas, a symbolic attachment to an ancestral land; and a sense of solidarity on the part of at least some sections of the group.[35] They comment:

> This brings out the importance of shared myths and memories in the defi-
> nition of *ethnies,* and the subjective identification of individuals with the
> community; without the shared myths and memories, including myths of
> origin and election, and the sense of solidarity they engender, we would be
> speaking of an ethnic category rather than a community.[36]

Similarly, Jonathan Hall argues that "the connection with a specific territory and the common myth of descent" remain distinctive characteristics of ethnic groups, even if one does not subscribe to a primordialist
position.[37]

Mason, writing with an eye to the Greek use of *ethnos,* also emphasizes the importance of common traditions:

> Each *ethnos* had its distinctive nature or character (*physis, ethos*), expressed
> in unique ancestral traditions (*ta patria*), which typically reflected a shared
> (if fictive) ancestry (*syggeneia*); each had its charter stories (*mythoi*), customs,
> norms, conventions, mores, laws (*nomoi, ethē, nomima*), and political arrange-
> ments or constitution (*politeia*).[38]

He goes on to add that

> an ancient *ethnos* normally had a national cult ... involving priests, temples,
> and animal sacrifice. This cannot be isolated from the *ethnos* itself, since
> temples, priesthood and cultic practices were part and parcel of a people's
> founding stories, traditions, and civic structures.[39]

Already in Herodotus (8.144) the Athenians reassure the Spartans of
their common Greekness (*to Hellēnikon*):

> We are all one in blood and one in language, those shrines of the gods
> belong to us all in common, and the sacrifices in common, and there are
> our habits, bred of a common upbringing.[40]

Mason adds, however, that "cult and *ethnos* may be distinguished for our
purposes, partly because there was no one-for-one match between a

people and a single cultic system,"[41] but the Judean *ethnos* was an exception in this regard.

Even Josephus, writing after the destruction of Jerusalem, was concerned to defend "the antiquity of our Judean race (*to genos hēmōn*), the purity of the original stock, and the manner in which it established itself in the country which we occupy today" (*Ag. Ap.* 1.1).[42] His treatise *Against Apion* is largely concerned to refute hostile accounts of Judean origins, but also includes a lengthy exposition of the laws and way of life, including the temple cult (which was no longer functioning when the treatise was written) (2.151–238). John Barclay comments that "Josephus does not weaken the significance of descent or territory in Judean identity,"[43] and that "the term *Ioudaios* has not become an indicator merely of 'religion' but retains its connection with kinship and even land."[44] Accordingly, he opts for the translation "Judean." But he also notes that "Josephus' use of the 'constitutional' model allows for an expansion in the definition of ethnicity,"[45] and that "the apparently close tie between ancestry and culture is loosened" by acknowledgment of people from other nations who adopt Jewish laws. "Purity is a matter not only of ancestry (cf. I.30) but also of law-observance."[46] In short, what we call "religion" was embedded in the whole web of ethnic identity, but it was an essential component of that identity. To say that "Judaism" did not exist as an unembedded religion, however, is not to say that Judaism, as the distinctive way of life of the Judean people, did not exist at all.[47]

### A CONSTITUTIONAL MODEL

Barclay's reference to "the constitutional model" is made in the introduction to his commentary on Josephus's tractate *Against Apion*. Josephus develops this model of the Judean way of life in the second book of the treatise, in his rejoinder to the critiques of Apollonius Molon and Lysimachus (*Ag. Ap.* 2.145–286).[48] He undertakes to give an account of "the whole structure of our constitution (*peri tēs holēs hēmōn katastaseōs tou politeumatos*) and about its individual parts" (2.145). Barclay introduces his summary of this account as follows:

> Here Moses is presented as the original "legislator" (*nomothetēs*), whose constitution embraces all features of the Judean life, from their religious rites to their social behavior, from their domestic customs to their stance towards foreigners. The political category makes Judeans comparable to other peoples, especially within the Greek tradition. The legislator Moses can be favorably compared with Lycurgus or Solon.[49]

The "constitution" that establishes "the singularity of our life-style" (1.68), is, in effect the Law or Torah of Moses. This is the ancestral law of the Judeans, and it can also be called "our ancestral philosophy" (1.54; 2.47). It is possible for foreigners, especially Greeks, "to come over to our laws" (2.123). "Affinity is not a matter of birth alone (*ou tō genei monon*), but also of choice in life-style" (2.209–10).[50] A similar claim had been made for Greek culture by Isocrates in the fourth century B.C.E.: "Those who are called 'Hellenes' are those who share our culture (*paideusis*) rather than a common biological inheritance (*koinē physis*)."[51]

In his classic study of conversion, published in 1933, Arthur Darby Nock distinguished between two kinds of religion in the ancient Mediterranean world. The first kind was linked to particular ethnic groups. The second, which he dubbed "prophetic," was a matter of individual choice, and included Judaism, Christianity, the Greek philosophical schools, and cults such as those of Isis and Mithras.[52] Nock distinguished between Judaism and Christianity, as he realized that Judaism in practice remained predominantly the religion of a particular people. He drew attention, however, to a phenomenon in the Hellenistic-Roman world that was not confined to Judaism or Christianity, but was related to the social and political changes brought on first by the spread of Hellenism and then by the Roman Empire.

Common descent and shared history are still important for Josephus, and for Judeans in general, but he also allows for an elective approach that views Judaism as a philosophy or way of life. The view of Judaism as a philosophy is found already in the mid-second century B.C.E. in the

*[handwritten margin notes: "Way of life / philosophy / Conflicts with" and "New perspecte + in line with Moser's critique"]*

Jewish philosopher Aristobulus, who wrote: "All philosophers agree that it is necessary to hold devout convictions about God, something which our school prescribes particularly well."[53] The ethnic dimension of this "philosophy" is not thereby eliminated. Judaism remained an "ethno-religion." But the perception of a comprehensive way of life, whether conceived as law or as philosophy, that was not necessarily dependent on blood and descent, represents a significant development in the understanding of Jewish ethnicity in the Hellenistic age.

### ANCESTRAL LAWS

The idea that the ethnicity of local peoples found expression in their ancestral laws, *patrioi nomoi,* is characteristic of the Hellenistic world. It was the ancestral laws of the Judeans that Epiphanes proscribed in his decree. The concept of ancestral laws (or ancestral constitution, *patrios politeia,* or customs, *ta patria*) was derived from classical Greece.[54] Thucydides (8.76) reports that in Samos the oligarchy was deposed because they had done wrong in abolishing the *patrioi nomoi.* When Andocides was on trial for impiety, he cited an earlier decree of Teisamenos that stated that "the Athenians shall conduct their affairs in the traditional manner (*kata ta patria*)" (Andocides 1.83). "Ancestral laws" usually meant "laws hitherto in effect,"[55] and they provided the framework for political action. Beginning with Herodotus, Greek ethnography expressed a respectful interest in the laws and customs of other peoples.[56]

Josephus claims that Alexander the Great visited Jerusalem, and that "when the High Priest asked whether they might observe the ancestral laws and in the seventh year be exempt from tribute, he granted all this" (*Ant.* 11.338). This whole narrative is highly legendary; it is unlikely that Alexander went to Jerusalem in person. As Erich Gruen has put it, "Alexander's visit to Jerusalem is outright fabrication."[57] The idea that the conquering king, however, would affirm the right of the conquered city to observe its ancestral laws is quintessentially Hellenistic. Elias Bickerman demonstrated that the first favor bestowed by a Hellenistic king on a conquered city—and the basis of all other favors—was the re-establishment of the municipal statutes. In virtue of the conquest, the subjugated city was no longer entitled to its institutions and laws, and it regained these only by means of an act promulgated by its new master.[58]

There are plentiful examples.[59] When Philip V of Macedon gained control of the island of Nisyros in 201 B.C.E., he proclaimed to the inhabitants that "the king has re-established among us the use of the ancestral laws which are currently in force."[60]

When Antiochus III conquered Jerusalem in 198 B.C.E. he issued a proclamation that "all who belong to the people are to be governed in accordance with their ancestral laws" (Josephus, *Ant.* 12.142).[61] The proclamation assumed that such laws already existed. Already at the beginning of the Hellenistic age Hecataeus of Abdera had written about Moses as the lawgiver of Judea.[62] Hecataeus seems to have had information of uneven quality. Judea, he wrote, had been settled by people who had been aliens in Egypt but were driven out. Moses, the head of the colony, founded Jerusalem, among other cities, and built the temple there. He organized the twelve tribes and regulated matters of worship. Hecataeus added a famous comment: "The sacrifices that he established differ from those of other nations, as does their way of living, for as a result of their own expulsion from Egypt he introduced an unsocial and intolerant mode of life." Despite that judgment, the account is quite positive, and the tone is that of a neutral observer.[63] For our purposes, the significant point is that Jerusalem and Judea were believed to have ancestral laws derived from Moses as early as 300 B.C.E.

## "JUDAISM" IN THE MACCABEAN CRISIS

It was these ancestral laws that were at issue in the Maccabean crisis of the second century B.C.E. The ancestral way of life that had been acknowledged and even enjoined by Antiochus III came under attack a generation later during the reign of his son, Antiochus IV Epiphanes.[64]

The attack came in two phases. The first phase was initiated by Judeans. 1 Maccabees refers to them as "lawless men who persuaded many, saying 'Let us go and make a treaty with the nations (*ethnē*) around us, because ever since we separated from them, many evils have come upon us" (1 Macc 1:11). 1 Maccabees mentions only two of the measures they took: they built a gymnasium, and undid the marks of their circumcision. From the viewpoint of 1 Maccabees, both of these were boundary markers that distinguished Judeans from Gentiles.

2 Maccabees develops this episode in greater detail. It identifies the protagonist as Jason, brother of Onias, who promised to increase the tribute and pay an additional sum in addition "if he might be given permission to set up a gymnasium and ephebeum and to register the Jerusalemites as Antiochenes." When the king assented, he set himself

> to convert his countrymen to the Greek way of life (*eis ton Hellēnikon charaktēra*). He set aside the established royal laws favorable to the Judeans, which had been obtained through John, father of Eupolemus.... He broke down the lawful constitution and introduced new customs contrary to the law. (2 Macc 4:10)

2 Maccabees also dwells on the gymnasium and its disruptive effect on the temple cult, and also notes the fashion of wearing the Greek hat.[65] The enthusiasts for the gymnasium "valued as nothing the customs their fathers honored and coveted only Greek honors as worthy of attainment" (4:19).

Both 1 and 2 Maccabees depict Jason's reform as an attempt to overthrow the ancestral laws and change the Judean way of life, so that it was no longer distinctive among the peoples of the region.

2 Maccabees describes the adoption of the new way of life as *Hellēnismos,* exemplified in enthusiasm for the gymnasium and the Greek hat (2 Macc 4:13). It also introduces for the first time the corresponding term *Ioudaismos.* Judas Maccabee and his followers "strove zealously on behalf of Judaism" (*huper tou Ioudaismou,* 2:21). He admitted into his army those who had remained *en tō Ioudaismō* (8:1). The elder Razis, who meets

*[handwritten marginalia: "what do we mean by this — It is a way of life"]*

a gruesome death in 2 Maccabees 14, had been accused of *Ioudaismos* in his youth, and had risked body and soul on its behalf. Mason argues vigorously that these terms should not be translated "Hellenism" and "Judaism."[66] Rather, they refer to *activities*—the promotion of Greek and Judaic ways, respectively. Judas sought people who "had persisted in *the Judaizing* [programme] ... not simply *remaining Ioudaioi,* but striving to bring back other Judaeans and reinstate the ancestral laws."[67] Mason consequently cautions against "adopting the word as if it were generally understood to mean the entire culture, legal system, and 'religion' of the Judaeans."[68] It "is not then 'Judaism' as a way of life," he writes, "but a newly coined counter-measure against *Hellēnismos*."[69] But even if we grant the active connotation of these words, they can hardly be emptied of cultural content. *Hellēnismos* still implies a concept of an entire culture that was being advocated, and conversely *Ioudaismos* is not simply agitation, even anti-Hellenistic agitation, but the advancement of the ancestral way of life of the Judeans.[70] In the words of Daniel Boyarin, it refers to "the entire complex of loyalties and practices that mark off the people of Israel."[71] Whether or not we should accept that *Ioudaismos* has the "static" sense of "Judaism" in 2 Maccabees, it implies a clear understanding of a well-defined Judean way of life. As Danny Schwartz has argued,

> "Judaism" in 2 Maccabees seems to mean what it means for us; something which one can practice, to which one can remain devoted; something to which a wicked king might forbid people to declare allegiance (6:6) but to which some, especially in villages outside the king's supervision, might nonetheless remain loyal (8:1). There is no reason to turn it into doing something to others.[72]

Judas Maccabee, however, did not take up arms against Jason's reform. The question arises, to what degree did Jason actually repudiate the ancestral laws? The erection of the gymnasium and the pursuit of physical exercise were not forbidden in the Torah, although they were alien to its spirit. The most direct violation of the Torah mentioned in either book of Maccabees concerns the attempt to undo circumcision mentioned in

1 Macc 1:15: literally, "they made themselves foreskins." Since circumcision had long been regarded as a symbol of the covenant, in effect a boundary marker, this action could reasonably be interpreted as a repudiation of Judean identity.[73] This would be in accordance with the wish attributed to the reformers to undo the separation from the Gentiles. It should be noted, however, that at least in the first century C.E. it was possible to argue that one could serve God without circumcision (quite apart from the case of Saint Paul, in the story of the conversion of the royal house of Adiabene).[74] 2 Maccabees acknowledges that some of the "Hellenizers" were reluctant to participate in the cult of pagan deities. When Jason sent a delegation to the games at Tyre with 3,000 silver drachmas for the sacrifice to Heracles, the delegates diverted the money to fitting out triremes (2 Macc 4:18–20).

It is clear that Jason wanted to reform the Judean way of life, but it is not so clear that he wanted to repudiate it completely, as the books of Maccabees imply. The changes in the sphere of religion and culture seem to have been limited to the gymnasium and related activities. There is no indication that Jason interfered with the traditional festivals or the temple cult.[75] As Victor Tcherikover noted, the reform was political and cultural, but not specifically religious, in the sense that it did not involve any conspicuous change in the temple cult.[76] Erich Gruen concludes that 2 Maccabees "has vastly overrated a crisis that few at the time seem to have found particularly alarming."[77]

There is also no evidence that Jason compelled anyone to participate in the activities in the gymnasium. Danny Schwartz argues plausibly that "it is doubtful that all Jerusalemites were forced to become citizens of the new city and to participate in its institutions; those who wanted to go on observing the ancestral ways were certainly allowed to do so."[78] The reorganization may have had the effect of marginalizing traditional observance, but it lacked the element of compulsion that would have provoked resistance. Those who flocked to the gymnasium presumably still thought of themselves as *Ioudaioi,* and did not entirely repudiate the traditional way of life.

## THE DECREES OF EPIPHANES

Neither is there any evidence that Menelaus initially sought to change the nature of the temple cult. Only after civil war broke out between Jason and Menelaus during Epiphanes's second invasion of Egypt did the situation change. As 2 Maccabees tells it,

> When news of what had happened reached the king, he took it to mean that Judea was in revolt. So, raging inwardly, he left Egypt and took the city by storm (5:11). Not long afterwards, he sent the Athenian elder to compel the Jews to forsake the laws of their fathers and cease to live by the laws of God. (6:1)

As Robert Doran has shown, 2 Maccabees provides a coherent account that is plausible in the Seleucid context:

> Thinking the city was in revolt, Antiochus IV took it by storm and abrogated the gift of allowing the city to live by its ancestral laws, as his father had done formerly to Apollonia at Rhyndacos.[79]

Instead, he imposed new laws that included cultic celebration of the king's birthday, sacrifices to Zeus, and processions in honor of Dionysus.

The account in 2 Maccabees sheds light not only on the new observances introduced by Epiphanes, but also on the understanding of ancestral law in Judea in the early second century B.C.E. Doran summarizes:

> The ancestral laws abrogated included circumcision, Sabbath observance and kosher regulations. It appears that these were attacked not because Antiochus IV was persecuting the Jewish religion, but because circumcision affected citizenship, Sabbath observance affected the civic economy, and kosher regulations affected cultic meals.[80]

One might equally well argue that these practices were singled out because of their symbolic value as boundary markers of Judean ethnicity. For the same reason, it was forbidden to have copies of the Torah, the iconic representation of the Judean way of life (1 Macc 1:56). These were the practices most widely associated with Judaism. What Antiochus wanted to break down was the ancestral laws and way of life of Judea and thereby the distinctive identity of the rebellious people.[81] In addition to practices like circumcision and Sabbath observance, the king also struck at the temple cult, the most prominent public expression of the Jewish way of life, both by forbidding the traditional offerings and by requiring sacrifices to foreign gods. His attention to the cult was the counterpart of the decree of his father, Antiochus III, who had made special provision for it when he affirmed the ancestral laws.

The decrees of Antiochus differed from the reforms of Jason in two crucial respects. First, they involved compulsion and the use of force. Second, they suspended the traditional festivals and imposed a new form of cult. According to 2 Macc 6:9 these decrees were also enforced in the neighboring Greek cities. There is no indication that Antiochus systematically pursued Judeans throughout his empire. His actions were a local punishment for perceived rebellion, but they did constitute an attempt to erase the traditional Jewish way of life in Judea, and perhaps in surrounding areas.

The fact that these actions, unlike the reforms of Jason, sparked a rebellion gives us some indication of what the rebels regarded as essential to their identity. Not all elements in the ethnic repertoire were weighted equally. The distinctive identity of the people of Judea was not seriously threatened by the introduction of a gymnasium, or by the Greek language, but it was seriously threatened by the disruption of the traditional cult.[82] This is even more obvious in the book of Daniel, which barely acknowledges Jason's reform but attaches pivotal importance to the desecration of the temple by "the abomination that makes desolate."[83]

The books of Maccabees see continuity between the reforms of Jason and the decrees of Antiochus. Both were calculated to change the identity of the people of Judea by making them more like the surrounding nations. E. J. Bickerman and Martin Hengel even thought that the decrees of Antiochus were suggested by Menelaus, as a means of completing the transformation of Jerusalem into a Hellenistic polis.[84] There is some support for this view in the sources. According to 2 Macc 13:4 the Seleucid general Lysias told Antiochus V Eupator that Menelaus was "the cause of all the trouble." Josephus elaborates: "by persuading the king's father to compel the Jews to abandon their fathers' cultic observance (*thrēskeia*)" (*Ant.* 12.384–85). The great majority of the sources, however, Jewish and pagan, place the ultimate responsibility with the king.[85] But whether Menelaus was to blame or not, the royal decrees mark a serious escalation of the assault on the ancestral laws. Jason undermined the status of those laws by changing the constitution of Jerusalem, but he does not seem to have been intent on violating them, and it is not clear that he replaced them with a new constitution, as was later done by the Athenian elder. Antiochus Epiphanes wanted to put an end to the distinctive Judean way of life, which was quite a different matter.

## THE CENTRALITY OF THE ANCESTRAL LAW

1 and 2 Maccabees differ in manifold ways in their accounts of the crisis. The family of Mattathias has a central role in 1 Maccabees. In 2 Maccabees, the deaths of the martyrs play the crucial role in achieving the salvation of the people. As Danny Schwartz has argued, 2 Maccabees is more "religious" in its attention to sin and atonement, miracles and apparitions, and the like.[86] But the two books seem quite in agreement on the centrality of the Law. 1 Maccabees is greatly concerned with the territory of the land of Israel, and also with the "seed" of the Maccabean family (5:62). It makes no reference to the Jews of the diaspora. Yet its rallying cry was the defense of the ancestral laws. 1 Maccabees has Mattathias cry out: "Let everyone who is zealous for the law and supports the covenant come out with me!" (1 Macc 2:27). The Maccabees were not necessarily bound by the letter of the law. They famously made an exception for fighting on the Sabbath: "If we do as our brethren have done and refuse to fight with the Gentiles for our lives and our ordinances, they will quickly destroy us from the earth" (2:40–41). Yet they

attempted not only to defend but to impose "the Jewish way of life" within the territory they controlled. According to 1 Maccabees, they

> struck down sinners in their anger and lawless men in their wrath; the survivors fled to the Gentiles for safety. And Mattathias and his friends went about and tore down the altars; they forcibly circumcised all the uncircumcised boys that they found within the borders of Israel.... They rescued the law out the hands of the Gentiles and kings. (1 Macc 2:44–47; cf. Josephus, *Ant.* 12.278)

To be a *Ioudaios,* according to 1 Maccabees, it was not enough to live in the land of Judah, or even to be of the seed of Abraham. One had to observe the law of Moses, at least in its most symbolically significant details. Conversely, while the protagonists of 2 Maccabees are devotees of *Ioudaismos,* its story is focused on the city of Jerusalem and its temple. It is doubtful then whether anything is gained by contrasting the "Judeans" of 1 Maccabees with the "Jews" of 2 Maccabees. Both books allow for the possibility of conversion, in the case of Antiochus Epiphanes in 2 Maccabees, and in the case of those who were forcibly circumcised in 1 Maccabees. Neither understands Judean identity purely in primordialist terms of land and blood, although 1 Maccabees leans more in that direction than does 2 Maccabees. Both regard life according to the ancestral laws as essential to what it means to be a *Ioudaios.* The advocacy of the Law in both books of Maccabees may be viewed as instrumentalist, insofar as it tried to identify what it meant to be a *Ioudaios* with the observance of the Mosaic Torah. But it also appealed to a tradition that already had a long history.

The terminological debate about the translation of *Ioudaios,* then, is ultimately misleading, insofar as it suggests that a clean distinction can be made between the views of Judaism as an *ethnos* and as a religion. Cohen is right that Judaism from the Maccabean period on was an ethno-religion, but I will argue that it was already that in the Persian period. Once the Law/Torah of Moses became accepted as the ances-

Way of life + choke prominent
for Collins

tral law of the Judeans, it was possible to become "Jewish" or "Judean" in virtue of observance of that law, regardless of birth or genealogy (although a strand of Jewish tradition, beginning with Ezra, resisted that possibility). It remains true, as both Cohen and Mason realize, that the religious and cultural aspects of Judaism remained embedded in a historical community that was predominantly shaped by ethnic descent and original geographical provenance. Mason is right to insist on the ethnic character of Judaism, and his use of the translation "Judean" is a useful reminder of that character. But what we call "religion" was an important element in ethnic identity, and Lee Levine has argued with some justification that "there is ample evidence to assume that the religious component among Jews (or Judaeans, if one wishes) was a far more prominent and salient characteristic than for other contemporary ethnic groups."[87] It was certainly a prominent aspect of the ancestral law of Judea that was attributed to Moses. Different elements in the ethnic repertoire could be emphasized at different times and places. Judaism could even be presented as a philosophy in the Hellenistic diaspora. But even there, the religious and cultural aspect of Judaism was never entirely separated from the ethnic ties of land and blood. This, I would think, has not changed in the modern era.

The articulation of the Judean way of life in terms of ancestral laws derived from Moses was arguably the most distinctive development in Second Temple Judaism. It was not an innovation of the Hellenistic period. Its roots must be traced at least to the Persian, and arguably to the Neo-Babylonian, period. In the following chapters we will consider how the Torah came to have such a definitive role in ancient Judaism.

What is religion for Collins

# CHAPTER I

# Deuteronomy and the Invention of the Torah

The people of Israel and Judah had a distinct ethnic identity long before the Law of Moses was formulated, at least as we have it in the Bible. There is general consensus that that identity took shape in the last centuries of the second millennium B.C.E., but opinions differ widely as to whether anything can be said about it with confidence.[1] The stele of Merneptah is usually accepted as confirming the existence of an entity called "Israel" in the late thirteenth century B.C.E., but it tells us no more than the name, and even the reading of the name is disputed.[2] A certain amount can be said, on the basis of archaeology, about the cultural "stuff" that characterized the central highlands in this period—housing structures, pottery, diet, and so on.[3] Some features of this culture were distinctive, and may have been ethnic markers (e.g., the apparent absence of pig bones suggests an avoidance of pork). The fact that the Philistines were uncircumcised may go some way to explaining the importance of circumcision in later Jewish tradition. But as Ann Killebrew acknowledges, "Attempts to locate Israel's ethnogenesis in the small Iron I villages in the hill-country and marginal regions ultimately go back to the biblical narrative as recounted in the books of Joshua and Judges."[4] These books, however, date from many centuries later.

In the first half of the first millennium B.C.E., Israel and Judah were kingdoms. Their inhabitants were largely defined by their allegiance to these kingdoms and by their distinctive, though by no means exclusive, devotion to the god YHWH. They had their distinctive customs and practices, largely centering on the cult, but these were not codified in the form of a law until late in the monarchic period. If we may judge by the biblical record, Israelite and Judean identity was largely shaped by traditional stories, which we now have in the Pentateuch and in the case of Judah also in the books of Samuel and Kings. Here again we are dependent on sources that attained their final form after the demise of the monarchies. The manner in which these stories took shape is arguably the most complicated and contested topic in all of biblical scholarship.[5] Our present concern, however, is not with the narratives, important though these undoubtedly were, but with the attempt to formulate the Israelite/Judahite way of life as law.

## THE SINAI REVELATION

On the canonical biblical account, the Law was first revealed to Moses on Mount Sinai, as recorded in Exodus 19–24.[6] This account includes the theophany in chapter 19, the Decalogue in chapter 20, the Book of the Covenant in 20:22 to 23:33, and an account of the sealing of the covenant in chapter 24. This picture is complicated, however, by several factors.

All scholars agree that the account is composite. (Witness the number of times Moses ascends the mountain.) The older documentary hypothesis, which dominated scholarship from the late nineteenth to the mid-twentieth century, recognized brief framing elements as Priestly (Exod 19:2; 24:15b, 17–18). The account of the theophany was assigned to J or to JE, the Decalogue to E, and Exodus 24 to some combination of J and E. The Book of the Covenant was viewed as an older legal collection.[7] Exodus 34 was thought to contain the Yahwist Decalogue. In the words of S. R. Driver, "In its original form 34[1–4, 10–28] was J's account of the original establishment of the covenant at Sinai ... and

*[handwritten: When did Israel distinguish itself from the nations?]*

*[handwritten: SC = 8th cent.]*

parallel to the narrative of E in 20²²-23³³ 24³⁻⁸."[8] According to the neo-documentary hypothesis of the early twenty-first century, however, no law is given at Sinai in the J source. The theophany is "simply a display of Yahweh's presence before the Israelite people."[9] The covenantal laws in Exod 34:11–26, which have often been attributed to J, are now widely regarded as "a late revision and redactional adaptation of earlier texts."[10] In this regard it should be noted that in some old poetic texts, such as Deut 33:1–2 or Judges 5:4–5, Sinai appears as a mountain to the south of Israel from which Yahweh marches forth as a divine warrior to aid his people. Sinai appears to have been a place of theophany before it was associated with the giving of the law.[11]

On all versions of the documentary hypothesis, the laws of Exodus 20–23 are firmly entrenched in E, where the mountain is called Horeb, as also in Deuteronomy.[12] Scholars who do not subscribe to the documentary hypothesis also recognize that this material, or most of it, is older than D and P. Erhard Blum concludes that "the synoptic evidence gives preference to some form of Exod 20 as the Vorlage of Deut 5," although he finds indications of later transformations in Exodus 20 as well.[13] Likewise Reinhard Achenbach writes: "If we compare Dtn 5,23–30 with the parallel story in Ex 20,18–21 it is obvious that in the Exodus-Version we have the older tradition of the narrative."[14]

## THE BOOK OF THE COVENANT

Regardless of whether the laws in Exodus 20–23 were part of the E source or were independent traditions until they were edited into the Pentateuch or Hexateuch, we do not know the context in which they were originally formulated, or what kind of authority they enjoyed. A wide range of settings has been proposed for the Book of the Covenant. Most scholars agree that these laws were reworked in Deuteronomy, and so can hardly be later than the middle of the seventh century B.C.E.[15] A terminus a quo is more difficult to establish. The laws presuppose a settled society, and obviously do not reflect the life of tribes wandering

*[handwritten margin note: earliest]*

in the wilderness. David Wright has demonstrated in detail that the Book of the Covenant, which on his view includes the Decalogue, is heavily influenced by the Laws of Hammurabi.[16] Wright argues that such borrowing was most likely to have occurred in the Neo-Assyrian period, "some time between 740 and 640 B.C.E. and perhaps close to 700," a time at which Israel, in extremis, and Judah had of necessity extensive contact with Assyria.[17] David Carr, who accepts the dependence on Hammurabi, argues that since there is little reflection of the monarchy, the laws better fit "the still peripheral character of the monarchy in the tenth and ninth centuries than the more developed monarchy and urban situation of the late eighth to seventh centuries."[18]

Carr is more optimistic than Wright "about the possibility of oral-written transmission of Mesopotamian traditions such as Hammurabi from the Levantine Bronze Age city-states where they are attested in an Iron II context."[19] Yet as Wright remarks, "It is hard to imagine why and how a premonarchic or even incipient monarchic society would produce a collection resembling LH [the Laws of Hammurabi] and other cuneiform collections."[20] Similarly, Jean-Louis Ska remarks that "the first redaction of the code could hardly have occurred before the 7th or 8th century B.C.E. because it requires a sufficiently developed legal and literary culture, which according to recent research could not have existed earlier."[21] Ska also notes that the attention to slaves and foreigners presumes a society with great social disparities, such as is presupposed in the eighth-century prophets.[22]

The most remarkable feature of the laws in Exodus, however, when viewed against the background of ancient Near-Eastern law, is that they are not promulgated by the order of a king, but by God. Despite occasional suggestions that the code should be associated with the founding of the Northern Kingdom by Jeroboam or the reform of Hezekiah,[23] it is not in fact attributed to any king. Some scholars, such as Carr, have inferred that these laws must date from a time before the monarchy was firmly established. Yet, as Douglas Knight has argued,

there is not much in the Book of the Covenant that can be traced unequivo-
cally to the villages of ancient Israel. As a whole, this text is a literary arti-
fact and does not necessarily bear resemblance to any actual legal formula-
tions or practices of the period.[24]

A more plausible time might be found after the collapse of the Northern Kingdom. Alternatively, the laws might have been formulated by
scribes or priests who were critical of the kingship in the manner of the
prophets.[25]

The consensus of contemporary scholarship is that neither the great
Mesopotamian law "codes," such as that of Hammurabi, nor the laws of
Exodus functioned as statutory law, or were binding on judges.[26] The
king, rather than a law code, was the source of legal authority. As Martha Roth has noted, "Whether or not the king was always himself an
active participant in the administration of the legal system, he was
always its guardian, for the application of justice was the highest trust
given by the gods to a legitimate king."[27] Judges relied on their sense of
the mores of a community rather than on written law. Written laws are
never cited as decisive in trial scenes, and sometimes cases are decided
in contradiction of what is written.[28] Law collections were descriptive
rather than prescriptive. They may have been "an aid for applying the
law, but not a rule."[29] Bernard Jackson has suggested four kinds of use
for written laws in the ancient Near East, including Israel: monumental,
archival, didactic, and ritual.[30] They might serve as royal propaganda,
or serve various uses for scribes or priests. But they did not function as
the law of the land in a prescriptive sense. Jackson refers to the laws of
Exodus as "wisdom-laws," with the implication that they functioned in
a way similar to Proverbs: they helped inform the wise person, but did
not determine right conduct automatically.[31]

> The earliest forms of judicial dispute resolution rely upon intuitions of jus-
> tice against a background of custom, rather than analysis of linguistically
> formulated rules.[32]

Michael Satlow argues that the function of these laws was largely educational: "Whether or not these laws were ever enforced in Israel, they
served a role in the education of Israelite scribes—the code was another
text to know, copy, and learn to rework."[33]

Konrad Schmid argues that this situation changed when the Book of
the Covenant took on the character of divine law. "The theologizing of
the law," he writes, "was accompanied by a completely altered conception of law."[34] The nonprescriptive character, he claims,

> changes the moment the Book of the Covenant, especially through the
> introduction in Exod 20:22—21:1 and the insertion of the second person,
> becomes "divine law" and thus simultaneously the standard for the rest of
> the further history of law in the Old Testament, which as a consequence
> necessarily becomes an interpretation of the more ancient divine law.[35]

It remains possible, however, that the Book of the Covenant was originally conceived as divine law. It must have been proposed on some
authority, and no other authoritative source of law is known in the biblical tradition. But in any case it is not apparent that these laws sud-
denly became prescriptive (rather than "wisdom-laws") when they
were promulgated as divine law, or that this led to a new concept of law.
Rather, the character of these laws remains the same, whether they are
thought to have been promulgated at Sinai or not.

The claim of divine revelation with respect to the Book of the Covenant can be seen as directly analogous to the claims of the prophets: an
attempt to trump the prevailing social order by appeal to a higher
authority.[36] But it is not apparent that the claim that these laws were
divinely revealed was universally accepted, any more than the claims
of the prophets that their words were "the word of the Lord." Eventually, when these laws are embedded in the Torah they attain official status as part of the Law of Moses, but official recognition of these laws is
not clearly attested before the time of Ezra. (Whether the use of the
Covenant Code in Deuteronomy constitutes an acknowledgment of its
authority, or rather subverts whatever authority it had, is a disputed

issue.[37])We simply do not know what status either the "Book of the Covenant" in isolation or the Elohist document enjoyed (assuming that there was such a document). The mere claim that certain laws were divinely revealed was never enough to establish their authority in Israelite or Judean society, unless that claim was endorsed by an authority with the power of enforcement.

The Book of the Covenant can never have been viewed as a comprehensive statement of the requirements of the covenant in any case. Neither the Decalogue nor the Covenant Code is designed to distinguish Israel from its neighbors, although the Decalogue includes some distinctive provisions, such as aniconism and Sabbath observance. Both documents are too elliptic and random in the topics they discuss to constitute a statement of Israelite identity. They may be viewed as the earliest step toward formulating the ancestral laws of Israel or Judah, but we do not know what status they enjoyed before the compilation of the Pentateuchal Torah.

## JOSIAH'S REFORM

A much more substantial formulation of the law of Moses is found in Deuteronomy. This is the first book of the Pentateuch to use the word torah in the sense of "law code" (Deut 17:19–20; 28:58; 29:19; 21:11–12).[38] Elsewhere in the Pentateuch the word refers to specific instructions, especially priestly instructions, such as "the torah of the guilt offering."[39] We shall also encounter torah as a term for wisdom instruction in Proverbs.[40] In the book of Joshua we read of "the book of the law of Moses" (*sēper torāt Moshe,* Josh 8:21; 23:6), in 1 Kgs 2:3 of "the law of Moses," and "the book of the law" (*sēper ha-tōrah*) occurs in the account of the reform of Josiah in 2 Kings 22–23. Deuteronomy is the only book of the Pentateuch that is ascribed to Moses (not as author but as the record of the words that he spoke). The word "Torah" is only applied to the whole Pentateuch by extension from Deuteronomy.[41]

For the last two centuries, since the dissertation of W.M.L. de Wette, the nucleus of Deuteronomy has been associated with the cultic reform of King Josiah in 621 B.C.E.[42] The reform is reported in 2 Kings 22–23 and 2 Chronicles 34–35. The account in Chronicles, however, cannot be regarded as a source of independent historical information.[43]

In 2 Kings 22–23, two distinct accounts may be distinguished: one tells of the discovery of "the book of the law," and the other describes the cultic reforms of Josiah in 23:4–20.[44] There is no mention of the book of the law in 23:4–20. 2 Kgs 23:17 notes that what Josiah does at Bethel had been predicted by a "man of God," implying that it was thereby authorized, but without referring to an authoritative book.

The content of the book is only indicated indirectly. Josiah is gravely concerned because his ancestors have not obeyed its words. The prophetess Huldah is more explicit about the cause of divine wrath:

> Because they have abandoned me and have made offerings to other gods, so that they have provoked me to anger with the works of their hands, therefore my wrath will be kindled against this place. (2 Kgs 22:17)

In response to this book, however, Josiah

> made a covenant before the Lord, to follow the Lord, keeping his commandments, his decrees, and his statutes, with all his heart and all his soul, to perform the words of this covenant that were written in this book. (23:3)

There can be little doubt that the "book" referred to in this passage is supposed to be Deuteronomy, in some form.[45] Also, when the king commands the people to observe the Passover "as prescribed in this book of the covenant" (23:21), it is clear that some form of Deuteronomy is implied, from the perspective of the author of Kings.

Whether Josiah himself was actually inspired by a law book, however, is more controversial. Norbert Lohfink claimed to identify a "short story (Kurzgeschichte) concerning the discovery of the Torah and the sealing of the covenant."[46] He supposed that it was "composed shortly after the events that it relates, perhaps as a memorandum, perhaps as propaganda."[47] In favor of an early date for the finding narrative is the assurance given to Josiah by Huldah that "I will gather you to your ancestors, and you shall be gathered to your grave in peace" (2 Kgs 22:20). Lohfink comments that "it is hardly conceivable that the text would have been composed in this form after the sudden death of Josiah at Megiddo."[48] Conversely, he questioned whether the "reform report" was a preexisting source. He noted that "the schematic presentation of the destruction of cult objects gives indication of relationship to Deut 9:21" (the destruction of the golden calf), and that "many, though not all, cultic matters that are mentioned hearken back to details already provided in the Books of Kings."[49]

Other scholars, however, have been disposed rather to see the reform report as older and the account of the finding of the law as a later, Deuteronomistic elaboration.[50] Lauren Monroe suggests that the reassurance given to Josiah by Huldah relates not to the manner of his death but to his burial.[51] One might argue that the point of the reassurance is that Josiah would not live to see the destruction of Jerusalem, and indeed that the passage presupposes both the destruction and Josiah's premature death.[52] The motif of book-finding is widely attested in ancient Near Eastern literature as a way to legitimate religious and political changes.[53]

### EXCURSUS
#### A Cultic Reform?

Some scholars hold that the material in 2 Kgs 23:4–20 provides the oldest account of the reform.[54] This is largely a matter of purifying the Jerusalem temple, by expunging the cults of Baal, Asherah, and the host of heaven. Josiah is also said to depose the "pagan priests" (*kᵉmārîn*) who had been appointed by the kings of Judah, and to defile the high places (*bāmôth*). The words *kᵉmārîn* and *bāmôth* do not occur in Deuteronomy, but Deuteronomy 12 urges the Israelites to demolish completely all the places where the nations served their gods, "on the mountain heights, on the hills and under every leafy tree."[55] They are urged to "break down their altars, smash their pillars, burn their sacred poles with fire, and hew down the idols of their gods" (Deut 12:3; cf. 7:5). Polemic against the high places is widespread in the books of Kings, beginning with the "sin of Jeroboam" in 1 Kgs 12:31. (These high places could be devoted to Yahweh as well as to foreign gods.[56]) According to 2 Kgs 23:14, when Josiah defiled the high places east of Jerusalem he "broke their pillars in pieces, cut down their sacred poles, and covered the sites with human bones." While the correspondence is not exact,[57] it is difficult to deny some measure of Deuteronomic influence on the account of the reform.

Monroe acknowledges that 2 Kgs 23:4–20 "clearly conjures Deuteronomy's destructive imagery,"[58] but she points out that "many of the modes of defilement that Josiah employs in his reform have no precedent in the laws of Deuteronomy."[59] She notes especially "references to burning, beating, scattering, casting of dust, and defiling," which she takes to reflect "apotropaic rites of riddance intended to contain contagion and eliminate dangerous forces," and to be typical of Priestly traditions rather than Deuteronomy.[60] Moreover, the attention to the host of heaven in 2 Kings 23 is not anticipated in Deuteronomy. Monroe then proposes that an older account of the purification of the cult was redacted by a Deuteronomistic editor.[61] On her reconstruction, the older account dealt with the purification of the temple by the elimination of astral worship and the defilement of *bāmôth*, including those on the Mount of Olives, and the *bāmāh* in Bethel. The Deuteronomistic editors

> rework the pre-existent themes of purification of the Jerusalem cult and consolidation of priestly authority into a scathing critique of Judah's civic and religious leadership, and they re-present Josiah as the only king in Israel's history to abide in the law of Moses "with all of his heart and all of his being."[62]

### Archaeological Evidence

There is unfortunately little archaeological evidence for Josiah's reform. William Dever's archaeological commentary on 2 Kings 23 is an attempt to document the various practices that Josiah is said to have attacked, not to document the attack itself.[63] Finds that at one time seemed to provide confirmatory evidence have now been discredited. A great horned altar at Beersheba seems to have been disassembled at some time in the eighth century.[64] The shrine at Arad, whose destruction had been dated to the time of Josiah, is now said to have been dismantled and buried under a layer of earth some time toward the end of the eighth century, possibly during the reign of Hezekiah.[65] The fact that it was not restored may reflect a gradual tendency toward centralization, but not to a sudden action on the part of Josiah.[66] In view of the lack of primary archaeological evidence, some scholars dismiss the whole reform story as improbable.[67]

Christoph Uehlinger, however, finds some evidence of cultic reform in seals and bullae. Seals from the eighth and early seventh centuries often use astral symbolism. "Through this striking astral imagery, deities of the night with the moon god of Harran at their pinnacle, entered the foreground in a way scarcely known before."[68] By the end of the seventh century, however, astral symbolism, and also anthropomorphic and theriomorphic representation, had gone out of vogue in Judah.

The seals are at best very indirect evidence for Josiah's reform. Ultimately we can only assess the historical plausibility of the account in 2 Kgs 23:4–20, even if it was edited later. Uehlinger notes that

> at least two measures appear to be directed against cult practices or institutions whose introduction in Judah must have been originally connected with the Assyrian expansion and the accompanying reception of Assyro-Aramean traditions of astral cults: the removal of the horses and chariots of the sun-god (v. 11) and the suppression of the k$^c$marim priests (v.5).[69]

These practices and institutions had lost their plausibility with the waning of Assyrian influence, and mainly concerned the Jerusalem temple. Uehlinger also allows that the importance of Asherah seems to have declined at the end of the First Temple period, although specific evidence to link the decline to the actions of Josiah is lacking.[70] It is apparent from Jeremiah that goddess worship in some form ("the queen of heaven") persisted into the sixth century, although in Jeremiah 44 women complain that they have fared less well since they ceased to venerate her.[71] Whether this disruption of goddess worship was due to the actions of Josiah we can only guess.

### Centralization?

The meager archaeological evidence adduced by Uehlinger concerns the purification rather than the centralization of the cult, and much of 2 Kgs 23:4–20 is also concerned with purificatory measures. Even Monroe, however, allows that some high places were also destroyed. The destruction of the high places in effect prohibits sacrifice outside of Jerusalem, and this has been taken, since de Wette, as the implementation of Deuteronomy 12: "Take care that you do not offer your burnt offerings at any place you happen to see. But only at the place that the Lord will choose in one of your tribes—there you shall offer your burnt offerings and there you shall do everything I command you" (Deut 12:13–14). The celebration of the Passover in 2 Kgs 23:21–23 also presupposes the centralization of the cult in Jerusalem. In the "reform report" of 23:4–20, centralization is hardly the primary concern, but it does seem to have been one of Josiah's objectives.[72]

The question is whether the destruction of the high places necessarily presupposes a law of centralization such as we find in Deuteronomy 12. Reinhard Kratz has argued that

> the programme of cultic centralization in Deuteronomy and the reports of putting such a centralization into practice that are found in the books of Kings are related to each other—despite all terminological and subject related differences. The programme of cultic centralization can stand for itself; the reports of its implementation, however, cannot: it is impossible to change the order of events. Deuteronomy has to come first and the verdict on kings in the annalistic frame of the book of Kings is derived from it.[73]

This argument, in itself, does not determine what role Deuteronomy might have played in Josiah's reform. Kratz considers two possible

*But why can't [tee] be a real reform for its own purposes to, that later DH writers repurpose their own[?]*

explanations for the centralization of the cult: either it is "a reaction to the downfall of Samaria and is meant to bind the northern Israelites, who have lost a political and religious home, to Judah and Jerusalem," or it is a reaction to the downfall of Jerusalem and "has the purpose of warning against the decentralization threatened as a result."[74] He favors the latter, opting for "an early exilic dating of Ur-Deuteronomy as a response to the threatening downfall."[75] This reconstruction would seem to relegate Josiah's reform to the realm of fiction, at least as it relates to the centralization of the cult. But it shows that much depends on the dating of the core of Deuteronomy. If it is an exilic composition, obviously it could not have served as the basis for a reform in 621 B.C.E. If it dates from the waning years of the Assyrian empire, then it is at least possible that it could have inspired Josiah's reform, although that conclusion would not follow necessarily.

## THE EARLIEST STRATUM OF DEUTERONOMY

Neither de Wette nor any of his followers supposed that all of Deuteronomy as we know it was available to Josiah. The original book of the law (Urdeuteronomium) would have consisted of laws now found in Deuteronomy 12–26. Scholars differ in their precise reconstruction, but there is a good measure of consensus on the main lines.[76] Two sets of literary relationships are especially important for this body of material. On the one hand, it "was a revision and supplement of the Covenant Code."[77] The key to this revision was largely supplied by the centralization of the cult in Deuteronomy 12, as can be seen most clearly in the law for the Passover in Deut 16:1–8.[78] On the other hand, there is clear influence of Neo-Assyrian treaty texts, specifically of the so-called Vassal Treaty of Esarhaddon (VTE).[79] This treaty is known from at least ten copies, and was evidently widely published. The most recently discovered copy is from Tell Tayinat, in present-day Turkey.[80] The dependence of Deuteronomy on the Assyrian treaties was demonstrated by Moshe Weinfeld in 1972,[81] and has been documented repeatedly by Eckart Otto.[82]

The influence of the Assyrian treaties has been challenged, most forcefully by Carly Crouch.[83] The objections are partly that there were many treaties current, and that the allusions are not necessarily to the VTE,[84] and partly that the correspondences are not so explicit that the readers of Deuteronomy would recognize them. The latter point calls for some caution in speaking of the "subversive" role of Deuteronomy. The essential point, however, is that the drafters of Deuteronomy conceived of the kind of loyalty demanded by YHWH by analogy with the loyalty demanded by the Assyrian king, whether their readers recognized the allusions or not.

The Esarhaddon "treaty" is essentially an oath of loyalty imposed on Assyria's vassals to ensure that they will recognize Esarhaddon's son Ashurbanipal.[85] They are commanded to "love Ashurbanipal" as themselves: "You shall hearken to whatever he says and do whatever he commands, and you shall not seek any other king or other lord against him" (VTE 195–97). They are to teach these provisions to their sons and grandsons. Compare Deuteronomy 6:

> Hear O Israel: Yahweh is our God, Yahweh alone.[86] You shall love Yahweh your God with all your heart, with all your life and with all your might.... Keep these words that I am commanding you today on your heart and teach them to your sons. (Deut 6:4–7)[87]

Further striking parallels are found between the warnings against prophets in Deuteronomy 13 and the injunctions against seditious talk in VTE 108, and between the curses in Deuteronomy 28 and VTE 419–30.[88] Crouch has shown that correspondences are not exact, and do not suggest simple translation, but most scholars have found them persuasive nonetheless.[89] If the Assyrian parallels are accepted, the relevant form of Deuteronomy would have included the Shema in Deut 6:5–6, and the curses in Deuteronomy 28, as well as some form of the laws in Deuteronomy 12–26.

Otto has argued that this adaptation of Assyrian propaganda served a subversive purpose. It accepted the concept of loyalty due to a sovereign, but applied it to Yahweh rather than to Ashurbanipal. Otto sees even the idea of cultic centralization as a reflection of Assyrian influence. As the god Ashur was worshipped in only one place, so now would Yahweh be.[90] Whether the Assyrian parallel is directly relevant to the program of centralization may be questioned; the Assyrians did not forbid all sacrificial worship elsewhere.[91] To speak of "subversion" is also an overstatement. Deuteronomy is not anti-Assyrian propaganda, but it adapts the Assyrian understanding of kingship, in good postcolonial mimicry,[92] and applies it to Yahweh's relation to Israel. As Otto has noted, "The specific Judean feature with respect to the idea of covenant was … the creation of an alliance between the deity and the people while disregarding the king, who functioned in the Assyrian context as sole covenantal partner."[93] But Deuteronomy not only disregarded the Assyrian king; it also and more immediately disregarded the king of Judah.

The use and adaptation of the Assyrian loyalty oath is highly compatible with a date around the time of Josiah.[94] Esarhaddon's treaty dates to 672 B.C.E. Jeffrey Stackert infers a date ca. 670 for the earliest stratum of Deuteronomy.[95] This would require extraordinary alacrity on the part of the Judahite scribes. The date of the treaty provides at most a terminus a quo, and only if the dependence is on this specific treaty. But the material would have lost much of its relevance after the collapse of the Assyrian Empire. The years of Assyria's decline, between the death of Ashurbanipal in 627 and the fall of Nineveh in 612 B.C.E., provide the most plausible setting for an expression of Judahite defiance. Philip Davies objects that "to be valid, this argument has to show that knowledge of such literary forms vanished at a certain point,"[96] but as Otto counters, "The decisive texts of the neo-Assyrian royal ideology had no late-Babylonian or Persian afterlife, and even if Judaeans would have had access to texts of Assyrian royal ideology in post-Assyrian times, there was no reason for them to return to this Assyrian ideology, when it was already politically overcome, outdated, and no longer of any relevance."[97]

Several scholars, nonetheless, have opted for an exilic or postexilic date for the earliest stratum of Deuteronomy.[98] Juha Pakkala argues that "the monarch plays no role in Urdeuteronomium."[99] Neither is there any indication of state organization. There is no mention of Judah, Jerusalem, or the temple itself. The entity that is addressed is Israel rather than Judah. All of this could also be said of the Book of the Covenant, and indeed king and the temple are missing from the entire Pentateuch. In Deuteronomy as we have it, all this is required by the fictive setting in the land of Moab,[100] and the analogy with the Book of the Covenant should caution against hasty assumptions of an exilic or postexilic date. Pakkala also points to the positive replies of the authorities in Jerusalem and Samaria to the Judeans in Elephantine in support of their request to rebuild their temple, but he misses the crucial detail that no animal sacrifice was to be practiced there. The fact that Deuteronomy speaks of "Israel" rather than Judah is not problematic in the time of Josiah. It may be an affirmation of pan-Israelite identity after the collapse of the Northern Kingdom.[101] Neither is it difficult to find a rationale for the centralization of the cult in the late preexilic period. In fact, the way to centralization had arguably been paved by Sennacherib's destruction of the Judean countryside eighty years earlier.[102] It is true that there are few references to a reform in the literature of the Babylonian period, but Jer 8:8 ("How can you say we are wise, and we have the law of the Lord?") seems to imply that "the law of the Lord" had recently acquired a new status, or at least was being promoted by some of Jeremiah's contemporaries.

Of the objections raised against a Josianic date for Urdeuteronomium, the most intriguing concerns the curtailment of the powers of the king. It is generally recognized that "the king as presented here differs enormously from that of the usual ancient Near Eastern concept of the king as the chief executive in all aspects of the nation's life."[103] He must not acquire many horses, which is to say he must not equip an army, nor many wives, which is to say that he must not form alliances, nor gold and silver. Moreover, Deuteronomy undercuts the king's judicial function.

In the words of Bernard Levinson, "The suppression of any mention of the conventional royal mandate to hear cases and to defend the rights of the marginalized is so systematic as to constitute an intentional rejection of that norm."[104] This rejection is not just found in the law of the king, in Deut 17:14–20, but is entailed in the whole judicial system of Deuteronomy.[105] Neither is the king given any role in the cult. Rather he must have a copy of the law written for him, and he must subordinate himself to it. He becomes, in effect, a constitutional monarch, and the law becomes the definition of what it means to be an Israelite.[106]

Should we suppose that such a law was accepted by Josiah? Patricia Dutcher-Walls has argued that the ideology of kingship reflected in Deut 17:16–17 (the restrictions on horses, wives, and wealth) "appears to have adapted its own concept of kingship to the necessary requirements of survival for a monarch on the periphery of the major world empire of its time." The restrictions "support a strategy of acquiescence to the domination of Assyria and an ideology that strictly defines the external relationships of the kingdom."[107] This interpretation runs counter to Otto's view of the subversive use of Assyrian ideology, but even if Otto overstates the subversive potential, there is little else in Deuteronomy to suggest acquiescence to foreign powers—in contrast to Jeremiah, where it is quite explicit.

Davies's argument that "there are no plausible explanations why a king should accept a reform that deprives him of the essential powers of monarchy, justice and warfare"[108] retains its force.[109] Rainer Albertz suggests that "the most probable period for dating the Deuteronomic law of the kings [is] the reigns of Jehoiakim and Zedekiah, when Shaphanide scribes, who are the best candidates for having written the Deuteronomic law, resisted the ruling kings."[110] In that case, we need not suppose that the king endorsed the law, or that it carried any authority. It was rather a utopian vision of an ideal Israel, proposed in stark contrast to the royal ideology of Judah.

In view of the adaptation of Assyrian ideology, the original core of Deuteronomy must be dated to the seventh century, but it is unlikely

*What about or Leuchter - Dtr response to Sohs reformn) Class dual theories*

that it was promulgated by Josiah. It seems undeniable that Josiah made some attempt to purify the Jerusalem temple and to destroy other places of worship in the vicinity of Jerusalem. Whether he derived authority for these actions from a law book is difficult to say. If he did, it need hardly have been more extensive than Deuteronomy 12. It may be that the king's cultic reforms were sufficient to win him credit with the authors of 2 Kings, who then co-opted him as the only king who observed the law. The actions attributed to Josiah in 2 Kings 22–23 do not conform perfectly to Deuteronomy. Notably, Deuteronomy accords the king no role in the cult, whereas Josiah took it upon himself to control it.[111] As Gordon McConville remarked, "Deuteronomy's king is nothing like King Josiah."[112] The king's deference to the law was probably augmented in later editions of the story of the reform.

On this reconstruction, the original core of Deuteronomy was a document analogous to the older Covenant Code, which it revised and supplemented. It was a programmatic, utopian document, which proposed a view of Israelite society that was very different from the kingdom of Judah. Most importantly, however, it shifted the locus of loyalty for Israel/Judah. Hitherto, Judahites had been defined as subjects of the Davidic king. Deuteronomy professed allegiance only to God.[113]

## IDENTITY FORMATION IN DEUTERONOMY

Crouch has written of Deuteronomy as an "identity formation project."[114] It pursues its goal by homogenizing Israelite cult as exclusive Yahwism, centralizing that cult around a single approved place of worship, a common mythology of origins (the exodus), and the regulation of a wide array of practices. It is characterized by the language of brotherhood, conceiving Israel as a large extended family, and differentiates throughout between Israelites and foreigners. Some scholars have seen in Deuteronomy an early form of nationalist identity.[115] Crouch objects that the "Israel" with which Deuteronomy is concerned is not a collection of ardent Israelites, battling for political autonomy, but a community which is in contention with itself, over itself. The focus, in other words, is not the protection of an Israelite state against one or more foreign states, but the preservation of an Israelite cultural identity threatened by exposure to and the temptation to adopt practices considered non-Israelite. This is ethnic identity, not nationalist identity.[116]

Nonetheless, Deuteronomy is predicated on the imminent possession of the land. In the original core of Deuteronomy the land is taken for granted. Concern for possession of the land comes to the fore more in the Deuteronomistic History, both in references to the promise to the fathers in the Deuteronomistic frame of Deuteronomy,[117] and, most explicitly, in the book of Joshua. If this is not nationalism, it is something akin to it, despite the prevailing view that nationalism is a modern phenomenon.[118]

Crouch is right, however, to insist that "the Deuteronomic entity called 'Israel' is not coterminous with Judah or its population."[119] It is not the case that Deuteronomy is concerned with religion rather than with ethnic identity.[120] Rather, religion, specifically the monolatrous cult of Yahweh, is a key element in the ethnic identity that is being proposed. This proposal is instrumentalist, insofar as it advocates one view of Israelite identity rather than others. It does not represent the status quo in preexilic or exilic Judah.[121] But it should not be viewed in reductionist terms. Inevitably, Deuteronomy entails a redistribution of power in Judahite society, diminishing the power of both the king and the paterfamilias, but it is a comprehensive attempt to define an ethnic culture in terms of a law that is claimed to be ancestral.

## THE EXPANSION OF DEUTERONOMY

On Otto's reconstruction,

> the real career of the book of Deuteronomy started in the exilic period with the end of the royal dynasty and its state, and the end of the temple, which was supposed to be the centre of an Israel assembled around it.[122]

Now it was framed as a revelation to Moses on Mount Horeb, promulgated to Israel in Moab, outside the land of Israel. It is also possible that the original laws of Deuteronomy were already assumed to be Mosaic, especially if the Book of the Covenant was already integrated into the Elohist source. Deuteronomy draws heavily on the Elohist. In the words of Joel Baden, "Virtually every aspect of E's Horeb narrative is present in D."[123] At no point are the laws in either the Book of the Covenant or Deuteronomy attributed to anyone other than Moses.

In any case, it is clear that the book of Deuteronomy was expanded and edited after the destruction of Jerusalem. The strongest evidence for an exilic redaction is found in the reformulation of the covenant in the land of Moab, in Deuteronomy 29–30, introduced in 28:69 (Heb. = 29:1 Eng.) as "the words of the covenant that the Lord commanded Moses to make with the Israelites in the land of Moab, in addition to the covenant that he had made with them at Horeb." As Dominik Markl has argued, the rhetorical dynamics of this covenant can be viewed on two levels, as addressed to the Moab generation in the literary context of the book and also to the actual addressees in the exile:

> Moses' digression to the future in the centre of the speech (Deut 29:2–31:6—30:10) relates to the experience of the addressees—exile (esp. Deut 29:27) and restoration. (Deut 20:1–10)[124]

Deut 29:21–32 (22–23 Eng.) warns:

> The next generation, your children who rise up after you, as well as the stranger who comes from a distant country, will see the devastation of that land and the afflictions with which the Lord has afflicted it—all its soil burned out by sulfur and salt, nothing planted, nothing sprouting, unable to support any vegetation, like the destruction of Sodom and Gomorrah.

They will then conclude: "It is because they abandoned the covenant of the Lord, the God of their ancestors, which he made with them when he brought them out of the land of Egypt" (29:24; 23 Eng.). But there is still hope:

When all these things have happened to you, the blessings and curses that I have set before you, if you call them to mind among all the nations where the Lord your God has driven you, and return to the Lord your God, and you and your children obey him with all your heart and with all your soul, just as I am commanding you today, then the Lord your God will restore your fortunes and have compassion on you, gathering you again from all the peoples among whom the Lord your God has scattered you. (Deut 30:1–3)

Markl concludes:

> Deuteronomy 29–30 constructs its implicit audience as a community that is supposed to identify with experiencing a situation of exile at the turning point to restoration (29:24–30:10). These chapters encourage the people to commit themselves to the Moab covenant and the torah of Deuteronomy.

In the exilic context, without king or temple, the Law provided a new identity for the remnant of Judah.[125] "Israel" was still a people bound by blood ties, and closely identified with the land. Most fundamentally, however, Israel was the people bound exclusively to the God Yahweh by covenant.[126]

### THE COMPOSITE TORAH

Deuteronomy was the original book of the Torah of Moses. But the Torah as it eventually took shape contained much more than the Deuteronomic law. It also included the foundational narratives of Genesis and Exodus. In the Torah as it took shape in Babylon, the Deuteronomic law was balanced by the Priestly document, which extended from creation to Sinai.[127] Otto regards P as "a counter-programme to the deuteronomistic book of Deuteronomy."[128] It certainly had different emphases, giving far more weight to ritual and purity, which were the primary concern of priests. P agreed with D, however, that the exile was punishment for failure to keep the commandments that God gave to Moses on Mount Sinai.[129]

Both D and P were concerned with boundary markers that would distinguish Israel from the nations, and prevent the exiles from disappearing through assimilation, as had happened with the exiles from the Northern Kingdom in the Assyrian period. The primary boundary marker in Deuteronomy is the exclusive allegiance to one God, Yahweh, and this is also basic to the Priestly tradition. Deuteronomy strikes a belligerent pose toward the nations inhabiting the land, although the belligerence may have been primarily directed against Israelites or Judeans who did not subscribe to the Deuteronomistic restriction of worship to Yahweh alone at his single sanctuary, "insiders who pose a threat to the hierarchy that is being asserted."[130] Fatefully, however, it enjoined the Israelites: "Do not intermarry with them, giving your daughters to their sons or taking their daughters for your sons" (Deut 7:3). It also imposed ethnic restrictions on admission to "the assembly of the Lord" (23:3–8): Ammonites and Moabites were excluded, although, remarkably enough, Edomites and Egyptians were acceptable. These restrictions would be fundamental for Ezra, who would extend them to all foreigners.

The Priestly tradition contributed distinctive boundary markers that would become definitive for Judaism in the succeeding centuries. As Thomas Römer has noted, P "insists that all major 'identity markers' for the nascent Judaism are given during the origins stage, before entering the land and before the creation of an Israelite or Judean state."[131] The Sabbath is grounded in the account of creation. Circumcision is prescribed for Abraham and his descendants (Gen 17). Neither Sabbath nor circumcision was invented as late as the Babylonian exile, but they acquired new significance as boundary markers in the exile.[132] The Passover is integrated into the story of the exodus. Dietary restrictions are prescribed already for Noah after the flood. The list of forbidden foods, including pork, that had most influence on later tradition is found in Leviticus 11, but the other foundation stone of later kosher laws, the prohibition of boiling a kid in its mother's milk, is found in Exod 23:19 (in the book of the covenant) and in Deut 14:21.

Perhaps the greatest riddle of the Torah is how the diverse theologies, especially those of D and P, came to be combined in a single book. The Persians, like the Greeks after them, were content to let subject peoples live by their ancestral laws. Whether one subscribes to the theory of Persian authorization of the Pentateuch or not,[133] the stamp of Persian approval was necessary if one formulation of the ancestral laws of Judah was to attain official recognition. In the late sixth and early fifth centuries there were several different models of Jewish identity on offer—not only the contrasting views of the Deuteronomists and the Priestly tradition but also a restoration movement in Judah in which the Torah does not seem to have played any important part. The party that gained Persian approval had the opportunity to impose its view as the official "ancestral law" of Judah.

It would seem that various parties, including the Deuteronomists and the Priestly tradents, joined forces in order to elevate the Torah of Moses as the official statement of Judahite ancestral law. They did not, however, attempt to iron out their differences. Rather, they created a composite document, in which their differing theologies, including the older Yahwist and Elohist ones, stood in tension. Albertz has suggested, somewhat facetiously, that the composite Torah was compiled by a commission:

> With a touch of imagination one could suppose that these majority parties in the council of elders and the priestly college each appointed a commission of professional theologians and entrusted it with working out a foundation document for Israel on the basis of existing traditions which could command an internal majority and at the same time was a suitable model for the central Persian authorities.[134]

One might, perhaps, compare the commission appointed by Darius to collect the laws of Egypt.[135] But whatever the process by which the Torah was compiled, it is clear that it included diverse, unreconciled perspectives. In the words of Ska, "The Pentateuch was a 'compromise' between various tendencies and just like all compromises, it had to take into account different perspectives."[136] There was, then, a measure of religious pluralism built into the Torah.[137] One might not suspect this from reading Ezra, but the potential for pluralism would be exploited in time in the ways in which the Torah was construed and interpreted.

# CHAPTER 2

# Torah in the Persian Period

Judean identity was not always formulated with reference to the Law of Moses. The Book of the Law is conspicuous by its absence in the literature of the restoration period, at the end of the sixth century B.C.E. The books of Ezra and Nehemiah represent its introduction as an innovation later in the Persian period.

## THE EARLY PERSIAN PERIOD

According to Nehemiah 8, when the people came to study the words of the Torah with Ezra on the second day of the seventh month, they found it written that they should live in booths during the festival of the seventh month (Neh 8:13). The remarkable thing about this account is that no one in Jerusalem seems to have been aware of such a law until they found it written in the book. In fact, the whole mission of Ezra is predicated on the fact that the book of the Torah was not known in Jerusalem before his arrival.

The impression of novelty associated with Ezra's introduction of the Law is all the more surprising in that Ezra 3 reports that a generation earlier Joshua son of Jozadak and Zerubbabel son of Shealtiel had "set out to build the altar of the God of Israel, to offer burnt offerings on it, as prescribed in the law of Moses, the man of God" (Ezra 3:2). Moreover, they had kept the Feast of Booths, as prescribed, and offered all the sacrifices "according to the ordinance." Michael Satlow is surely right when he suggests that this passage reflects the assumptions of the author of the book of Ezra, writing at least a generation later, rather than what actually happened in the late sixth century.[1] It would be remarkable indeed if the early returnees were guided by the Law of Moses, and yet it was forgotten by the middle of the following century.

Our primary sources for the period of the restoration are found in the prophetic books of Haggai, Zechariah, and Third Isaiah. As David Carr has remarked, these books "lack the kind of Torah focus seen in later texts."[2]

Haggai is primarily preoccupied with the issue of rebuilding the temple, with a brief appendix on the restoration of the monarchy. The question of familiarity with Pentateuchal texts arises in the second chapter, when he tells his audience to "ask the priests for a ruling" on two issues concerning purity. In their commentary on Haggai in the Anchor Bible series, Carol and Eric Meyers claim that

> the clarity of the priestly response is based upon pentateuchal texts.... Haggai's use of a priestly ruling based on cases found in Leviticus and Numbers presupposes an awareness on the part of his audience of the existence of those texts and their validity for the community, if not a familiarity with the actual content of those texts. Pentateuchal law was obviously a factor in the community life of the early restoration period with respect to priestly responsibilities.

They infer that "an authoritative legal system, probably some form of the Pentateuch, existed."[3] But Haggai makes no reference to a written law. The *torah* in question is a matter of priestly judgment.[4] To be sure, the role of the priests in giving *torah* is affirmed in Lev 10:10–11, but the specific issues posed by Haggai are not discussed there. The second issue, corpse contamination, is discussed in Num 19:11–13, but the appeal in Haggai is not to the Law of Moses but to the judgment of the priests. Far from attesting to knowledge of the Pentateuch, Haggai presupposes a system where a written book is superfluous. No doubt the priests were informed by the kind of traditions that are also found in Leviticus, but there is no indication here that their authority derived from any book, or specifically from the Law of Moses.

In Zechariah, too, the emphasis is on the temple and the restoration of the monarchy.[5] There is a reference to the Torah in Zech 7:12 ("They had made their hearts adamant in order not to hear the Law"), but this is part of the redactional frame of the oracles, of uncertain date, and cannot be ascribed to the prophet Zechariah.[6] The core visions in Zech 1:7–6:15 never refer to the Torah.[7] Here again the Meyers have tried to find a reference to the Torah in an enigmatic vision in Zech 5:1–4. The prophet sees a flying scroll, and is told:

> This is the curse that goes out over the face of the whole land; for everyone who steals shall be cut off according to the writing on one side, and everyone who swears falsely shall be cut off according to the writing on the other. (Zech 5:3)

The Meyers take "curse" here as representing "covenant in its breach,"[8] and the references to stealing and false swearing as metonymical references to the Torah. They infer:

> Perhaps, already in the middle of the exile the Pentateuch had assumed its enduring position as the beginning of an account of Israel from its prehistory through its termination with the collapse of Judah (as recorded in 2 Kgs 25). In any event, given Darius's concern that indigenous legal systems be made authoritative for the people who had traditionally adhered to them, it is reasonable to suppose that the Torah literature, or at least, the legal portions thereof, is the specific body of law represented by the scroll of the prophet's vision. This would appear to mean that biblical authority is being promulgated in this vision only for Yahwists resident in Yehud.[9]

They support this inference in part by the belief that Darius I of Persia tried to codify the laws of the subject peoples, a view that we will discuss below in connection with the mission of Ezra. Even if Darius had requested a codification of the laws of Judah, this would not have produced an authoritative law instantaneously in the time of Haggai and Zechariah. But reference, in a vision, to prohibitions of stealing and swearing can hardly be construed as a promulgation of "biblical authority." Even if the scroll were to contain the full Decalogue, which it does not, this would still be far short of an affirmation of the authority of the entire Pentateuch or Torah. To speak of "biblical authority" in this context is blatantly anachronistic.

Third Isaiah does not mention the Torah at all.[10] It does, of course, touch on issues that are also treated in the Torah, and here again there is a tendency in scholarship to assume that it is engaging in exegesis. Isaiah 56:1–7 takes a position contradictory to Deut 23:2–9 on the question of who may be admitted to the assembly of the Lord. Several scholars have argued that these texts, together with Ezek 44:6–9 constitute an exegetical chain.[11] In the words of Joachim Schaper, "What we have in Ezek 44:6–9 and Isa 56:1–8 are two interpretations of Deut 23:2–9 that are mutually exclusive."[12] But as Christophe Nihan has pointed out, the passages in Deuteronomy 23 and Isaiah 56 do not have a single term in common.[13] (In contrast there are several cross-references between Isaiah 56 and Ezekiel 44.) It is difficult then to regard Isaiah 56 as a reinterpretation of Deuteronomy. Moreover, as Michael Fishbane has acknowledged, Isaiah 56 is not presented as the interpretation of anything, but as an oracle from God.[14] (The same is true of Ezekiel 44.) The issue of admission to the assembly was evidently disputed, and the postexilic prophets may well have known Deuteronomy 23. Saul Olyan points out that Isa 56:3–4, which affirms that the eunuch has a place in the temple, can be read as a contradictory allusion to Deut 23:2 ("No one whose testicles are crushed or whose testicles are cut off shall be admitted to the assembly of the Lord"), although here again the terminology is different.[15] But even if Isaiah 56 has Deuteronomy 23 in view, it can hardly be regarded as an interpretation. Far from treating Deuteronomy as authoritative scripture, it flatly contradicts it. Neither is there any appeal to the Law of Moses in Ezekiel 44.

Isa 56:1–7 does not appeal to the Torah of Moses as such. It does, however, appeal to the covenant. Eunuchs and foreigners may be admitted to the house of the Lord if they keep the Sabbath, "choose the things that please me," and hold fast to the covenant (Isa 56:4, 6). Beyond the observance of the Sabbath, the requirements of the covenant are not specified. Joseph Blenkinsopp comments that "in contrast to the Priestly prescriptions in the Pentateuch ... Sabbath observance and not circumcision is here the criterion of membership in the community."[16] It is possible, of course, that circumcision is entailed in "keeping the covenant." But even if the covenant is presumed to be the one God made with Moses, the lack of appeal to the Torah of Moses is notable. The Law of Moses, in its written form, was not the touchstone for Judean identity in the early restoration period, before the coming of Ezra.

## THE JUDEANS OF ELEPHANTINE

The Law of Moses is also conspicuous by its absence from the archive of the Judean garrison at Elephantine (Yeb) in Upper Egypt.[17] This community is known from a cache of Aramaic papyri that spans the fifth century B.C.E.[18] It had its own temple in honor of Yahu (or Yaho), the traditional god of Israel, which had been built before Cambyses came to Egypt, where sacrifices and offerings were made, until it was eventually burned down by the local Egyptians.[19] But the garrison also apparently contributed funds to the cults of other, Aramean deities, Anath-Bethel and Eshem-Bethel.[20] (There were nearby Aramean temples to Bethel, the Queen of Heaven, Banit, and Nabu.[21]) Moreover, Judeans at Elephantine swore oaths by several other deities, including Anath-Yahu, whose name is reminiscent of preexilic inscriptions that mention "Yahweh and his Asherah."[22] While there are several items that relate to cultic matters, there are no copies of the Torah or any part of it, and the correspondence does not refer to the Torah.[23]

The authors refer to themselves as *Yehudayya',* Judeans, even though there are indications that their ancestors came from the region of

Bethel.[24] When their temple was burned down, they appealed to the authorities in Samaria and Jerusalem, apparently unaware of the restriction of sacrificial worship to one place in Deuteronomy 12. There are references to distinctively Israelite or Judean practices such as the Passover, the Feast of Unleavened Bread, and the Sabbath (but not circumcision!), and André Lemaire has argued that Judean ethnicity at Elephantine "was mainly apparent as marked by religion and ritual."[25] But there is nothing to indicate that these Judeans had in their possession a copy of the Torah of Moses. Neither do they betray any awareness of the patriarchs, Moses, David, or even, despite their observance of the Passover, the story of the exodus.[26] They did have a copy of the sayings of Aḥikar, and an Aramaic copy of the Behistun inscription. As A. E. Cowley put it, "The literary pieces … are evidently of non-Jewish origin, but they show nevertheless the kind of literature which was current in the community."[27]

The so-called Passover Papyrus is especially interesting in this regard. This is a letter sent by one Hananiah to "my brothers Jedaniah and his colleagues of the Judean garrison," transmitting an instruction allegedly sent by the king to Arsames, governor of Egypt:

> Now you thus count four[teen days of Nisan … ] and from the 15th until the 21st day of [Nisan.… ] be pure and take heed. Any work do n[ot do … ] do not drink, anything of leaven do not eat … sunset until the 21st day of Nisa[n …b]ring (the leaven) into your chambers and seal it up during [these] days.[28]

We do not know for sure who this Hananiah was, but he was evidently a person of some importance. Nehemiah had a brother Hanani (Neh 1:2; 7:2), and it is possible that this is the same person, but this cannot be verified.[29] Nehemiah also mentions a Hananiah who was commander of the citadel in Jerusalem (Neh 7:2). Another text from Elephantine speaks of trouble with the local Egyptians "since the time that Hananiah came to Egypt."[30] It is unlikely that instructions on the observance of Unleavened Bread were sent on the initiative of the king. Presumably the Persian officials signed off on the initiative of some Judeans who sought to impose standard observance on outlying communities. We might suppose that this was a consequence of the attempts of Ezra and Nehemiah to impose the Torah in Judah. Bezalel Porten went so far as to claim that "the letter of Hananiah would have been written under the impact of the canonization of the Torah,"[31] but this is clearly anachronistic.

The view that Hananiah was bringing the provisions of the Torah to Elephantine encounters some anomalies. First, there is no reference in the papyrus to the Law of Moses; the authority invoked is that of the Persian king. Second, the extant text does not actually mention Passover; it only deals with the Feast of Unleavened Bread or Mazzoth. Neither does it specify whether Passover and Mazzoth should be celebrated together or whether the Passover should be celebrated in the temple or in the family. Reinhard Kratz infers that the papyrus shows no awareness of Deuteronomy 16 or Exodus 12–13.[32] Some of the provisions are not found in the Torah, but only in the Mishnah (the prohibition of drinking anything fermented), and others were prohibited later (sealing up leaven in chambers).[33] There are two ostraca from Elephantine that mention Passover, but they make no reference to Mazzoth.[34] Kratz concludes that while the papyrus deals with a matter that is discussed in the Torah, it is not based on the stipulations of the Torah.

This conclusion is open to question, however. The references to the fourteenth and fifteenth days of the month seem to reflect Lev 23:5–6: "In the first month, on the fourteenth day of the month, at twilight, there shall be a Passover offering to the Lord, and on the fifteenth day of the same month is the festival of Unleavened Bread to the Lord; seven days you shall eat unleavened bread." In fact, it is likely that the major purpose of the letter was to communicate the correct dates for Passover and Mazzoth in accordance with Priestly legislation. It is remarkable, however, that the papyrus does not invoke the authority of the Torah or cite its specifications exactly. It would seem that the authorities in Jerusalem were unwilling to go to the expense and trouble of making a copy of the Law, in whatever form it existed, for the benefit of a remote community.

Kratz argues that the case of the Sabbath, too, was not greatly different in Elephantine from what it was in Jerusalem.[35] We find references
to the Sabbath on ostraca, but Judeans at Elephantine engaged in trade
and transportation and stocked warehouses on the Sabbath.[36] Kratz
comments: "In this respect, they were no different from the Judeans or
the people of Tyre mentioned in Neh 13:15–16."[37]

Julius Wellhausen deemed the Judeans of Elephantine to be a "strange
vestige of pre-legal Hebraism," and a "fossil remnant of not yet reformed
Judaism in a distant land."[38] Most scholars have agreed, whether they
trace these "Judeans" to the Northern or Southern Kingdom.[39] Kratz,
however, argues that they "do not just represent an earlier form of the religion of preexilic Israel or preexilic Judah respectively," and suggests that

> even in their own time they were not exceptional. Rather they seem to
> have been compatible with the Jewry represented by the leading figures in
> Jerusalem and Samaria to whom they addressed their letters.[40]

He infers that the Torah of Moses did not play an important role yet in
the Persian provinces of Yehud and Samaria.

It is not apparent, however, that the leading figures in Judah and
Samaria regarded them as entirely compatible. When the temple was
burned down, the Judeans appealed to Bagohi, governor of Judah and
the High Priest. As Satlow has observed, "This indicates that they did
not, apparently, know the Pentateuch as it survives today."[41] The appeal
was to no avail. Three years later they appealed again to Bagohi, and to
the sons of the governor of Samaria.[42] They replied, not by letter, but by
an oral communication recorded in a memorandum:

> Let it be an instruction to you in Egypt to say to Arsames about the altar-
> house of the God of Heaven, which was built in the fortress of Yeb ... to
> rebuild it in its place as was before, and they may offer the meal-offering
> and incense upon the altar as formerly was done.[43]

The High Priest is not cited in the reply, and there is no mention of animal sacrifices. A subsequent petition to Arsames specifically promised

that no animal sacrifices would be offered in the restored temple.[44] The compromise may have been necessary to appease the priests of the ram-god Khnum, but it may also have been required by the authorities of Jerusalem.

Whatever the authorities in Jerusalem may have thought of the Judeans at Elephantine, the latter may not have been as greatly at odds with the situation in Judah as they might initially seem. What the books of Ezra and Nehemiah show, taken at face value, is, first, that the Torah was virtually unknown in Judah before the coming of Ezra, and, second, that the reforms of Ezra were ephemeral. We find Nehemiah, who is usually dated some thirteen years after Ezra, fighting with people who persisted in marrying non-Judeans: "I contended with them and cursed them, and beat some of them and pulled out their hair" (Neh 13:25). This does not necessarily show that the Torah was unknown in Nehemiah's time, but that many Judeans, including some of the high priestly family, did not feel any obligation to let it regulate their behavior. We do not, of course, know how the people berated by Nehemiah would have identified themselves, but they were presumably Judeans or Judahites. The people at Elephantine, who celebrated the Passover, do not even refer to the common Israelite/Judean myth of origin in the exodus, in the extant papyri. The papyri may not give us the full picture, but they show that it was possible to be "Judean" in the fifth century without reference to the Law of Moses.

## EZRA

At some point in the Persian period, the Law of Moses attained new status, as can be seen from the evidence of the Hellenistic period considered in the introduction to this book. In biblical tradition, that development is associated with the book of Ezra.

The book of Ezra claims that in the seventh year of Artaxerxes, Ezra, a scribe skilled in the Law of Moses, brought a copy of that law to Jerusalem. The account bristles with historical difficulties.[45] It is uncertain whether the reference is to the first or second Artaxerxes. The majority view favors the first, and this would place Ezra's mission in 458 B.C.E., but the seventh year of Artaxerxes II, or 398 B.C.E., is also possible.[46] For our present purpose, the difference is not of great importance: the Torah gained its official status some time in the mid- or late Persian period. More seriously, the letter that Artaxerxes allegedly gave to Ezra is unlikely to be authentic, at least in its extant wording.[47] The king is too generous to be credible,[48] and the decree has several echoes of biblical language.[49] Nonetheless, it is difficult to believe that the story would have been invented out of whole cloth. It is apparent that by the Hellenistic period the law of Moses had gained official status as the ancestral law of Judah. While the biblical account is embellished in its details, it remains the only account we have of how this came about.

The decree of Artaxerxes has given rise to a controversy as to whether the Torah received official authorization by the Persian rulers as the law of the land in Judah.[50] A text preserved in a Hellenistic papyrus, on the reverse of the Demotic Chronicle, records an order by Darius I, dating from 519 B.C.E., that scholars among the soldiers, priests, and scribes of Egypt write out the law of Egypt from olden days to the forty-fourth year of Pharaoh Amasis, or 526 B.C.E.[51] The laws were collected and written in Aramaic and demotic over a sixteen-year period, from 519 to 503. They included the laws of temples as well as the laws of the people.[52] Peter Frei argued that this constituted a "codification" of Egyptian laws, and noted that Diodorus counted Darius as the sixth lawgiver of the Egyptians.[53] Some Egyptologists see it as a more limited measure: a catalogue of exemptions and entitlements, intended to aid the Persians in controlling the sources of wealth.[54] It does, in any case, indicate an interest on the part of the Persians in the laws of Egypt.

Some biblical scholars have inferred that the Persians would have taken a similar interest in the laws of all subject peoples. On this scenario, the Pentateuch would have been drafted in response to a Persian demand, and then authorized by the emperor.[55] It is noteworthy, however, that the Torah was not translated into Aramaic. In fact there is little evidence of a consistent Persian policy empire-wide.[56] Rather, Persian authorities typically responded to proposals by local officials. Even in Frei's model, "authorization ... means that the imperial authority issues in writing a norm proposed by subordinates.... Subordinates could apply to the king or to the easier-to-reach satrap and ask him for an authorization fixed in writing."[57] On this understanding, the Torah was composed by Judean scribes in Babylon and presented to the king by Ezra for authorization. It should be noted that there does not appear to have been any comprehensive code of Persian law before the Parthian period.[58]

Even if the Torah had been composed on the initiative of Judean exiles, Ezra presumably required Persian permission in order to give it any authority at all.[59] James Watts infers that "the Persians may have designated the Pentateuch as the 'official' law of the Jerusalem community simply as a token of favor, with little or no attention to that law's form or content."[60] Kyong-Jin Lee sees the Persian authorization as an act of royal propaganda. By equating the law of Ezra's God and the lot of the king, the king announced himself as the divinely authorized champion of law, and reaffirmed his legitimacy as the ruler of the land.[61]

The idea that Persian rulers lent their authority to local rulings derives support from the so-called Passover Papyrus at Elephantine, discussed above, which transmits instructions to the "Judeans" (*Yehudayya*') in Elephantine about the correct observance of the Feast of Unleavened Bread in the name of the king.[62] The "Passover Papyrus" is interesting not only in its use of royal authorization but also in the attempt to regulate the behavior of Judeans outside the land of Judah by Judean law. The papyrus is dated to the fifth year of Darius II, several decades after the mission of Ezra, if that is correctly dated to 458 B.C.E. It should be noted, however, that the authorities in Jerusalem did not provide a copy of the whole Torah, but only attempted to regulate a particular festival.

In contrast, the decree of Artaxerxes in Ezra 7 confers wide-ranging, even comprehensive authority.[63] Ezra is authorized to

appoint magistrates and judges who may judge all the people in the province Beyond the River who know the laws of your God; and you shall teach
those who do not know them. All who will not obey the law of your God
and the law of the king, let judgment be strictly executed on them, whether
for death or for banishment or for confiscation of their goods or for impris-
onment. (Ezra 7:25)

This decree seems to grant Ezra authority over the entire satrapy, but
as Blenkinsopp remarks, "It seems tolerably clear that only those 'familiar with the law of our God' are intended, that is Jews and proselytes
(*gerim*) insofar as those came under the law."[64] The decree did not apply
to non-Judeans. In any case, the aim is to regulate Judean life as a
whole, and thereby prescribe a comprehensive way of life.

It is generally assumed that Ezra's law book was something close to
our Pentateuch, even if not in its final form.[65] Blenkinsopp concludes
that "the law" in Ezra-Nehemiah is basically "Deuteronomic law supplemented by ritual legislation in the Pentateuchal corpora convention-
ally designated P and H."[66] He adds, however, that this conclusion is
"complicated by another factor: those indications in Ezra-Nehemiah of
practice in accord with neither Deuteronomic nor Priestly law."[67] There
are several discrepancies between the actions of Ezra and Nehemiah
and the Torah as we have received it.[68] Stipulations regarding the Feast
of Booths "according to the Law" (Neh 8:13–18) are different from what
we find in the Torah. The prohibitions against intermarriage go beyond
Deuteronomy (Neh 10:31), and making purchases on the Sabbath is not
actually prohibited in the Pentateuch (Neh 10:32). The annual temple tax
in Nehemiah 10 is a third of a shekel, rather than a half, as in Exod 30:13,
and the wood offering (also in Nehemiah 10) lacks scriptural support. In
the words of Schaper, "Some [texts] that refer to torah, in fact *refer to no
known (quasi)-canonical or otherwise authoritative text.*"[69] Juha Pakkala finds
"that in no single case does the quotation or purported quotation correspond exactly to a known pentateuchal text. Only in one case is it une-
quivocally clear which passage of the Pentateuch was used: Neh 13:1–2 is
quoting Deut 23:4–6. Even in this case, the text in Neh 13:1–2 differs from

the known versions of Deut 23:4–6."[70] The most notable discrepancy is the absence of Yom Kippur from the festivals of the seventh month in Nehemiah 8, although there is a day of repentance and fasting on the twenty-fourth (rather than the tenth) day of the month. It is apparent that the cultic calendar had not yet been finalized.

The issues raised by the other discrepancies are more complex. Fishbane has argued that at least some of them may have been derived exegetically from the text as we know it.[71] So, for example, Neh 8:14, which says that "they found it written in the law … that the people of Israel should live in booths during the festival of the seventh month," is "a verbatim citation" from Lev 23:42 ("You shall live in booths for seven days"). Nehemiah differs from Leviticus with regard to *what* should be gathered, the *kinds* of branches to be gathered, and *how* they should be used.[72] Fishbane argues that the variations may be a matter of interpretation of Leviticus 23.[73] In the case of intermarriage, he argues that "the mechanism for prohibiting intermarriage with the Ammonites, Moabites, etc. was an exegetical extension of the law in Deut. 7:1–3 effected by means of an adaptation and interpolation of features from Deut. 23:4–9."[74] Deuteronomy 23 bars Ammonites and Moabites from the assembly of God, but not Egyptians, who are also excluded in Ezra. Fishbane explains the ban on Sabbath purchases, which is admittedly not found in the Torah, by reference to Jer 17:21–22, which forbids carrying burdens on the Sabbath day. According to Neh 8:8, the Levites read from the Torah *mephorash*, an expression variously translated as "with interpretation" or "distinctly." We are also told that they gave the sense, so that the people understood the reading. Fishbane argues that

> even though the precise meaning of the preceding terms remains in question, the way these activities are referred to leaves little doubt that they express developed and well-known exegetical procedures.[75]

But as Michael LeFebvre has argued, "The fact remains, however, that nowhere in Ezra-Nehemiah is such an exegetical activity actually indicated."[76] The reading by the Levites in Nehemiah 8 is more easily understood as translation. Moreover, even Fishbane's ingenuity cannot explain away some discrepancies, such as the date of Yom Kippur. LeFebvre rightly concludes that the kind of exegetical procedure Fishbane assumes here is anachronistic, and is not attested before the second century B.C.E.[77]

There is no doubt that the authors or editors of Ezra-Nehemiah regarded some form of the Law of Moses as authoritative. It may be that the Law known to them was different, at least in some cases, from that which has come down to us.[78] It may also be, as Schaper has argued, that "the reference to an alleged written text simply seems to serve the aim of lending greater authority to a rule that actually has no support in authoritative texts."[79] Even in that case, the frequent use of the formula *kakathub*, as it is written, testifies to the new authority of written scripture as a point of reference for Judean practice in the mid- to late fifth century B.C.E.[80]

LeFebvre has argued that the Torah was viewed in this period as "a collection of historic descriptions, not as a prescriptive code,"[81] as indeed written laws had traditionally been regarded in the ancient Near East. Yet it is clear that Ezra expects people to act in accordance with "what is written in the Law of Moses," even if this does not always correspond to what we find in the text. The Law is taken as prescriptive in some cases, but the enforcement is highly selective. Ezra focuses his attention on the festivals, and then on the problem of intermarriage, which were issues of great symbolic importance.

RESHAPING JUDEAN IDENTITY

Ezra's use of the Torah lends itself readily to analysis in terms of identity formation and boundary maintenance.[82] More specifically, it lends itself well to an analysis "that recognizes the socially constructed nature of ideas of 'Self' and 'Other,' and the malleability of boundaries that separate groups," because of the obvious concern for self-definition and the introduction of novel criteria for group boundaries.[83]

Coming from the Babylonian diaspora, Ezra was obsessed with maintaining clear boundaries between Judeans ("the holy seed") and others. (Not all Judeans in Babylon necessarily shared this obsession, but such concerns often arise in exilic communities.[84]) Daniel Smith-Christopher argues that Ezra's use of exclusive language and his strong action against intermarriage "all add up to a self-conscious community that is occupied with self-preservation, both as a pure community in a religious sense and also preservation in a material sense."[85] More specifically, Katherine Southwood attributes Ezra's concerns to the experience of "return migration."[86] She notes the frequency of references to "the children of the Exile, or Golah." The life of the exiled community (or a segment thereof) is regarded as definitive for what it means to be a Judean, and the community existing in Judah is measured and judged by reference to this ideal.[87]

On his arrival in Jerusalem, Ezra discovered that

> the people of Israel, the priests, and the Levites have not separated themselves from the peoples of the lands with their abominations, from the Canaanites, the Hittites, the Perizzites, the Jebusites, the Ammonites, the Moabites, the Egyptians and the Amorites. For they have taken some of their daughters as wives for themselves and for their sons. Thus the holy seed has mixed itself with the peoples of the lands, and in this faithlessness the officials and leaders have led the way. (Ezra 9:1–3)

Ezra is appalled at the discovery, and proceeds to take drastic steps to remedy the situation.

The issue at stake is characterized in the book of Ezra as one of purity. In a bold and innovative move it declares that Israelite "seed" is holy, and that it is defiled by intermarriage.[88] Olyan attributes this move to "expansive and creative exegesis of earlier texts such as Lev 18:24–30, Deut 23:4–9, and Deut 7:1–6."[89] It is certainly true that Ezra invokes the authority of the Torah, and that his position goes beyond what we find in the actual texts of the Torah. How far the justification of this position is exegetical seems to me questionable. Ezra seems to rely on the thrust of the older texts rather than on literal application, so it is free exegesis, at best. In doing so, he subordinates the text of the Torah to the perceived need for a clearly articulated Judean identity. Restrictions placed on interaction with outsiders can be generalized and expanded. He treats the Torah as a malleable instrument, a point that Olyan readily acknowledges.[90]

Over against the "holy seed" or "the people of the Golah/Exile," Ezra sets "the people of the land," identified as Canaanites, Hittites, and so on. Many scholars have suspected, with Smith-Christopher, that

> some of these "mixed" marriages … were probably not "mixed" at all in any truly racial/ethnic sense of the term, and may well have represented marriages between Jews who were not a part of the exilic-formed "Sons of the Golah," with those who were.[91]

The "people of the Golah" set the norms for what it meant to be Judean. Those who did not belong to the community of returned exiles were not to be trusted, and indeed could be labeled as "Canaanites" or other traditional enemies of Israel. Ezra depicts a struggle to refashion Judean identity by bringing it into conformity with the ideals and practices of his party of returned exiles.

Similar concerns are in evidence in Nehemiah 13, where Nehemiah tries to enforce strict observance of the Sabbath and expresses concern that the children of some Judeans could not speak "the language of Judah." Nehemiah also appeals to the Torah (Deut 23:3) as a warrant for evicting Tobiah the Ammonite from quarters in the Jerusalem temple, although Tobiah was surely a worshipper of YHWH.[92]

The authority of the Torah is fundamental to the reform of Ezra. In the matter of mixed marriages, the people defer to the authority of Ezra, and ask that things be done "according to the Law" (Ezra 10:3). In Nehemiah 8, Ezra reads to the people from the book, and afterward "the heads of ancestral houses of all the people, with the priests and the Levites, came together to the scribe Ezra in order to study the words of the Law" (Neh 8:13). The Levites, we are told, helped the people understand the Law when it was read to them in public. But as Kyong-Jin Lee has observed, "There is no record that Ezra launched a massive educational campaign to inform the people of the content of the Torah."[93] Satlow has emphasized that very few people in Persian Yehud could read.[94] In such a society, the general populace was heavily dependent on the word of the scribe and the priest. Conformity to the "Law of Moses" was primarily a matter of cultic observance (including Sabbath observance in Nehemiah), which had great symbolic value, and of boundary maintenance (avoidance of mixed marriage, language), and was essentially a matter of conformity to the dictates of the religious authorities.

Ezra's reform appears to have been short-lived. Most of the problems he tried to address were still there to confront Nehemiah thirteen years later, on the usual dating of Ezra. But his installation of the Law of Moses as the normative expression of the Judean way of life would endure, regardless of whether the populace, or even the authorities, observed it in detail. Henceforth, the Torah would at least have iconic status as the ancestral law of Judah, in the sense that it would be treated with deference and respect even when it was not observed in detail.[95]

To return to the issues discussed in the introduction, the adoption of the law of Moses as the law of Judah was a huge step in making Judaism into a religion. Henceforth it would be possible to argue that observance of the Law was more important to "Jewish" identity than geographical provenance or even ethnic descent.[96] "Judaism" could exist outside the land of Judah, and it could, at least potentially, be universalized. Of course geographical and genealogical considerations would remain important. In Shaye Cohen's term, Judaism was and would remain an "ethno-religion." But Judean ethnicity would no longer be defined only in primordial terms. There was now available a "constitutional" model of what it meant to be a Judean.

It is somewhat ironic that Ezra, as he is portrayed in the book of Ezra, seems to view Judean ethnicity in ultraprimordialist, even genealogical, terms. The complaint that leads to the mass divorce of foreign wives is that "the holy seed has mixed itself with the peoples of the land" (Ezra 9:2). The intention of Ezra's reform was to distinguish Judeans from other peoples by keeping this "holy seed" pure. The Law of Moses would often be used in later times as an instrument to separate Jew from Gentile. But contrary to Ezra's apparent intention, it would also make it possible to be a Judean regardless of whether one came from "the holy seed" or not.

_Judaism_

CHAPTER 3

# The Persistence of Non-Mosaic Judaism

From the Persian period forward, there was an officially recognized expression of Judean identity, in the form of the ancestral laws. Moses was credited as the author of these laws. It is reasonable to assume that that they bore some resemblance to what we know as the Torah or Pentateuch, although there was still some textual fluctuation well into the Hellenistic period. But even when allowance is made for some variation in the formulation of the Torah, the great bulk of Jewish literature that has survived from the Hellenistic period onward relies in some way on the Torah of Moses as a foundational document.

The centrality of the Torah in the later Second Temple period has led one strand of scholarship to suppose that there existed already in this period a normative form of Judaism, which would reach its definitive expression in the writings of the rabbis. The classic expression of this strand of scholarship is George Foot Moore's _Judaism in the First Centuries of the Christian Era._ Referring to the Persian, Greek, and Roman periods, Moore wrote:

> In these centuries, past the middle of which the Christian era falls, Judaism brought to complete development its characteristic institutions, the school and the synagogue.... Through the study of the Scriptures and the discussions of generations of scholars it defined its religious conceptions,

its moral principles, its forms of worship, and its distinctive type of piety, as well as the rules of law and observance which became authoritative for all succeeding time. In the light of subsequent history, the great achievement of these centuries was the creation of a normative type of Judaism and its establishment in undisputed supremacy throughout the wide Jewish world. This goal was not reached without many conflicts of parties and sects and more than one grave political and religious crisis, but in the end the tendency which most truly represented the historical character and spirit of the religion prevailed, and accomplished the unification of Judaism.[1]

Moore realized that this form of Judaism did not take its definitive shape until the Mishnah, but as Seth Schwartz has remarked, Moore's view of Judaism in the Second Temple period is "teleologically rabbinotropic."[2] The same might be said of E. P. Sanders's argument that there was a common theology in the late Second Temple period. Sanders recognizes that the rabbinic literature cannot be assumed to provide "an accurate picture of Judaism or even of Pharisaism in the time of Jesus and Paul."[3] He also recognizes that Jewish literature from this period, including the Tannaitic literature, is varied. Yet he argues that "a common pattern can be discerned which underlies otherwise disparate parts of Tannaitic literature,"[4] which he describes as "covenantal nomism."

At the opposite end of the spectrum from Moore is the position of Jacob Neusner:

> There never has been a single encompassing Judaism, present beneath the accidents of difference. There have only been diverse Judaisms. But these Judaisms do form a whole; seen all together over time and in comparison to other religion-cultures, these Judaisms do bear traits that distinguish all of them from all other religion-cultures and permit us to identify the Judaisms as a cogent set of systems.[5]

"A Judaism" for Neusner is

> a single religious system. It is composed of three elements: a worldview, a way of life, and a social group that, in the here and now, embodies the whole. The worldview explains the life of the group, ordinarily referring to

God's creation, the revelation of the Torah, the goal and end of the group's life in the end time. The way of life defines what is special about the life of the group. The social group, in a single place and time, then forms the living witness and testimony to the system as a whole.[6]

Neusner was closely associated for many years with the theoretician of religion Jonathan Z. Smith. Smith, too, spoke of "Judaisms," as an illustration of a broader argument in favor of polythetic, rather than monothetic, taxonomies. Noting the varied ways in which ancient Jewish authors interpreted circumcision, Smith wrote:

> The wide range of uses and interpretations of circumcision as a taxic indicator in early Judaism suggests that, even with respect to this most fundamental division, we cannot sustain the impossible construct of a normative Judaism. We must conceive of a variety of early Judaisms, clustered in varying configurations.[7]

For all their mutual admiration, however, Smith and Neusner held rather different views of what constituted a religion, or a Judaism. For Neusner, it was a system. For Smith, in contrast, it was a "'heap of rubbish,' a 'tangle,' a 'hotch-potch.'"[8]

Neusner's argument that we should speak of Judaisms in the plural has not won many followers. (Gabriele Boccaccini is the most notable exception.) His argument that the concept of "Judaism" is extrapolated from individual "Judaisms" is surely backwards: to speak of "a Judaism" presupposes the overarching concept of Judaism in the singular. While Neusner recognizes three components of a religious system, his distinction of different "Judaisms" favors worldview over practice. This is explicitly the case in Smith's admittedly brief discussion. Different groups that share the practice of circumcision but explain it differently are said to constitute different "Judaisms." Seth Schwartz declares, with some justification, that this is "precisely wrong."[9] The same evidence that Smith used to argue for plural "Judaisms" could be used to argue for the prevalence of "common Judaism," since regardless of how they explained it, all these groups followed a common practice. The notion of "common Judaism" was developed by E. P. Sanders to describe the practices and rudimentary beliefs that all Jews had in common.[10] In the words of Morton Smith, "Down to the fall of the Temple, the normative Judaism of Palestine is the compromise of which the three principal elements are the Pentateuch, the Temple, and the *'amme ha'arets*, the ordinary Jews who were not members of any sect."[11] It is of interest that for Neusner "a Judaism" ordinarily affirms the revelation of the Torah. This point undercuts to a great degree his insistence on the difference between the various "Judaisms."

Jonathan Z. Smith and Neusner made a valuable contribution in noting that common practices did not always entail common worldviews. This proves to be true even among people who all agree on the primary importance of the Torah. A more fundamental question, however, is whether there existed in the Second Temple period any forms of Judaism that did not accord primary importance to the Torah of Moses, and indeed whether any such group could or would be recognized as Jewish, or Judean, at all.

We have already seen that the earliest phase of postexilic Judaism was not regulated by the Torah, and that the people of Jerusalem do not seem to have been familiar with it when Ezra introduced it in the mid-fifth century B.C.E. The Judeans of Elephantine do not seem to have had a copy of it, and were only informed about regulations for Unleavened Bread, and probably for the Passover, by a decree brought from outside, as late as 419 B.C.E. But was it still possible to live as a Judean without according primary importance to the Torah of Moses in the late Persian and Hellenistic periods?

The centrality of the Torah for most of Judaism in the Hellenistic period is not in dispute. Nonetheless, there are exceptions, at least in the pre-Maccabean period. One major example, enshrined eventually in the biblical canon, is provided by the wisdom tradition prior to Ben Sira. Another significant example can be found in the Enoch tradition. Some of the stories from the eastern diaspora (Esther; Daniel 1–6) also lack explicit acknowledgment of the Torah.

## THE WISDOM TRADITION

The early wisdom books now included in the Bible do not refer to distinctive Israelite or Judean traditions at all. In the words of James Crenshaw,

> The existence of a body of literature that reflects specific interests at variance with Yahwistic texts in general seems to argue strongly for a professional class of sages in Israel. Within Proverbs, Job, and Ecclesiastes one looks in vain for the dominant themes of Yahwistic thought: the exodus from Egypt, election of Israel, the Davidic covenant, the Mosaic legislation, the patriarchal narratives, the divine control of history, and movement toward a glorious moment when right will triumph. Instead, one encounters in these three books a different world of thought, one that stands apart so impressively that some scholars have described that literary corpus as an alien body within the Bible.[12]

David Carr argues, plausibly, that the absence of the Torah in this material is due to the fact that it originated before the Torah attained its central importance:

> In the beginning, there were various forms of textual "wisdom" in which Torah is either not reflected at all or is reflected in very subtle ways.... Just as Mesopotamian and Egyptian (educational) systems began with proverbs, instructions, and hymns as their foundational texts, it is likely that Israel ... likewise started with some of the texts we now see in Proverbs and Psalms, these texts serving as foundational texts for the rest of the curriculum.[13]

At least in the case of Qoheleth (Ecclesiastes), we have to assume that an independent wisdom tradition, with no explicit acknowledgment of the Torah, persisted into the Hellenistic period.

This situation changed in the second century B.C.E., when Ben Sira famously declared that all wisdom is "the book of the covenant of the Most High God, the law that Moses commanded us" (Sir 24:23). By this time the Torah was incorporated into the educational curriculum of the sages, as an important source of wisdom.[14] The association of wisdom and Torah is also attested in the Dead Sea Scrolls in 4Q 525.[15] Even 4QInstruction, which does not thematize the Torah, clearly draws on it.[16] It should be said that Ben Sira uses the Torah as a source of wisdom rather than law, but he clearly subscribes to the view that the Torah of Moses has iconic status as an expression of the traditional Judean way of life.

Some scholars find the fusion of wisdom and Torah already in the later stages of the book of Proverbs. Bernd Schipper notes the echoes of Deuteronomy in Proverbs 6:20–23:

(20) Keep, my son, your fathers *mitsvot,* forsake not your mother's *torah.*

(21) Bind them always upon your heart, tie them about your neck.

(22) When you walk about it will guide you, when you lie down it will watch over you, when you wake up it will converse with you,

(23) for the *mitsvah* is a lamp, and the *torah* is a light, and disciplinary reproof is a way to life.[17]

Similar echoes of Deuteronomy can be found in the wisdom instructions in Proverbs 3 and 7: "The three wisdom instructions share a number of terms like *torah,* in 3,1; 6,20; 7,2; *mitsvot* in 3,1; 6,20; 7,1 and the injunction to bind the Torah upon the heart (6,21), to 'inscribe it on the tablet of the heart' (verbally in 3,3, and 7,3) or 'to tie them about your neck' (3,3 and with exactly the same wording in 6,21)."[18] These and other observations support the view that Proverbs is alluding to Deuteronomy. Schipper concludes: "The crucial point is that by this intertextual allusion the *mitsvot* of the father and the *torah* of the mother come close to the *torah* and *mitsvot* of God. Even if they appear in the text strategy of Proverbs as a parental instruction, this instruction refers to the will of JHWH."[19] Wisdom has become "a hermeneutic of Torah." Schipper even claims that Proverbs 6 prioritizes Torah over wisdom. Similarly, Stuart Weeks argues that Proverbs is "trying to assert some sort of connection between proper instruction and the Law."[20]

In fact, however, Proverbs refers neither to the Torah of Moses nor to the Torah of YHWH, but to the teaching and instructions of the parents (or the sage *in loco parentis*). As Michael Fox has noted, the terms *torah* and *mitsvah* in Proverbs refer to authoritative injunctions, not suggestions or recommendations, but do not refer to law or legally enforceable ordinances.[21] It is authoritative teaching, but its authority derives from human teachers, not from divine law given on Sinai. Insofar as Proverbs uses language derived from Deuteronomy, this means, in the words of Fox, "only that terms of honor learned from the one book are *used in the other*."[22] (It should be noted that Deuteronomy itself borrows language from the wisdom tradition, and claims to show the wisdom and discernment of Israel.[23]) The sages were familiar with Deuteronomy, but they do not invoke it as divine revelation. Rather, they claim for their own *torah* or teaching what Deuteronomy claims for its Torah. No doubt, in rabbinic times, or perhaps even in the period of the Scrolls, the use of words like *torah* and *mitsvah* would evoke the Torah of Moses,[24] but this was not necessarily the case in the circles in which Proverbs was composed.

The relation of Qoheleth to the Torah has also been a matter of controversy. Many scholars see an allusion to Genesis 2–3 in Qoh 3:20: "All go to one place; all are from the dust, and all turn to dust again";[25] or to Deut 23:22–24 in Qoh 5:3–4, which warns that one should fulfill a vow without delay.[26] But while Qoheleth may know Genesis and Deuteronomy, he hardly treats them as Torah, or acknowledges them as authoritiative. As Bernard Levinson has commented, "While Qoh 5:3–4 cites Deuteronomy's law of vows, it does not do so because of the authority of Scripture as much as because of the law's reasonableness."[27] As Weeks has commented, until the closing verses of the book, Qoheleth shows no obvious interest in the Torah at all.[28]

The main controversy about Qoheleth's attitude to the Torah concerns the epilogue in Qoh 12:13: "The end of the matter, all has been heard. Fear God and keep his commandments for that is the whole duty of everyone." Most scholars regard the epilogue as a corrective coda added by an editor, not as a summary of the sage's teaching.[29] Even Fox, who argues that it was part of the original composition, sees the epilogue as an attempt to win acceptance for the book by a gesture toward conventional piety.[30] It is true that this epilogue does not contradict the sayings of Qoheleth, since he never disparages the keeping of commandments.[31] Yet, as Choon-Leong Seow has noted, it puts a different spin on Qoheleth's work by associating the fear of God with keeping the commandments.[32] As Weeks has noted,

> To fear and obey God is to act in a way that characterizes almost any ancient piety, but the specific formulation here, "keep his commandments," is so quintessentially Deuteronomic (see, for instance Deut 4:40; 7:9; 13:5; 26:18) that it could hardly but have been read by early Jewish readers as a reference to the Torah, and the author of the verses must surely have been aware of these connotations. Although Qohelet might allow the possibility of divine communication and commands, it is very doubtful that his thought has any place for the concept of a Torah, or its many implications.[33]

Gerald Sheppard argued that the epilogue finds its closest parallels in Ben Sira, and is therefore a secondary addition to the book.[34] In contrast, Thomas Krüger argues that one can also interpret verse 13 as "a purely pragmatic recommendation to all people in daily life to hold 'undogmatically' to the religious and cultural norms that they find in their particular living environment."[35] In that case, however, it would no longer bespeak a Torah-centered piety.

The wisdom tradition, at least before Ben Sira, is not an attempt to formulate Judean identity. We simply do not know whether the sages and their students were circumcised and kept the Passover. It would be hasty to infer that they did not. Nonetheless, it is significant that a whole area of instruction in the Second Temple period could proceed without reference to the Torah. The Torah was not the only possible framework for teaching fear of the Lord. Crenshaw is surely right that the canonical wisdom books exhibit a worldview that is quite different from that of the Torah, and as such represent a different construal of "Judaism" from what we find in the books of Maccabees or even in the wisdom literature itself from the second century B.C.E. on.

## ENOCHIC JUDAISM

A more controversial instance of non-Mosaic Judaism is provided by the early literature in the name of Enoch. Gabriele Boccaccini has argued at length that the books of Enoch attest to a tradition that extended over centuries, possibly beginning as early as the fourth century B.C.E. and extending into the first century C.E.[36] He recognizes that this was "a complex and dynamic trend of thought ... and therefore cannot be fit entirely into a unitary scheme or a universal definition." Yet

> its generative idea ... can be identified in a particular conception of evil, understood as an autonomous reality antecedent to humanity's ability to choose, the result of "a contamination that has spoiled [human] nature," an evil that "was produced before the beginning of history."[37]

He associates this tradition with a movement of dissent within the priesthood, reflected in the strong interest in the calendar and a statement in the Animal Apocalypse that all the offerings in the postexilic temple were polluted and impure (1 Enoch 89:73).[38] According to Boccaccini, writings preserved in 1 Enoch were the constitutive documents of this tradition, but not the only ones. He finds the same conception of evil in some books in which the figure of Enoch was not central (Jubilees, Testaments of the Twelve Patriarchs) or was even missing (4 Ezra). He also argues that this Enoch tradition was in fact the early Essene movement.[39]

Boccaccini's wider claims, which go beyond the actual Enochic writings, and identify Enochic Judaism with early Essenism, have been widely criticized, and need not detain us here.[40] The further "Enochic Judaism" is extended beyond the book of 1 Enoch the more problematic it becomes. The writings that make up 1 Enoch, however, are closely bound together by recurring motifs and allusions, and several of them envision a distinct group of righteous within Israel.[41] The Book of the Watchers (1 Enoch 1–36) refers to "the plant of righteousness and truth" (10:16). In the Apocalypse of Weeks (1 Enoch 93:1–10 and 91:11–17), the elect are "the chosen righteous from the chosen plant of righteousness" (93:10). The Animal Apocalypse (1 Enoch 85–90) speaks of "lambs" whose eyes are opened (90:6). Even the Similitudes of Enoch, which are later in date than any other part of 1 Enoch by at least a century, seem to envision the righteous as a community. It is not unreasonable, then, to suppose that these books of Enoch were composed within a movement of some sort, although continuity becomes problematic in the case of the Similitudes. For the present, however, I want to focus on the earliest components of the collection: the Book of the Watchers, the Astronomical Book, the Apocalypse of Weeks, and the Animal Apocalypse.

This corpus has some distinctive features. One is the prominence of the story of the Watchers, developed from the enigmatic account of the "sons of God" in Gen 6:1–4, which seems to provide a distinctive explanation for the prevalence of evil in the world. Another is the degree of interest in otherworldly geography. These features of 1 Enoch are distinctive even in the context of apocalyptic literature, as exemplified by the book of Daniel. Moreover, the negative reference to the temple in the Animal Apocalypse (1 Enoch 89:73) implies a rupture with what was arguably the most central symbol in Judaism at that time. The most obvious and basic distinguishing trait of this literature, however, is the fact that Enoch is the mediator of revelation, rather than Moses or any other figure drawn from Israelite tradition. This in turn raises the question of the status of the Mosaic, Sinaitic revelation in these books. Was this group Enochic, in the sense that it looked on the legendary patriarch as the primary mediator of revelation? Or was the invocation of the antediluvian hero merely a literary device in books that were solidly grounded in the Mosaic covenant?

Scholarship on this issue has in fact been rather evenly divided.[42] On the one hand, George Nickelsburg has argued that Enochic wisdom was an alternative to the Mosaic Torah.[43] On the other, E. P. Sanders[44] and Mark Elliott[45] have viewed it as an example of covenantal nomism. The division of opinion is most acute in the case of the early Enochic Book of the Watchers (1 Enoch 1–36).

At the core of this book is the story of the fallen angels, in 1 Enoch 6–11. This is usually regarded as an extrapolation from the story of the sons of God in Genesis 6,[46] although J. T. Milik famously argued that the Enochic story was older than the variant in Genesis.[47] The account of Enoch's ascent to heaven has various points of contact with prophetic traditions.[48] In his subsequent tour with an angelic guide he is shown a holy mountain in the center of the earth, which is evidently Mount Zion, and beside it a cursed valley, presumably Ge Hinnom or Gehenna.[49] He also sees the Garden of Righteousness, and the tree of wisdom, from which

> your father of old and your mother of old, who were before you, ate and learned wisdom. And their eyes were opened, and they knew that they were naked, and they were driven from the garden. (1 Enoch 32:6)

Moreover, the opening chapters of the Book of the Watchers are a virtual tissue of biblical allusions, and Lars Hartman has argued that they find their referential background in covenant renewal ceremonies and that the entire passage must be understood in a covenantal context.[50]

It is widely recognized that the story of the Watchers weaves together two distinct strands, in one of which Shemihazah is the leader of the fallen angels, while in the other the leader is Asael.[51] Helge Kvanvig has offered a sophisticated argument that Genesis 6 depends on the Shemihazah story, but that the Book of the Watchers as we have it presupposes the Priestly source in Genesis.[52] Even if this is accepted, however, it only affirms the priority of a few verses in 1 Enoch (6:1–2; 7:1–2). Much of the Book of the Watchers clearly depends on what we know as the biblical text. This is not to say, however, that it is exegetical in intent or that it presupposes the authority of the Mosaic Torah. James Kugel, who more than any other scholar has made the case for the exegetical character of the Pseudepigrapha, grants that 1 Enoch may well have passed on traditions originally unrelated to the biblical text.[53] There is, to be sure, an exegetical element in the story. In the Book of the Watchers, the flood is clearly the consequence of the sins initiated by the sons of God, while this connection is not explicit in Genesis: the connection in the Book of the Watchers is most probably inferred from the juxtaposition in Genesis. But there is no biblical basis at all for the stories of Asael and Shemihazah, the leaders of the fallen angels. The ascent of Enoch and his tour of the extremities of the earth are spun off from the biblical statement that he "walked with elohim" (Gen 5:22), but many of the details of these chapters (e.g., the geography of chapters 17–19 or the discussion of the chambers of the dead in chapter 22) have little basis in biblical tradition.[54]

## A DISTINCT FORM OF JUDAISM?

The "chosen righteous from the chosen plant of righteousness," or the elect group envisioned in 1 Enoch, understood themselves as descendants of Abraham, the chosen plant of righteousness. In the Animal Apocalypse, and in the Apocalypse of Weeks, it is quite clear that they are an offshoot of historic Israel. Yet, as Nickelsburg has observed, the only *explicit* reference to the Sinai covenant appears in the Apocalypse of Weeks in 1 Enoch 93:6, which says that "a covenant for all generations and a tabernacle" will be made in the fourth week. The Animal Apocalypse, in contrast, which clearly knows the story of the exodus, refers to the ascent of Moses on Mount Sinai ("and that sheep went up to the summit of a high rock," 1 Enoch 89:29) but conspicuously fails to mention either the making of a covenant or the giving of the law. At no point is there any polemic against the Mosaic Torah, but it is never the explicit frame of reference. In this respect, the Enochic literature stands in striking contrast to Jubilees, which retells the stories of Genesis from a distinctly Mosaic perspective, with explicit halakic interests.[55] The revelation to Enoch is prior to that of Moses and in no way subordinated to it. As Nickelsburg has argued, "The general category of covenant was not important for these authors."[56] The word is rare. To quote Nickelsburg again:

In short, the heart of the religion of *1 Enoch* juxtaposes election, revealed wisdom, the right and wrong ways to respond to this wisdom, and God's rewards and punishments for this conduct. Although all the components of "covenantal nomism" are present in this scheme, the word *covenant* rarely appears and Enoch takes the place of Moses as the mediator of revelation. In addition, the presentation of this religion is dominated by a notion of revelation—the claim that the books of Enoch are the embodiment of God's wisdom, which was received in primordial times and is being revealed in the eschaton to God's chosen ones.[57]

The understanding of the relationship between the elect and God may be covenantal, in the sense that it is based on laws that entail reward or punishment as their consequences, but it is not based on the Mosaic covenant, which was so widely accepted as the foundation of Jewish religion in the Hellenistic period.

It is often argued that the reason that 1 Enoch is not specifically Mosaic is simply a reflection of its pseudepigraphic setting in the prediluvian period.[58] But the choice of pseudonym and setting is not incidental. By choosing to attribute vital revelation to a figure who lived long before Moses, long before the emergence of Israel as a people, the authors of the Enoch literature chose to identify the core revelation, and the criteria for judgment, with creation, or the order of nature as they understood it, rather than with anything distinctively Mosaic.

Discussion of "Enochic Judaism" suffers from the fact that the Enochic books provide no account of a social organization or of the rituals that "the chosen righteous" observed. We can only discuss "world view," and any inferences about the social location of the authors are hazardous. They are often thought to be priests, who were alienated from the Jerusalem temple. The clearest evidence of alienation is the criticism of the offerings in the Second Temple in the Animal Apocalypse. The Book of the Watchers describes the heavenly abode as having an outer court, a central chamber, and an inner chamber, or holy of holies, like the earthly temple.[59] The Apocalypse of Weeks (1 Enoch 91:13) envisions an eschatological temple, and the Animal Apocalypse

(1 Enoch 90:28–29) speaks of an eschatological "house," which is variously interpreted as a temple or a city.[60] It has been suggested that the story of the fallen angels, who took human wives, was an allegory for priests who entered into forbidden marriages.[61] Martha Himmelfarb notes that the "fit" is not exact: angels were not supposed to marry at all.[62] Nonetheless she accepts the suggestion and suggests that "the Book of the Watchers believes that priests should marry only women from priestly families."[63] She also argues that the Book of the Watchers depicts Enoch as a priest, because he is cast in the role of intercessor for the fallen angels/priests, who should be interceding for him.[64] But in fact Enoch is never called a priest in the Book of the Watchers, but rather a righteous scribe. If the story of the Watchers implies a criticism of priests at all, the point would be that the priesthood has failed, and nonpriestly scribes need to intervene. While it is clear enough that the people who produced the early Enoch literature were not associated with the Jerusalem temple, and were critical of it at least in the Animal Apocalypse, it is not at all clear that they were dissident priests or engaged in a sustained polemic against the Jerusalem priesthood.[65]

The authors were evidently familiar with at least parts of what we know as the Torah. The Book of the Watchers demonstrably depends on Genesis. The Apocalypse of Weeks and the Animal Apocalypse summarize what we know as the biblical tradition, although the latter, remarkably, fails to mention the giving of the Law in its account of the theophany at Mount Sinai (1 Enoch 89:28–35). (The Apocalypse of Weeks, in contrast, refers to "a covenant for all generations.") The most extensive engagement with the history of Israel is found in the later apocalypses, which date to the time around the Maccabean revolt. Andreas Bedenbender speaks of "the fundamental change Enochic Judaism underwent in consequence of the Maccabean uprising."[66] He also regards the prefatory chapters in 1 Enoch 1–5, which castigate humanity because it has not "acted according to his commandments" (5:4), as a *Mosaisierung* of the Book of the Watchers.[67] As in the case of the wisdom literature, we appear to have a tradition that was not originally focused on the Torah of Moses but that eventually integrated it into its repertoire. Even in the later stages of the tradition, however, the Enochic literature never acquires the kind of halakic interest that we find in Jubilees or in some works from Qumran, and the Torah plays no significant role in the Similitudes of Enoch, which is usually dated to the early first century c.e.[68] Like the earlier Enochic books, the Similitudes speak of "the righteous and chosen" rather than of Israel, and their primary opponents are "the kings and the mighty."[69] The Similitudes are not found among the Dead Sea Scrolls, and they may testify to the persistence of a form of Judaism that was not focused on the Torah of Moses into the first century of the Common Era.

## TALES OF THE EASTERN DIASPORA

A third area where reference to the Torah is conspicuously absent is constituted by tales set in the eastern diaspora.

Not only does the book of Esther not mention the Torah: it does not even mention the name of God. The closest the book comes to mentioning God is the response to Esther that if she does not act, "relief and deliverance will rise for the Jews from another quarter" (Esth 4:14), and Fox deems it "certainly incorrect" to read this as an allusion to God.[70] Moreover, the only religious rites mentioned in the book are fasting and mourning rituals (Esth 2:1–3, 16), and at the end, the new festival of Purim.[71] Nonetheless, the book evinces a high degree of solidarity among the Judeans, and a very distinct identity, that has even, inappropriately, been dubbed "nationalistic."[72] When Haman takes offense at Mordechai's refusal to bow down to him, he resolves to destroy all Judeans. Mordechai warns Esther that even in the king's palace she cannot escape the fate of her people, and she proceeds to risk her life on their behalf. In the end, the king allows Judeans in every city of his empire to assemble and destroy any force that might attack them (Esth 8:11), but not, it should be noted, to return to Judah, or to enjoy independence within the empire. Most notable for our purposes is the way Haman characterizes the Judeans to the king:

> There is a certain people scattered and separated among the peoples in all the provinces of your kingdom; their laws are different from those of every other people, and they do not keep the king's laws, so that it is not appropriate for the king to tolerate them. (Esth 2:8)

We should like to know what these laws were. The charge is triggered by Mordechai's refusal to bow down to Haman. Presumably the Judeans had ancestral customs, and while these may have corresponded to traditional Jewish observances, we are not actually told what they were. Esther does not seem to worry about *kashruth* when she becomes queen. The Judeans of Susa may have been like their counterparts in Elephantine, who also had strong solidarity and were recognized as a group apart by their neighbors. There is no indication that they were bound by the Torah of Moses, if they knew of its existence. Modern interpreters who read from a canonical perspective may make subtle intertextual connections with other biblical books. Timothy Beal claims that

> Esther is in subtle dialogue with many other biblical texts, including the Joseph narratives, Samuel, and Deuteronomy, as well as, to some extent, wisdom literature and the Exodus/Passover traditions. These intertextual dimensions integrate the book of Esther within the larger dialogical space of canonical Scripture.[73]

So, for example, he finds in the hiddenness of God in Esther an allusion to Deut 31: 16b–18, where God threatens to hide his face if the Israelites should break the covenant. The allusion is in the eye of the canonical interpreter. Esther does not refer to a covenant at all. There is, to be sure, a well-known generic affinity between the story of Esther and that of Joseph,[74] but that does not require that Esther is relating to the Joseph story as canonical scripture.

The stories in Daniel 1–6 are also silent on the subject of the Torah. Unlike Esther, Daniel is uninhibited in his piety. As in Esther, refusal to bow down or worship, in this case before a statue, is a nonnegotiable aspect of Judean identity. Apart from that, Daniel is a willing and loyal courtier. As the courtiers of Darius the Mede remark in chapter 6, "We shall not find any ground for complaint against this Daniel unless we find it in connection with the law of his God" (Dan 6:5).[75]

Should we assume that "the law of his God" is the law of Moses? The strongest evidence in favor of an association with Mosaic law is in chapter 1, where Daniel resolves "that he would not defile himself with the royal rations of food and wine" (Dan 1:8), and asks for a diet of vegetables instead. Some scholars have argued that this is a gesture of resistance, by refusal to eat the royal food,[76] but it is difficult to avoid the suspicion that *kashruth* is involved. Yet wine is not prohibited in Leviticus, and a vegetarian diet is not required.[77] Daniel's concern goes beyond the prohibitions of Leviticus. This concern arises only in Daniel 1, which is written in Hebrew, and is not reflected in the Aramaic tales. In the tales, Daniel's only distinctively Jewish observance is that he prays three times a day toward Jerusalem, a practice that lacks any basis in the Torah (Dan 6:10). It seems likely, then, that the Persian word *dat*, "law," is used here in the general sense of religious practice.[78] The issues that arise in diaspora life, in Daniel as in Esther, do not arise from the Torah, but from rivalry with other courtiers, and from the erratic behavior of Gentile kings. Despite the prediction of an ultimate "kingdom of God" in Daniel chapter 2, Daniel does not seek Judean independence any more than Esther did. Eschatology is deferred.[79] What is needed for the present is a favorable monarch. All of this changes in the visions in the second half of the book of Daniel, where foreign rule appears as beasts rising from the sea, and where "those who forsake the holy covenant" (Dan 11:30) are regarded with contempt. In the tales in Daniel 2–6, Daniel and his companions are assured in their Jewish identity, but the Law of Moses is never invoked, and does not seem to be a factor in their lives.

The tales from the eastern diaspora, in Esther and Daniel, assume that Judeans had distinctive customs, but betray no awareness of the book of the Torah of Moses, as such. Qoheleth or the author of the Book of the Watchers may well have regarded the Torah as one source of wisdom among many, but they do not accord it a primary role in shaping their identity. All of this is very different from the kind of legal, halakic, use of the Torah that is exemplified, if only selectively, in Ezra, and that later becomes typical, in the Dead Sea Scrolls and in the rabbinic corpus.

# CHAPTER 4

# Torah as Narrative and Wisdom

The Torah always included other material besides law.[1] The narratives preserved in the books of Genesis and Exodus shape Jewish identity at the most basic level. These stories were older than the laws of Deuteronomy and the Priestly code. The exodus story was obviously important for the Judean exiles and returnees in the early Persian period. Both Second Isaiah (Isa 40:3; 43:16–17; 51:9–11, etc.) and Zechariah (2:6) invoke the exodus in their exhortations to their compatriots to leave Babylon and return to Judah.

Regardless of how we reconstruct the composition of the Torah, it clearly contained "two competing myths of [Israelite] origins" in the phrase of Thomas Römer.[2] One of these consists of the stories of patriarchal wanderings in Genesis, the other of the story of the exodus from Egypt. Neither of these was invented in the Babylonian period. If one holds to any version of the documentary hypothesis, they had long been combined in the Yahwist and Elohist sources. They are also combined in the Priestly strand of the Pentateuch, which may be roughly contemporary with Deuteronomy in its various stages.[3] Both myths of origin took on new significance in the light of the exile. In Römer's view, the exodus tradition, filtered through the Deuteronomic strand, had special significance for the exiles:

The Exodus and conquest story affirm the right to possess the land through an ideology of colonization. Yhwh brought Israel out of Egypt to give them the land; he will also bring back the members of the "true Israel" from Babylon, and they will possess the land again.[4]

In contrast, Ezek 33:24 claims that "the inhabitants of these ruins in the land of Israel" appeal to the example of Abraham: "Abraham was only one, yet he possessed the land, but we are many; to us the land has been given for a possession." But the wanderings of the patriarchs could also be taken as a precedent for those who returned from Babylon. The Priestly account of Abraham claimed that he came from "Ur of the Chaldees" (Gen 11:31). Indeed the precedent of the patriarchs was a better model for the returning exiles, insofar as they did not set out to slaughter the inhabitants of the land, in the manner of Joshua. Both stories, in any case, would be mined as models of Jewish identity throughout the Second Temple period. Neither was the exclusive property of one party.

The narrative traditions of the patriarchs and exodus were eventually given stable form in the Torah. It is now apparent from the Dead Sea Scrolls that the text was not finalized until the Hasmonean era, but the stories were well established long before that time. My concern here is with the ways in which these stories were used in the late Persian and early Hellenistic periods.

### "REWRITTEN BIBLE"

The late Geza Vermes drew attention to a category of texts from the Second Temple period that engage in extensive paraphrase of older scriptures. He introduced the label "rewritten Bible," and applied it to Jubilees, the Genesis Apocryphon, the *Biblical Antiquities* of Pseudo-Philo, and the *Antiquities* of Josephus.[5] The designation is problematic, since what was rewritten was not yet the "Bible," and so scholars increasingly refer to these writings as "rewritten scriptures."[6] The rewriting has much in common with what we find in expansionistic texts of the Torah, such as the Samaritan Pentateuch or the fragmentary 4QReworked Pentateuch found at Qumran. It involves harmonizing, rearranging, and expansion. Some scholars see a spectrum, which ranges from minor editorial changes in the received text to changes so extensive that they are deemed to constitute independent works.[7] In the case of 4QReworked Pentateuch, the current consensus is that this was intended to be an improved edition of the Pentateuchal text.[8] Most of the texts called "rewritten scriptures," however, are distinct compositions, based on the older texts but not intended to replace them.

There has been extensive debate about the extent and definition of this category of writing.[9] It is not strictly a literary genre.[10] Individual compositions tend to follow the genre of the prototype.[11] A great amount of Jewish literature from the late Second Temple period is based on older scriptures in one way or another. For example, the fragments of Hellenistic Jewish literature preserve retellings of stories about the patriarchs and the exodus not only in narrative form, but also in epic poetry and even in the form of a tragedy.[12] There is no question in these writings of replacing the original scriptures: they simply present (and often embellish) these stories in ways that render them more interesting for a Hellenized audience, and use them to reshape Jewish identity in a diaspora setting. They treat the scriptures as sources for their literary imagination. This is also true of Josephus's great retelling of biblical history in his *Antiquities*, which was one of the works originally categorized as "rewritten Bible" by Vermes. These works may have an exegetical dimension, insofar as they sometimes try to resolve problems in the scriptures, but they are not primarily works of exegesis. They are new compositions that draw their source material from the traditional scriptures, supplemented by other sources.

It is now generally acknowledged that the canon of Jewish scriptures as we know it did not take shape until the late first century C.E., at the earliest.[13] The Torah, however, was regarded as authoritative from the Persian period onward. It was, to be sure, authoritative in legal matters, but we may also think of it as canonical in a literary sense. "A canon," writes Robert Alter, "is above all a transhistorical textual community.

Knowledge of the received texts and recourse to them constitute the community, but the texts do not have a single authoritative meaning."[14] This looser sense of authority, which treats the received texts as resources for a literary imagination, is very widely attested in ancient Judaism, including the Scrolls.

In this chapter I wish to draw attention to two bodies of material that draw on older scriptures, or at least on the traditions contained therein, but are notably lacking in halakic interest. The first is the corpus of Aramaic texts found in the region of Qumran. The second is the later Hebrew wisdom tradition beginning with Ben Sira, and including texts found in the Scrolls. I will conclude the chapter with some reflections on the book of Tobit.

### THE ARAMAIC CORPUS

Fragments of 129 Aramaic manuscripts are found in the Scrolls, of which approximately 87 are well enough preserved to be studied.[15] These are in various genres, including targumim, narrative compositions, and visionary texts.[16] A number of them draw on material we know from the Torah, especially the stories about the primeval history and the patriarchs. Katell Berthelot claims that "nearly half of the compositions in Aramaic from Qumran refer to the book of Genesis."[17] This corpus includes the Enochic Book of the Watchers, which we considered in the previous chapter. The Book of the Watchers uses the story of the fallen angels, which it probably knew from a text of Genesis, as a jumping-off point, but is a free composition, drawing on various traditions. Some of the other Aramaic texts follow the older scriptures much more closely.

### THE GENESIS APOCRYPHON

One such text is the Genesis Apocryphon. Fragments of twenty-two columns were found in Qumran Cave 1, but the scroll was originally

longer.[18] The surviving fragments of the Genesis Apocryphon correspond to Gen 5:18–15:8. They can be divided into three cycles, dealing
with Enoch, Noah, and Abram.[19]

The Enoch cycle is very fragmentary, and much of the surviving
text deals with the birth of Noah. Lamech suspects that "the conception was from the Watchers, and the seed from Holy Ones" (2:1). His
wife, Bitenosh, indignantly reminds him of the pleasure of their intercourse, and swears that the seed is his own. Lamech appeals to his
father, Methuselah, who in turn appeals to his father, Enoch. Enoch
tells him to assure Lamech that the child is his own.

The Noah cycle is introduced in 5:29 as "a copy of the words of
Noah." Noah speaks in the first person and testifies that the Holy One
had instructed him in the ways of truth, and he held fast to righteousness. While this feature may be regarded as an expansion of the brief
statement in Gen 6:9 (Noah was a righteous man, blameless in his generation), much of the story is paralleled neither in the Bible nor in other
books such as Enoch and Jubilees that touch on the career of Noah. The
text is enlivened by dreams, both nonsymbolic and symbolic. No mention is made of Noah's drunkenness and nakedness (Gen 9:21–23).

The highlight of the Abram cycle is the sojourn in Egypt (cols. 19–20).
The biblical text mentions that the Egyptians saw that Sarah was very
beautiful (Gen 12:14). The Apocryphon describes her beauty in detail, in
the style of a *wasf* (a traditional Arabic style of descriptive poetry; *wasf*
love poems typically comment on the different parts of the body of the
beloved).[20] The Apocryphon comments on the various parts of Sarah's
body: "How graceful are her eyes, and how precious her nose …, how
lovely is her breast and how beautiful her white complexion." Abram is
warned in a dream of the danger that could arise from Sarah's beauty, so
his deception in passing her off as his sister is justified.

Moshe Bernstein has pointed out that the classification "rewritten
Bible" fits the Abram cycle much better than the earlier columns.[21] He
regards the Enoch and Noah cycles as "parabiblical" in the sense that
they have a jumping-off point in the biblical text, but do not follow it

closely.[22] While the Apocryphon exhibits some points of similarity with targum and midrash in the way it treats the text of Genesis, it cannot be assigned to either genre.[23]

Daniel Machiela argues that the Apocryphon is an exegetical work, and "was meant to be read *alongside* the authoritative text, and not instead of it."[24] He is certainly right that it was not intended to replace Genesis. The question is rather what kind of authority it claims. It is not apparent that it is an exegetical work, written to explicate a text that is regarded as sacred scripture. Rather, it is a literary work in its own right, which views Genesis as a fount of literary tradition that nourishes the imagination, but allows the later writer considerable freedom. It is written to edify, in part, but also simply to entertain.

### THE ARAMAIC LEVI DOCUMENT

Another Aramaic text that is based in some way on the Torah is the Aramaic Levi Document.[25] Two leaves pertaining to this text were found in the Cairo Geniza, one of which is now in Oxford, in the Bodleian Library, while the other is in Cambridge. The Qumran fragments were originally related to three manuscripts, 1Q21, 4Q213, and 4Q214, but the Cave 4 manuscripts were each divided into three in the official edition, so that now seven manuscripts are distinguished.[26] Moreover, a manuscript of the Greek Testament of Levi from Mount Athos has two long additions after T. Levi 2:3 and 18:2, parts of which correspond to the Geniza material and to the Qumran fragments. The transmission history of this text is obviously fluid, and all the witnesses do not necessarily constitute a single text. While it is related to the Greek Testament of Levi, and may have been one of its sources, it is now agreed that this document is not a testament.[27]

The story is narrated by Levi in the first person, in autobiographical form. In part it is based on Genesis 34 and 37. As in the Genesis Apocryphon, there is a concern for edification. Levi and Simeon are absent when Joseph is sold into slavery. Henryk Drawnel claims that the killing of the Shechemites (Genesis 34) is presented as a positive action.[28] This, however, is not clear in the fragmentary text of the Cambridge manuscript. All that is preserved is that Levi, Jacob, and Reuben spoke to the Canaanites with wisdom and understanding that they should become circumcised so that they would all be like brothers. Presumably the story went on to tell of the killing of the Canaanites, as in Genesis 34, but unfortunately this part of the story is not preserved. So we do not know how the killing was portrayed.

Aramaic Levi, in its various witnesses, contains several passages that have no parallel in the text of Genesis. These include a prayer, a vision of the heavens, an account of Levi's ordination, a long wisdom instruction delivered by Isaac, a wisdom poem recited by Levi, and predictions of the future. Because of the lengthy wisdom passages, Drawnel calls the Levi Document as a whole a wisdom text.

The instruction of Isaac is largely concerned with "the law of the priesthood."[29] This is concerned with the types of wood suitable for offering, and the correct way to sacrifice animals. These instructions are being passed down from one generation to another. Isaac says he learned from Abraham what he is now passing on. As befits a priestly instruction, it is concerned with impurity and proper marriage. Levi is reminded that his seed is holy. There is then a greater concern for detailed halakah than what we find in 1 Enoch or the Genesis Apocryphon, but it is specifically priestly halakah.[30] This lore is passed on within priestly families. It is not an exposition of the Torah. The events narrated and their dates are paralleled in Jubilees. The direction of influence between the two works is disputed.[31] Aramaic Levi does not, however, follow the text of Genesis nearly as closely as does Jubilees. While both works derive from a priestly tradition, the Levi Document is more directly concerned with the priesthood and with technical aspects of priestly lore.

The Aramaic Levi Document is more directly didactic than the Book of the Watchers or the Genesis Apocryphon. Drawnel tentatively classifies it as "a pseudepigraphic autobiography with a didactic poem and prophetic speech at its end,"[32] although he also calls it a "wisdom text." He argues that it grew in "the Levitical milieu in which priestly education, metro-arithmetical training, and scribal ideals were transmitted," and infers that "the proper context for the education is the Levitical priestly family."[33] Its distinctively priestly character sets it apart from other wisdom literature. No doubt the author knew the text of Genesis, more or less as we know it, but he is concerned with the transmission of tradition rather than with the exegesis of scripture.

## TORAH AND WISDOM

The sapiential character of the Aramaic Levi Document provides a segue to the fusion of wisdom and Torah that we find in the Hellenistic period, most famously in Ben Sira.

We have noted that already in Ezra the authority of the Torah is invoked even for measures that do not actually correspond to the text of the Pentateuch as it has come down to us. Again, although Antiochus III declared that the people of Judea should conduct their affairs in accordance with their ancestral laws (Josephus, *Ant.* 12.142), his decree is mainly concerned with the upkeep of the temple. One of his provisions restricted access to the temple and banned the flesh of certain animals from Jerusalem. As Elias Bickerman noted, there is no precept excluding foreigners from the temple in the law of Moses.[34] Neither is the prohibition of the flesh or hides of certain animals explicit in the Torah. In these and other cases the Torah is assumed to extend to customs that are not actually found in it. (This is still true of Josephus.) The "Torah of Moses" had taken on an iconic status whereby it stood for the entire Judean way of life, whether specific provisions were actually found in the text or not.

The iconic character of the Torah is also in evidence in some of the psalms from the Second Temple period. Psalm 119 uses the word Torah twenty-five times, a usage that Jon Levenson described as "like a mantra,"[35] and also uses several terms such as *mishpat* and *mitsvah* as rough equivalents.[36] Yet, Levenson argues, "the psalmist's Torah lacks a constant identity."[37] It can refer variously to received tradition or cosmic or natural law or unmediated divine teaching.[38] The psalmist declares his love for the Torah, and says that "your commandments make me wiser than my enemies," but he gives no examples of the specific commandments. In the words of Kent Reynolds, the Torah is "greater than the sum of the parts."[39] It is a comprehensive expression of the will and revelation of God.

In Psalm 19, which draws some of its terminology from Psalm 119, this comprehensive concept of the Torah becomes an object of praise:

> The Torah of the Lord is perfect, reviving the soul;
> the decrees of the Lord are sure, making wise the simple,
> the precepts of the Lord are right rejoicing the heart ...
> More to be desired are they than gold, even much fine gold;
> Sweeter also than honey, and drippings of the honeycomb.
>
> (Ps 19:7–10)

Anja Klein has noted that the praise of the Torah here has a close parallel in the self-praise of the Lady Wisdom in Proverbs 8, notably in the comparison with gold, but also in general terminology.[40] Klein refers to this as a sapiential interpretation of the Torah: "Drawing on the portrayal of wisdom in Proverbs 8, the Torah from Psalm 119 is set as an absolute and attracts both characteristics and predications of classic wisdom."[41] The Torah is analogous to personified wisdom, as an abstraction that represents a whole way of life. The way of life summed up in the Torah is somewhat different from that described in Proverbs, since it affirms the specifically Israelite laws of the Pentateuch, but the psalm is not concerned with the details. Rather, it uses the Torah as an icon, which is treated with great respect and deference but not examined for the specificity of its commandments.

## BEN SIRA

Klein also notes affinities between Psalm 19 and Ben Sira, notably in the praise of God as lord of creation in Sir 42:15–43:33. Ben Sira famously identifies wisdom with the Torah of Moses. The praise of wisdom as a cosmic force in creation in chapter 24 concludes, rather counterintuitively, by saying that "all this is the book of the covenant of the Most High God, the law that Moses commanded us as an inheritance for the congregation of Jacob." The force of the identification is endlessly debated. Does it mean that the Torah is all the wisdom you need, or that all wisdom is ipso facto Torah?[42] Klein writes that "the Law comes into play as a way of practicing wisdom" and that "the encompassing quality of wisdom manifests itself in the guidelines of the Law."[43] But as Ben Wright observes in the same volume, Ben Sira never explicitly cites material from the Torah, and Torah is only one of several sources of wisdom.[44] Wright grants that references to law, commandments, statutes, and so on should be read as references to the Mosaic Torah, but he is unsure just what that encompasses. In any case, performance of the Law is not the only way that wisdom can be actualized. The sapiential tradition and the created order are also sources of wisdom.[45]

But while I would argue that Ben Sira subsumes Torah under wisdom, rather than vice versa, his understanding of wisdom is distinctly different from that of Proverbs or Qoheleth. The very fact of acknowledging the Torah of Moses as a source of wisdom brought him closer to the orbit of the Deuteronomic tradition. Entailed in that acknowledgment was an affirmation of the election and special status of Israel.[46] The great figures of Israel's history were recast as examples of wisdom in action, but they were given a role that had no precedent in the older wisdom tradition. Ben Sira does not take over the treaty framework of Deuteronomy, and does not invoke curses on those who fail to follow his teachings. The *Tun-Ergehen Zusammenhang* of traditional wisdom was enough to constitute a general similarity of outlook with the Deuteronomic tradition. Whether Ben Sira can be said to exemplify "covenantal nomism" in the manner of E. P. Sanders, however, is debatable. Despite his great respect for the Torah of Moses, he does not cast his teaching in a covenantal context. It is still presented as teaching for individuals, even, perhaps, for an elite segment of Judean society.

Wright is probably correct that

> the increasing authority of the Torah and the growing importance of Torah-piety in ... Second Temple Judaism worked to make the Torah an indispensable source of wisdom for a sage like Ben Sira.[47]

Even the authors of non-Mosaic writings, such as Qoheleth and the Book of the Watchers, drew on the writings of the Torah in various ways. Where Ben Sira differed from these writers was in his explicit acknowledgment of the status of the Torah. In this, I suspect, he was influenced by his social location. His admiration for the high priest Simon suggests that he was a retainer, who enjoyed and depended on the patronage of the priestly establishment in Jerusalem in a way that the authors of Qoheleth and the Enochic writings did not. Consequently, he had to acknowledge the wisdom of the official "ancestral laws" of Judah, more explicitly than some of his contemporaries.

But Ben Sira's use of the Torah still seems to be largely iconic. It is a formal acknowledgment of the superiority of Mosaic wisdom, but it is far removed from the kind of obsession with the details of Mosaic law that we will find in some of the Dead Sea Scrolls. Halakic Judaism, the view that Judaism is defined primarily by Mosaic law, as law, had not yet become dominant in Judah when Ben Sira wrote.

## WISDOM TEXTS IN THE SCROLLS

The Dead Sea Scrolls include several wisdom texts that had not been previously known.[48] These texts are not necessarily sectarian. 4QInstruction has much in common with the Hodayot and with the Instruction on the Two Spirits, but it may have been a source on which the sectarian authors drew rather than a sectarian composition.[49] The other wisdom texts that are most immediately relevant to our subject, 4QBeatitudes (4Q525) and 4Q185, also lack clear indication of sectarian origin, although they are not incompatible with sectarian provenance either.

The longest of these texts, 4QInstruction, draws on the Torah implicitly at various points, but does not acknowledge it explicitly at all.[50] The most striking example is found in 4Q417 1 i 16–18.[51] The passage speaks of an engraved law that is decreed by God for all the wickedness of the sons of Seth (or Sheth), and a book of remembrance that is written before him for those who keep his word. This is also called "the Vision of Hagu" or Meditation. The passage continues:

> And he gave it as an inheritance to *enosh* with a spiritual people, for according to the likeness of the Holy Ones is his inclination [or, he formed him]. Moreover, the Hagu (Meditation) was not given to the spirit of flesh, for it did not know the difference between good and evil according to the judgment of its spirit.

*Enosh* can be read as a proper name, referring to the son of Seth, grandson of Adam, who is mentioned in Gen 4:26; 5:6–7, 9–11.[52] But the word is also used in the context of creation in the Instruction on the Two Spirits in the Community Rule, which says that God created *enosh* to rule the world (cf. Gen 1:28). If we take the word in the latter sense, then the following phrase, "for according to the likeness of the Holy Ones is his inclination [or, he formed him]," can be seen as a paraphrase of Gen 1:27, which says that God created Adam (or humankind) "in the image of God." The Qumran text understands this as in the image of the Holy Ones or angels, rather than in the image of the Most High. A second allusion to the creation story is provided by the statement that the spirit of flesh did not distinguish between good and evil. Here we have a clear allusion to Genesis 2–3. God did not forbid humanity to eat of the tree of the knowledge of good and evil, according to this text, but some human beings, those who had a "spirit of flesh," failed to grasp the distinction. The spirit of flesh, however, stands in contrast to a "spiritual people" or "people of spirit," associated with *enosh*, who were deemed worthy to receive the revelation, and who presumably recognized the difference between good and evil.

4QInstruction conflates the two accounts of creation in Genesis, since it uses the word *yatsar*, "to fashion," from Gen 2:7, to describe the creation in the image of God. But it still distinguishes between two kinds of human being who are created: the spiritual kind, whose creation is reported in Genesis 1, and the fleshly kind described in Genesis 2–3. Only the fleshly kind fails to recognize the difference between good and evil, in accordance with the story in Genesis 2–3. The author is clearly working with the Genesis story, but is also innovating, by introducing an incipient dualism.

An even bolder reinterpretation of Genesis is found in the Instruction on the Two Spirits in the Community Rule. There the statement that God created *enosh* to rule the world is followed by the claim that he

> has appointed for him two spirits in which to walk until the time of His visitation: the spirits of truth and injustice. Those born of truth spring from a fountain of light, but those born of injustice spring from a source of darkness. All the children of righteousness are ruled by the Prince of Light, and walk in the ways of light, but all the children of injustice are ruled by the Angel of Darkness and walk in the ways of darkness. (1QS 3:15–21)

There is no precedent for warring spirits of light and darkness in the Jewish tradition. On the contrary, this concept has its closest parallel in Persian dualism, as has often been noted.[53] And yet the passage is also an interpretation of Genesis, as we might expect in an account of the creation of humanity. Dependence on Genesis is signaled most clearly in the statement that God created man to rule the world. But even the doctrine of the two spirits should be understood in the context of the ongoing debate about the meaning of Genesis 1–3 and the origin of evil in Ben Sira and in the wisdom texts from Qumran.

The most explicit acknowledgment of the Torah in the wisdom texts from the Scrolls is found in 4Q525.[54] This text echoes Psalm 1, which praises those who meditate on the law of the Lord, but it correlates that with the pursuit of wisdom:

> Blessed is the man who attains Wisdom, and walks in the law of the Most High. (frag. 2 ii 3)

The passage that follows may apply equally to wisdom and Torah:

> and directs his heart to her ways, and is constrained by her discipline and always takes pleasure in her punishments . . . for he always thinks of her and in his distress he meditates on her.[55]

William Tooman construes this to mean that "the written Torah is the source of wisdom and Torah piety is its sign and substance."[56] Similarly, George Brooke relates the language of "walking in her ways" to the concept of halakah:

> The halakhah is based on practical advice for everyday living which is the application of various of the principles underlying the Torah, rather than the application of individual rulings (*mishpatim*) or statutes (*huqim*).[57]

Brooke is certainly right that the text does not refer to individual rulings or statutes, but for that reason it is misleading to refer to it as "halakic exegesis."[58] Rather, 4Q525 uses Torah as an "ideological sign," in the phrase of Carol Newsom, interchangeably with "wisdom."[59] The term "righteousness" is a similar "ideological sign" that signifies an approach to life, which may be construed quite differently by different groups. As Hindy Najman has put it,

> Torah was not limited to a particular corpus of texts but was inextricably linked to a broader tradition of extrabiblical law and narrative, interpretation, and cosmic wisdom.[60]

The idea of Torah, like personified Wisdom, signifies an approach to life, but is not analyzed in detail. The language of 4Q525 is much more heavily indebted to Proverbs than to the laws of the Pentateuch, but by identifying wisdom with Torah it claims for the wisdom tradition the authority of God's revelation to Moses on Mount Sinai.

Another wisdom text from Qumran, 4Q185, does not refer to Torah as such, but urges its readers to "draw wisdom from the [p]ower of our God, remember the miracles he performed in Egypt." (1–2 i 14).[61] As Tooman puts it, "The excerpt is a complex conflation of locutions from scriptural poems that recite the history of Israel for pedagogic purposes, texts like Ps 78, 105, and 106."[62] It also refers to "the way he commanded to J[acob] and the path which he decreed to Isaac" (1–2 ii 4). Tooman infers: "Wisdom, in so far as this author is concerned, is the proper possession of Israel."[63] Here the reference is not specifically to the laws revealed at Sinai, but rather to the Pentateuchal narratives. It does not necessarily follow that "worldly wisdom of the international type is surely excluded," as Tooman assumes.[64] But at least in the fragments that have survived, the Torah appears to be the primary source of wisdom.

### TORAH AND WISDOM IN TOBIT

A rather different fusion of Torah and wisdom is found in the book of Tobit, a novella set in the eastern diaspora. Tobit is portrayed as almost obsessive in his observance of the Mosaic Law, in the opening chapter of the book. He is the only one of his tribe who went regularly to Jerusalem on feast days, even though he lived in the Northern Kingdom of Israel, carrying tithes and offerings "in keeping with the decree set down about them in the Law of Moses" (1:8). His marriage to a woman from his kindred, and his abstention from the food of the Gentiles, even in exile, are further indications of his fidelity to the Law. It is somewhat surprising, then, that the law does not figure more prominently in the instructions that Tobit gives to his son Tobias, before the latter sets out on his journey. He warns his son to be mindful of the Lord, and not to sin or transgress his commandments (4:5), but this is no more than what we might find in a wisdom book such as Proverbs. Tobit's own injunctions are called "commands" in 4:19. Some of the material is common to the Torah and to traditional wisdom: the need to honor parents, avoid illicit sex, or to give the laborer his due. Tobit emphasizes almsgiving, in a way that goes far beyond what we find in the Torah, but is paralleled in Ben Sira. The Hebrew word *tsedaqah*, "righteousness," is sometimes rendered as "almsgiving" in the Greek translation. Tobit's statement that "almsgiving delivers from death" is derived from Proverbs, which says that "righteousness delivers from death" (Prov 11:4). In light of Tobit's Torah piety in chapter 1, it is striking that he does not warn his son to keep the Sabbath or observe any specific ritual commandment. In contrast, the instruction of Abraham to Isaac in Jubilees 21 is largely preoccupied with sacrificial ritual, but also addresses idolatry, purity, and the need to separate from the mass of humanity.

In view of the difference between the Deuteronomistic frame and the folkloristic core of the book, it is likely that we should distinguish two redactional stages in Tobit.[65] The Torah, however, is by no means absent from the core narrative.

There is one quite distinctive commandment in Tobit's instruction: "Above all, take a wife from among the descendants of your ancestors, and do not marry a foreign woman who is not of your father's tribe" (4:12).[66] In this, he seems to be guided by the example of the patriarchs in Genesis rather than by that of Ezra. The concern is not to avoid foreign women because of the danger of idolatry, but rather to maintain the bonds of tribal society. Endogamy, however, is presented as a divine command. The angel Raphael tells Tobias that Sarah's father, Raguel, "will not be able to withhold her from you or betroth her to anyone else without incurring death according to the ordinance of the book of Moses" (6:13). The Torah does not, in fact, prescribe the death penalty in connection with the obligation to keep the family's inheritance within the tribe. It would seem that "the book of Moses" in Tobit does not point to specific biblical law, but rather to ancestral traditions, which derive authority from Moses even when they go beyond what is written in the Torah.

The "law of Moses" is invoked again in connection with the wedding of Tobias and Sarah. Raguel tells Tobias that "she has been given to you according to the ordinance of the book of Moses" (7:11) and then tells him to "take her to be your wife according to the Law and the ordinance written in the book of Moses" (7:12).[67] The marriage ceremony is never actually spelled out in the Torah. Deuteronomy 24 mentions a bill of divorce, so we may infer that written marriage contracts were the norm, at least in the Second Temple period. In Tobit, however, reference to the Law of Moses is not to a specific law, but to traditional custom, which is given the aura of Mosaic authority. The Torah is invoked in connection with the wedding in another way in the prayer of Tobias, when Adam and Eve are recalled as the paradigm of marriage.

The author of Tobit was evidently familiar with "the book of Moses" in some form. Beyond explicit reference to Genesis in the prayer of Tobias, the story is clearly influenced by patriarchal narratives, especially Isaac's quest for a wife. The biblical narrative has some halakic implications, especially in the matter of endogamy, but more typically it is a source of wisdom and guidance by the precedents it provides. It can embrace Jewish tradition broadly, even including details that are not actually found in the written Torah.[68]

In all of the literature surveyed in this chapter, the Torah provides the context for Jewish life, by providing precedents and sapiential advice. The emphasis is on Torah as wisdom rather than as law. This emphasis was broadly typical of the ways in which the Torah was used in the early Hellenistic period. We will find a quite different emphasis in the period after the Maccabean revolt.

# CHAPTER 5

# Torah as Law

The Maccabean revolt was fought in defense of the right of Judeans to live according to their ancestral law, or at least that is how it is presented in 1 Maccabees. "Let everyone who is zealous for the law and supports the covenant come out with me," says Mattathias in 1 Macc 2:27. A major objective was to cleanse the temple that had been polluted and to restore a legitimate cult (1 Macc 4). The rededication of the temple by Judas would be commemorated by the festival of Hanukkah. The Maccabees were hardly scrupulous in their observance of the Law. They famously decided to fight on the Sabbath so that they would not be wiped out by the Seleucids. But they insisted on some level of observance, at least where key symbols were at issue. Mattathias and his friends went around and tore down the pagan altars that had been set up at the king's command, and forcibly circumcised all the boys who had been left uncircumcised because of the king's decree.[1] This aggressive policy was continued by his sons. Josephus tells us that when John Hyrcanus conquered the Idumeans, about 128 B.C.E., he

> permitted them to remain in their country so long as they had themselves circumcised and were willing to observe the laws of the Jews. And so, out of attachment to their ancestral land, they submitted to circumcision and to having their manner of life in all other respects made the same as

that of the Judaeans. And from that time on they have continued to be Judaeans.[2]

Similarly, when Aristobulus conquered the Itureans in 104–103 B.C.E., "he compelled the inhabitants, if they wished to remain in their country, to be circumcised and to live in accordance with the laws of the Judaeans."[3] Later, when the inhabitants of Pella refused to accept the laws of the Judeans, Alexander Jannaeus destroyed the city.[4] He also launched attacks against the Hellenistic cities of the coastal plain and Transjordan. On the one hand, these actions drew a sharp line between Judeans and other inhabitants of the region. On the other, they provide the first instance of the incorporation of large bodies of Gentiles into Judaism. As Shaye Cohen has observed, this process has two aspects, change of citizenship or political enfranchisement and religious conversion.[5] Cohen regards this development as a

> limitation of the role of ethnicity in Judaean identity.... But by investing Judaean identity with political or cultural (religious) content, the Hasmoneans were able to give outsiders an opportunity to attain membership in Judaean society.[6]

Rather than viewing this as a limitation of the role of ethnicity, however, it would be more correct to say that the Hasmoneans did this by taking a constructivist, or even instrumentalist, view of Judean ethnicity.[7] Moreover, cultural or religious content had never been lacking in Judean identity.

The Hasmoneans expanded the borders of Judea. John Hyrcanus conquered Samaria and Idumea. Josephus credits Aristobulus with the conquest of the Itureans, but archaeological evidence is lacking. The high point of Hasmonean expansion came in the reign of Alexander Jannaeus. Again, there is little archaeological evidence of his conquest of Galilee, but it clear that Galilee was under Hasmonean control by the end of his reign, as can be seen especially from the spread of Hasmonean coins. Some sites went out of use; others received new populations, and new settlements appeared. The Jewish character of Galilee in the Roman period had its roots in Hasmonean colonization.[8] Besides political expediency, the Hasmoneans were guided by an ideal but loosely defined sense of the traditional boundaries of Israel. 1 Macc 15:33–34 has Simon Maccabee declare:

> We have neither taken any other man's land, nor do we hold dominion over other people's territory, but only over the inheritance of our fathers. On the contrary, for a certain time it was unjustly held by our enemies; but we, seizing the opportunity, hold fast to the inheritance of our fathers.

Some of the archaeological findings suggest a heightened concern for purity. Stepped pools (often called *miqvaoth*) first appear in the Hasmonean period.[9] Stone vessels, which were important for purity, proliferate even more in the late first century B.C.E., when Herod's rebuilding of the Jerusalem temple led to increased quarrying of limestone.[10] Hellenistic amphorae, which were very common in Jerusalem in the period between 180 and 150 B.C.E., are virtually absent in Hasmonean Jerusalem, and are also unattested in the Hasmonean palaces.[11] The language of purification plays an important part in the account of the actions of Judas in 1 Maccabees, most obviously in connection with rededication of the temple (4:41–52).

## THE TEMPLE SCROLL AND JUBILEES

Concern for purity also comes to the fore in the literature of the Hasmonean era. Two "rewritten Bible" texts, the Temple Scroll and Jubilees, are major witnesses to this development.[12] Both of these texts were written in Hebrew. While they are found in the Dead Sea Scrolls, and the Temple Scroll is only known from the Scrolls, neither is thought to have been a product of the sectarian movement known from the Damascus Document and Community Rule. Both clearly draw on the traditional Torah, but neither is presented as a work of exegesis.

The Temple Scroll takes its name from the instructions for building the sanctuary, but these occupy only a portion of the text (2:1–13:8 and

30:3–47:18). Other major sections are devoted to the calendar (13:9–30:2), purity laws (48:1–51:10), laws of polity (51:11–56:21 and 60:1–66:17), and the Torah of the King (57–59).[13] The Temple Scroll attempts to integrate the laws in Exodus, Leviticus, and Numbers, dealing with the sanctuary, the festivals, sacrifices, and purity. It practices what Lawrence Schiffman has called "a distinct form of harmonistic exegesis," mainly on legal materials.[14] For example, 11QT 53:4–8 adds to the Deuteronomic permission of secular slaughter the provision that the blood be covered with dust, by analogy with the slaughter of wild animals in Lev 17:13. This kind of harmonistic exegesis is broadly typical of the Samaritan Pentateuch and the text known as 4QReworked Pentateuch.[15]

The Temple Scroll, however, is not presented as exegesis. While we do not have the opening column, and so cannot be sure how the text is introduced, the speaking voice throughout is that of God. There is a passing reference to "Aaron your brother" in TS 44:5, and another to "those things which I tell you on this mountain" in TS 51:6. From these it appears that the discourse is addressed to Moses on Mount Sinai, but Moses is never mentioned by name. Schiffman actually suggests that the apparent allusions to Moses are mere lapses, where the author had not fully revised his sources.[16] Hindy Najman argues that "by means of the second person singular pronoun, the reader is placed in the position of Moses, as the addressee of divine revelation on Mount Sinai."[17] But she also recognizes that Moses is only the implicit initial addressee. The Temple Scroll appeals to a higher authority than Moses, by appealing directly to God. The Temple Scroll claims for itself the status of Torah. Several passages demand that the Israelites observe "the regulation of this law" (50:5–9, 17). It also refers to itself as "this Torah" (56:20–21; 59:7–10). TS 54:5–7 appropriates the warning of Deut 13:1: "All the things which I order you today, take care to carry them out; you shall not add to them nor shall you remove anything from them." The question arises whether it was intended to replace the Torah. The main argument that it was not so intended is that there are many basic issues that it does not address. It does not, for example, reproduce the Ten

Commandments. The traditional Torah also presupposed some basic matters, such as the law of divorce, which is only acknowledged indirectly in Deuteronomy 24. The author of the Temple Scroll apparently felt that the Ten Commandments were so familiar that they could be taken for granted. It may be that "the *Temple Scroll* is meant to stand alongside the Torah, to supplement and explain it,"[18] but it surprising that it does not acknowledge the older scripture at all.

There can be little doubt in any case that the Temple Scroll was meant to be decisive on the matters it addressed. It is also reasonable to assume that the topics it singled out were those it regarded as most important. These were primarily concerned with the temple and cult, purity issues, and governance, especially the role of the king.

The date of the Temple Scroll is a matter of controversy. Hartmut Stegemann argued for a date as early as 400 B.C.E., but there is no specific evidence in support of such an early date.[19] The question is complicated both by the manuscript evidence and by the use of sources. In addition to 11QTemple a and b (11Q19 and 11Q20), there are three other relevant manuscripts:[20] 11Q21 (dubbed a "*Temple Scroll*-Like Document" by James Charlesworth),[21] 4Q365a ("*Temple Scroll* Source or Divergent Copy"),[22] and 4Q535 ( = 4QRouleau du Temple, "*Temple Scroll* Source or Earlier Edition").[23] 4Q524 is variously taken as the oldest copy of the Temple Scroll, as a possible source or early edition, or simply as a related text. It contains close parallels to TS 59–66, but also significant discrepancies. The text is fragmentary, but it clearly parallels the "law of the king" and also some of the Levitical laws. It reworks passages from both Deuteronomy and Leviticus. Émile Puech dates the script to 150–125 B.C.E., and takes it to be a copy of an even earlier manuscript.[24] Others allow for a slightly later date, but "no later than the last quarter of the second century B.C.E."[25] The law of the king in the Temple Scroll, however, is often thought to be a polemic against the Hasmonean rulers, because it proposes "a king subject to the priesthood and free from all cultic activities."[26] To quote Florentino García Martínez, "The need for reformulating the biblical data with respect to royalty seemed more pressing once the Maccabees attained national independence than had been the case during the Persian period or under Ptolemaic or Seleucid dominion."[27] Despite this argument, García Martínez pushes the date back to the Maccabean era, and suggests that the reformulation of the law of the king may have been prompted by the discussions leading to the investiture of Simon. Schiffman argues, more cogently, that "we must see the composition of the law of the king as taking place no earlier than the second half of the reign of John Hyrcanus."[28] There is general agreement that the Temple Scroll is "presectarian" in the sense that it predates the "new covenant" known from the Scrolls. The dating of this and other texts has often been influenced by the assumption that the sect originated in a dispute over the high priesthood when the Hasmoneans assumed office. That assumption, however, is unfounded.[29] There is no need to push a "presectarian" text such as the Temple Scroll back to the mid- or early second century B.C.E. The reformulation of the law of the king in the Temple Scroll is likely to presuppose the development of Hasmonean rule, and is not likely to be earlier than the reign of John Hyrcanus.

The date of Jubilees is also controversial. James VanderKam argued for a date between 161 and 140 B.C.E., with a preference for the earlier part of that period, on the basis of implicit allusions to the Maccabean wars.[30] Even if these allusions are correctly identified, this would only argue for a *terminus post quem*. The oldest copy, 4Q216, dates from the late second century.[31] George Nickelsburg argued that Jub 23:9–32 was a polemic against the Hellenizers before the Maccabean revolt.[32] Menahem Kister, in contrast, argued that the revolt is not mentioned because it was already long past.[33] Doron Mendels argued that Jubilees 38, which refers to the subjection of the Edomites, presupposes the conquest of Idumea by John Hyrcanus, about 125 B.C.E.[34] None of these arguments is conclusive.[35] The question is further complicated if we acknowledge redactional layers in Jubilees, as Michael Segal and James Kugel have argued.[36] Nonetheless, a date in the Hasmonean period, probably in the last quarter of the second century B.C.E., seems plausible. There is general agreement that Jubilees is older than the sectarian scrolls from Qumran. It seems to be cited as an authoritative text in the Damascus Document (CD 16:3–4). It has much in common with the Temple Scroll, and is probably roughly contemporary with it.[37]

Jubilees retells the story of Genesis and Exodus, through Exodus 19. Unlike the Temple Scroll, it explicitly acknowledges "the first law" (Jub 6:20–22; 30:12). But it too is presented as a revelation, delivered to Moses by the angel of the presence. While it presupposes the validity of the first law, it supersedes it at some points. VanderKam has aptly described it as "Moses trumping Moses."[38] In this respect, it resembles the appeal to higher revelation that we will find in the Dead Sea Scrolls, and more generally in apocalyptic writings such as 4 Ezra and 2 Baruch.[39] Especially noteworthy is Jubilees's appeal to what is written on the heavenly tablets (Jub 3:10, 31; 4:5, 32; etc.).[40] The tablets contain the "testimony," which complements the Torah. VanderKam argues that the content of Jubilees itself corresponds to the "testimony," although it may not exhaust it.[41] David Lambert, more precisely, relates it to the narrative part of the Torah, which complements the commandments.[42]

One of the distinctive features of Jubilees is that it tries to show that the laws revealed to Moses were already observed by the patriarchs, and even in the creation stories.[43] The account of creation in Jubilees 2 highlights the Sabbath, and the book concludes with instructions for the Sabbath in chapter 50.[44] Halakic rules are woven into the narrative. So, for example, we read that Adam was created in the first week but Eve in the second, "and that is why the commandment was given for women to keep in their uncleanness—seven days for a male and fourteen days for a female." Adam was brought into the garden after forty days, but Eve only on the eightieth day, "and that is why the commandment is written on the heavenly tablets about a woman that gives birth" that she will be impure twice as long after the birth of a female as after the birth of a male (Jub 3:8–13). In this case, Jubilees grounds the law of Leviticus 12 in the story of creation. In other cases, it expands or elaborates the law. So, for example, we are told, apropos of the primal couple's discovery of their nakedness, that it is prescribed in the heavenly tablets that all those familiar with the law should cover their shame and not uncover themselves as the Gentiles do (Jub 3:31). The festivals, and rituals such as circumcision, are a focus of attention throughout. Jubilees defends a 364-day calendar, which is also presupposed in the Temple Scroll and the Dead Sea Scrolls, and warns against "the feast of the Gentiles" and the aberration of the moon (6:32–38). The dominant concerns of the book may be illustrated from the last words of Abraham, in chapters 20–22. Abraham warns his sons to practice circumcision, renounce fornication and uncleanness, refrain from marriage with Canaanite women, avoid idolatry, eat no blood, and perform washings before and after sacrificing. Marriage with Gentiles is emphatically forbidden in the story of the destruction of Shechem (chap. 30).[45]

Jubilees is especially concerned with matters of purity. Noah tells his grandsons that the flood had come about because of fornication, uncleanness, and all iniquity, all of which were exemplified by the Watchers, or fallen angels (Jub 7:21). Bloodshed had defiled the earth. The prohibition of fornication and bloodshed is addressed to all humanity.[46] Likewise, when Jubilees inveighs against the sin of Reuben, we are told that it is written on the heavenly tablets that a man should not lie with his father's wife. This is an abomination for anyone, because "they are guilty of uncleanness on the earth" (Jub 33:10). But injunctions against impurity apply all the more to Israel. Moses is told to tell the Israelites:

> And there is no sin on earth they can commit greater than fornication, for Israel is a holy nation to the Lord its God, and a special nation of his own, and a priestly and royal nation for his possession, and no such uncleanness should be seen in a holy nation. (Jub 33:20)

Jubilees is equally vehement on the subject of intermarriage:

> If there is a man in Israel who wishes to give his daughter or his sister to any foreigner, he is to die. He is to be stoned.... The woman is to be burned.... The man who has defiled his daughter within all of Israel is to

be eradicated because he has given one of his descendants to Molech. (Jub 30:7, 10)[47]

Simeon and Levi acted rightly in slaughtering the people of Shechem, "so that it might never happen again in Israel that an Israelite virgin should be thus defiled" (Jub 30:6). In the biblical text, Jacob grumbled that their actions had made him odious to the inhabitants of the land (Gen 34:30), and condemns their violence in the Blessing of Jacob in Gen 49:6. In Jubilees, however, their deeds are "reckoned to them as righteousness and accounted to their credit" (Jub 30:17). Their zeal is compared to that of Phinehas, who, like Levi, was rewarded with the priesthood (18).[48]

For Jubilees, Israelites and Gentiles are distinct "seeds."[49] The angels tell Abraham that it is through Isaac that his descent will be traced:

> And we told him that all the descendants of his other sons would be Gentiles, and be reckoned with the Gentiles, although one of Isaac's sons would become a holy seed, and not be reckoned with the Gentiles: he would become the Most High's portion, and all his descendants settled in that land which belongs to God, so as to be the Lord's special possession, chosen out of all nations, and to be a kingdom of priests and a holy nation. (Jub 16:17–18)

This is a heightened version of Ezra's idea of a holy seed. In the words of Kugel, Israel is holy

> virtually in the sense of angelic, a people whose existence and function on earth is comparable to that of God's own sacred hosts on high. As a result, any mingling—particularly any sexual union—between an Israelite and a foreigner is monstrous. *Jubilees* defines such unions as "unclean" and "an abomination," an act of "fornication" that belongs to the same order of sexual sacrileges as incest, bestiality, and the other forbidden unions of the priestly code.[50]

In all of this, Jubilees is concerned to draw a clear line between Israel and the Gentiles,[51] even to the point of denying the possibility of conversion.[52] Indeed, Christine Hayes argues that "the need for Israel to separate itself from the nations," typified by Abraham, is "the single most important issue in *Jubilees*."[53]

Jubilees is often seen as a reaction against the Hellenizing trends in the period before the Maccabean revolt.[54] The rationale for the so-called Hellenistic Reform in 1 Macc 1:11 was that things had gone badly for the Judeans because of their separation from the Gentiles. Jubilees argued the reverse. Martha Himmelfarb has argued that it was rather a reaction to the incorporation of Idumeans and other Gentiles into Judaism in the Hasmonean period, while granting that this is not incompatible with the view that it was a reaction to the spread of Hellenism.[55] On either view, it is clear that while Jubilees appears to take an extremely primordialist view of Jewish ethnicity, basing it on genetic descent from Abraham, it is actually quite constructivist, even instrumentalist. It is arguing for one rather extreme view in the context of a much broader debate about what Judean identity entailed.

Himmelfarb insists, with reason, that Jubilees is not a sectarian text, because it "insists that all Jews were singled out by god from the beginning of the world, and they continue to be his holy people for all time."[56] Unlike the apocalypses of Enoch and Daniel, Jubilees does not distinguish between a doomed majority and a righteous remnant:

> After this they will turn to me from among the Gentiles with all their heart and with all their soul and with all their strength; and I will gather them from among all the Gentiles, and they will seek me, and I will let them find me. (Jub 1:15)

The Deuteronomic language suggests the restoration of the whole people. The final acceptance of the whole people, however, is conditional on their turning to God, which entails their acceptance of the rigorist interpretation found in Jubilees, and also the 364-day calendar, which differed from that observed in the Jerusalem temple. It is true that Jubilees shows no sign of sectarian organization, but its distinctive interpretation of the Torah surely contained the seeds of sectarianism. There is at least tension between the belief that all those descended from Abraham through Isaac are elect, and the insistence on a strict, separatist ideology, which left little room for Judeans with a more open attitude to the Gentiles.

## COMMON JUDAISM AND THE RISE
## OF SECTARIANISM

While G.F. Moore's idea of a "normative" Judaism in the late Second Temple period has been generally discredited,[57] E.P. Sanders has argued forcefully that one can speak of "normal" or "common" Judaism, on which the priests and people agreed, and which was based on the Torah, the temple, and the ordinary Judeans who were not members of any sect.[58] This common Judaism was manifested especially in practices: Sabbath observance, circumcision, observance of the festivals, avoidance of pork, support for the temple, and so on. Eric Meyers and Jürgen Zangenberg have argued that the idea of a common Judaism is corroborated by the archaeological record, noting the spread of stepped pools, stone vessels, synagogues, ossuaries, and so on beginning in the Hasmonean period.[59] Shaye Cohen has shown that the conception of a common Judaism receives strong support from the comments of Greek and Latin authors.[60]

While it is certainly true that some practices were common to all Judeans or Jews, the Law was also a source of division. Josephus first mentions the sects in the context of Jonathan Maccabee's rule in *Antiquities* 12.171. Whether this is reliable information about the date at which the sects arose may be doubted. In the *Jewish War*, Josephus introduces them much later, in the context of the early first century C.E. Joseph Sievers has argued persuasively that the notice in *Antiquities* 12 is a secondary addition, and out of context.[61] Josephus elsewhere states that the sects existed "from the most ancient times" (*Ant.* 18.11). He does not appear to have actually known when they arose.[62] There is ample evidence, however, that the sects were flourishing by the end of the Hasmonean era. Josephus reports a dispute between John Hyrcanus and the

Pharisees, which arose even though "he was a disciple of theirs and greatly beloved by them" (*Ant.* 13.289–91). A Pharisee named Eleazar told the king that he should give up the high priesthood and be content with governing the people, because his mother had allegedly been a captive. This led to a rift, and Hyrcanus was persuaded "to join the Sadducean party and desert the Pharisees, and to abrogate the regulations which they had established for the people and punish those who observed them" (*Ant.* 13.298). Josephus adds an explanatory note:

> For the present I wish merely to explain that the Pharisees had passed on to the people certain regulations handed down by former generations and not recorded in the Laws of Moses, for which reason they are rejected by the Sadducean group, who hold that only those regulations should be considered valid which were written down (in Scripture) and that those which had been handed down by the fathers need not be observed. And concerning these matters the two parties came to have controversies and serious differences, the Sadducees having the confidence of the wealthy alone but no following among the populace, while the Pharisees have the support of the masses. (*Ant.* 13.297–98)[63]

There was bitter conflict between the Pharisees and rulers during the reign of Hyrcanus's son Alexander Jannaeus, and at one time it erupted into open rebellion. The rebels called on the Seleucid Demetrius Akairos for help, but their strategy backfired, as the people rallied against the Seleucid invader. Jannaeus, we are told, had some eight hundred of his enemies crucified (*Ant.* 13.380). On his deathbed, however, he advised his widow, Salome Alexandra, to "yield a certain amount of power to the Pharisees, for if they praised her in return for this sign of regard, they would dispose the nation favorably toward her" (*Ant.* 13.401). He added that he "had come into conflict with the nation because these men had been badly treated by him" (*Ant.* 13.402). After his death she appointed Hyrcanus II as high priest, but

> she permitted the Pharisees to do as they liked in all matters, and also commanded the people to obey them; and whatever regulations, introduced by the Pharisees in accordance with the tradition of their fathers,

had been abolished by her father-in-law Hyrcanus, these she again restored. And so, while she had the title of sovereign, the Pharisees had the power. (*Ant.* 13.408–9)

From all of this it would seem that "common Judaism" was not quite so harmonious as some scholars would have us believe, and that sectarian divisions had a significant bearing on the interpretation of the Law. While the Sadducees claimed to follow the written law, they inevitably relied on traditions of interpretation. Equally, the traditions of the fathers, on which the Pharisees relied, were grounded in interpretations of the scriptural texts.

It is not clear whether there was any attempt to enforce a particular interpretation of the Law outside of the temple area, but if Josephus is to be trusted on this point, the sympathies of the common people were with the Pharisees. Accordingly, Martin Hengel and Roland Deines have argued that what E. P. Sanders regards as "common Judaism" was essentially "Pharisaic Judaism."[64] They attribute the proliferation of ritual baths, stone vessels, and synagogues to Pharisaic influence. This view is vigorously contested by Zangenberg, who points out that the Pharisees were not the only people interested in ritual purity, and that there is no clear evidence linking them to the development of the synagogue.[65] In fact, stepped pools and stone vessels were compatible with more than one interpretation. The evidence for Pharisaic hegemony does not derive from material culture, but from Josephus. For our present purpose, however, whether these developments were due to sectarian preference is not so important. What is important is that the heightened scrutiny of the Torah as religious law had an impact on the common people and also generated sectarian division among the religious experts.

The clearest evidence that disputes over the exact interpretation of the Torah were a (not necessarily the only) factor in sectarian disputes is provided by the Dead Sea Scrolls, especially by 4QMMT ("Some of the Works of the Law"), which is a treatise addressed to a leader of Israel, presumably a high priest, urging him to accept the writer's interpretation of the Law rather than that of a third party.[66] Part of the text deals with the religious calendar. The sectarian Scrolls generally attest to a calendar of 364 days (as do the Temple Scroll and Jubilees), whereas the traditional calendar observed in the temple had 354. The main body of 4QMMT, however, deals with some twenty issues bearing on holiness and purity, sacrifice and tithing, forbidden sexual unions, and so forth. In all cases, the views of the "we" group are stricter than those of their opponents. Several of the issues discussed in 4QMMT appear again in rabbinic literature. The views of the third party, to which MMT is opposed, generally correspond to those of the rabbis, and are widely assumed to be those of the Pharisees. Jacob Sussmann, followed by Schiffman, argued that the viewpoint advanced in MMT corresponded to that of the Sadducees, even if the group in question was Essene.[67] The Essenes shared the Saducean view on these issues.

The sectarian movement described in the Dead Sea Scrolls, usually assumed to be the Essenes, distinguished between that which was revealed (*nigleh*) and that which was hidden (*nistar*).[68] The written laws were known to all Israel. The hidden laws were only revealed to the sectarians (CD 3:12–16). It is apparent that in many cases these hidden things were "revealed" through exegesis, and were understood to be implicit in the text of the Torah. In CD 6:2–11 the process of revealing the hidden things is symbolized as digging a well, alluding to Num 21:18.[69] The well is the Torah, and those who dig it are "the penitents of Israel," while a special role is reserved for an authoritative teacher called "the Interpreter of the Torah" (*doresh ha-Torah*).

Danny Schwartz has argued that there was a fundamental difference between the attitude to law of the priestly groups (Sadducees and Essenes; the Temple Scroll and CD are both in the priestly camp) and that of the Pharisees and later rabbis.[70] In his view, the priestly halakah was realistic, whereas that of the Pharisees and rabbis was nominalistic. In other words, the priestly legal system was bound to nature and reality. A nice example of this is found in the prohibition of remarriage while the first wife was alive in CD 4:20–21: "The foundation of the creation (*yesod ha-b'ri'ah*) is 'male and female he created them' (Gen 1:27)." Concern for the order of nature underlies the insistence on the 364-day calendar. If human bones are impure, animal bones must be impure too. Intermarriage is absolutely excluded in such texts as Jubilees and 4QMMT by analogy with the separation of species in creation.[71] The Pharisees and rabbis, in contrast, held that such issues, including calendrical matters, were for authoritative interpreters to decide. Schwartz has been criticized for overstating his case.[72] As he now admits, "Some rabbinic laws seem to assume that law conforms to nature."[73] The rabbis are not invariably opposed to the realist perspective, but weigh it among other considerations. Nonetheless, the distinction stands as a broad generalization.[74]

Hayes has argued that what is at issue here is "the role of epistemological certainty in determining the content of the law."[75] If legal principles exist in nature, and have independent reality, they cannot be subject to negotiation. This conflict of legal epistemologies was a significant factor in the rise of sectarianism in the late Second Temple period.

A plausible occasion for an appeal such as we find in 4QMMT is provided by the switch of official allegiance from the Sadducees to the Pharisees after the death of Alexander Jannaeus.[76] If the Essenes, who are generally assumed to be the authors of 4QMMT, shared the legal traditions of the Sadducees, they would have viewed the switch of allegiance with alarm. In their view, the Pharisees were "seekers after smooth things,"[77] and the Hasmonean rulers were putting the welfare of Israel in jeopardy by following their rulings. Hence their appeal to the ruler/high priest to recognize that their (Essene/Sadducean) interpretations were the right ones.

Many of the issues in dispute in 4QMMT seem trivial to the modern reader (e.g., the purity of liquid streams), although some, such as the calendar, are of obvious importance. Dispute about specific interpretations is not incompatible with an underlying common Judaism. There was no dispute between the rival sects about circumcision or the importance of the Sabbath, or the need for ritual washing, although the specific requirements might vary. But even as the Torah provided the basis for cohesion in Judaism, it also provided the impetus for division. Judaism was not only a matter of practice. Beliefs were important too, as Jonathan Klawans has recently reminded us.[78] Judaism could tolerate some diversity of opinion on matters of belief—whether there would be one or two messiahs, the role of supernatural forces in human affairs, and so on. But as Morton Smith famously said, "Touch the Law and the sect will split."[79] The range of tolerance on legal issues was narrow, among people who were zealous for the Law.

## THE PAPYRI FROM THE ROMAN PERIOD

We should not assume that all the inhabitants of Judea were as zealous for the Law as the author of 4QMMT. The discussions in the Scrolls represent a religious elite, who are concerned with matters of principle. For example, the Damascus Document engages in a discussion as to whether one may marry one's niece (CD 5:7–11). This is a theoretical question, not an actual legal case. For insight into the practice of law in Judea, we have to wait until the documents from the early second century C.E., found in the region of the Dead Sea.[80] These include more than a hundred legal documents—sales documents, marriage documents, and the like. More than one-third of the legal documents are written in Greek. (The others are in Hebrew, Aramaic, or Nabatean Aramaic.) All of this material comes from a time after the end of Judean independence, and so the context is very different from that of the sectarian scrolls. Much of the discussion of these papyri has focused on the question of whether they conform to Roman law or rather correspond to Jewish law, as found later in the Mishnah and Talmud. At the outset, it must be noted that the only court mentioned is that of the Roman governor of Arabia. After the Roman incorporation of Nabatea in 106 C.E., contracts were increasingly written in Greek, even when the parties to them did not know that language. This was necessary so that they would be recognized as valid. The contracts and legal documents "bear a striking resemblance to their Egyptian counterparts."[81] It should also be noted that rabbinic law, which is often adduced as representative of "Jewish law" in this context, was not yet written down when these documents were drawn up. Hannah Cotton has argued:

> Even when the provisions in the documents do resemble what came to be normative Jewish law, we cannot assume without further proof that what we are witnessing is the influence of Jewish law on the documents rather than the reverse: the halakha adopted the legal usage of the documents, which, in their turn, reflect the legal usage of the environment.[82]

The most interesting and controversial issues raised by the papyri concern marital law. The marriage contracts written in Aramaic have a distinctively Jewish character. Two of these contracts (DJD 2, no. 20 and p. Yadin 10) contain the formula "that you will be my wife according to the law of Moses and the Jews." These contracts also refer to "the money of your *ketubbah*." Cotton infers that the rabbinic marriage contract had indeed by then developed its own special form.[83] She doubts, however, that it was normative at this time. None of the five marriage contracts written in Greek is a translation of an Aramaic *ketubbah*. The formula referring to the law of Moses is absent from all of them.

Jacobine Oudshoorn concludes from her review of the papyri that "under Roman rule substantive arrangements referred to indigenous law," but she bases her conclusion on the fact that they do not follow Greek or Roman precedent in a rigid way. In fact, the papyri seem to take a flexible attitude to laws. While they sometimes correspond to later rabbinic law, this is not true on the whole. If they reflect indigenous law, then Jewish law had not yet taken the form we know from rabbinic literature in a consistent way.[84]

These papyri raise many interesting issues that go beyond the bounds of the present book. These include a possible case of bigamy, the practice of unwritten marriage, and whether women could initiate divorce.[85] All of these issues are disputed and complex, but they reflect a world that is very different from that of the Dead Sea Scrolls.

# CHAPTER 6

# Torah and Apocalypticism

In 1903, the German scholar Wilhelm Bousset ignited a controversy when he published an account of the religion of Judaism in the New Testament period that was based on the Pseudepigrapha rather than on the rabbinic writings.[1] The Pseudepigrapha were writings attributed to ancient figures such as Enoch, which had come to light in the course of the nineteenth century. Many of them had an apocalyptic character, which is to say that they purported to contain supernatural revelations, concerning either the end of history or otherworldly regions. They had been preserved by Christians, in such languages as Ethiopic, Old Church Slavonic, and Syriac, but they contained only isolated references to Christ or to distinctively Christian beliefs, and these references could be explained as interpolations.[2] The basic texts appeared to be Jewish rather than Christian, but they bespoke a view of Judaism very different from that of the rabbis.

Bousset's book was greeted by a storm of protest from Jewish scholars, who claimed that it had missed the center of Jewish religion.[3] Bousset responded that one must differentiate between the piety of the scribes, which became normative after 70 C.E., and the more diverse popular piety of the earlier period.[4] In the short term, the Jewish objections seemed to carry the day. George Foot Moore, an authoritative Christian scholar of Judaism, wrote:

The censure which Jewish scholars have unanimously passed on *Die Religion des Judentums* is that the author uses as his primary sources almost exclusively the writings commonly called Apocrypha and Pseudepigrapha, with an especial penchant for the apocalypses; and only secondarily and almost casually the writings which represent the acknowledged and authoritative teaching of the school and the more popular instructions. This is much as if one should describe early Christianity using indiscriminately for his principal sources the Apocryphal Gospels and Acts, the Apocalypses of John and Peter and the Clementine literature.[5]

The discovery of the Dead Sea Scrolls, which brought to light for the first time a significant corpus of literature in Hebrew and Aramaic from the period around the turn of era, provided a unique opportunity to assess this controversy.

## AN APOCALYPTIC MOVEMENT?

The first two decades of research on the Scrolls, after the initial discovery in 1947, were distinguished by the fact that no Jewish scholars were included in the official editorial team.[6] This was due to the political situation after the partition of Palestine; the Scrolls, with few exceptions, were under Jordanian control. Naturally, the Christian scholars were attracted especially by those aspects of the Scrolls that showed affinities with Christianity, and these were especially the apocalyptic aspects. A classic formulation of the relation between the Scrolls and Christianity was provided by Frank Moore Cross in 1958. Cross wrote that "the Essenes prove to be the bearers, and in no small part the producers, of the apocalyptic tradition of Judaism."[7] "In some sense," he added, "the primitive Church is the continuation of this communal and apocalyptic tradition."[8] Like the Essenes, the early Christians believed they were living in the end of days, and this belief shaped the way they lived. Both were "apocalyptic communities."

After the 1967 war, however, Jewish scholars became increasingly involved in the study of the Scrolls. In part, their interest was stimulated by the publication of the Temple Scroll, which was seized by Yigael Yadin from the dealer Kando in Bethlehem.[9] This was the longest of all the Scrolls, and it was primarily concerned with matters of religious law, or halakah. Gradually, Israeli scholars were invited to join in the work of editing the Scrolls. Collaboration between John Strugnell, of the official editorial team, and a young Israeli scholar Elisha Qimron led to a joint paper at a conference in Jerusalem in 1984 on the text called 4QMMT ("Some of the Works of the Law"), which has been discussed in the previous chapter.[10] This text outlined a series of more than twenty issues on which the sectarians disagreed with other Jews of the time. Many of these concerned issues of purity. Calendrical differences were also important. It became clear that the sectarian movement described in the Scrolls had come into being because of halakic disputes with other Jewish parties, notably the Pharisees. It had not come into being because of messianic beliefs or belief in the imminence of the eschaton. Neither had it had its origin in disputes over the high priesthood, as was popularly believed.

In the wake of the publication of 4QMMT, the balance of scholarly opinion shifted, and focused increasingly on those aspects of the Scrolls that show continuity with rabbinic Judaism. It had always been obvious that the sectarians attached great importance to the Law. The Damascus Document speaks of a "new covenant in the land of Damascus," and the Community Rule (*Serek ha-Yaḥad*) begins with a covenant renewal service. E. P. Sanders argued in 1977 that "common Judaism" was characterized by "covenantal nomism."[11] He found this pattern not only in the rabbinic literature but also in most of the Pseudepigrapha (with the exception of 4 Ezra) and in the Dead Sea Scrolls. Sanders's view of Judaism focused on practice rather than belief. Apocalyptic speculations about the heavens or the end of history tell us little about the practices people observed, and were therefore, in his view, less important.

But while the centrality of the Law in the Scrolls is not in doubt, there remain considerable apocalyptic elements that give the Scrolls a character that is significantly different from that of the rabbis. Indeed,

Seth Schwartz has argued that "apocalyptic mythology" and "covenantal ideology" are incongruous systems:

> The covenant imagines an orderly world governed justly by the one God. The apocalyptic myth imagines a world in disarray, filled with evil; a world in which people do *not* get what they deserve. God is not in control in any obvious way; indeed the cosmology of the myth is dualist or polytheist.[12]

Nonetheless, the sectarians known from the Scrolls seem to have combined the two. In what follows we will focus on the apocalyptic elements in the Scrolls and ask how they fit into the overall ideology of the sect. These elements are of two kinds. First, the collection includes several apocalyptic writings that were probably not authored by the sectarians themselves. Second, while no clear examples of apocalypses have been found in the sectarian Scrolls, many of these writings exhibit what may be called an apocalyptic worldview.

## THE APOCALYPTIC HERITAGE OF THE SCROLLS

Eight copies of the book of Daniel have been identified among the Scrolls,[13] and seven manuscripts containing various parts of 1 Enoch in Aramaic.[14] These writings were composed about a century before most of the Scrolls were written. It is often suggested that they are representative of the circles from which the sect emerged. The Enochic writings have been especially controversial in this regard. Some of them speak of the emergence of an elect movement in Israel in the Hellenistic period. So, for example, the Apocalypse of Weeks says that in the seventh "week," which represents the postexilic period, at its end, "the chosen will be chosen as witnesses of righteousness from the everlasting plant of righteousness, to whom will be given sevenfold wisdom and knowledge" (1 Enoch 93:10). Similarly, the Animal Apocalypse, an elaborate allegorical overview of history, speaks of "lambs," who begin to open their eyes, late in the postexilic period. Several scholars have suggested that these passages refer, if not to the Essenes themselves, at least to a movement that was a precursor of the sect known from the Scrolls. (Compare the Damascus Document, column I, which speaks of a "plant root" that arises from Aaron and Israel.) Gabriele Boccaccini has gone so far as to claim that these Enochic texts were actually Essene: "Enochic Judaism is the modern name for the mainstream body of the Essene party, from which the Qumran community parted as a radical, dissident, and marginal offspring."[15] Boccaccini's thesis is complex, and has been widely criticized.[16] The Essenes are known to us from Philo, Josephus, and Pliny. The sect described in the Scrolls has been identified as Essene on the basis of similarities between these accounts and the descriptions of the sectarian community, especially that of the Community Rule (1QS).[17] There is no basis for attributing the Enochic writings to the Essenes, or for regarding "the Qumran community" as a splinter group from the larger Essene movement. That said, however, it is clear that the writings of Enoch are important for the sectarians. They are not uniquely important—the book of Daniel, which cannot be ascribed to the same movement as the books of Enoch, is no less important. Similarities can be traced between the Scrolls and various bodies of literature. The Scrolls cannot be explained solely as the continuation of the Enoch tradition. But the Enoch tradition is important nonetheless. This is of interest especially since the themes of law and covenant that are central to the sectarian Scrolls scarcely appear at all in the Enochic tradition.[18]

The influence of Daniel and Enoch on the sectarian Scrolls is manifested in several ways.[19] There are explicit citations of Daniel in 4Q174, the Florilegium (citing Dan 12:10, with an allusion to Dan 11:32), and in 11QMelchizedek, which refers to "the anointed of the spirit, of whom Daniel spoke." Dan 11:33 says that "the wise among the people" (*maśkîlē 'am*) will instruct the many (*rabbîm*)." In the Community Rule, *maśkîl* is a title for a community official, and the *rabbîm* are the rank and file of the community. The sectarian Scrolls polemicize against "seekers after smooth things" (*dōrešē chalāqôt*)—a possible echo of the statement in Daniel that many would join the wise *bachalaqlāqlôt* (insincerely). The opening column of the War Scroll draws heavily on Daniel 11. It refers to the "violators of the covenant," and describes the time of battle as a time of distress (Dan 12:1). There is mention of the Kittim in both texts. The archangel Michael, who arises in victory in Dan 12:1, is also exalted in 1QM 17:7. It has been argued that "the eschatological vision of the *War Scroll* is predicated on an actualizing interpretation of Daniel's unfulfilled prophecy."[20] Moreover, Daniel's interpretation of dreams may be a model for *pesher*-style exegesis of prophetic texts. The concept of *raz*, "mystery," is important for both Daniel and the Scrolls.

More broadly, the sectarian Scrolls derive from the apocalypses the idea that history is divided into periods, and that the final period is at hand. Perhaps the most important idea inherited from the apocalypses is the belief that the righteous are destined for a blessed afterlife with the angels after death (Dan 12:3; 1 Enoch 104:2, 4). The sectarians, however, appear to have believed that they were participating in the angelic life already in the present in their community, and that death was of no account.[21]

The books of Daniel and Enoch were not the only apocalyptic writings preserved among the Scrolls.[22] Two other Aramaic texts mention Daniel (4Q243–44; 4Q245).[23] Both contain extended prophecies of history, written after the fact (*ex eventu*). It is not apparent that either depends directly on the canonical book of Daniel, and their view of history seems somewhat different.[24] Another Aramaic text predicts the advent of a figure who will be called the Son of God, and who should be identified with the Davidic messiah.[25] In this case several phrases recall the biblical book of Daniel (e.g., "His kingdom will be an everlasting kingdom"), and it is possible that the text is an interpretation of the vision in Daniel 7, but this cannot be shown conclusively. All these texts are fragmentary, and crucial elements are missing at the beginnings and ends, so that it is difficult to determine their genre with any precision, although they obviously bear some affinity to the Daniel tradition.

Also fragmentary are compositions related to Jeremiah (Apocryphon of Jeremiah C) and Ezekiel (4QPseudo-Ezekiel), preserved in

4Q383–91.[26] There is controversy as to just how many texts should be distinguished in this lot.[27] 4Q390 resembles apocalypses of the historical type insofar as it divides history into jubilees.[28] Here again it is difficult to determine whether the text should be regarded as an apocalypse because of the fragmentary condition of the text.[29] The Ezekielian fragment (4Q385–86) appears to understand Ezekiel 37 as referring to the resurrection of individuals rather than to the communal restoration of Israel as envisioned in the biblical text.[30]

Related to the Enoch tradition are nine fragmentary manuscripts of the book of Giants, one of which (4Q530) contains a vision of the divine throne that has close parallels in Daniel 7 and 1 Enoch 14.[31]

Also of note is a fragmentary Aramaic text called 4QFour Kingdoms[a-b] ar (4Q552–53), in which four kingdoms are symbolized as four trees.[32] The motif of four kingdoms is familiar from the book of Daniel, where they are identified as Babylon, Media, Persia, and Greece. In 4QFour Kingdoms, only the first kingdom is clearly identified, as Babylon, which is then said to rule over Persia. Émile Puech, in the DJD edition, restored Media as the second kingdom, but this is unlikely, since Persia has already been subsumed under Babylon. Moreover, the second tree appears in the West. Bennie Reynolds has argued persuasively that it should be identified as Greece.[33] The third and fourth kingdoms are not preserved. They may have been identified with the Ptolemies and the Seleucids, or perhaps with the Seleucids and Rome, but in any case they do not simply reproduce the four kingdoms of Daniel.

The full significance of these fragmentary apocalyptic texts has yet to be fully explored. They suggest that there was a good deal more apocalyptic literature in circulation in the last centuries before the turn of the era than was known before the discovery of the Scrolls. The fact that most of these texts are in Aramaic (except for the Jeremianic and Ezekielian fragments) suggests that they were not composed within the community of the new covenant.[34] This does not necessarily mean that they are all older than the sectarian texts. The sectarian communities were not sealed so effectively that they could not have acquired texts that were composed outside their bounds. But the sectarians do not appear to have composed literature in Aramaic. It remains true that there is no undisputed case where an apocalyptic text, ascribed pseudonymously to an ancient figure, was composed within the sectarian community. A few scholars have argued for the sectarian provenance of 4Q390.[35] It does not refer to sectarian structures, but has many motifs that are paralleled in the sectarian Scrolls, especially the Damascus Document.[36] Even if 4Q390 is deemed to be sectarian, however, such compositions were evidently atypical of the sect.

## REVELATION IN THE SCROLLS

The apocalyptic writings are typically presented as revelations mediated by a venerable figure from the past (Enoch, Daniel, Jeremiah). In the Aramaic writings, the emphasis is not usually on the Torah. In contrast, the Torah has primary importance in the sectarian texts. 4Q390, which complains that "they will break all my laws and my precepts" (frag. 2, line 5) aligns with the sectarian texts in this regard. The sectarians, to be sure, had their own distinctive interpretation of the Torah, but for this they relied on the authority of their Teacher. The Damascus Document expounds Num 21:18, "a well which the princes dug, which the nobles of the people delved with the staff," as follows: "The well is the law, and those who dug it are the converts of Israel ... and the staff is the interpreter of the law, of whom Isaiah said 'he produces a tool for his work'" (CD 6:3–8).

The pesher on Habakkuk says that God made known to the Teacher "all the mysteries of the words of his servants the prophets" (1QpHab 7:4), and that the words of the Teacher were from the mouth of God (1QpHab 2:2). Steven Fraade has objected that "not a single Qumran sectarian scroll is explicitly attributed to the authorship of the Teacher."[37] But he was nonetheless regarded as the source of an authoritative tradition that continued after his death. As Samuel Byrskog has argued, it is likely that there were channels besides the written records by which the Qumranites could recognize the traditions from the Teacher.... There were presumably oral means of communicating the traditions' attachment to the Teacher.[38]

In any case, it is apparent that the sectarians did not usually attribute their teachings pseudonymously to ancient visionaries. Rather they presented them as interpretations of the Torah, in a tradition derived from the Teacher.

Nonetheless, these interpretations too were subsumed under a higher revelation, and assumed a view of the world that was apocalyptic, in the sense that human behavior was shaped by supernatural forces and subject to a judgment that would determine the fate of individual human beings for all eternity.

### THE APOCALYPTIC WORLDVIEW OF THE SECT

The *locus classicus* of the sectarian worldview is the Instruction on the Two Spirits in columns 3 and 4 of the Community Rule. According to this passage, God appointed for humanity

> two spirits in which to walk until the time of his visitation: the spirits of truth and injustice. Those born of truth spring from a fountain of light, but those born of injustice spring from a source of darkness. All the children of righteousness are ruled by the Prince of Light and walk in the ways of light, but all the children of injustice are ruled by the Angel of Darkness and walk in the ways of darkness.
>
> The children of darkness are destined for an abyss of darkness, while the children of light are promised eternal enjoyment with endless life. God has divided humanity between the two spirits until the time of the end, but then God in the mysteries of his knowledge and in the wisdom of his glory has determined an end to the existence of injustice and at the appointed time of the visitation he will obliterate it forever. (1QS 4:18–19)

This passage is not found in all copies of the Community Rule, and its importance for the worldview of the sect has been questioned.[39] In

German scholarship, it is often regarded as a relic of an older tradition that was incorporated whole, but was not a product of the sect.[40] It is certainly a distinctive composition, but nothing like it is known in ancient Judaism outside of the Scrolls. As we shall see, it fits a sectarian mind-set remarkably well, and pending evidence to the contrary, it must be assumed to be a sectarian composition.

While the Instruction expresses an apocalyptic view of the world, it is not overtly indebted to Daniel or Enoch, but rather draws on traditions known from Zoroastrianism. The fullest Zoroastrian sources date from a much later time,[41] but the essential dualism is reflected already in the Gathas, and in an account preserved by Plutarch, who cites Theopompus (ca. 300 B.C.E.) as his source.[42] The affinity to Persian dualism was pointed out by the German scholar K. G. Kuhn shortly after the text was published, and remains compelling.[43] As Albert de Jong has shown, in both the Community Rule and Persian dualism

> the two spirits are wholly opposed to each other and do not share a single common trait. They are associated with two distinct realms, described in (predictable) opposing terms. The one is described as "truth," has his origins in a source of light, and is located—occasionally—in the highest realms of reality, being with God. The other is described as "deceit," has his origins in a source of darkness, and belongs, more clearly, to a lower realm (the "abyss") where darkness itself is located.[44]

The association of the two spirits with light and darkness is found in Plutarch's account.

The Jewish text adapts the dualism of the two spirits for its purpose. Not only is there a supreme creator God above the two spirits, but God assigns human beings to one or the other lot. In Persian tradition, people were supposed to choose between them. As de Jong points out, "The Zoroastrian sources ... do not at any moment suggest that Ahura Mazda has pre-ordained everything."[45] The human ability to choose is also presupposed in the Testament of Amram, a fragmentary Aramaic text found at Qumran that has been dated to the late third or early second century B.C.E.[46]

Whatever the origin of the Instruction on the Two Spirits, its placement in 1QS shows that at some time it was regarded as important by community leadership. Moreover, similar cosmic dualism is found in the War Scroll, and there are allusions to the Instruction on the Two Spirits in several other texts.[47]

Dualistic elements also appear in the Damascus Document, which is a strongly covenantal text. One recension of the Document begins with an exhortation "for the So]ns of Light to keep apart from the wa[ys of Darkness."[48] CD 5:17–19 portrays the struggle between Moses and Aaron and the Egyptian magicians Jannes and Jambres in terms of the struggle between the Prince of Light and Belial. CD 2:2–13 is introduced as an address to those who enter the covenant. It does not mention spirits of Light and Darkness, but it has a strongly deterministic tone. It is possible that these references were introduced secondarily into the Document,[49] but in any case they show that at some point dualistic theology played an important part in the sectarian worldview.

## COVENANTAL NOMISM

The problem presented by this dualistic and deterministic theology is that it sits uneasily beside the emphasis on Torah and covenant that is undeniably central to the sectarian Scrolls.[50] E. P. Sanders demonstrated persuasively that most Jewish literature in the late Second Temple period was characterized by "covenantal nomism."[51] This pattern was set out especially in the book of Deuteronomy. At its heart was the demand for obedience to the commandments, with curses for disobedience and blessings for observance. Sanders insisted that

> entrance into the covenant was prior to the fulfillment of commandments; in other words, that the covenant was not earned, but that obedience to the commandments is the consequence of the prior election of Israel by God.[52]

Again,

> the election was of all Israel.... The individual's place in God's plan was accomplished by his being a member of the group.... The question is whether or not one is an Israelite in good standing.[53]

While Deuteronomy envisioned the consequences of the covenant in this-worldly terms, many Jews in the later Second Temple period believed in resurrection and a differentiated afterlife. In the rabbinic literature, the pervasive view is that "all Israelites have a share in the world to come" (Sanhedrin 10.1).

E. P. Sanders argued that the Scrolls could be subsumed under the pattern of covenantal nomism, but since the sectarian movement broke away from the rest of Judaism, some modification of the understanding of the covenant would seem to be required. The Scrolls refer to the covenant in two distinct ways. In some passages, the covenant is the one God made with Moses, but it contained hidden provisions that were revealed only to the members of this community. According to CD 3:12–15,

> But with those who remained steadfast in God's precepts, with those who were left from among them, God established his covenant with Israel forever, revealing to them hidden matters in which all Israel had gone astray: his holy Sabbaths and his glorious feasts, his just stipulations and his truthful paths, and the wishes of his will which man must do in order to live by them.

The sectarians believed that they had the only correct interpretation of the Torah of Moses, even though it was meant for all Israel. Consequently, the members are said to enter the covenant for all Israel (CD 15:5) and take "the oath of the covenant which Moses established with Israel, the covenant to return to the Torah of Moses with all one's heart and with all one's soul" (CD 15:8–9). Also, the sectarians believed that all Israel would walk according to their regulations in the end of days (1QSa 1:1–2).[54]

In other passages, however, we read of a *new* covenant (1QpHab 2:3), sometimes specified as "the new covenant in the land of Damascus" (CD 6:19; 8:21; 20:12).[55] Even if all Israel *should* follow the "correct" interpretation of the Torah, it was painfully obvious that it did not. Consequently, returning to the Law of Moses is in fact equivalent to joining the new covenant. It required admission to a voluntary association, with its own rituals for admission and expulsion, and instruction in the rulings peculiar to that association.[56] Similarly in 1QS 5:8–9,

> Whoever enters the council of the *yaḥad* enters the covenant of God.... He shall swear with a binding oath to revert to the Law of Moses, according to all that he commanded, with whole heart and whole soul, in compliance with all that has been revealed of it to the sons of Zadok, the priests who keep the covenant ... and to the multitude of the men of their covenant.

The expression "their covenant" is telling. Even though it is identified as "the covenant of God," it is defined by the distinctive interpretation of the *yaḥad*.

There is some ambiguity as to how one became a member of this new covenant. In the Damascus Document, the members are sometimes called the penitents or returnees of Israel. They realized their iniquity and their guilt (CD 1:8–9). Yet we are told that God raised them up, and raised up a Teacher of Righteousness to guide them. Conversely, others failed to join the new covenant because "God did not choose them at the beginning of the world, and before they were established he knew their deeds" (CD 2:7–8). There is a dialectic between human merit and divine grace, between free will and determinism. Human beings are assigned to one lot or the other, but they are nonetheless held responsible for their actions.

The sectarian understanding of the covenant, then, differed from that of common Judaism in some crucial respects.

First, one had to believe in a further, higher revelation, which disclosed not only the interpretation of the Torah but the mystery of God's purpose in the world, as we find it laid out, for example, in the Instruction on the Two Spirits. It also includes the mysteries of the heavenly, angelic world, which we glimpse in the Songs of the Sabbath Sacrifices and in the Hodayot, which speak of fellowship with the angels,[57] and the belief that God will intervene at the appointed time to destroy the wicked.[58] The idea of a higher revelation is quintessentially apocalyptic, although the manner of revelation in the Scrolls is not described as it is in the apocalypses.

Second, membership of the "new" covenant did not extend to all Israel, but only to the elect whom God had chosen. The degree to which this election allowed for human free will is unclear. The claim that people were predestined enabled the sectarians to accept the fact that many in Israel did not accept their interpretation of the Torah, even though it seemed to the sectarians to be manifestly right.

Third, final verification of the true understanding of covenant would have to wait until the eschatological future, when God would finally bring an end to wickedness. It would then be clear that not all Israel had a share in the world to come.

### INCONGRUOUS SYSTEMS

Seth Schwartz has argued that the doctrine of the two spirits is only the "most poignant and self-conscious form" of "the juxtaposition of incongruous systems" that characterized much of Judaism around the turn of the era.[59] In his view, what he calls "the apocalyptic myth" in all its forms is in "stark contradiction of the covenantal ideology."[60] It appears to allow far less room for human agency than the traditional covenant, and to operate with different criteria as to what qualifies one for salvation in the world to come.

All religions live with traditions that are not fully consistent with each other, and Judaism in this era was no exception. But while the "apocalyptic myth" was fundamentally different from the traditional, Deuteronomic covenant, they are not merely juxtaposed in the Scrolls, but integrated in a way that has its own coherence. Those who entered the covenant affirmed their election, and their allegiance, to the lot of light, and this was regarded as meritorious, even though they were predestined to do so. Conversely, those who rejected the covenant or defected from it displayed the abject nature that had been assigned to their lot, and were rightly cursed for it  The new covenant, in short, operated differently from Deuteronomy. Election was not only an offer made by God to select humans, but actually determined their fate. As Jeremiah might have said, it was a covenant written in the heart (Jer 31:33). The covenant left to human free choice had long ago been shown to be a failure.

To qualify for a blessed hereafter, it was no longer sufficient to belong to the ethnic people of Israel. One must now be a child of light, in good standing with a community of the new covenant. The categories of sons of light and sons of darkness were not universalistic. Gentiles were assumed to belong to the sons of darkness, except for the poorly documented case of proselytes.[61] (Unlike Jubilees, the sectarians do not appear to have excluded the possibility of conversion.) But not all Judeans could be counted among the sons of light.

The idea that only the righteous within Israel would be saved was not peculiar to the sect known from the Scrolls. Ezekiel had already suggested as much when he claimed that an angel had marked those who grieved over the abominations of Jerusalem and saved them from destruction at the hands of the Babylonians (Ezek 9:4–5). But there can be no doubt that the belief that did most to undercut the covenantal solidarity of Israel was the belief in judgment after death, and opposing fates for righteous and wicked. In Daniel 12, the wise (but not all Jews) will shine like the brightness of the firmament, but those who awake to shame and everlasting contempt surely include the violators of the covenant. When Dan 7:27 speaks of a kingdom that is given to the people of the holy ones of the Most High, this is not just a national Jewish kingdom without qualification. It is doubtful whether the Hasmonean kingdom would qualify. The people of the holy ones are assumed to be Judeans, to be sure, but not all Judeans are included, only those who align themselves with the holy ones.[62] Similarly in the Enoch litera-

ture, the antithesis is between the righteous and the wicked. Enoch
assures the righteous:

> I know this mystery. For I have read the tablets of heaven, and I have seen
> the writing of what must be, and I have seen the things that are written in them
> and inscribed concerning you—that good things and joy and honor have
> been prepared and written down for the souls of the pious who have died.
> (1 Enoch 103:2–3)

The belief in the judgment of the dead and a consequent differentiated afterlife was introduced into Judaism in the apocalyptic writings
of Daniel and Enoch. It spread, in time, to groups that might not be
considered strictly apocalyptic. Israel Yuval claims that the Pharisees
"believed that only the righteous shall be worthy of a place in the world
to come."[63] The evidence is indirect. Yuval seems to infer it from the
importance the Pharisees attached to the observance of the Torah.
Moreover, the passage in the Mishnah that says that all Israelites have a
share in the world to come goes on to say that one who denies the resurrection has no share in the world to come (as well as one who denies
that the Law is from heaven, and an Epicurean).[64] This would seem to
exclude the Sadducees. The judgment scenes in the Gospels are also
based on individual merit rather than on membership of a covenant
people. Nonetheless, Paul affirms that "all Israel will be saved," even
though he also claims that "a hardening has come upon part of Israel"
(Rom 11:26).[65] His affirmation surely shows that the expectation that all
Israel has a share in the world to come was indeed widespread in the
first century, although it was evidently rejected by sectarian groups,
such as those described in the Dead Sea Scrolls.[66]

## APOCALYPTICISM OUTSIDE THE SCROLLS
### *The Similitudes of Enoch*

The apocalyptic worldview was not confined to the circles associated
with the Dead Sea Scrolls. In fact, as already noted, the sectarians do

not appear to have produced apocalypses. We do, however, have a number of apocalypses that were either contemporary with the Scrolls, or were produced a little later, after the destruction of Jerusalem.

The Similitudes of Enoch (1 Enoch 37–71) have not been found among the Scrolls.[67] The work should most probably be dated to the early or middle first century C.E., before the Jewish revolt, to which it makes no reference, and was evidently written in Aramaic, although no fragments have survived. (The work is preserved in Ethiopic.) Like the older Enochic literature, it makes no overt reference to the Law. It speaks repeatedly about "the righteous and the chosen," but they are characterized primarily by their faith: they believe in the name of the Lord of Spirits, and in another heavenly figure called "that Son of Man," (an allusion to the figure in Daniel 7), who is their heavenly counterpart and vindicator. (He is also called "the Righteous One.") The kings and the mighty of the earth, who trust in their own works, do not believe in these heavenly figures, or in the future judgment, but they will be confounded when they see "that Son of Man" sitting on the throne of glory and presiding at the judgment. The righteousness of the "righteous," then, is grounded in their steadfast belief that there will be such a judgment, that the kings and the mighty will be overthrown, and that they themselves will be vindicated.

In an epilogue to the Similitudes, Enoch is taken up to heaven, where he is greeted by an angel, who tells him: "You are the Son of Man who was born to righteousness" (71:14). The interpretation of this acclamation has been endlessly disputed.[68] Nothing in the preceding chapters suggested that the "Son of Man" was really the exalted Enoch, and indeed the majority reading in 1 Enoch 70:1 makes a clear distinction between Enoch and the Son of Man. There are literary grounds for suggesting that this passage is a secondary addition to the Similitudes, since it constitutes a second epilogue to the work. It may have been intended to counter the identification of Jesus with the Son of Man in the Gospels, although this is speculative. It is also possible that the expression "Son of Man" is used here in a nontitular sense, meaning "human being." It is used in this way in 1 Enoch 60:10, based on the usage of the book of Ezekiel. In this case, the point would be that Enoch is perfectly righteous, like the heavenly Son of Man. There is in any case a homology between the righteous in heaven and the righteous on earth. Enoch is told:

> all will walk on your path since righteousness will never forsake you
> with you will be their dwelling and with you, their lot,
> and from you they will not be separated forever and forever and ever.
> And thus there will be length of days with that son of man
> and there will be peace for the righteous,
> and the path of truth for the righteous,
> in the name of the Lord of Spirits forever and ever.
>
> (1 Enoch 71:17)

The hope of the righteous in the Similitudes of Enoch is not overtly based on the Torah of Moses. This is quite exceptional, however, in the first century C.E.[69] In contrast, the Law plays a central role in two apocalypses composed after the destruction of Jerusalem, 4 Ezra and 2 Baruch.[70]

### 4 Ezra and 2 Baruch

Ezra, to whom the book of 4 Ezra is ascribed, was remembered in Jewish tradition as the one who restored the Law after the exile. He has no hesitation in affirming the justice of God. "You have been just in all that has come upon us," he prays. "You have dealt faithfully, and we have acted wickedly" (Neh 9:33). In 4 Ezra, however, he has a very different profile.[71] He questions the justice of letting Babylon ( = Rome) triumph over Israel. Israel may have sinned, but was Babylon really better? In effect, he accuses God of abandoning the covenant. He does not deny the prevalence of sin, but he argues that humanity is not capable of keeping the Law because of the evil heart, and Israel is no better off than the Gentiles in this respect. The angel Uriel tries to counter Ezra's arguments, without much success.[72] Only when he is overwhelmed by visionary experience does Ezra resign himself to God's ways.[73]

Ezra eventually gets to play the role of the restorer of the Law.[74] Since the Torah has been burned, Ezra is commissioned to replace it. He takes five scribes and dictates to them for forty nights, having imbibed a fiery liquid. In all, ninety-four books were written. Then the Most High instructs Ezra:

> Make public the 24 books that you wrote first and let the worthy and the unworthy read them, but keep the seventy that were written last, in order to give them to the wise among your people. For in them are the springs of understanding, the fountains of wisdom, and the river of knowledge. (4 Ezra 1:45–47)

The twenty-four public books are what we know as the Hebrew scriptures. (4 Ezra, along with Josephus, *Against Apion,* is one of the earliest witnesses to a "canon," limited to a specific number of books.) But these are not the books that contain the fountain of wisdom. That is to be found in the books reserved for the wise, presumably books like 4 Ezra itself. In short, the revealed Torah does not suffice to understand the way of the Lord. A higher revelation is necessary. For 4 Ezra, Torah is not simply the Pentateuch, but embraces all of wisdom, somewhat in the manner of Ben Sira, although the latter sage had no cache of books reserved for the wise.[75]

2 Baruch is closely related to 4 Ezra. Both works were most probably written in Hebrew, but they only survive in translations.[76] In both, the first destruction of Jerusalem at the hands of the Babylonians serves as a prism for reflections on the destruction by the Romans. Both receive enlightenment and comfort through visions.

2 Baruch, however, does not engage in the skeptical questioning of either God or the Law that we found in 4 Ezra. On the contrary, he affirms in the letter that concludes the book, "We have nothing now save the Almighty One and his Law" (2 Bar 85:3). The eschatological revelations are clearly subordinated to the observance of the Law. The book fits the pattern of covenantal nomism, since salvation depends on the mercy of God for those within the covenant who are basically obe-

dient. The Law is correlated with wisdom, in the tradition of Deuteronomy and Ben Sira. Dependence on Deuteronomy is explicit at several points (e.g., 2 Bar 19:1; 84:1–6). Matthias Henze comments that 2 Baruch

> breaks down any potential conflict that might exist between apocalyptic and Mosaic authority, and instead incorporates the latter into the former, fully endorsing the single authoritative status for the Torah and turning it into the centerpiece of his apocalyptic program.[77]

Nonetheless, the traditional Deuteronomic covenant is also modified here. It must be buttressed by the apocalyptic revelations that Baruch receives. The covenantal people is not simply coterminous with the Jewish people. It consists of those who observe the Law, with the inclusion of proselytes and the exclusion of apostates. The promised salvation is in the world to come rather than this world, and it concerns not only the future of the covenant people but also the destiny of the individual. Even when the centrality of the Torah is affirmed in the apocalyptic tradition, as it is in both 4 Ezra and 2 Baruch, and also in the Dead Sea Scrolls, it must still be supplemented by a higher revelation that puts the old covenantal identity of Israel in a new perspective.

# CHAPTER 7

# The Law in the Diaspora

The earliest account of the origin of the people of Judea by a Greek author was written by Hecataeus of Abdera in the reign of Ptolemy I, in the context of his description of Egypt.[1] Hecataeus had some Judean source, probably oral,[2] but much of his information seems to be derived from Egyptians.[3] On his account, various foreigners were expelled from Egypt in a time of pestilence. The most outstanding of them went to Greece and some other places, "but the greater number were driven into what is now called Judaea."[4] The leader of the colony was Moses, who is admired for his wisdom and courage. Moses is credited with founding Jerusalem and establishing the temple, but he is also said to have drawn up the laws of the Judeans and ordered their political institutions. Hecataeus speaks admiringly of Moses's monotheism and aniconism, but emphasizes that the laws of the Judeans are different from those of other people. He comments that "as a result of their own expulsion from Egypt, he [Moses] introduced an unsocial and intolerant mode of life."[5] Yet, as Erich Gruen remarks, "none of this implies animosity on Hecataeus' part, let alone anti-Semitism."[6] The report as a whole is neutral, even admiring on occasion. It ends with the comment that many of the traditional practices became disturbed when Judea became subject to foreign rule.

Hecataeus evidently had information of uneven quality. Of interest to us here, however, is the fact that at the beginning of the Hellenistic era it was widely known that Judeans lived by a code of laws derived from Moses. Hecataeus was aware that this code existed in written form. He writes that "at the end of their laws there is even appended the statement: 'These are the words that Moses heard from God and declares unto the Jews.'"[7] It is unlikely, however, that Hecataeus actually read these laws. They had not yet been translated into Greek when he wrote.

### THE SEPTUAGINT

According to the legend preserved in the *Letter of Aristeas,* the Greek translation of the Judean laws was undertaken at the behest of Ptolemy II Philadelphus (285–247 B.C.E.) for the sake of ensuring the comprehensiveness of the collection of books in the library of Alexandria. The account must be dated more than a century after the supposed translation.[8] Most modern scholars have been inclined to dismiss it as historical evidence. As Gruen put it, "The tale, of course, should not be confused with history."[9] Recently Tessa Rajak, while granting that the story is oversimplified, has argued that it is not impossible.[10] Regardless of the supposed royal involvement, it is generally agreed that the translation was completed by the mid-second century B.C.E., since it is presupposed in the work of Demetrius the Chronographer. Demetrius is usually dated to the time of Ptolemy IV (221–204 B.C.E.), since he reckons the time from the fall of Samaria to that Ptolemy's reign.[11] From that point on, the Greek translation of the Torah is presupposed in virtually all Hellenistic Jewish literature. Indeed, some of that literature is only recognized as Jewish because of its use of the Septuagint.

### THE TORAH IN HELLENISTIC JEWISH WRITINGS

The writings of the Hellenistic diaspora appropriate the Torah of Moses in various ways.[12] In many, such as Ezekiel the Tragedian or the romance of *Joseph and Aseneth*, it is a source of stories about the past, retold in various genres, which provided an essential ingredient for ongoing identity. In some, there is an attempt to treat the Law as a work of philosophy, a tendency that reached its climax in the works of Philo. Many of these writings address questions of ethics, whether directly or indirectly. In general, but with some exceptions, they tend to bypass the distinctive Jewish laws and dwell on the importance of monotheism and matters of social and sexual morality. We do not find in the diaspora the kind of detailed halakic discussions of the correct interpretation of the laws that are characteristic of the Dead Sea Scrolls, for example, in 4QMMT or the Damascus Document. Philo, to be sure, expounds the "special laws" in great detail, but the tone of his discussion is expository rather than polemical, as it is in the Scrolls.

A few examples may suffice.[13] In the *Sibylline Oracles*, we are told that the destruction of the Romans will be brought about by their "unjust haughtiness," homosexuality, and greed (3:182–90).[14] The Greeks are condemned for idolatry (3:545–55), and several nations are denounced for homosexuality and idolatry and "transgressing the holy law of immortal God, which they transgressed" (3:599–600). The conduct required by the sibyl is summarized in 3:762–66:

> But urge on your minds in your breasts and shun unlawful worship. Worship the Living One. Avoid adultery and indiscriminate intercourse with males. Rear your own offspring and do not kill it, for the Immortal is angry at whoever commits these sins.

It may be argued that this passage is ostensibly addressed to Gentiles, and that this explains the failure to mention the Sabbath or circumcision, but at least the passage indicates what the author regarded as the significant differences in conduct between Jews and Gentiles. Similarly, in the *Sibylline Oracles* 3:218–47, the sibyl sings the praises of the Jews, without mentioning them by name. They are always concerned with good counsel and noble works, and not with astronomy or "the astrological predictions of the Chaldeans." She goes on to praise their righteousness and concern for the poor, "fulfilling the word of the great God, the hymn of the law." In all of this, the Law is of central importance. The sibyl refers explicitly to the law given to Moses on Mount Sinai (3:255–58). Only the Jews, in contrast with "Phoenicians, Egyptians and Romans, spacious Greece and many nations of others," observe the Law (3:597–98). Jews too are subject to punishment if they fail to observe the Law, as seen from the Babylonian exile. They are called on to "remain trusting in the holy laws of the great God" (3:283–84). Yet the Law also applies to Gentiles. The sibyl seems to assume that the basic requirements of the Law are known to everyone by nature, an assumption also found in Wisdom of Solomon 13 and in Romans 1. The basic sin is idolatry. Sexual practices judged as deviant are high on the list. Other practices such as Chaldean divination are occasionally condemned. While the sibyl insists that the true Law is the Law of Moses, she treats it in practice as natural law. At the end, God "will put in effect a common law for men throughout the whole earth" (3:757–58). Nonetheless, the vision of salvation is unambiguously Judeo-centric. The other nations are called on to send their offerings to the temple and to ponder the Law of the Most High God (718–19).

A further illustration may be drawn from the *Sentences of Pseudo-Phocylides*.[15] Again, the work is presented as that of a pagan author. In fact, the Jewish origin is betrayed only by a few sayings that clearly echo the Septuagint (e.g., v. 140: "If a beast of your enemy falls on the way, help it to rise"; cf. Exod 23:5). There are exhortations to justice in verses 9–21 that have strong biblical overtones. Yet the distinctive laws of Judaism, such as Sabbath and circumcision, are ignored. Again, we might suppose that the omissions are required by the pseudonym: to insist on distinctive Jewish practices would undermine the illusion of pagan authorship. Pseudo-Phocylides does not explicitly acknowledge the Law of Moses at all. Yet it shares considerable material with Philo's *Hypothetica* 7.1–9 and Josephus's *Against Apion* 2.190–219, both of which are explicitly presented as summaries of the Law.[16] Philo begins with a list of offenses for which the penalty is death, and boasts of the clarity and simplicity of the Law. The list begins with sexual offenses:

If you are guilty of pederasty or adultery or rape of a young person, even of a female, for I need not mention the case of a male, similarly if you prostitute yourself or allow or purpose or intend any action which your age makes indecent, the penalty is death.

The following section focuses on household rules ("wives must be in servitude to their husbands ... "). Philo touches here on distinctively Jewish matters relating to dedicated property, but discussion of household roles is commonplace in Hellenistic moral literature.[17] He then proceeds to "a host of other things which belong to unwritten customs and institutions or are contained in the laws themselves."[18]

Not everything in these laws is derived, or derived directly, from the Torah. Philo has a negative formulation of the Golden Rule: "What a man would hate to suffer he must not do himself to others." Other non-biblical injunctions include the obligation to give fire and running water to those who need them, not to deny burial or disturb the place of the dead. Some other prohibitions, such as those of abortion and abandoning children, are quite typical of Hellenistic Judaism, but are not explicitly found in the Torah. Other items, such as the concern for nesting birds, have a clear biblical basis.[19]

Josephus gives a fuller exposition of the Law, beginning with the conception of God and the temple cult. He proceeds to marriage laws and, like Philo, emphasizes the death penalty for sexual offenses. He claims, inaccurately, that the Law forbids abortion and orders that all children be brought up. Also like Philo, he insists that the Law requires that people provide fire, water, and food to those who need them, and not leave a corpse unburied. Some of these laws correspond to unwritten laws attributed to Buzyges, the legendary hero of an Attic priestly tribe.[20] As Gregory Sterling has put it, "Ethical codes began with the Torah, but they did not end there. The issue was how to extend biblical material so that it would address contemporary concerns."[21]

The summaries of the Law by Philo and Josephus, and the teaching of Pseudo-Phocylides, have much in common.[22] In addition to monotheism, all three emphasize sexual matters (adultery, homosexuality, rape of a virgin, abortion). Philo and Pseudo-Phocylides forbid emasculation. Josephus and Pseudo-Phocylides forbid sexual relations with a pregnant woman. The common material extends to the duties of parents and children, husband and wife, the young and their elders, and the burial of the dead. Conspicuously lacking are discussions of the most distinctive practices of Judaism, such as circumcision and the Sabbath. Philo follows his epitome of the laws with a discussion of the Sabbath in *Hypothetica* 7.10. But if these three authors shared a common source, as seems likely, the discussion of the Sabbath does not seem to have been part of it.

It would of course be very rash to assume that the Sabbath and circumcision were not important to Jews in the Hellenistic diaspora. Philo famously criticized the extreme allegorists, "who, regarding laws in their literal sense in the light of symbols belonging to the intellect, are over-punctilious about the latter, while treating the former with easygoing neglect,"[23] and he expounds the laws in detail in four books in the *Special Laws*. The *Letter of Aristeas* feels obliged to offer an allegorical interpretation of the food laws, but it is clear that the continued practice of those laws was presupposed.[24] *Joseph and Aseneth*, which I date to the late Ptolemaic period,[25] emphasizes the possibility of rapprochement between Jew and Gentile,[26] but Joseph does not compromise on *kashrut*, and it is clear that Aseneth is absorbed into the family of Jacob.[27] The need for circumcision was the subject of dispute in the case of the royal house of Adiabene in the first century C.E., but the stricter view, that held to the requirement, prevailed.[28] The Roman satirists, also in the first century, clearly associated Judaism with distinctive practices, among which circumcision and Sabbath observance figured prominently.[29] Even Josephus boasts that

> the masses have long since shown a keen desire to adopt our religious observances; and there is not one city, Greek or barbarian, nor a single nation, to which our custom of abstaining from work on the seventh day has not spread, and where fasts and the lighting of lamps and many of our prohibitions in the matter of food are not observed.[30]

It is possible, of course, that Jewish practice may have varied with time and place, but the persistence of the practices should warn us against inferring any neglect of them from their absence in much of the literature.

Nonetheless, the tendency in the literature to emphasize the broader concerns of the Law, and to focus on matters that might also be of concern to Gentiles, is noteworthy. It accords with the tendency to associate the law of Moses with the law of nature. This tendency is most explicit in Philo. Philo claims that

> the cosmos is in harmony with the law and the law with the cosmos, and the man who observes the law is at once a citizen of the cosmos, directing his actions in relation to the rational purpose of nature, in accordance with which the entire cosmos also is administered.[31]

The lives of the patriarchs are included in the Torah because

> first, he wished to show that the enacted ordinances are not inconsistent with nature; and secondly that those who wish to live in accordance with the laws as they stand have no difficult task, seeing that the first generations before any at all of the particular statutes was set in writing followed the unwritten law with perfect ease, so that one might properly say that the enacted laws are nothing else than reminders of the life of the ancients, preserving to a later generation their actual words and deeds. (*Abr* 5)

The view that one who lived in accordance with the laws of nature in effect fulfilled the law of Moses creates a common framework for Jewish and Gentile ethics. This should not be confused with assimilation, however. Jewish Hellenistic literature invariably emphasizes issues on which it is critical of majority practice in the Gentile world—idolatry, homosexuality, exposure of infants, and so on. Even Philo, who is rightly regarded as a model of cultural convergence,[32] says that in an ideal world "each nation would abandon its peculiar ways, and throwing overboard its ancestral customs, turn to honoring our laws alone."[33] But the boundary markers that are emphasized are not the obvious ritual ones, but

ritual vs ethical

rather a distinctive stance on ethical issues that were, or should be, of concern to everyone. In this way, Jews could engage deeply with Hellenistic culture while still maintaining a distinctive identity.[34] Judaism is construed, or at least presented, as an ethical system that is comparable but superior to that of the Greeks. This construction of Judaism is evident in Philo's claim that synagogues were places of ethical instruction:

> For what are our houses of prayer in various cities but schools of prudence, courage, moderation, justice, piety, holiness, and every virtue by which our obligations to humanity and the Deity are understood and properly performed?[35]

The insistence that the Law of Moses was a written copy of the natural law was, to be sure, paradoxical.[36] One doubts that any Hellenistic philosophers would have found it persuasive. Nonetheless, it was essential to the construction of Jewish identity that we find in Philo, and in a more inchoate form in other writers from the Hellenistic diaspora.

Sterling has offered an interesting comparison between the ways the Law is construed in the literature from the diaspora and in the Dead Sea Scrolls. On the one hand, he finds that some of the same texts figure prominently in both corpora, especially Leviticus 19–20 and Deuteronomy 22, all of which deal with sexual issues. He also notes some shared laws that do not have a direct biblical base, such as restrictions on lawful sexual intercourse, although it is not clear that the rationale for the restriction was always the same. (For example, Josephus recognizes sexual intercourse as legitimate only if it is intended to produce children.[37] Pseudo-Phocylides condemns "shameful" types of intercourse. The Damascus Document says that anyone who "approaches his wife to fornicate, not according to the command" must be expelled from the community.[38]) Despite these shared features, however, the understanding of the Law in the two corpora was very different. While both found ways to extend the Law to address new situations, they did so in different ways. The sectarians of the Scrolls relied on authoritative interpretations or inspired exegesis. Some things were revealed to the community that were hidden even from the rest of Israel. The diaspora authors, in contrast, incorporated moral traditions from the larger Hellenistic world (such as the laws of Buzyges or the household codes) into their summaries of the Law. The sectarians intensified the notion of holiness. The diasporic authors paid little attention to matters of holiness and purity.

We might add another notable difference. The sectarian authors were greatly concerned with the details of the Law, most conspicuously in 4QMMT. The writers from the diaspora, in contrast, focus on broader issues. "Among the vast number of particular truths and principles," writes Philo, "there stand out practically high above the others two main heads: one of duty to God as shown by piety and holiness, one of duty to men as shown by humanity and justice."[39] The distinction of underlying principles was not necessarily peculiar to diaspora Judaism, but it stands in contrast to the kind of intensive halakic exegesis that we find in the Scrolls. As Hindy Najman has argued in the case of Philo, the Law of Moses is not "reducible to a code of rules. Instead the rules have weight insofar as they direct us towards the virtuous life."[40]

### A POLITIKOS NOMOS?

A quite different perspective on the use of the Torah in the diaspora, however, is opened up by the papyri. In his introduction to *Corpus Papyrorum Judaicarum* (*CPJ*), Victor Tcherikover wrote:

> Jews in Egypt, like their brethren everywhere in the Diaspora, lived in communities, i.e. in separate semi-political organizations, having their own laws and customs, buildings and institutions, leading personages and officials.[41]

He continued:

> As to the legal basis of Jewish communities in Egypt, there was no need for the Ptolemaic government to establish new principles of legislation, since many other national groups had a similar legal status. The Hellenistic world was accustomed to a political institution called a *politeuma*. The term

had several meanings, but the most usual was an ethnic group from abroad enjoying certain rights and having its domicile inside a *polis* or country.[42]

Tcherikover supposed that *politeumata* were granted by the king the right to live according to their ancestral laws. It is well known that the Persians, and the Hellenistic kingdoms after them, allowed subject peoples to live according to their ancestral laws. In the case of Judah/Judea, the authorization of the Torah as the king's law is narrated in Ezra 7. In the Hellenistic period, Antiochus III confirmed the right to live according to ancestral law when he conquered Jerusalem in 198 B.C.E.[43] Tcherikover concluded: "Yet 'the ancestral laws' as concerning Jews could have had only one meaning: Jewish autonomous organization based on the laws of Moses."[44] So "the Torah was the fundamental law of all Jewish communities in Egypt."[45] Aryeh Kasher developed this idea to claim that Jews in Egypt had "an independent judicial system and community establishment, on the basis of the right to preserve ancestral customs."[46]

Joseph Mélèze-Modrzejewski developed the legal understanding implicit in Tcherikover's claims. He argued that the Law of Moses had the status of a *politikos nomos,* that is, of a subsidiary law of an immigrant group.[47] He pointed to the collection and translation of Egyptian laws under Darius I, and then to demotic papyrus fragments from Hermopolis, and a Greek papyrus from Oxyrhynchus, which he takes to be fragments of an old casebook compiled by Egyptian priests. The edict of the king was supreme, but for matters not addressed by royal edict, the courts relied on local traditional law. The hierarchy involved is spelled out in a papyrus from 226 B.C.E., relating to a case between Jewish litigants:

> And whereas the code of regulations [*diagramma*] ... directs us to give judgments in a ... manner on all points that any person knows or shows us to have been dealt with in the regulations of King Ptolemy [*diagrammata*], in accordance with the regulations; and on all points not dealt with in the regulations, but in the civic laws [*politikoi nomoi*] in accordance with these laws; and on all other points to follow the most equitable view.[48]

In the event, the accuser withdrew from the proceedings, and so we do not know what law would have applied.

A second papyrus, *CPJ* I 128, provides more substance for Modrze-jewski's view. This concerns a woman named Helladote who had married a Jew named Jonathas, apparently by "the law of the Jews." Jonathas had apparently divorced her unilaterally, in accordance with Jewish law, as found in Deut 24:1, whereas current Greek custom recognized the equality of husband and wife in divorce proceedings. Helladote's appeal was based on the discrepancy between Jewish and Greek law. Modrzejewski concludes:

> Thanks to this misadventure, we have been able to learn a most important fact: Jewish Law, that is, the Greek Torah, had truly become a "civic law," *politikos nomos*, among other "civic laws" applicable to Greek-speaking immigrants.[49]

This papyrus, however, is "the only instance in the Greek papyri of Jewish national law being applied to the legal life of members of the Jewish community."[50] Other texts from *CPJ* show Jews charging the usual Ptolemaic rate of 24 percent for loans, even to fellow Jews.[51] Even in the case of the Helladote papyrus, we do not know how, or on what basis, the judges decided the case.

THE HERAKLEOPOLIS PAPYRI

Since Modrzejewski's comments, however, a new corpus of papyri has become available, from a Jewish *politeuma* at Herakleopolis.[52] Prior to the discovery of these papyri, the existence of Jewish *politeumata* in Egypt had been controversial. In a sharp critique of Kasher's work, Constantine Zuckerman found no evidence that *politeumata* had judicial powers.[53] The study of the Idumeans of Memphis by Dorothy J. Thompson Crawford also took a restrictive view of the *politeuma*.[54] All known instances involved a military body, but were embedded in a local network of civil-ian members of the same ethnic group who were not members of the *politeuma* itself. A synthesis was attempted by Gerd Lüderitz, who posited two distinct types of *politeumata*.[55] The first was "a political body which is part of the administrative apparatus of a Greek polis,"[56] while the second was a private, often cultic, association. Lüderitz viewed the Jewish *politeumata* as closer to the second type, but he allowed that they might have had administrative authority in some cases.[57]

The publication of the papyri from Herakleopolis in Middle Egypt established beyond doubt that there was such a thing as a Jewish *politeuma*. It also showed that the archons of a *politeuma* could have judicial authority. The *politeuma* at Herakleopolis, which the editors tentatively identified as a military colony,[58] did not include all Judeans in the area. Since Judeans from neighboring Aphroditopolis and Oxyrhynchus made appeals to the archons in Herakleopolis, it is apparent that not every Judean community had its own *politeuma*. It appears that the jurisdiction of the archons extended to non-Judeans in cases where Judeans were involved. The editors note three petitions by Judeans that involve non-Judeans, but in no case was a petition to the archons filed by a non-Judean.

The implications of these papyri for the use of the Torah in Hellenistic Egypt have been interpreted variously. James Cowey and Klaus Maresch claimed that the *politeuma* basically followed Ptolemaic legal practice.[59] Kasher, nonetheless, claimed that his views had been vindicated.[60] Sylvie Honigman argued that the Jewish character of these papyri is primarily a matter of religious belief, cultic practice, and marriage customs:

> What did these Jews have in mind when invoking their *patrios nomos?* Probably something much less clearly defined than modern scholars, readers of the Mishnah and Talmud, would like them to. As long as the faith in the God of the Jews (see the oath) was respected, as long as some specific customs directly bearing on family life (law of marriage) were carried on, an unconscious process of progressive assimilation into local legal practices could be set in motion.[61]

KUGLER

This reading of the papyrological evidence has been challenged in a series of essays by Rob Kugler.[62] While Kugler grants that "the Judeans of Heracleopolis drew heavily on the hybrid Greco-Egyptian common law of the Ptolemaic kingdom," he claims that "they also relied on the juridical norms of their Judean ancestry to achieve their litigation goals."[63]

The clearest instance of a Jewish juridical norm is found in *P. Polit. Iud.* 4. A member of the *politeuma* named Philotas had courted Nikaia, daughter of Lysimachos. Her father, he claims, gave her to him, along with the agreed dowry. "Not only did we make determinations/oaths in common, but also according to the law an oath became binding." Yet "after a short time, without cause, Lysimachos joined Nikaia to another man before receiving from me the customary writ of separation."[64] The reference to the writ of separation (*apostasiou to biblion*) is a clear allusion to Deut 24:1. The word used for oath (*horismos*) is unusual, paralleled in this sense only in LXX Num 30:3. Kugler regards this as a subtle way to strengthen the claim that the oath could not be broken.[65]

Despite these allusions to the Torah, however, Kugler recognizes that "the petition echoes a cornucopia of customary norms for marriage agreements with roots in Egyptian, Greek, and Judean practices."[66] The courtship, as distinct from arranged marriage, reflects Egyptian culture, the oath and negotiated dowry conform to Greek and Egyptian practice, and the formula "with which I was satisfied" is Egyptian. Nonetheless, the legal basis for the petition would seem to be that Lysimachos broke an oath and did not provide a writ of separation. So it would seem that Philotas based his case on a Jewish understanding of marriage. We do not know, however, whether his argument was successful, or whether the archons decided the case on the same basis.

Three petitions (*P. Polit Iud.* 3, 9, and 12) refer to the defendant's failure to honor an ancestral oath (*horkos patrios*). Kugler takes this as a likely reference to LXX Num 30:3, which emphasizes the binding character of oaths:

All three petitions are from Judeans who were engaging in ordinary transactions unaddressed by the Torah; yet in all three cases the parties validated their transactions with an oath normed by the Greek Torah's
stipulations.[67]

Cowey and Maresch had already noted that "the custom of writing a
contract under oath is exceptional in Ptolemaic Egypt, since at this
time Greeks did not resort to oaths in legal practice."[68] Here at least we
have a distinctive Jewish practice, but the appeal to the Septuagint is
indirect at best—Numbers 30 does not refer to contracts. The phrase
*horkos patrios* is not biblical, but is paralleled in Hellenistic Egypt.[69]

Other cases that allegedly appeal to Jewish law are less clear.[70]

*P. Polit. Iud.* 7 involves a dispute over a girl whose father had died.[71]
The plaintiff, Dorotheos, was the brother-in-law of the father, and
cared for him during the latter's final illness. He also redeemed the
daughter from debtor's prison. The father gave the daughter into the
charge of Dorotheos, "on account of what I had expended for the two of
them" and because of his confidence in his sister, the wife of Dorotheos.
The mother of the girl sent her to live with her (the mother's) sister
instead. Dorotheos appealed to the archons for justice. Kugler argues
that the daughter was given to Dorotheos "not as a household servant,
as was warily suggested by the editors, but as an orphan to her guardian."[72] He construes this as a combination of the Greek customary law
pertaining to the guardianship of an orphan (a minor predeceased by
her father) and a Torah stipulation, the duty of an individual to care for
destitute kinfolk (LXX Lev 25:35–38). He detects an allusion to LXX
Lev 25:35 in the use of the phrase *par'emoi* in the papyrus (Lev has *para
soi*) because the dative is rare, though not unattested, after *para*.[73] He
also argues that guardianship was a burden, and that Dorotheos would
not have sought it if it had not been required by the Torah. But the
papyrus clearly implies that the presence of the daughter would to
some degree repay Dorotheos for his expenditures, so the editors were
probably correct to suppose that she would stay with him as a servant,
even if the relationship was informal. It seems gratuitous to suppose

that Dorotheos was motivated by the Torah, and implausible to think that anyone would detect a subtle allusion to Leviticus in the use of the dative after *para*. Even if Dorotheos was influenced by the Torah's concern for orphans, he does not make that the legal basis for his appeal. In this case, the archons awarded custody to Dorotheos because the father had given the girl into his care.

Kugler finds another allusion to the Torah in a papyrus that is not part of the corpus *P. Polit. Iud.*, but contains a petition from a Judean named Peton, from Phnebieus in the Heracleopolite nome.[74] The complaint concerns an official named Apollonios who seized, or "distrained," some of his property until he should pay rent a second time. Here, Kugler grants:

> Most of the episode Peton describes is more or less typical practice according to Ptolemaic administrative law relating to the collection of debts, enforcement of work agreements, and the gathering of rental income.[75]

He suggests, however, that there is an alternative way to read the petition. The term used for "seize" or "distrain," *enechurazein*, is used in the Septuagint to translate the Hebrew *chabal*, "to take in pledge," probably because it was the appropriate Ptolemaic administrative term. The Torah places limitations on the practice, in such cases as the taking of a neighbor's garment (Exod 22:25–26), or of a mill or millstone, "for that would take a life" (Deut 24:6), or of forcible entry to seize the pledge (Deut 24:10–11). Kugler infers: "Whatever Ptolemaic administrative law says about the behavior of Apollonios in demanding a second rental payment, his means of obtaining it was illegal under Judean law."[76] Kugler himself admits that this reasoning is speculative. Even the Torah does not forbid distraint outright, and there is no indication that any Pentateuchal law would apply in this case. At most we might think that a Jew familiar with the Torah on these issues would find distraint distasteful, but that would not provide a legal argument in this case, even in a court that recognized the Torah.

Kugler adduces several other supposed instances of Torah influence in the papyri, but the argument always rests on the recognition of subtle allusions, not on the legal basis of the claim.[77] At most we may suspect that the plaintiffs' sensibility was informed by familiarity with the Torah, but it is not invoked as a legal basis.

Kugler finds only one petition in the Herakleopolis archive, *P. Polit Iud.* 8, that seems to contradict the ancestral law in providing for interest on a loan. But he also recognizes that in some papyri the petitioner's legal reasoning exhibits nothing distinctively Jewish, and makes no appeal to customary or legal norms derived from the Torah.[78]

In all of this, the only clear appeal to Jewish law is in *P. Polit. Iud.* 4, in the matter of a writ of separation. (The use of the *patrios horkos* shows the persistence of a distinctively Jewish custom, but is not so directly based on Jewish law.) Like *CPJ* I 128, adduced by Modrzejewski, this case shows that Jews could on occasion appeal to Jewish law, but the instances are strikingly rare.[79] It is also important to remember that even these cases do not show that the archons based their legal decisions on the Torah. It may be that some of the other cases adduced by Kugler reflect a sensibility informed by the Torah. Indeed, it is now commonly recognized that even in ancient Israel the laws of the Torah often functioned as wisdom rather than as positive law.[80] That is also how the Torah functions in texts like the *Sentences of Pseudo-Phocylides.*

## A BROADER MEANING OF TORAH

Even Tcherikover and Modrzejewski, who championed the view that Judeans in Egypt enjoyed legal autonomy, recognized that the papyri rarely refer to Jewish law. Tcherikover found "two contradictory tendencies in Egyptian Jewry: the desire to follow old national and religious tradition, and the desire to participate vigorously in all aspects of Hellenistic life."[81] Tcherikover supposed, gratuitously, that Jewish communities as a whole followed the first tendency, "but individual Jews, when faced with the innumerable petty problems of everyday life, were more disposed to follow the second."[82] Modrzejewski noted that "in the practice of law, the choice of language and of formulae is determinative. Language is the vehicle of law. Jews who drew up Greek contracts followed Greek law."[83] Both scholars cited the Talmudic principle that "the law of the land is law."[84]

None of this is to dispute the centrality of the Torah in the life of diaspora Jews.[85] It is certainly pervasive in the literature, although I have argued that it is most often construed as wisdom or natural law, rather than positive law. Insofar as echoes of the Torah can be found in the papyri, it functions as instructional or inspirational material rather than as the basis of legal action, with few exceptions. We may compare this conclusion with that of Seth Schwartz apropos of the legal papyri from the Judean desert:

> "Torah" does of course refer to the Pentateuch, but it had a rather broader meaning, too, referring to the entire body of traditional Jewish legal practice, which varied from place to place and time to time, and also in respect to the closeness of its relationship with the Pentateuch.... "Torah" was a set of negotiations between an authoritative but opaque text and various sets of traditional but not fully authorized practice.[86]

This approach to the Law is very different from the kind of intensive halakic scrutiny familiar to us from the Dead Sea Scrolls, but it is broadly typical of much of Second Temple Judaism in Judea as well as in the diaspora.

EXCURSUS
*Marriage and Conversion*

Another aspect of the Torah in the diaspora, one that bears directly on the question of ethnicity, is illustrated by *Joseph and Aseneth*, which is the most elaborate story of conversion that has come down to us from antiquity.[87] The story has been a subject of controversy in recent years.[88] The textual history is exceptionally complicated. The earliest manuscript evidence is a Syriac translation from the sixth century C.E.[89] In part because of the lateness of the textual witnesses, there is ongoing debate as to whether the composition should be regarded as Jewish or Christian. The original editor, Pierre Battifol, regarded it as Christian,[90] but the great majority of scholars have taken it as Jewish. The possibility of Christian provenance has been raised again vigorously by Ross Kraemer and Rivka Nir,[91] but it remains a minority position.[92] If the original work is Jewish, it is almost certainly earlier than the diaspora revolt of 115–118 C.E. Since it presupposes the Septuagint, it can hardly be earlier than the second century B.C.E. Egypt is by far the most likely place of origin.[93] I presuppose arguments I have offered elsewhere for the Jewish provenance of the story, granting the possibility of some Christian embellishments (such as the cross that is drawn on the honeycomb in 16:17), and I assume a date in the late Ptolemaic or early Roman period, with a preference for the former.[94]

*Joseph and Aseneth* has two episodes that are distinct but by no means unrelated. The first of these, in chapters 1–21, explains how the marriage of Aseneth to Joseph came about. The second, in chapters 21–29, recounts the story of ensuing conflict with Pharaoh's sons, in which Joseph's brothers are divided. The first episode has an obvious jumping-off point in the Joseph story in Genesis. According to Gen 41:45, Pharaoh gave Joseph Aseneth daughter of Potipher, priest of On (later Heliopolis), as wife. For interpreters of the Hellenistic and Roman periods, this brief notice posed a problem: "How did Joseph, an Israelite, marry an Egyptian woman, who was the daughter of an Egyptian priest, particularly in light of numerous biblical prohibitions against such marriages."[95] The story resolves this problem by explaining that Aseneth underwent a conversion experience, abandoned idolatry, and came to worship the God of Israel. The story, then, is at once a romance or love story, which has much in common with Hellenistic romances that became popular from the first century B.C.E. onward,[96] and a story of religious conversion. The second episode does not arise from an obvious problem in the biblical text, but it explains how Joseph rather than Pharaoh's son became ruler of Egypt. It would be reductionistic, however, to say that either episode exists primarily to resolve an exegetical problem. The biblical text provides a starting point, but the story goes on to address issues that are not adumbrated in Genesis at all.

At the beginning of the story, Aseneth is described as a virgin of eighteen years and very beautiful. Her beauty, however, is unlike that of the Egyptians, but in all respects like that of Hebrew women, a detail that points to Jewish rather than Christian authorship. She is said, however, to be boastful and arrogant and devoted to the worship of innumerable Egyptian deities. When her father tells her about Joseph, she responds with disdain, dismissing him as an alien and a fugitive and a shepherd's son. When she sees him, however, she is struck with remorse, for he appears to her "like the sun from heaven on its chariot," and she recognizes that he is a "son of God."

Her repentance is not triggered only by the recognition of Joseph's quasi-divine status, but also by the sting of rejection. Joseph disdains Egyptian women, and has been warned by his father to guard against the strange woman. Even when he is assured that Aseneth will not molest him, and he agrees to welcome her as a sister, he still refuses to kiss her, for

> it is not fitting for a man who worships God, who will bless with his mouth the living God and eat the blessed bread of life and drink a blessed cup of immortality and anoint himself with blessed ointment of incorruptibility to kiss a strange woman who will bless with her mouth dead and dumb idols and eat from their table bread of strangulation and drink from their libation a cup of insidiousness and anoint herself with ointment of destruction. (8:5–7)

He softens the blow, however, by praying to the Lord to bless her and

> make her alive again by your life, and let her eat your bread of life and drink your cup of blessing and number her among your people that you have chosen before all things came into being, and let her enter your rest which you have prepared for your chosen ones and live in your eternal life for ever (and) ever. (8:9)

Aseneth retires in confusion.

The initial mutual dislike of the future lovers is a stock theme in romances, ancient and modern. Here it is overlaid with other connotations. Aseneth initially despises Joseph as a foreigner, and one of lowly status besides. Joseph has general contempt for Egyptian women, but his objection to Aseneth is more specific: he refuses to associate with idolators. It is an abomination to him to eat with Egyptians, and he refuses to do so, even when he is a guest in an Egyptian home. This mutual disdain is bound up with perceptions of ethnicity, but the critique of idolatry introduces a criterion that is traditionally termed "religious."

The initial characterization of the protagonists might suggest a rather antagonistic relationship between Hebrews and Egyptians, and John Barclay has gone so far as to claim that *Joseph and Aseneth* as a whole is an instance of "cultural antagonism."[97] Joseph's view of the Egyptian gods, and indeed the view espoused by the narrator, would seem to leave little room for mutual respect. Remarkably enough, Pentephres, father of Aseneth, even though he is an Egyptian priest, shows nothing but admiration for Joseph. But in any case, mutual antagonism is the starting point of the story, not its culmination. One might argue that the purpose of the narrative is to show how this antagonism may be overcome.[98]

The antagonistic ways of life are spelled out clearly by Joseph, in terms of food, drink, and ointment. One side eats the bread of life, drinks the cup of immortality, and uses the ointment of incorruptibility. The other eats food that has been strangled, drinks insidious libations, and uses the ointment of destruction. There has been endless debate as to whether the reference here is to specific cultic activities.[99] On the one hand, the mention of the table of idols and of libations evokes pagan sacrificial meals, although the "ointment of destruction" is puzzling.

Analogies with ritualized meals among the Qumran covenanters, Therapeutae, or early Christians break down on the mention of anointing. On the contrary, "grain, wine and oil" are viewed as staples of life as early as the book of Hosea (Hos 2:8). Randall Chessnut has argued persuasively that in various ancient Jewish sources, oil ranks with food and drink as those items deemed most vulnerable to pagan defilement, and conversely, if used properly, as representative items to express a distinctive Jewish identity.[100]

If the reference is to a ritual meal, it is to one that is not otherwise attested. It seems safer to conclude that the contrast is between two ways of life. Sacrificial meals are characteristic of the pagan way, but in the case of the Jewish (or Judean) way, the point is simply to underline the importance of commensality.

*Joseph and Aseneth*, however, does not speak of the bread of commensality, but of the bread of life and the cup of immortality. Analogies with the Gospel of John come to mind, but the hope of immortality is well attested in Hellenistic Judaism. The assumption here is that the Jewish/Judean way of life leads to eternal life, while the worship of idols leads to death. The transformation of Aseneth is twofold. On the one hand, it involves integration into a social community, as indicated by the emphasis on commensality. On the other hand, it qualifies her for eternal life. The dual goals of the transformation are explicit in Joseph's prayer for Aseneth in 8:9: number her among your people, and let her enter into your rest and live in your eternal life.

Aseneth now goes into seclusion and engages in repentance and mortification that mark the complete repudiation of her former life. She throws away her finery and puts on a black robe of mourning. She also throws out her idols. She throws her food to strange dogs, lest her own dogs be contaminated by food sacrificed to idols. In the prayer that follows, she also claims that her mother and father have repudiated her because she destroyed their gods (11:5; 12:12). There is no indication of such repudiation in the actual narrative; on the contrary, her parents rejoice in her marriage to Joseph. The prayer here seems to draw on a traditional motif, which was probably grounded in the experience of many proselytes. Philo praises proselytes who abandon "their kinsfolk by blood, their country, their customs, and the temples and the images of their gods, and the tributes and honors paid to them."[101] It is apparent that to become a proselyte to Judaism had social and ethnic implications in the Hellenistic world.

There is no public ritual to mark Aseneth's transition to Judaism. A man would presumably have been circumcised. Proselyte baptism is not attested in Judaism until the second century C.E.[102] The fact that Aseneth does not undergo baptism weighs heavily against the suggestion that the book is of Christian origin.

Instead, she has a mystical encounter with an angel. The angel informs Aseneth that her repentance has been accepted by God. As a result her name has been written in the book of the living in heaven, and will not be erased forever (15:4). Henceforth,

> you will be renewed and formed anew and made alive again, and you will eat blessed bread of life and drink a blessed cup of immortality, and anoint yourself with blessed ointment of incorruptibility.

She is given a new name, "City of Refuge," "because in you many nations will take refuge in the Lord Most High."

She is not, however, given bread to eat or a cup to drink. The bread, cup, and ointment evidently do not refer to a special initiatory meal, but to the ongoing practice to which she will be introduced. Instead, the angel gives her to eat from a mysterious honeycomb that appears miraculously in her storeroom. The symbolism of the honeycomb has been much disputed.[103] On the one hand, it recalls the manna in the exodus story. On the other, it may be associated with the goddess Neith, whose symbols included the bee. Its significance in this story is stated explicitly:

> For this comb is (full of) the spirit of life. And the bees of the paradise of delight have made this from the dew of the roses of life that are in the paradise of God. And all the angels of God eat of it and all the chosen of God and all the sons of the Most High, because this is a comb of life, and everyone who eats of it will not die forever (and) ever. (16:14)

Aseneth can now partake of the food of the angels. Like Joseph, whose appearance is angelomorphic, she has made the transition to a higher life.[104]

Her transformation, however, is not a private experience for herself alone. Two details in the encounter with the angel point to its broader social significance. One is her new name, "City of Refuge," which is said to mean that she will be a refuge for Gentiles who attach themselves to the Most High God in the name of repentance (15:7).[105] This would seem to imply that Aseneth is a paradigmatic proselyte, whose example provides a supportive precedent for others who abandon idolatry. We may infer that proselytes needed support. On the one hand, they were likely to be repudiated by their own people; on the other, not all Judeans were receptive to them. The example of Aseneth, however, showed that proselytes had divine approval and could overcome any opposition that they might encounter.

## The Wedding

The second encounter of Joseph and Aseneth is free of the suspicions and misunderstandings of their first meeting. The angel has also spoken to Joseph. Joseph kisses Aseneth and imparts to her the spirits of life, wisdom, and truth (19:11). Their union is celebrated by Pharaoh, who affirms that Joseph is the firstborn son of God. No mention is made of separate tables for Hebrews and Egyptians at the marriage feast. The cultural antagonism portrayed at the beginning of the story has disappeared.

## Families and Conflicts

The second major episode in *Joseph and Aseneth* deals with the acceptance of Aseneth in the family of Jacob. Aseneth wants to meet Jacob, "because your father Israel is like a father to me and a god" (22:3). He receives her with open arms.

Her reception by Jacob's family is not without tensions, however. Pharaoh's son, the jilted suitor of Aseneth, seeks to kill Pharaoh and kidnap Aseneth. He seeks the help of Levi and Simeon but is rejected.

but the sons of Jacob's maidservants, Dan and Gad, Naphtali and Asher, are envious, and hostile to Joseph and Aseneth. The plot against Pharaoh fails, and Naphtali and Asher have second thoughts. The other brothers and Pharaoh's son ambush Aseneth, but Levi and the other brothers come to the rescue. Aseneth persuades them not to return evil for evil, but to leave their punishment to the Lord, for they are, after all, brothers (28:14).[106] Moreover, Levi tries to save the life of Pharaoh's son who was wounded in battle, reasoning that "if he lives, he will be our friend after this, and his father Pharaoh will be like our father" (29:4). The son dies, but Joseph succeeds to the throne until Pharaoh's younger son comes of age (somewhat belatedly, forty-eight years later).

The final episode makes clear the communal, ethnic dimension of Aseneth's conversion.[107] She is absorbed into a new family, even if she is not initially welcomed by everyone. It should be noted, however, that Joseph speaks of Pharaoh as "like our father." There are also familial bonds between the Hebrews and the Egyptians. The emphasis is on reconciliation, not cultural antagonism. Intermarriage is possible, even if it presents difficulties. It remains true, of course, that such reconciliation is possible only on Jewish terms. Intermarriage is only possible with those who renounce idolatry and worship the God of Israel. But the tone of the narrative is affirmative nonetheless. As Gruen put it, "The fable plainly promotes concord between the communities," even while "it asserts the superiority of Jewish traditions and morality."[108]

While the story cannot be read as a simple political allegory, the last episode inevitably brings to mind the warrior-priests of the Jewish community at Leontopolis.[109] It imagines a situation when Judeans in Egypt were a military force to be reckoned with, as they were until the end of Ptolemaic rule. Josephus claims that in the mid-second century B.C.E. "Ptolemy Philometor and his consort Cleopatra entrusted the whole of their realm to Jews, and placed their entire army under the command of Jewish generals, Onias and Dositheus" (*Ag. Ap.* 2.49). Even if the claim is exaggerated, it still reflects a time when Judeans enjoyed military prominence in Egypt. The episode in *Joseph and Aseneth* is far more intelligible in a Jewish than in a Christian context, and suggests a date in the century before rather than after the turn of the era.[110] In this context, the story is at pains to emphasize the loyalty of the Israelites, under the priestly leadership of Levi. Indeed, their loyalty is greater than that of Pharaoh's own son—a claim that does not seem unreasonable in view of the internecine strife of the late Ptolemaic era. It is also at pains to claim that the sons of Jacob use their military ability sparingly as a matter of last recourse, and pose no threat to Pharaonic (Ptolemaic?) rule.

It is clear then that conversion as envisioned by *Joseph and Aseneth* had an essential ethnic component. It entailed aggregation to a different ethnic group, with all the tensions that involved. In that sense, it vindicates the argument of Steve Mason and others that to be a Judean meant first of all to belong to a people whose ancestral homeland was in Judea, even if one joined that people by conversion.

But it is equally true that the conversion of Aseneth involves a spiritual transformation that is traditionally described as "religious." Her transformation is defined first of all by the repudiation of idolatry and acceptance of the God of Israel. She is not only gathered to the chosen people; she also gains access to eternal life, and is given to eat the food of angels. Indeed she is transformed already in this life to the angel-like state that Joseph also enjoys. We need not infer that all proselytes, or all Judeans, were thought to be like angels. Joseph and Aseneth are exceptional characters, specially favored by, and close to, God. Joseph is repeatedly said to be God's firstborn son. But then we should remember that in Exod 4:22 it is Israel that is declared to be God's firstborn son. Joseph may be an idealized representative of Israel, but he is a representative nonetheless, and Aseneth likewise is an idealized proselyte. Israel, in *Joseph and Aseneth*, is an ethnic group, but an ethnic group with heightened spiritual significance. In Shaye Cohen's terminology, it is an "ethno-religion," whose distinctive character lies not only in shared descent and traditional customs but also in a spiritual dimension that finds expression in the angelomorphic character of its leading representatives.

CHAPTER 8

# Paul, Torah, and Jewish Identity

### PAUL AND THE LAW

According to the Acts of the Apostles, when the apostle Paul went up to Jerusalem after he had been preaching in Greece and Asia Minor, he was warned by those who received him that he had acquired a reputation among those who were zealous for the Law:

> They have been told that you teach all the Jews living among the Gentiles to forsake Moses, and that you tell them not to circumcise their children or observe the customs. (Acts 21:21)

They advised him to go through a ritual of purification with four men who were under a vow, so that "all will know that there is nothing in what they been told about you, but that you yourself observe and guard the law" (21:24), even though Gentiles who had become believers (in Christ) were only required to "abstain from what has been sacrificed to idols and from blood and from what is strangled and from fornication" (21:25). Paul complied, but some Jews from Asia who saw him in the temple seized him, shouting:

> Fellow Israelites, help! This is the man who is teaching everyone everywhere against our people, our law, and this place; more than that he has actually brought Greeks into the temple and has defiled this holy place! (21:28)

The resulting tumult attracted the attention of the Roman tribune. Paul defended himself by recounting how he had changed from being zealous for the Law to being a believer in the risen Jesus, and an apostle to the Gentiles. His opponents insisted that such a person should not be allowed to live. Eventually Paul appealed to the emperor, protesting that he was a Roman citizen. The incident led to his being sent as a prisoner to Rome, where, according to tradition, he would meet his death.

Philipp Vielhauer, in a famous article published in 1950, argued that Acts depicts Paul as a Jewish Christian, who was loyal to the Law and stressed its validity for Jews.[1] For Vielhauer, this was a misconception. Paul in fact had taught that the Law was not the way of salvation and that Jewish customs were a matter of indifference. The author of Acts had failed to grasp Paul's rejection of the Law. More than half a century later, however, Paul's actual attitude to the Law remains a disputed issue, and the pendulum of scholarly opinion has swung toward the view that he did not reject the Law or question its validity for Jews.

When Vielhauer wrote in the mid-twentieth century, he could assume a consensus understanding of Paul's view of the Law, based on the Lutheran tradition. This understanding was based on such passages as Gal 2:16, "A person is justified not by the works of the Law but through faith in Jesus Christ," and 3:10, "All who rely on the works of the Law are under a curse." Judaism was viewed as a legalistic religion, where people tried to earn salvation by keeping the Law, but could not succeed in doing so. In the English-speaking world, at least, this view of Judaism was overturned in the 1970s by Krister Stendahl's essays,[2] and especially by the work of E. P. Sanders.[3] Sanders described the pattern of ancient Judaism as "covenantal nomism." Obedience to the Law was the condition for remaining in the covenant. It did not *earn* covenantal status, which was conferred by divine grace.[4] Paul did not find the Law burdensome. He claimed to be blameless with respect to it (Phil 3:6). He continued to view it as holy and just and good (Rom 7:12). As Sanders famously put it, for Paul the only thing wrong with Judaism was that it was not Christianity.[5] (This is sometimes called the "Christological" view of Paul's attitude to the Law. Paul did not find fault with Judaism but believed he had found a better way.)

This reevaluation of Judaism gave rise to what James D.G. Dunn called the "new perspective" on Paul.[6] Dunn lauded Sanders's work, but felt that he portrayed Paul as arbitrary in abandoning Judaism for something else:

> The Lutheran Paul has been replaced by an idiosyncratic Paul, who in arbitrary and irrational manner turns his face against the glory and greatness of Judaism's covenant theology and abandons Judaism simply because it is not Christianity.[7]

In Dunn's view, Sanders has "Paul making an arbitrary jump from one system to another."[8] Dunn argued that what Paul meant by "works of the Law" was those practices such as circumcision that served as identity markers for Judaism. These practices, including food laws and purity regulations, created a barrier between Jews and Gentiles. What Paul objected to was not the Law as such but Jewish particularism, the view that the covenant was reserved for Jews. Here again he disagreed with Sanders:

> When Sanders says, "Israel's failure is not that they do not obey the law in the correct way, but that they do not have faith in Christ," I disagree. Paul does criticize his fellow Jews for "not obeying the law in the correct way." (Rom. 3.27, 31; 9:30–2; Gal. 3.10–11)[9]

Sanders, in fact, added a second consideration in his book *Paul, the Law, and the Jewish People*:

> The argument is that one need not be Jewish to be "righteous" and is thus against the standard Jewish view that accepting and living by the law is a sign and condition of favored status.[10]

In a similar vein N. T. Wright argued that the problem lay with Judean attachment to a "national, ethnic, and territorial identity."[11]

Other scholars went further. Lloyd Gaston[12] and John Gager[13] argued that Paul's focus was on the justification of Gentiles. Christ was

God's solution for Gentiles, while the Law remained valid for Jews. Gager claimed that

> Paul never speaks of Israel's ultimate redemption as a conversion to Christ. In line with this, an increasing number of readers have spoken of two ways or paths to salvation—through Christ for Gentiles, through the law for Israel.[14]

Paul did not conceive of separate or divided paths as the final word. Gager points to 1 Cor 15:24 ("Then comes the end, when he (Christ) hands over the kingdom to God the Father"). Gager comments: "In this eschatological scenario, even Christ is subordinated in a way that finally reveals Paul as a thoroughly Jewish monotheist."[15] In the end, there are not two peoples of God but one. Jews and Gentiles—humanity in its entirety—form one corporate body, not identical with Israel and certainly not with any Christian church. They are seen as common heirs ("the Jew first and then the Greek"—Rom. 1:16; 2:10) of the divine promise to Abraham as the children of God (Rom. 8:19).

Even farther along this trajectory, Matthew Thiessen suggests that "Paul's opposition to Gentile Christians' adopting Jewish customs and identity may be better understood as a variation on the genealogical exclusivism of contemporaneous forms of Judaism."[16] Thiessen supposes that Paul's position was similar to that of Jubilees, which only recognized circumcision when it was performed on the eighth day. Membership of the covenant people was reserved for native-born Jews. Thiessen argues that the thinking of Luke and Paul "had much in common with the most stringent forms of Judaism, which conceived of Jewishness in genealogical terms."[17] In a similar vein, Magnus Zetterholm cites a third-century C.E. midrash that says that "the Torah is betrothed to Israel and is like a married woman with respect to the nations of the world."[18] Christine Hayes argues that in Paul's view Jews should not

> desire to be free of Torah observance, for it is a privilege that marks their greater proximity to the divine. Paul's vision of the distinct demographic groups in the end-time kingdom may well be predicated on a system of

concentric circles of proximity to the Holy One and *maintained by genealogical distinction.*[19]

This line of argument represents one extreme in the current debate, but increasingly scholars try to interpret "Paul within Judaism," to borrow from the title of a recent volume edited by Mark D. Nanos and Magnus Zetterholm.[20] Among the more notable attempts is that of Daniel Boyarin, who sees Paul as a *Ioudaios,* but specifically as a Hellenistic *Ioudaios,* who argues for a spiritualized, universalizing Judaism, as opposed to the carnal Israel preserved in the (later) rabbinic tradition.[21] At the other extreme from the position of Thiessen, Hayes, and Zetterholm, Joshua Garroway has argued that Paul's Gentile converts had a hybrid identity, "neither Jew nor Gentile, but both," and insists that "many of the terms he uses to describe his charges are undeniably Jewish in nature."[22]

The topic of Paul and the Law continues to give rise to a vast bibliography and nuanced arguments. I cannot pretend to engage the debate in all its complexities here. Instead, I would like to consider whether the discussion of Torah and Jewish identity developed in the present book can shed any light on Paul's attitude to the Law.

## A FOCUS ON GENTILES

Paul was a religious thinker rather than a political one. No doubt, his thought had political implications,[23] but he was primarily concerned with salvation and justification before God, not with Jewish rights in the Roman Empire. In this respect, he resembled the sectarians of the Dead Sea Scrolls, although they had more overt long-term political ambitions. He accepted the basic premises of apocalypticism. The goal of life was resurrection and eternal life in the presence of God. Christ had been raised as the first fruits of those who had died (1 Cor 15:20), and so the end of the ages was at hand. Those who were still alive at the coming of the Lord would be caught up to meet the Lord in the air (1 Thess 4:17). Unlike most apocalyptic writers, however, Paul was intensely concerned with the salvation of the Gentiles.[24] (The classic texts for the ingathering of the nations are found in prophetic rather than apocalyptic literature, and to some degree also in literature from the diaspora such as *Sibylline Oracles* 3.[25]) I accept the view that has gained ground steadily in recent decades that the question of the salvation of the Gentiles was the question that drove his agenda, and led to conflict with respect to the role of the Torah. Paul does not seek to dissuade Jews from observing the Law. His own observance of the Torah is a more controversial question. His clearest statement on the subject is in 1 Cor 9:19–23:

> For though I am free with respect to all, I have made myself a slave to all, so that I might win more of them. To the Jews I became as a Jew, in order to win Jews. To those under the law I became as one under the law (though I myself am not under the law) so that I might win those under the law. To those outside the law I became as one outside the law (though I am not free from God's law but am under Christ's law) so that I might win those outside the law. To the weak I became weak, so that I might win the weak. I have become all things to all people, that I might by all means save some. I do it all for the sake of the gospel, so that I may share in its blessings.[26]

It seems clear from this passage that Paul did not consider himself bound by the law of Moses, except insofar as it overlapped with the law of Christ, although he observed it in some circumstances to avoid giving scandal. His observance depended on the context in which he was operating.[27]

## CIRCUMCISION AND THE LAW

Much of the controversy in Paul's letters is focused specifically on circumcision. While circumcision can represent the whole Law by metonymy, some passages seem to make a distinction between circumcision and the requirements of the Law. So in Rom 2:27, Paul allows for the possibility that some who are physically uncircumcised may keep the Law. He goes on to say that

a person is not a Jew who is one outwardly nor is true circumcision something external and physical. Rather, a person is a Jew who is one inwardly,
and real circumcision is a matter of the heart—it is spiritual and not literal.
(Rom 2:28–29)[28]

Again, in 1 Cor 7:19 we read, "Circumcision is nothing, and uncircumcision is nothing, but obeying the commandments of God is everything,"
as if circumcision were not included in "the commandments of God."[29]

As Sanders noted, Paul's ethical admonitions are in accord with the
Law and Jewish tradition to a remarkable degree,[30] and he never
explains how one who does not accept circumcision can fulfill the
Law.[31] All of this might lend support to Boyarin's view that what is at
issue is a spiritual versus literal view of the Law, or it might be taken to
indicate that Paul was concerned with the spirit of the Law rather than
the letter. Alternatively, it might lend support to Dunn's view that Paul
was not objecting to the observance of the Law as such, but to specific
features. Circumcision, the Sabbath, and the food laws certainly were
boundary markers in the eyes of the Gentiles, and also in the eyes of
many Jews. Of course the boundary markers have significance precisely
because they stand for a whole way of life. It is not just particular
observances that are at issue. Rather, according to Dunn,

> it is two ways of looking at the law as a whole which [Paul in Romans 3:27]
> sets in opposition: when the law is understood in terms of works it is seen as
> distinctively Jewish and particular features come into prominence (in par-
> ticular circumcision); but when the law is understood in terms of faith its
> distinctive Jewish character ceases to hold center stage, and the distinc-
> tively Jewish works become subsidiary and secondary matters which cannot
> be required of all and which can be disregarded by Gentiles in particular
> without damaging (indeed thereby enhancing—v 32) its faith character.[32]

### THE DIASPORA CONTEXT

Paul's view of the Torah must be seen against the background of the
Hellenistic Jewish diaspora, discussed in the preceding chapter. Much

of the literature of the Egyptian diaspora is ostensibly addressed to Gentiles.[33] Think, for example, of the *Third Sibylline Oracle* or the *Letter of Aristeas*. This literature typically pays little attention to the ritual law and focuses instead on such issues as the avoidance of idolatry, and ethical issues such as homosexuality and the exposure of infants.[34] (The *Letter of Aristeas* is exceptional in addressing the food laws explicitly.[35]) These issues might be controversial in the Gentile world, but they were issues on which enlightened Gentiles might, conceivably, appreciate the Jewish position. The Hellenistic Jewish writers did not envision that the Gentiles would become Jews, just that they would come to acknowledge the God of Israel. This is true even in the eschatological time. So, for example, the *Third Sibylline Oracle* depicts the flocking of the nations to the temple in the eschatological period in terms reminiscent of Isa 2:2–4, Micah 4:1–4, and similar passages in the prophets.[36]

Both Jewish and Gentile writers attest to the fact that many Gentiles took an interest in Jewish laws and customs, and sympathized with Judaism in various ways.[37] Josephus could boast:

> The masses have long since shown a keen desire to adopt our religious observances; and there is not one city, Greek or barbarian, nor a single nation, to which our custom of abstaining from work on the seventh day has not spread, and where fasts and the lighting of lamps and many of our prohibitions in the matter of food are not observed. (*Ag. Ap.* 2.282)[38]

Much of the Roman evidence suggests a benign curiosity, but it could, on occasion, lead to full conversion. Juvenal writes scathingly:

> Some who have had a father who reveres the Sabbath worship nothing but the clouds and the divinity of the heavens, and see no difference between eating swine's flesh, from which their father abstained, and that of humans; and soon they lay aside their foreskins. Being wont to flout the laws of Rome, they learn and practice and revere the Jewish law, and all that Moses committed to his secret volume: not to show the ways to anyone who does not practice the same rites and to lead only the circumcised to the desired fountain. But the father is to blame, who devoted every seventh day to idleness, keeping it apart from all the concerns of life. (*Satires* 14.96–106)

Circumcision evidently was a more significant ethnic marker than the Sabbath. One who "laid aside his foreskin" had, in effect, become a Jew.

The significance of circumcision in the world of the first century C.E. is also in evidence in the story of the conversion of the royal house of Adiabene, recounted by Josephus in *Antiquities* 20.2.3–4 (24–48).[39] A Jewish merchant named Ananias "visited the king's wives and taught them to worship God after the manner of the Jewish tradition." He also won over Izates, the crown prince. The queen, Helena, had been converted by another Jew. When Izates wanted to be circumcised, however, his mother tried to stop him, fearing that his subjects would not tolerate the rule of a Jew over them. Ananias supported her, partly out of self-interest, since he feared he would be blamed if there was a revolt, but also because he held

> he could worship God (*to theion sebein*) even without circumcision if he had fully decided to be devoted to the ancestral customs of the Jews, for this was more important than circumcision.

Izates was persuaded for the time being, but later another Jew, Eleazar, came from Galilee. He had a reputation for being very strict about the Law, and persuaded Izates that circumcision was indeed necessary. Izates complied, and happily his mother's fears were not realized.

Izates, to be sure, was an atypical proselyte, since he was about to become king, and his conversion had political implications, but the advice given by Ananias cannot be entirely dismissed as a matter of expediency.[40] Ananias was not alone in thinking that one could worship God without circumcision. Philo acknowledges that

> there are some who, regarding laws in their literal sense in the light of symbols of matters belonging to the intellect, are overpunctilious about the latter while treating the former with easy-going neglect. (*Migr.* 89)

Philo is critical of such people, although he shares their understanding of the significance of circumcision:

It is true that receiving circumcision does indeed portray the excision of pleasure and all passions, and the putting away of impious conceit. (*Migr.* 92)

He argues, however, that outward observances resemble the body, and the inner meanings the soul, and that bodily rituals should not be neglected.[41] Yet he does not simply defend circumcision as a sign of the covenant, or question that the allegorizers are still authentic Jews. He is at pains to explain circumcision in terms that would appear respectable to an educated Greek, according primacy to its allegorical significance, and even noting its hygienic value.[42] The difference between Ananias and Eleazar in the story of Izates may reflect the differences between the attitude of the diaspora literature in general and the stricter insistence on the details of the Law that we find in the Hebraic literature such as Jubilees or the Dead Sea Scrolls.[43]

Frank Thielman has argued that the issue between Paul and his opponents was to a large degree a difference between two Jewish ways of looking at the Law. He finds it difficult to see any great difference between what Paul says in Gal 5:14 ("For the whole law is summed up in a single commandment, 'You shall love your neighbor as yourself'"), and what Philo describes as the principal theme of sermons heard in the synagogues of 'every city':

> But among the vast number of particular truths and principles there studied, there stand out practically high above the others two main heads: one of duty to God as shown by piety and holiness, one of duty to men as shown by humanity and justice. (*Spec Leg* 2.62–3[282])[44]

When Paul spells out his instructions to the Thessalonians he focuses on a few ethical issues (avoiding sexual immorality, loving their brethren, behaving properly toward outsiders) in a way that resembles the common ethic of Hellenistic Judaism (1 Thess 4:2–12). Should we infer that Paul has adopted positively the typical Hellenistic Jewish view of the Law, and that what he was rejecting was the focus on the detailed observance of the Law, with its emphasis on purity and ritual matters, such as we find, for example, in the Dead Sea Scrolls?

## THE WORKS OF THE LAW

In the epistles to the Romans and Galatians Paul uses the phrase "works of the Law" with a negative connotation, in opposition to faith.[45] So, for example, Gal 2:16:

> We have come to believe in Christ Jesus so that we might be justified by faith in Christ, and not by doing the works of the law, because no one will be justified by the works of the law.

The expression "works of the Law," or its Hebrew equivalent, finally turned up in a Jewish writing from the late Second Temple period, in 4QMMT, where it refers to some twenty rulings, on which the sectarian author disagreed with other Jews.[46] The text itself seems to have been sent to a ruler of Israel, probably a high priest, as an appeal to him to recognize that the sectarian rulings are right. At the end of the document the author says:

> Now, we have written to you some of the works of the Law, those which we determined would be beneficial for you and your people, because we have seen that you possess insight and knowledge of the Law. Understand all these things and beseech Him to set your counsel straight and so keep you away from evil thoughts and the counsel of Belial. Then you shall rejoice at the end time when you find some of our words to be true. And *it will be reckoned to you as righteousness,* in that you have done what is right and good before Him, to your own benefit and to that of Israel.[47]

According to MMT, it is precisely the observance of "works of the Law" that is reckoned as righteousness. There is no reason to think that Paul had these specific works of the Law in mind, but the Qumran text can reasonably be taken as indicative of the kind of mentality Paul was contending with.[48]

Before 4QMMT was published, Dunn had argued that the phrase referred to those aspects of the Law that were ethnic markers. Some of the rulings mentioned in MMT might be thought to fit this category (avoidance of Gentile grain and Gentile sacrifice), but most do not (e.g., the purity of liquid streams).[49] Dunn nonetheless maintained his inter-pretation: "In both cases the rulings and practices (works) have been focal points of dispute within the community, sufficient indeed to cause a separation in the wider community."[50] The difference, according to Dunn, is that 4QMMT is concerned with an intra-Jewish dispute, where the issue hangs on finer points of halakah, rather than on the separation of Jew and Gentile, as in Galatians. But while both MMT and Galatians are concerned with points in dispute, it is by no means clear that the expression "works of the Law" refers only to such points, or that the phrase is shorthand for "disputed works of the Law."

The "works of the Law" in 4QMMT are concerned with matters of purity and ritual in minute detail. The approach to the Law in MMT, or other texts such as Jubilees that witness to the halakic turn in the post-Maccabean era, stands in stark contrast to that of the diaspora literature that tends to construe the Torah in terms of ethical principles. It is true that the usual ethnic markers of Judaism, such as circumcision, are among the specific commandments often passed over in the diasporic summaries of the Law, but at least in 4QMMT "works of the Law" are not necessarily ethnic markers. The ethos of a text like 4QMMT is exclusivist, insofar as it excludes those who do not abide by its strict rul-ings. Michael Bachmann speaks of "halakically-based exclusivism."[51] If we take the scroll from Qumran as our guide to the meaning of the expression "works of the Law," it would seem to mean the observance of specific commandments or *mitsvot,* including especially matters relating to ritual and purity. The point at issue, in the Pauline polemic, then, is the contrast between two ways of construing the Law, one focusing on moral issues ( = faith, or the law of Christ) and the other focusing on details of ritual and purity laws, such as we find in 4QMMT, which was representative of a trend in Palestinian Judaism in the period after the Maccabean revolt.[52] "Nationalism" or "particularism" was not the pri-mary issue, although a focus on the specific, detailed laws would indeed lead to an exclusivistic view of Judaism.

Paul himself had been devoted to the works of the Law in his earlier life.[53] In Phil 3:5 he says that he was circumcised on the eighth day, a member of the tribe of Benjamin, "a Hebrew born of Hebrews, as to the law, a Pharisee, as to zeal, a persecutor of the church, as to righteousness under the law, blameless." In Gal 1:13 he says "I advanced in Judaism beyond many among my people of the same age, for I was far more zealous for the traditions of my ancestors." If he abandoned this way of life, however, it was not because he encountered Hellenistic Judaism of the Philonic type.[54] It was rather because of what he experienced as a revelation of Jesus Christ.

### PAUL'S REVELATION

Paul is quite explicit in his claim that he had received a higher revelation: "The gospel that was proclaimed by me is not of human origin; for I did not receive it from a human source, nor was I taught it, but I received it through a revelation of Jesus Christ" (Gal 1:12). For Paul, this gospel involves a new life, expressed as participation in the death and resurrection of Jesus:

> Do you not know that all of us who have been baptized into Christ Jesus were baptized into his death? Therefore we have been buried with him by baptism into death, so that just as Christ was raised from the dead by the glory of the Father, so we too may walk in newness of life. For if we have been united with him in a death like his, we will certainly be united with him in a resurrection like his. (Rom 6:3–5)[55]

This way of life supersedes the way of life prescribed by the Law. Christ, says Paul, is "the end (*telos*) of the Law."[56] Whether *telos* here is understood as the temporal end or as the goal toward which the Law was striving, it is clear that for Paul the Law has been superseded. Life "in Christ" is now on offer as a new possibility, and for this life the old rituals have lost their significance. "For in Christ Jesus neither circumcision nor uncircumcision counts for anything; the only thing that counts is faith working through love" (Gal 5:6; compare 1 Cor 7:19). The Law had served its purpose for a time:

> Before faith came, we were imprisoned and guarded under the law until faith would be revealed. Therefore the law was our disciplinarian until Christ came, so that we might be justified by faith. But now that faith has come, we are no longer subject to a disciplinarian, for in Christ Jesus you are all children of God through faith. (Gal 3:23–26)

Once Christ had come, faith in him was as necessary for Jews as it was for Gentiles. Paul writes to the Galatians:

> We ourselves are Jews by birth and not Gentile sinners; yet we know that a person is justified not by the works of the law but through faith in Jesus Christ. (Gal 2:15–16)

Jews could continue to observe their traditional customs, but this would not "justify" them before God or bring them to salvation. According to Paul, this gospel "is the power of God for salvation to everyone who has faith, to the Jew first and also to the Greek" (Rom 1:16).

In light of such passages as these, the argument of Gaston and Gager that Paul envisioned separate paths for salvation for Jews and Gentiles cannot be maintained. That argument rests heavily on the assumption that since Paul is writing to Gentiles, his words are valid only for Gentiles, but, as Thielman argued cogently,

> Paul may have had occasion to discuss concepts of universal significance in order to address the specific situation of Gentiles in Galatia or Rome or Philippi. So in Phil. 2:11 when Paul says "every knee shall bow, whether heavenly, earthly, or subterranean, and every tongue shall confess that Jesus Christ is Lord to the glory of God the Father," we should not infer that he means every Gentile knee shall bow and tongue confess, even if he is addressing a predominantly Gentile church.[57]

I can only agree with Boyarin's assessment, that the Gaston-Gager proposal is certainly a moving attempt to rescue Paul from charges of anti-Semitism and thus save him for modern Christians. Ultimately, however, it has proven exegetically unconvincing.[58]

Equally unconvincing, in my judgment is the suggestion of Thiessen and Hayes that Paul held a strict genealogical view of Judaism that precluded the circumcision, and thereby the conversion, of Gentiles to Judaism. The strand of Jewish tradition that held such a view (Ezra, Jubilees, the Dead Sea Scrolls) was not concerned with the salvation of the Gentiles at all. Paul never suggests that circumcision, and the attendant admission to the covenant people, are privileges that are denied to Gentiles. Hayes seeks to address his failure to do so by arguing that

> Paul does not want to describe Torah observance in a manner suggestive of privilege lest Gentiles aspire to the regimen of Torah observance that is not, in his view, open to them.[59]

To this end, he rhetorically denigrates the Law on occasion, drawing on the Greek dichotomy between the (superior) unwritten natural law and written, positive law. This argument comes close to making Paul seem duplicitous; at least he withheld an essential part of his theology from his contemporary readers (and confused future readers for two thousand years to come). I do not find it convincing. There is no reason to assume that the emphatic statement that neither circumcision nor uncircumcision counts for anything should be qualified so as to apply only to Gentiles.

What remains puzzling is why Paul posed such a sharp opposition between faith in Christ and the works of the Law as alternative ways to justification before God, so that "if you let yourselves be circumcised, Christ will be of no benefit to you" (Gal 5:2). Other Jews of the late Second Temple period had also believed they had a higher revelation, but saw it as supplementing the Torah.[60] The Teacher of the sect known from the Scrolls believed that God had opened his eyes to mysteries, but these largely concerned the interpretation of the Law. There is not much evidence to support the idea that the Law "would become obsolete in the messianic age under the direction of the expected prophet."[61] Even though the rules of the sectarian community in the Dead Sea Scrolls were valid "until the prophet comes, and the messiahs of Aaron and Israel," (1QS 9:11) it is not apparent that a new law would be issued at that time. Even the Gospel of Matthew, which also accepted the messiahship of Jesus, argued that not one jot or tittle of the Law should pass away "until all is accomplished" (Matt 5:18). Paul, however, saw these as mutually exclusive paths to salvation, at least for Gentiles. Jews could continue to observe the Law, on the understanding that neither circumcision nor uncircumcision ultimately matters. If Gentiles were to be circumcised, however, this would indicate that they were putting their trust in the Law as the way to justification.

Paul's vision of the risen Jesus convinced him that Christ had in fact been justified by God, and that therefore the faith of Christ had been validated as the way to justification.[62] But he also drew the conclusion that observing "the works of the Law," was not the way to salvation, since this was not the way of Christ. So Paul came to regard whatever advantages he had as a Torah-observant Jew "as loss because of Christ" (Phil 3:7). There is merit, then, in Sanders's idea that for Paul the problem with Judaism was that it was not Christianity, or more accurately that it lacked Christ. But when Paul came to believe that the way to justification was faith in Christ, he simultaneously concluded that no one, Jew or Gentile, was justified by "the works of the Law" (Gal 2:16). In that sense, there was something wrong with Judaism, or at least with Judaism construed as "works of the Law."

The resurrection of Jesus signaled the beginning of the eschatological period (1 Cor 15:20). One of the features of the eschatological age would be the gathering in of the Gentiles, in accordance with biblical prophecy, as Paula Fredriksen and others have argued.[63] Hence the urgency of the mission to the Gentiles.

Paul was not antinomian. He never intended to dispense with all law, and neither had Jesus. The summary commandment, "You shall love your neighbor as yourself," is also affirmed by Jesus in the Gospels (Matt 22:39; Mark 12:31), and was understood by Paul in light of the common ethic of Hellenistic Judaism, which included concern for sexual ethics, for example. But this broader ethic, which affirmed the spirit of the Law, was of value for Paul only insofar it encapsulated the "faith" of Christ.

## CHRIST FOLLOWERS AND JUDAISM

Paul did not envision that Gentile believers in Christ would convert to Judaism in the conventional way by being circumcised. Neither would they be regarded as "God-fearers" or some intermediate class affiliated with Judaism. "Christians" was not yet a category,[64] although believers in Pauline terms were "in Christ." How then did the new movement relate to the historic community of Israel/Judaism?

Much Pauline scholarship has held that Paul envisioned a new entity, freed from the constraints of ethnicity. The classic support for this view is found in Gal 3: 28: "There is no longer Jew or Greek, there is no longer slave or free, there is no longer male and female, for all of you are one in Christ Jesus." Hans Dieter Betz comments:

> There can be no doubt that Paul's statements have social and political implications of even a revolutionary dimension. The claim is made that very old and decisive ideals and hopes of the ancient world have come true in the Christian community. These ideals include the abolition of the religious and social distinctions between Jews and Greeks, slaves and freemen, men and women.[65]

Boyarin, a much less traditional interpreter of Paul, also argues that

> what motivated Paul ultimately was a profound concern for the one-ness of humanity. This concern was motivated both by certain universalistic tendencies within biblical Israelite religion and even more by the reinterpretation of these tendencies in the light of Hellenistic notions of universalism.[66]

Against this notion of the dissolution of ethnic identity in Paul, Caroline Johnson Hodge has argued that the letters of Paul are replete with ethnic reasoning, and still rely on a master narrative found in the Torah that privileges Israel. The point may be illustrated from Romans 11, where Paul speaks of grafting Gentile believers onto the olive tree/Israel.[67] Hodge assumes that "kinship and ethnicity are social constructions. While both of these, as categories of identity, claim a primordial or natural base, they are nevertheless human creations."[68] Paul's image of grafting is an example of "aggregative" ethnic self-definition.[69] Ethnic identity is constructed not by contrast with others but by affiliation, and one way of doing this is by "ethnic genealogies," whereby various ethnic groups are linked together as descendants of a common ancestor.[70] The common ancestor to whom Paul appeals is Abraham, "for he is the father of us all, as it is written, 'I have made you the father of many nations'" (Rom 4:16).[71] Those who share the faith of Abraham are said to be *ek pisteos Abraam* (4:16), a phrase that associates them with those who share the faith of Christ:

> Just as Abraham "believed God, and it was reckoned to him as righteousness," so you see, those who believe are the descendants of Abraham. And the scripture, foreseeing that God would justify the Gentiles by faith, declared the gospel beforehand to Abraham, saying, "All the Gentiles shall be blessed in you." For this reason those who believe are blessed with Abraham who believed. (Gal 3:6–9)[72]

Garroway pushes Hodge's idea even further:

> Paul does not furnish an Abrahamic lineage for his Gentile initiates with the intention of making them merely into a companion people to Israel; the idea of two covenanted peoples of God—an original and a belated one—would have been incomprehensible to Paul. Rather Paul insists upon the Abrahamic origins of baptized Gentiles because he believes that they have become a part of the genuine people of Israel. Faith, in Paul's view, turns Gentiles into authentic descendants of the patriarchs, authentic Israelites, authentically ethnic Jews, because the death and resurrection of Christ fundamentally altered the way that the identity of Israel was to be reckoned in the last stage of human history. Where descent from the patriarchs, genital circumcision, and observance of the Law had designated the extent

of Israel in previous generations, now each of those ethnic markers could be achieved through Christ and Christ alone. Faith in Christ made a person into a descendant from Abraham; faith in Christ made one circumcised; faith in Christ made it possible to observe the righteous dictates of the Law. Through Christ, Paul believed, Gentiles could become ethnic Jews through and through.[73]

Garroway's argument is skewed by his insistence that people were *genitally* circumcised by faith in Christ and became *physical* descendants of Abraham by faith in Christ,[74] even while admitting that the point is that they are *reckoned as if* they were circumcised,[75] and that Paul wants "to transform physical descent from an actual to a putative status,"[76] or reconfigure what *counts as* physical descent from the patriarchs."[77] The force of his argument, however, is that Paul is not creating a new *ethnos*, but redefining Israelite identity, or, as Garroway controversially claims, even Jewish identity.[78]

It seems clear enough that Paul was incorporating Gentile believers into Israel when he reckoned them as "seed of Abraham." Whether he would have regarded them as "ethnic Jews through and through" is more debatable. Abraham was a figure in the history of Israel, but before Moses and the Law. The entity into which believing Gentiles are grafted, then, is not Judaism as defined by its ancestral law, the Torah of Moses. It is still "the Israel of God," but it is also "a new creation," where no significance is attached either to circumcision or to uncircumcision (Gal 5:15–16, despite the circumcision of Abraham!).

As Garroway recognizes, Paul often refers to *Ioudaioi* in terms that distinguish them from Gentile believers.[79] There is only one passage where he seems to redefine the term. This is in Rom 2:29, cited above: "A person is a Jew who is one inwardly." Dunn already commented on this passage:

> Paul will not allow this false understanding of God's covenant righteousness to retain even the title "Jew." Not only is the requirement of circumcision to be redefined (properly defined) in a way which renders the outward rite unnecessary, but the very name "Jew" is to be redefined (properly

defined) also, as one whose Jewishness ( = praiseworthiness) is dependent
not on what spectators can see and approve, but on what God alone can see
and approve (the hidden secrets of the heart).[80]

Garroway, from a quite different perspective, agrees:

> Paul reconfigures Jewish identity so that its *sine qua non* is no longer the lit-
> eral circumcision of the penis, or the performance of the literal decrees of
> the Law, but a spirit-mediated circumcision and the consequent perfor-
> mance of the righteous decrees of the Law, which are presumably its moral,
> rather than ceremonial requirements.... Without the internal transforma-
> tion wrought by Christ, they [Jews] are no longer even Jews![81]

This is the only passage, however, that could be construed to mean that
Paul would deny the name *Ioudaios* to those who did not accept Christ,
and even here he does not say so explicitly. (Is the possibility excluded
that a traditional Jew could be circumcised at heart, even apart from
Christ?) In the great majority of passages, the term *Ioudaios* is reserved
for those whose identity is defined by the Law of Moses. In some passages, Paul speaks as if there is still a hierarchy, "to the Jew first, and
also to the Greek" (Rom 1:16).[82] Elsewhere, most notably in Gal 3:28, he
speaks as if the distinction had lost its significance. It is not apparent,
then, that Paul uses the terms Israel and *Ioudaioi* interchangeably. To
say that Gentiles who come to faith in Christ are incorporated into
Israel is not necessarily to say that they become Jews through and
through.[83]

Garroway is right, however, that Paul is attempting to redefine Israel,
even if not Judaism. In Rom 9:6–7, he declares: "For not all who are
from Israel are (truly) Israel, and not all children of Abraham are his
seed." In Romans 11, Paul insists that God has not rejected his people,
but he has redefined it. Branches were broken off the vine, because of
unbelief, so that Gentiles might be grafted in (Rom 11:19–20). Again,
"even those of Israel, if they do not persist in unbelief, will be grafted
in, for God has the power to graft them in again" (Rom 11:23). Here he is
evidently using "Israel" in the traditional, ethnic, sense. The statement

that all Israel will be saved (Rom 11:26) is usually read as an optimistic hope that all Jews will come to faith in Christ. In Garroway's view, it entails a revision of what it means to be "Israel": "An efflux of Jews and an influx of Gentiles is the process by which 'all Israel,' properly understood according to faith, will be saved."[84] In Rom 3:30, Paul insists that God "will justify the circumcised on the ground of faith and the uncircumcised through that same faith." "Do we then overthrow the law by this faith?" he asks. "By no means! On the contrary we uphold the law." But he evidently does not uphold the Law as the means to justification. As Boyarin puts it, "There is no more role for Israel as such in its concrete sense—except always for the promise of Romans 9–11 that in the end it will not be abandoned by coming to faith in Christ."[85] Boyarin expresses the contrast between traditional Judaism and Israel redefined in terms of the dichotomy of flesh and spirit.

Judaism "has been transcended by that which was its spiritual, allegorical referent always and forever: faith in Jesus Christ and the community of the faithful in which there is no Jew or Greek."[86] The community of the faithful is not quite the nonethnic utopia that this formulation may seem to imply, as its identity is still grounded in the story of Israel. But it is a redefined Israel, distinct from the historic, Torah-bound community of Judaism. Paul sometimes uses the language of flesh and spirit to express the contrast, for example, in Gal 3:5: "Having started with the Spirit, are you now ending with the flesh [by being circumcised]?"[87]

John Barclay objects that it is misleading to say that Paul is engaged in spiritualizing or allegorical hermeneutics. Paul, writes Barclay,

> was not reaching behind Jewish particulars to some abstract "essence" or disembodied "ideal": he was placing alongside the Jewish community another which was equally physical and embodied in social reality.... Paul's apparent allegorization of Jewish particulars is performed not in a quest for "the universal human essence," but to enable an alternative form of community, which could bridge ethnic and cultural divisions by creating new patterns of common life.[88]

For Barclay, this alternative community was multicultural, or multieth-
nic, and therefore something radically new. But Boyarin is not suggesting that the Pauline community was not embodied. What is at issue is
the sense in which this community is affiliated with Israel, and this
affiliation rests on a spiritual construal of Israel as opposed to the Judaism of the synagogues, or Israel according to the flesh. At the least, it
rests on a redefinition of Israel, which differed from the traditional
understanding of Judaism defined by its ancestral law.

### A THIRD RACE?

Eventually the emerging Christian community would itself come to be
regarded as a new *ethnos*, a "third race" or *genos*.[89] This fact has seemed
anomalous, insofar as Christianity has often been thought to transcend
ethnicity,[90] or to have swept ethnic and racial distinctions aside.[91] In
the words of Frances Young, Christians claim "that they are an ethnos,
a people, despite the evident fact that they have no common ethnic
roots."[92] Denise Buell has tried to resolve the anomaly by emphasizing
the constructed nature of ethnic identity, and noting the similarity of
the strategies and presuppositions of Christian historiographers to
those of Jewish, Greek, and Egyptian historians.[93] Nonetheless, the
Christian construction of ethnicity was distinctive insofar as it did not
appeal to blood and land, the staples of primordialist views of ethnicity,
even if it still appealed to the seed of Abraham in an imputed sense. As
we saw at the beginning of this book, Jewish or Judean identity could
also be construed in different ways. Christianity had much in common
with Judaism construed as a philosophy, or the "constitutional model"
that we find in Josephus's exposition of the Law.[94] No strand of Judaism,
however, even in the diaspora, entirely disregarded genealogical
descent and the memory of a common homeland as ingredients in ethnic identity.

Our concern here is with Jewish rather than Christian ethnic identity. Boyarin is surely right that "Paul's writing poses a significant chal-

lenge to Jewish notions of identity,"[95] and this remains true even if one does not subscribe to the view that Paul was impelled by a vision of human unity. Arguably, indeed, Paul's writings, and the movement that he fostered, posed a greater threat to Jewish or Judean identity than did Antiochus Epiphanes. Paul may not have objected to continued Judean observance of the Torah, but his arguments would surely have undermined its significance to a great degree. Those who followed Paul would base their identity not on the ancestral laws of the Judeans but on faith in Christ. On this premise, an eventual parting of the ways between Judaism and Christianity was inevitable.

# Epilogue

"The Deuteronomic entity called 'Israel' is not coterminous with Judah or its population," writes Carly Crouch.[1] The problem was not that some Judahites lived outside of Judah, but that some of the native population did not conform to Deuteronomic ideals. From the beginning, the Torah of Moses was an attempt to mold Judean identity in a particular way. There had been Judahites before Deuteronomy was composed, identified as such by their place of residence and political loyalty, and also by shared cultural traits including the (not necessarily exclusive) veneration of the God of the land, YHWH. There would still be Judeans well into the Second Temple period who did not define themselves by reference to the Torah (as seen in the earlier wisdom literature), and some even (in the case of Elephantine) who may not have been aware of its existence. Eventually, however, the composite Torah, which combined Deuteronomic and Priestly traditions, would come to be the dominant expression of Judean identity.

The Torah achieved its normative status in the Persian period. The biblical narrative ascribes this development to the initiative of Ezra, but it required a stamp of royal approval from the Persians. Ezra's use of the Torah, as depicted in the book that bears his name, was highly instrumentalist, and endeavored to impose a strict genealogical standard on

Judean identity. The result, however, was ambiguous. Most of the problems that Ezra sought to address persisted after his attempted reform. The most enduring part of his legacy was the new status accorded to the Torah of Moses. The idea that Judeans were those who lived by the Torah would in time facilitate the idea of conversion to Judaism, an idea that had no place in Ezra's ideology.

In the early Hellenistic period, the Torah seems to have been valued largely for its narratives and as a source of wisdom. In the Aramaic literature from this period it serves as a literary canon that shapes the imagination of the later writers. In contrast, there is relatively little emphasis on its legal requirements, which is not to say that these requirements were not observed to some degree. By the second century B.C.E., the Torah had acquired iconic status, in the sense that it was acknowledged with respect and deference, even when it was not examined in detail. The classic expression of this kind of deference toward the Torah is found in Ben Sira's famous wisdom hymn, which declares that "all this [wisdom] is the book of the covenant of the Most High God, the law that Moses commanded us" (Sir 24:23), even though Ben Sira never cites specific commandments.

In the second century B.C.E., however, life in Judea underwent a crisis in the reign of the Syrian king Antiochus Epiphanes. While the events that led to the crisis remain very much in dispute, it seems clear that Epiphanes thought that Judea was in revolt, and revoked the privilege of living according to the ancestral law, which had been affirmed by his father, Antiochus III. Accordingly, he attempted to suppress the traditional cult and its festivals, outlaw distinctive Judean customs such as circumcision and Sabbath observance and impose Greek observances in their place. These measures have often been viewed as a religious persecution. Scholars have increasingly come to recognize that they were primarily acts of political repression, intended to erase the identity of Judea as a separate people.

The repression failed, because of the resistance it encountered from the Maccabees. When the Maccabees came to power, however, they did not simply revert to the status quo. Wherever they ruled, they imposed observance of key features of the law of Moses, such as circumcision and Sabbath observance, that served as markers of Judean identity. Idumeans and Itureans who came under Hasmonean rule had to accept these customs if they wished to remain in their territories. In the course of the century of Hasmonean rule, we see the spread of immersion pools and stone vessels, indicating increased concern for purity.

It is also during this century that we see the rise of literature that was intensely concerned with halakah, or with the detailed interpretation of the laws of the Torah, especially those concerned with purity. We see this trend in such works as the Temple Scroll and Jubilees, and especially in the sectarian document 4QMMT. It is now apparent that disputes over the interpretation of the Torah were a major factor in the rise of sectarianism.

The Hasmoneans, who were not especially known for their piety, sponsored the Torah as an instrument for the unification of their people, and indeed succeeded in fostering a "common Judaism," marked by certain practices and beliefs. But even as it served to unite the people, the Torah also became a source of division. The division arose from differences in interpretation. There was also another factor. In some cases, people claimed to have a higher revelation that took precedence over the literal text of the Torah. In most cases, however, the higher revelation was thought to supplement and clarify the Torah, not to undermine it in any way, even if it imposed a distinctive interpretation. We find this complementary appeal to higher revelation especially in the Dead Sea Scrolls, but also in some of the apocalypses, including those written at the end of the first century C.E. after the fall of Jerusalem.

In the post-Maccabean period, there is a clear contrast between the way the Law was interpreted in the land of Israel and the way it was interpreted in the Hellenistic diaspora. Much of the diaspora literature is ostensibly addressed to Gentiles, and does not necessarily give a full picture of Jewish practice. This literature places its emphasis on the moral requirements of the Law, emphasizing the rejection of idolatry and certain sexual practices, including homosexual ones. Only rarely does it address the Jewish food laws, the Sabbath, or circumcision, and when it does, it explains them allegorically so as to give them moral significance. All of this literature takes issue with common Hellenistic practices, but the argument is couched in ways an enlightened Gentile might conceivably appreciate. Despite some claims to the contrary, it does not appear that the law of Moses was the common law in Judean communities in Egypt in this period. In most cases, Judeans followed local law, and this indeed was also true in Judea in the period after the fall of Jerusalem, if we may judge by the papyri found in the Judean desert.

The followers of Jesus of Nazareth, who believed he was the Messiah or Christ, created a significant upheaval in Jewish communities in the mid-first century C.E. As we have argued in the last chapter, the apostle Paul did not yet conceive of Christianity as a new religion. Rather, he conceived of Israel redefined in light of the coming of the Christ. The Israel of God would now be defined by faith in Christ, rather than by the ancestral law. In one passage (Rom 2:28–29) Paul seems to redefine what it means to be a *Ioudaios*, but most often he uses that term for those who live by the law of Moses. Israel redefined looked to Abraham rather than Moses as its ancestor, and would include Gentiles as well as Jews, while Jews would only qualify if they came to believe in Christ. Paul did not seek to dissuade Jews from keeping the commandments of the Torah, but he undercut the primacy of the ancestral law in defining the people of God. The law of Christ, as Paul understood it, bore considerable resemblance to the ethical Law of the Hellenistic diaspora, in contrast to the "works of the Law" of the type illustrated in the Dead Sea Scrolls. But even the ethical Law, in Paul's understanding, now derived its efficacy from faith in Christ. As Daniel Boyarin has noted, Paul's Gospel posed a considerable threat and challenge to Jewish identity in the mid-first century C.E.

This threat was compounded by the fact that within a couple of decades of the preaching of Paul the Judean homeland was ravaged, the temple destroyed, and all vestiges of political independence were lost. In the wake of that disaster, a Jewish apocalypticist lamented:

> But now the righteous have been gathered, and the prophets have fallen asleep. We, too, have left our land, and Zion has been taken from us, and we have nothing now except for the Mighty One and his Torah.[2]

The Mighty One and his Torah would, in fact, suffice. Judaism retains its vitality two thousand years later despite even greater challenges that have arisen over the centuries. The loss of the homeland contributed massively to the perception that Judaism had now become a "religion." There is no doubt that adherence to its ancestral law has been a key factor in the survival of Judaism in a world often hostile to it.

Even the loss of the homeland did not in fact erase the stubborn ethnicity in which Jewish tradition is rooted. The Torah itself affirms the link to the land and to genealogical descent, even if Gentile converts can also be aggregated to the *ethnos*. Jews remain the people who originated in Judea, even if they lived in diaspora for two thousand years. The links of blood and land have, of course, been reinvigorated by the rise of the state of Israel, but they have never been absent.

Conversely, the importance of the Torah for Jewish identity has not faded either. Whether it is possible to be Jewish (or Judean?) without regard to the law of Moses remains a vital existential question, likely to elicit passionate and contradictory answers. The duality of descent and provenance, on the one hand, and a normative way of life, on the other, remains a feature of Judaism. Both are intimately implicated in what it means to be a Jew.

# NOTES

## INTRODUCTION

1. See Peter Franz Mittag, *Antiochus IV. Epiphanes: Eine politische Biographie,* Klio: Beiträge zur Alten Geschichte, Beihefte, N.F. 11 (Berlin: Akademie, 2006), 214–24.

2. For a helpful survey and analysis, see Cynthia Baker, "A 'Jew' by Any Other Name?," *JAJ* 2 (2011): 153–80. See also Joshua D. Garroway, *Paul's Gentile-Jews: Neither Jew nor Gentile, but Both* (New York: Palgrave Macmillan, 2012), 22–23.

3. Shaye J. D. Cohen, *The Beginnings of Jewishness: Boundaries, Varieties, Uncertainties* (Berkeley: University of California Press, 1999), 70.

4. Ibid., 78–79.

5. Ibid., 104.

6. Ibid., 137.

7. Joseph Blenkinsopp, *Judaism: The First Phase; The Place of Ezra and Nehemiah in the Origins of Judaism* (Grand Rapids, MI: Eerdmans, 2009), 27.

8. Steve Mason, "Jews, Judaeans, Judaizing, Judaism: Problems of Categorization in Ancient History," *JSJ* 38 (2007): 457–512, here 457. For a similar perspective, see Philip F. Esler, "Judean Ethnic Identity in Josephus' *Against Apion*," in Zuleika Rodgers, with Margaret Daly-Denton and Anne Fitzpatrick McKinley, eds., *A Wandering Galilean: Essays in Honour of Seán Freyne,* JSJSup 132 (Leiden: Brill, 2009), 73–91.

9. Mason, "Jews, Judaeans, Judaizing, Judaism," 508.

10. Michael Satlow, "Jew or Judean?," in Caroline Johnson Hodge, Saul M. Olyan, and Daniel Ullucci, eds., *One Who Sows Bountifully: Essays in Honor of Stanley K. Stowers*, BJS 356 (Providence: Brown Judaic Studies, 2013), 165–74, argues that ancient ethnographers use *ethnos* for "a politically organized community residing in a particular territory" (168). In a clarification of his views, in "Ancient Jews or Judeans? Different Questions, Different Answers," *Marginalia*, August 26, 2014, Mason insists that he does not regard "Jews" as an incorrect translation; "it simply does not reflect as clearly the connection with place-bound identity that ancient authors assumed."

11. Daniel R. Schwartz, "'Judaean' or 'Jew'? How Should We Translate *ioudaios* in Josephus?," in Jörg Frey, Daniel R. Schwartz, and Stephanie Gripentrog, eds., *Jewish Identity in the Greco-Roman World*, AGJU 71 (Leiden: Brill, 2007), 3–27, esp. 17. So also Seth Schwartz, "How Many Judaisms Were There? A Critique of Neusner and Smith on Definition and Mason and Boyarin on Categorization," *JAJ* 2 (2011): 208–38, esp. 221–38. Adele Reinhartz, "The Vanishing Jews of Antiquity," *Marginalia,* June 24, 2014, states categorically that "to define Jew solely or even primarily in religious terms is simply wrong."

12. Schwartz, "'Judean' or 'Jew,'" 13–14.

13. Daniel R. Schwartz, "Judeans, Jews, and Their Neighbors: Jewish Identity in the Second Temple Period," in Rainer Albertz and Jakob Wöhrle, eds., *Between Cooperation and Hostility: Multiple Identities in Ancient Judaism and the Interaction with Foreign Powers,* JAJSup 11 (Göttingen: Vandenhoeck & Ruprecht, 2013), 13–31.

14. Ibid., 27. See now also his *Judeans and Jews: Four Faces of Dichotomy in Ancient Jewish History* (Toronto: University of Toronto Press, 2014), 16–19.

15. Compare the argument of Brent Nongbri, *Before Religion: A History of a Modern Concept* (New Haven, CT: Yale University Press, 2013). Cf. also Leora Batnitzky, *How Judaism Became a Religion: An Introduction to Modern Jewish Thought* (Princeton, NJ: Princeton University Press, 2011); Batnitzky argues that the idea that Judaism was a "religion" separable from politics and culture was invented by Moses Mendelsohn in the eighteenth century.

16. See Schwartz's rejoinder to Mason in "Appendix: May We Speak of 'Religion' and 'Judaism' in the Second Temple Period?," in his book *Judeans and Jews,* 91–112.

17. Satlow, "Jew or Judean?," 167, comments that ethnicity is no less problematic a category than religion.

18. John Hutchinson and Anthony D. Smith, introduction to Hutchinson and Smith, ed., *Ethnicity* (Oxford: Oxford University Press, 1996), 4.

19. David Goodblatt, *Elements of Ancient Jewish Nationalism* (Cambridge: Cambridge University Press, 2006), 14, holds that nationality is indistinguishable from ethnicity, following George De Vos, "Ethnic Pluralism: Conflict and Accommodation," in G. A. De Vos and L. Romanucci-Ross, eds., *Ethnic Identity: Creation, Conflict, and Accommodation*, 3rd ed. (Walnut Creek, CA, and London: Altamira, 1995), 24–25. Doron Mendels, *The Rise and Fall of Jewish Nationalism*, ABRL (New York: Doubleday, 1992; 2nd ed., Grand Rapids, MI: Eerdmans, 1997), 13–14, also uses the terms interchangeably.

20. Craig Calhoun, "Nationalism and Ethnicity," *Annual Review of Sociology* 19 (1993): 211–39, here 235: "Nationalism, in particular, remains the pre-eminent rhetoric for attempts to demarcate political communities, claim rights of self-determination and legitimate rule by reference to 'the people' of a country." See Katherine E. Southwood, *Ethnicity and the Mixed Marriage Crisis in Ezra 9–10: An Anthropological Approach* (Oxford: Oxford University Press, 2012), 32–33; C. L. Crouch, *The Making of Israel: Cultural Diversity in the Southern Levant and the Formation of Ethnic Identity in Deuteronomy*, VTSup 162 (Leiden: Brill, 2014), 88–93.

21. Dermot A. Nestor, *Cognitive Perspectives on Israelite Identity* (London and New York: T & T Clark International, 2010), 84–86.

22. Clifford Geertz, *The Interpretation of Cultures* (New York: Basic Books, 1973), 259. Compare already Edward Shils, "Primordial, Personal, Sacred, and Civil Ties: Some Particular Observations on the Relationships of Sociological Research and Theory," *British Journal of Sociology* 8 (1957): 130–45. Neither Shils nor Geertz necessarily shared this view of ethnicity, as can be seen from the reference to "assumed givens." See further Stewart Moore, *Jewish Ethnic Identity and Relations in Hellenistic Egypt: With Walls of Iron?* JSJSup 171 (Leiden: Brill, 2015), 7–44.

23. Jonathan M. Hall, *Ethnic Identity in Greek Antiquity* (Cambridge: Cambridge University Press, 1997), 17.

24. Hutchinson and Smith, introduction, 8; Jack Eller and Reed Coughlan, "The Poverty of Primordialism," in Hutchinson and Smith, *Ethnicity*, 45–51; Nestor, *Cognitive Perspectives*, 78–100; Southwood, *Ethnicity*, 19–41; Crouch, *The Making of Israel*, 84–87.

25. Denise Kimber Buell, *Why This New Race? Ethnic Reasoning in Early Christianity* (New York: Columbia University Press, 2005), 6.

26. Benedict Anderson, *Imagined Communities: Reflections on the Origin and Spread of Nationalism* (London: Verso, 1983).

27. Karl Deutsch, *Nationalism and Its Alternatives* (New York: Knopf, 1969), 3.

28. Fredrik Barth, "Ethnic Groups and Boundaries," in Hutchinson and Smith, *Ethnicity*, 75–83 ( = Barth, ed., *Ethnic Groups and Boundaries* [Boston: Little, Brown and Co., 1969], 10–19).

29. Fredrik Barth, introduction to *Ethnic Groups and Boundaries*, 38.

30. Compare Anathea Portier-Young, *Apocalypse against Empire: Theologies of Resistance in Early Judaism* (Grand Rapids, MI: Eerdmans, 2010), 110: "The content, markers, and boundaries of what it means to be 'Greek' and what it means to be 'Jewish' will be defined and demarcated differently at different moments and in different places."

31. Nestor, *Cognitive Perspectives*, 83, 92.

32. Abner P. Cohen, *Two-Dimensional Man: An Essay on Power and Symbolism in Complex Society* (London: Routledge & Kegan Paul, 1974), 91. See the discussion by Southwood, *Ethnicity*, 34–36; Nestor, *Cognitive Perspectives*, 92–93; Hall, *Ethnic Identity in Greek Antiquity*, 17.

33. A.P. Cohen, "Introduction: The Lesson of Ethnicity," in A.P. Cohen, ed., *Urban Ethnicity* (London: Tavistock, 1974), xiii.

34. Crouch, *The Making of Israel*, 86.

35. Hutchinson and Smith, *Ethnicity*, 6–7.

36. Ibid. The importance of belief in common descent for ethnic identity was emphasized already by Max Weber, *Economy and Society: An Outline of Interpretive Sociology* (Berkeley: University of California Press, 1978), 1:389.

37. Hall, *Ethnic Identity in Greek Antiquity*, 25.

38. Mason, "Jews, Judaeans, Judaizing, Judaism," 484.

39. Ibid.

40. Trans. David Grene, *Herodotus, The History* (Chicago and London: University of Chicago Press, 1987), 611; see 17.

41. Mason, "Jews, Judaeans, Judaizing, Judaism," 485.

42. Trans. H. St. John Thackeray, *Josephus*, vol. 1, *The Life; Against Apion*, LCL (1926; reprint, Cambridge, MA: Harvard University Press, 1976), 163.

43. John M.G. Barclay, *Flavius Josephus, Against Apion: Translation and Commentary* (Leiden: Brill, 2007), LXI.

44. Ibid., LX. It should be noted that Cohen did not claim that the ethnic connotations of the term died out, but that Judaism became an "ethno-religion."

45. Barclay, *Flavius Josephus*, LXI.

46. Ibid., LIX.

47. Daniel Boyarin, "Rethinking Jewish Christianity: An Argument for Dismantling a Dubious Category (to Which Is Appended a Correction of My

Border Lines)," *JQR* 99 (2009): 7–36, rightly insists on the embeddedness of religion but concludes: "It might seem then that Judaism has not, until some time in modernity, existed at all" (8).

48. Apollonius Molon was a rhetorician and grammarian who lectured in Rhodes and visited Rome in the early first century B.C.E., where Cicero was among his pupils. The identity of Lysimachus is uncertain. See Barclay, *Flavius Josephus*, 158–59.

49. Barclay, *Flavius Josephus*, LVIII.

50. Ibid., LIX.

51. Isocrates, *Paneg.* 50; trans. Jonathan Hall, *Hellenicity: Between Ethnicity and Culture* (Chicago: University of Chicago Press, 2002), 209.

52. Arthur Darby Nock, *Conversion: The Old and the New in Religion from Alexander the Great to Augustine of Hippo* (Oxford: Clarendon, 1933; reprint, Baltimore: Johns Hopkins University Press, 1988).

53. Aristobulus frag. 4, in Eusebius, *Praep. ev.* 13.12. See Carl Holladay, *Fragments from Hellenistic Jewish Authors,* vol. 3, *Aristobulus* (Atlanta: SBL, 1995), 175.

54. Hans G. Kippenberg, "Die jüdischen Überlieferungen als *patrioi nomoi*," in Richard Faber and Renate Schlesier, eds., *Die Restauration der Götter: Antike Religionen und Neo-Paganismus* (Würzburg: Königshausen und Neumann, 1986), 45–60; Bernd Schröder, *Die "väterlichen Gesetze": Flavius Josephus als Vermittler von Halachah an Griechen und Römer* (Tübingen: Mohr Siebeck, 1996), 176–206.

55. Alexander Fuks, *The Ancestral Constitution: Four Studies in Athenian Party Politics at the End of the Fifth Century B.C.* (London: Routledge and Kegan Paul, 1953), 40.

56. E.g., Herodotus 1.131: "The customs which I know the Persians to observe are the following … "

57. Erich Gruen, *Heritage and Hellenism: The Reinvention of Jewish Tradition* (Cambridge, MA: Harvard University Press, 1998), 195.

58. Elias J. Bickerman, "The Seleucid Charter for Jerusalem," in Bickerman, *Studies on Jewish and Christian History* (Leiden: Brill, 2011), 1:340. Compare John Ma, *Antiochus III and the Cities of Western Asia Minor* (Oxford: Oxford University Press, 2000), 112–13; Robert Doran, "The Persecution of Judeans by Antiochus IV Epiphanes: The Significance of 'Ancestral Laws,'" in Daniel C. Harlow, Karina Martin Hogan, Matthew Goff, and Joel Kaminsky, eds., *The "Other" in Second Temple Judaism* (Grand Rapids, MI: Eerdmans, 2011), 423–33, esp. 426–28.

59. Robert Doran, *2 Maccabees,* Hermeneia (Minneapolis: Fortress, 2012), 103.

60. Bickerman, "The Seleucid Charter for Jerusalem," 1:342, with other examples on p. 340. Bickerman's model is disputed by Sylvie Honigman, *Tales of High Priests and Taxes: The Books of the Maccabees and the Judean Rebellion against Antiochus IV* (Oakland: University of California Press, 2014), 303–6. She argues that the status of the conquered community was established by negotiation, not by unilateral decree. But a measure of negotiation is not incompatible with Bickerman's model, especially where the interpretation of the ancestral laws was involved. In the end, the king ruled by decree.

61. On the authenticity of the proclamation, see Bickerman, "The Seleucid Charter for Jerusalem."

62. Hecataeus *apud* Diodorus Siculus, *Hist.* 40.3; Menahem Stern, *Greek and Latin Authors on Jews and Judaism* (Jerusalem: The Israel Academy of Sciences and Humanities, 1974), 1:26–35.

63. John G. Gager, *Moses in Greco-Roman Paganism,* SBLMS 16 (Nashville: Abingdon, 1972), 26–37.

64. A different interpretation of the actions of Antiochus and the Maccabean response has recently been proposed by Honigman, *Tales of High Priests and Taxes.* See my article "Temple or Taxes? What Sparked the Maccabean Revolt?" in J.J. Collins and J.G. Manning, eds., *Revolt and Resistance in the Ancient Classical World and the Near East: In the Crucible of Empire* (Leiden: Brill, 2016), 189–201.

65. The broad-brimmed hat (*petasos*) was worn to protect the athletes' heads from the sun and was associated with Hermes. See Doran, *2 Maccabees,* 105.

66. Mason, "Jews, Judaeans, Judaizing, Judaism," 466–68.

67. Ibid., 467.

68. Ibid., 468.

69. Ibid., 467.

70. See Seth Schwartz, "How Many Judaisms?," 225–26. Schwartz rightly points out that in some cases, including 2 Macc 8:1 and 4 Macc 4:26, *ioudaismos* is most easily construed as "Judaism."

71. Boyarin, "Rethinking Jewish Christianity," 8.

72. Schwartz, "Judeans, Jews, and Their Neighbors," 23.

73. Cf. Josephus, *Ant.* 12.241.

74. Josephus, *Ant.* 20.34–48. See my essay "A Symbol of Otherness: Circumcision and Salvation in the First Century," in John J. Collins, *Seers, Sibyls, and Sages in Hellenistic-Roman Judaism,* JSJSup 54 (Leiden: Brill, 1997), 211–35, esp. 225–28; as well as the epilogue in this book.

75. Compare Victor Tcherikover, *Hellenistic Civilization and the Jews* (Peabody, MA: Hendrickson, 1999), 166.

76. Tcherikover, *Hellenistic Civilization*, 167.

77. Gruen, *Heritage and Hellenism*, 29. He finds 1 Macc more sober, but still subject to misinterpretation.

78. Daniel R. Schwartz, *2 Maccabees*. CEJL (Berlin: De Gruyter, 2008), 220.

79. Doran, "The Persecution of Judeans," 432.

80. Ibid.

81. See Portier-Young, *Apocalypse against Empire*, 140–210, on the logic of the Seleucid repression; she does not, however, advert to the most repressive tactic of all, the erasure of the subject people's identity.

82. See my article "Cult and Culture: The Limits of Hellenization in Judea," in John J. Collins, *Jewish Cult and Hellenistic Culture*, JSJSup 100 (Leiden: Brill, 2005), 21–43.

83. Dan 8:13; 9:27; 11:31. See my commentary, *Daniel: A Commentary on the Book of Daniel*, Hermeneia (Minneapolis: Fortress, 1993), 357–58.

84. E.J. Bickerman, "The God of the Maccabees," in Bickerman, *Studies in Jewish and Christian History*, 2:1025–1149, here 1124; Martin Hengel, *Judaism and Hellenism* (Philadelphia: Fortress, 1974), 1:287, 289. Mittag, *Antiochus IV*, 279–81, attempts to shift responsibility to the king's advisers, but cannot relieve the king of ultimate responsibility.

85. Collins, "Cult and Culture," 37–38. Pagan authors (Diodorus, Tacitus) tend to credit the king with trying to civilize the Judeans.

86. Schwartz, "Judeans, Jews, and Their Neighbors," 23–25.

87. Lee I. Levine, "Jewish Identities in Antiquity: An Introductory Essay," in Lee I. Levine and Daniel R. Schwartz, eds., *Jewish Identities in Antiquity: Studies in Memory of Menahem Stern*, TSAJ 130 (Tübingen: Mohr Siebeck, 2009), 31.

## CHAPTER 1. DEUTERONOMY AND THE INVENTION OF THE TORAH

1. For contrasting opinions, see Diana Edelman, "Ethnicity and Early Israel," in Mark G. Brett, ed., *Ethnicity and the Bible*, BibInt 19 (Leiden: Brill, 1996), 25–55; and Ann E. Killebrew, *Biblical Peoples and Ethnicity: An Archaeological Study of Egyptians, Canaanites, Philistines, and Early Israel, 1300–1100 B.C.E*, SBL Archaeology and Biblical Studies 9 (Atlanta: SBL, 2005), 149–96.

2. Edelman, "Ethnicity in Early Israel," 35–38.

3. E.g., Killebrew, *Biblical Peoples and Ethnicity,* 155–81; William G. Dever, *Who Were the Early Israelites and Where Did They Come From?* (Grand Rapids, MI: Eerdmans, 2003).

4. Killebrew, *Biblical Peoples and Ethnicity,* 185.

5. See Ernest Nicholson, *The Pentateuch in the Twentieth Century: The Legacy of Julius Wellhausen* (Oxford: Clarendon, 1998), and the diverse recent studies of Reinhard G. Kratz, *The Composition of the Narrative Books of the Old Testament* (London: Clark, 2005), 225–308; Konrad Schmid, *Genesis and the Moses Story: Israel's Dual Origins in the Hebrew Bible* (Winona Lake, IN: Eisenbrauns, 2010); David M. Carr, *The Formation of the Hebrew Bible: A New Reconstruction* (Oxford: Oxford University Press, 2011); and Joel Baden, *The Composition of the Pentateuch: Renewing the Documentary Hypothesis,* AYBRL (New Haven, CT: Yale University Press, 2012).

6. A full discussion of the literary structure and history of scholarship can be found in Thomas B. Dozeman, *Exodus,* Eerdmans Critical Commentary (Grand Rapids, MI: Eerdmans, 2009), 411–568.

7. Antony F. Campbell and Mark A. O'Brien, *Sources of the Pentateuch: Texts, Introductions, Annotations* (Minneapolis: Fortress, 1993), 43, 145–46, 187–89, following Martin Noth, *A History of Pentateuchal Traditions* (Englewood Cliffs, NJ: Prentice-Hall, 1972).

8. S.R. Driver, *Introduction to the Literature of the Old Testament* (Edinburgh: Clark, 1891), 39.

9. Baden, *The Composition of the Pentateuch,* 77.

10. Shimon Gesundheit, *Three Times a Year: Studies on Festival Legislation in the Pentateuch,* FAT 82 (Tübingen: Mohr Siebeck, 2012), 39.

11. See F.M. Cross, *Canaanite Myth and Hebrew Epic* (Cambridge, MA: Harvard University Press, 1973), 156–69; and especially Gerhard von Rad, "The Form-Critical Problem of the Hexateuch," in von Rad, *The Form-Critical Problem of the Hexateuch and Other Essays* (Edinburgh: Clark, 1965), 1–78.

12. Exod 3:1; 17:6; 33:6.

13. Erhard Blum, "The Decalogue and the Composition History of the Pentateuch," in Thomas B. Dozeman, Konrad Schmid, and Baruch J. Schwartz, eds., *The Pentateuch,* FAT 78 (Tübingen: Mohr Siebeck, 2011), 289–301, here 291. He assigns the non-Priestly material in Exodus 19–24 plus 32–34 to his Komposition D, presumably because of the covenantal theme. See Erhard Blum, "Israël à la montagne de Dieu: Remarques sur Ex 19–24; 32–34 et sur le contexte littéraire et historique de sa composition," in Albert de Pury, ed., *Le Pentateuque en question,* Le Monde de la Bible No. 19 (Geneva: Labor et Fides, 1989),

271–95. On the differences between the two presentations of the Decalogue, see Dominik Markl, "The Ten Words Revealed and Revised," in Markl, ed., *The Decalogue and Its Cultural Influence,* Hebrew Bible Monographs 58 (Sheffield: Sheffield Phoenix, 2013), 21–22.

14. Reinhard Achenbach, "The Story of the Revelation at the Mountain of God," in Eckart Otto and J. LeRoux, eds., *A Critical Study of the Pentateuch: An Encounter between Europe and Africa,* Altes Testament und Moderne 20 (Münster: Lit Verlag, 2005), 126–52, here 133. He supposes, however, that the Decalogue was introduced by the redactor of the Pentateuch.

15. Eckart Otto, "The Pre-Exilic Deuteronomy as a Revision of the Covenant Code," in Otto, *Kontinuum und Proprium: Studien zur Sozial- und Rechtsgeschichte des Alten Orients und des Alten Testaments* (Wiesbaden: Harrassowitz, 1996), 112–22; "Vom Bundesbuch zum Deuteronomium: Die deuteronomische Redaktion in Dtn 12–26," in Georg Braulik, Walter Gross, and Sean McEvenue, eds., *Biblische Theologie und gesellschaftlicher Wandel: Für Norbert Lohfink* (Freiburg: Herder, 1993), 260–78; Bernard M. Levinson, *Deuteronomy and the Hermeneutics of Legal Innovation* (Oxford and New York: Oxford University Press, 1997). The most notable exception is John Van Seters, *A Law Book for the Diaspora: Revision in the Study of the Covenant Code* (Oxford and New York: Oxford University Press, 2003), who tries to reverse the relationship. See the refutation by Bernard M. Levinson, "Is the Covenant Code an Exilic Composition?" in John Day, ed., *In Search of Pre-Exilic Israel* (London and New York: T & T Clark, 2004), 272–325. The Book of the Covenant is also dated to the postexilic period by Douglas A. Knight, *Law, Power, and Justice in Ancient Israel* (Louisville, KY: Westminster John Knox, 2011), 101–9.

16. David P. Wright, *Inventing God's Law: How the Covenant Code of the Bible Used and Revised the Laws of Hammurabi* (Oxford and New York: Oxford University Press, 2009).

17. Ibid., 91–120.

18. Carr, *The Formation of the Hebrew Bible,* 471. In his earlier work, *Writing on the Tablet of the Heart: The Origins of Scripture and Literature* (Oxford and New York: Oxford University Press, 2005), 165, Carr suggests that eighth-century Judah is a probable context for a form of the Covenant Code.

19. Carr, *The Formation of the Hebrew Bible,* 471. A small fragment of Hammurabi was found in Bronze Age Hazor.

20. Wright, *Inventing God's Law,* 97.

21. Jean-Louis Ska, *Introduction to Reading the Pentateuch* (Winona Lake, IN: Eisenbrauns, 2006), 214.

22. Similar dating is proposed by Frank Crüsemann, "Das Bundesbuch: Historischer Ort und institutioneller Hintergrund," in J. A. Emerton, ed., *Congress Volume: Jerusalem 1986*, VTSup 40 (Leiden: Brill, 1988), 27–41; and Rainer Albertz, *A History of Israelite Religion in the Old Testament Period* (Philadelphia: Westminster, 1994), 1:180–86.

23. Albertz, *A History of Israelite Religion in the Old Testament Period*, 1:182, sees the Covenant Code as the legal basis for Hezekiah's reform.

24. Douglas A. Knight, "Village Law and the Book of the Covenant," in Saul M. Olyan and Robert C. Culley, eds., *"A Wise and Discerning Mind": Essays in Honor of Burke O. Long*, BJS 235 (Providence, RI: Brown Judaic Studies, 2000), 163–79, here 178.

25. See Konrad Schmid, *The Old Testament: A Literary History* (Minneapolis: Fortress, 2012), 99, on analogies between the Book of the Covenant and Amos.

26. Joshua Berman, "The History of Legal Theory and the Study of Biblical Law," *CBQ* 76 (2014): 19–39; Michael LeFebvre, *Collections, Codes, and Torah: The Re-characterization of Israel's Written Law* (New York and London: Clark, 2006), 1–54; Eckart Otto, "Aspects of Legal Reforms and Reformulations in Ancient Cuneiform and Israelite Law," in Bernard M. Levinson, ed., *Theory and Method in Biblical and Cuneiform Law: Revision, Interpolation, and Development*, JSOTSup 181 (Sheffield: JSOT, 1994), 160–96, esp. 160–63; Otto, "Recht/Rechtswesen im Alten Orient und im Alten Testament," *Theologische Realenzyclopädie* 28 (Berlin: De Gruyter, 1997), 197–210; Schmid, *The Old Testament*, 97; Jean-Louis Ska, "The Law of Israel in the Old Testament," in Ska, *The Exegesis of the Pentateuch: Exegetical Studies and Basic Questions*, FAT 66 (Tübingen: Mohr Siebeck, 2009), 196–220.

27. Martha T. Roth, *Law Collections from Mesopotamia and Asia Minor*, 2nd ed., SBL Writings from the Ancient World 6 (Atlanta: Scholars Press, 1997), 5.

28. Lefebvre, *Collections, Codes, and Torah*, 35.

29. Jan Assmann, *Herrschaft und Heil: Politische Theologie in Ägypten, Israel und Europa* (Munich and Vienna: Hanser, 2000), 179; Schmid, *The Old Testament*, 97.

30. Bernard S. Jackson, *Studies in the Semiotics of Biblical Law*, JSOTSup 314 (Sheffield: Sheffield Academic Press, 2000), 121–41.

31. Bernard S. Jackson, *Wisdom-Laws: A Study of the Mishpatim of Exodus 21:1–22:16* (Oxford: Oxford University Press, 2006).

32. Ibid., 24.

33. Michael L. Satlow, *How the Bible Became Holy* (New Haven, CT: Yale University Press, 2014), 39.

34. Schmid, *The Old Testament*, 97. On the theologizing of law in the Covenant Code, see also Rainer Albertz, "Zur Theologisierung des Rechts im

Alten Israel," in Albertz, ed., *Religion und Gesellschaft: Studien zu ihrer Wechselbeziehung in den Kulturen des Antiken Orients*, AOAT 248 (Münster (Ugarit Verlag, 1997), 115–32.

35. Schmid, *The Old Testament*, 98.

36. Albertz, "Zur Theologisierung des Rechts," 122–23.

37. Eckart Otto, "The History of the Legal-Religious Hermeneutics of the Book of Deuteronomy from the Assyrian to the Hellenistic Period," in Anselm Hagedorn and Reinhard G. Kratz, eds., *Law and Religion in the Eastern Mediterranean from Antiquity to Early Islam* (Oxford: Oxford University Press, 2013), 211–50, here 213. For the view that Deuteronomy is intended to replace the Covenant Code, see Levinson, *Deuteronomy and the Hermeneutics of Legal Innovation*, 150.

38. Richard D. Nelson, *Deuteronomy*, OTL (Louisville, KY: Westminster John Knox, 2002), 225.

39. Moshe Weinfeld, *Deuteronomy 1–11*, AB 5 (New York: Doubleday, 1991), 17–18.

40. See the comprehensive study of Gunnar Östborn, *Tora in the Old Testament* (Lund: Ohlsson, 1945).

41. Weinfeld, *Deuteronomy 1–11*, 17.

42. W. M. L. de Wette, "Dissertatio critico-exegetica, qua Deuteronomium a prioribus Pentateuchi libris diversum, alius cuiusdam auctoris opus esse monstratur" (PhD diss., University of Jena, 1805). The identification was already suggested by Saint Jerome, Commentary to Ezekiel 1:1 and in a scholion to 2 Kgs 22 by Procopius of Gaza (ca. 500 C.E.). See Eberhard Nestle, "Miscellen," *ZAW* 22 (1902): 170–72. See also Dominik Markl, "No Future without Moses: The Disastrous End of 2 Kings 22–25 and the Chance of the Moab Covenant (Deuteronomy 29–30)," *JBL* 133 (2014): 711–28, here 716 n. 19.

43. On the secondary nature of the account in Chronicles, see Ralph Klein, *1 Chronicles*, Hermeneia (Minneapolis: Fortress, 2006), 23–26, 30–42; *2 Chronicles*, Hermeneia (Minneapolis: Fortress, 2012), 1–2, 499–508. So also Norbert Lohfink, "The Cult Reform of Josiah of Judah: 2 Kings 22–23 as a Source for the History of Israelite Religion," in Patrick D. Miller, Paul D. Hanson, and S. Dean McBride, eds., *Ancient Israelite Religion: Essays in Honor of Frank Moore Cross* (Philadelphia: Fortress, 1987), 459–75, here 460; W. Boyd Barrick, *The King and the Cemeteries: Toward a New Understanding of Josiah's Reform*, VTSup 88 (Leiden: Brill, 2002), 17–26.

44. Theodor Oestreicher, "Das deuteronomische Grundgesetz," *Beiträge zur Förderung christlicher Theologie* 27.4 (1923): 37–58, limited the "reform account"

to 23:4–14, and allowed for a redactional frame in 22:1–2 and 23:25–30. For various adaptations of his proposal, see Barrick, *The King and the Cemeteries,* 106–11; Thomas Römer, *The So-Called Deuteronomistic History: A Sociological, Historical, and Literary Introduction* (London and New York: T & T Clark, 2007), 51; Lauren A. S. Monroe, *Josiah's Reform and the Dynamics of Defilement: Israelite Rites of Violence and the Making of a Biblical Text* (New York: Oxford University Press, 2011), 16. See also the form-critical commentary by Burke O. Long, *2 Kings,* FOTL 10 (Grand Rapids, MI: Eerdmans, 1991), 258–85; and the review of scholarship by Michael Pietsch, *Die Kultreform Josias,* FAT 86 (Tübingen: Mohr Siebeck, 2013), 1–23.

45. Compare the typical Deuteronomic phraseology listed by Moshe Weinfeld, *Deuteronomy and the Deuteronomic School* (Oxford: Oxford University Press, 1972; repr., Winona Lake, IN: Eisenbrauns, 1992), 320–65, esp. 334, 336 ("with all heart and soul," "to keep the commandment(s) statutes/testimonies/judgments"). See further Markl, "No Future without Moses," 716–21.

46. Lohfink, "The Cult Reform of Josiah of Judah," 464.

47. Ibid.

48. Ibid., 463. So also Mordechai Cogan and Hayim Tadmor, *II Kings,* AB 11 (New York: Doubleday, 1988), 284, 295.

49. Lohfink, "The Cult Reform of Josiah of Judah," 464–65, citing H.-D. Hoffmann, *Reform und Reformen: Untersuchungen zu einem Grundthema der deuteronomistischen Geschichtsschreibung,* Abhandlungen zur Theologie des Alten und Neuen Testaments 66 (Zurich: Theologischer Verlag, 1980), 253. Similarly Erik Eynikel, *The Reform of King Josiah and the Composition of the Deuteronomistic History,* OTS 33 (Leiden: Brill, 1996), 351, regards the account of the reforms as a secondary addition. Pietsch, *Die Kultreform Josias,* 473–74, emphasizes the redactional elements and denies that an original report can be identified.

50. So Monroe, *Josiah's Reform,* 17; Barrick, *The King and the Cemeteries,* 119–43.

51. Monroe, *Josiah's Reform,* 17. Monroe notes the contrast with such kings as Jeroboam, Baasha, and Ahab, who did not receive proper burials, and with the disruption of graves in 2 Kgs 23:4–20.

52. Römer, *The So-Called Deuteronomistic History,* 51.

53. Wolfgang Speyer, *Bücherfunde in der Glaubenswerbung der Antike: Mit einem Ausblick auf Mittelalter und Neuzeit,* Hypomnemata 24 (Göttingen: Vandenhoeck & Ruprecht, 1970); B.-J. Diebner and C. Nauerth, "Die Inventio des *seper hatorah* in 2 Kön 22: Struktur, Intention und Funktion von Auffindungslegenden," *DBAT* 18 (1984): 95–118.

54. Barrick, *The King and the Cemeteries*, 141, suggests that the reform report derived ultimately from a royal memorial inscription.

55. Monroe, *Josiah's Reform*, 85, argues that "the preoccupation with *bamot* constitutes a particular interest unique to the Deuteronomistic historians that was independent on their reliance on Deuteronomic law and ideology," but this seems to be overstated.

56. Barrick, *The King and the Cemeteries*, 186, infers that Yahweh was worshipped on the high places from 2 Kgs 23:9, which implies that the priests were invited to come up to Jerusalem.

57. See Barrick, *The King and the Cemeteries*, 9.

58. Monroe, *Josiah's Reform*, 23.

59. Ibid., 24.

60. Ibid.

61. Ibid., 77–129. Christoph Hardmeier, "König Joschija in der Klimax des DtrG (2Reg 22f.) und das vordtr Dokument einer Kultreform am Residenzort (23,4–15*)," in Rüdiger Lux, ed., *Erzählte Geschichte: Beiträge zur narrativen Kultur im alten Israel* (Neukirchen-Vluyn: Neukirchener Verlag, 2000), 81–145, identifies a pre-Deuteronomistic core, with Deuteronomistic reworking, in 2 Kgs 23:4–15.

62. Monroe, *Josiah's Reform*, 89.

63. William G. Dever, "The Silence of the Text: An Archaeological Commentary on 2 Kings 23," in Michael D. Coogan, J. Cheryl Exum, and Lawrence E. Stager, eds., *Scripture and Other Artifacts: Essays on the Bible and Archaeology in Honor of Philip J. King* (Louisville, KY: Westminster John Knox, 1994), 143–68. See also Dever, *Did God Have a Wife?* (Grand Rapids, MI: Eerdmans, 2005), 289–91, and the critical comments of Pietsch, *Die Kultreform Josias*, 9–11.

64. Christoph Uehlinger, "Was There a Cult Reform under King Josiah? The Case for a Well-Grounded Minimum," in Lester L. Grabbe, ed., *Good Kings and Bad Kings* (London and New York: T & T Clark, 2005), 279–316, here 287. This essay was originally published as "Gab es eine joschijanische Kultreform? Pladoyer für ein begründetes Minimum," in Walter Gross, ed., *Jeremia und die "deuteronomistische Bewegung,"* BBB 98 (Weinheim: Beltz Athenäeum, 1995), 57–89.

65. Ze'ev Herzog, "The Date of the Temple at Arad: Reassessment of the Stratigraphy and the Implications for the History of Religion in Judah," in Amihai Mazar, ed., *Studies in the Archaeology of the Iron Age in Israel and Jordan*, JSOTSup 331 (Sheffield: Sheffield Academic Press, 2001), 156–78.

66. Nadav Na'aman, "The Abandonment of Cult Places in the Kingdoms of Israel and Judah as Acts of Cult Reform," *UF* 34 (2002): 585–602; Uehlinger, "Was There a Cult Reform?," 291.

67. So Herbert Niehr, "Die Reform des Joschija: Methodische, historische und religionsgeschichtliche Aspekte," in Gross, *Jeremia und die "deuteronomistische Bewegung,"* 33–55: "Eine Kultreform des Joschija, wie sie in 2Kön 22–23 berichtet wird, lässt sich historisch nicht nachweisen, sie ist sogar als historisch unwahrscheinlich zu qualifizieren" (51). Niehr relies on the minimalist reconstruction of the reform report by Christoph Levin, "Joschija im deuteronomistischen Geschichtswerk," *ZAW* 96 (1984): 351–71, who reduces the original account to seven (partial) verses.

68. Uehlinger, "Was There a Cult Reform?," 292.

69. Ibid., 300. Compare R. H. Lowery, *The Reforming Kings: Cults and Society in First Temple Judah,* JSOTSup 120 (Sheffield: Sheffield Academic Press, 1991), 208: "Josiah purged indigenous cults and Assyrian cults."

70. Uehlinger, "Was There a Cult Reform?," 307.

71. Jer 7:16–20; Jer 44:15–19, 25. The complaint is found in Jer 44:18. See the discussion by Susan Ackerman, *Under Every Green Tree: Popular Religion in Sixth-Century Judah,* HSM 46 (Atlanta: Scholars Press, 1992), 5–35.

72. Pietsch, *Die Kultreform Josias,* 474, affirms that purification and centralization of the cult go hand in hand.

73. Reinhard G. Kratz, "'The Peg in the Wall': Cultic Centralization Revisited," in Anselm C. Hagedorn and Reinhard G. Kratz, eds., *Law and Religion in the Eastern Mediterranean: From Antiquity to Islam* (Oxford: Oxford University Press, 2013), 251–85.

74. Ibid., 268; Kratz, *The Composition of the Narrative Books,* 133.

75. Kratz, *The Composition of the Narrative Books,* 133.

76. Eckart Otto, "The History of the Legal-Religious Hermeneutics of the Book of Deuteronomy from the Assyrian to the Hellenistic Period," in Hagedorn and Kratz, *Law and Religion,* 211–50, here 213–14, ascribes to "the pre-exilic book of Deuteronomy" the following passages: Deut 6:4–5*; 12:13–27*; 13:2–12*; 14:22–15:23; 16:1–17, 18—18:5*; 19:2–13*, 15–21:23*; 22:1–12*, 13–29; 23:16–26; 24:1–4, 6–25:4*, 5–10, 11–12; 26:2–13*, 20–24.

77. Otto, "The History of the Legal-Religious Hermeneutics," 213. For detailed demonstration, see Levinson, *Deuteronomy and the Hermeneutics of Legal Innovation.*

78. See further Otto, "The History of the Legal-Religious Hermeneutics," 215.

79. D. J. Wiseman, "The Vassal Treaties of Esarhaddon," *Iraq* 20 (1958): 1–99; S. Parpola and K. Watanabe, *Neo-Assyrian Treaties and Loyalty Oaths* (Helsinki: Helsinki University Press, 1988).

80. See F.M. Fales, "After Ta'yinat: The New Status of Esarhaddon's *adê* for Assyrian Political History," *Revue d'Assyriologie* (2012): 133–58.

81. Weinfeld, *Deuteronomy and the Deuteronomic School*, 59–129.

82. Eckart Otto, "Das Deuteronomium als Archimedischer Punkt der Pentateuchkritik: Auf dem Wege zu einer Neubegründung der De Wette'schen Hypothese," in M. Vervenne and J. Lust, eds., *Deuteronomy and Deuteronomic Literature: Festschrift C.H.W. Brekelmans,* BETL 133 (Leuven: Peeters, 1997), 321–39, esp. 325–33; Otto, "Die Ursprünge der Bundestheologie im Alten Testament und im Alten Orient," *Zeitschrift für Altorientalische und biblische Rechtsgeschichte* 4 (1998): 1–84; Otto, *Das Deuteronomium: Politische Theologie und Rechtsreform in Juda und Assyrien,* BZAW 284 (Berlin: De Gruyter, 1999), 14–90. For a lucid summary, see Römer, *The So-Called Deuteronomistic History,* 74–81.

83. C.L. Crouch, *Israel and the Assyrians: Deuteronomy, the Succession Treaty of Esarhaddon, and the Nature of Subversion,* SBL Ancient Near East Monographs 8 (Atlanta: SBL, 2014). So also Juha Pakkala, "Der literar- und religionsgeschichtliche Ort von Deuteronomium 13," in M. Witte, K. Schmid, D. Prechel, and J.C. Gertz, ed., *Die deuteronomistischen Geschichtswerke: Redactions- und religionsgeschichtliche Perspektiven zur "Deuteronomismus"-Diskussion in Tora und Vorderen Propheten,* BZAW 365 (Berlin: De Gruyter, 2006), 239–48; and C. Koch, *Vertrag, Treueid und Bund: Studien zur Rezeption des altorientalischen Vertragsrechts im Deuteronomium und zur Ausbildung der Bundestheologie im alten Testament,* BZAW 383 (Berlin: De Gruyter, 2008), 108–70. Crouch, *Israel and the Assyrians,* 1–13, provides a fuller overview of scholarship.

84. Eckart Otto, "Assyria and Judean Identity: Beyond the Religionsgeschichtliche Schule," in David S. Vanderhooft and Abraham Winitzer, eds., *Literature as Politics, Politics as Literatur: Essays in Honor of Peter Machinist* (Winona Lake, IN: Eisenbrauns, 2013), 339–47, here 343, allows that the motifs from VTE were expanded by motifs from the Aramean literary tradition in Deuteronomy 13. For a comprehensive collection of ancient Near Eastern treaties, see now Kenneth A. Kitchen and Paul J.N. Lawrence, *Treaty, Law, and Covenant in the Ancient Near East,* 3 vols. (Wiesbaden: Harrassowitz, 2012).

85. On the question of whether it is a loyalty oath or a treaty, see Otto, *Deuteronomium,* 15–32.

86. On the construal of this verse, see Nathan MacDonald, *Deuteronomy and the Meaning of "Monotheism,"* FAT 2/1 (Tübingen: Mohr Siebeck, 2003), 62–75.

87. W.L. Moran, "The Ancient Near Eastern Background of the Love of God in Deuteronomy," *CBQ* 25 (1963): 77–87.

88. H. U. Steymans, *Deuteronomium 28 und die adê zur Thronfolgeregelung Asarhaddons: Segen und Fluch im Alten Orient und in Israel,* OBO 145 (Freiburg: Universitätsverlag; Göttingen: Vandenhoeck & Ruprecht, 1995). Otto's suggestion that Deuteronomy 13* and 28* existed independently as a loyalty oath for Yahweh is unnecessary. See Römer, *The So-Called Deuteronomistic History,* 78; Kratz, "The Peg in the Wall," 254; Bernard M. Levinson and Jeffrey Stackert, "Between the Covenant Code and Esarhaddon's Succession Treaty: Deuteronomy 13 and the Composition of Deuteronomy," *JAJ* 3 (2012): 123–40.

89. Crouch, *Israel and the Assyrians,* 47–92.

90. Otto, *Deuteronomium,* 351.

91. Kratz, "The Peg in the Wall," 254–58.

92. For the concept of mimicry, see Homi K. Bhabha, *The Location of Culture* (London: Routledge, 1994); Stephen D. Moore, *Empire and Apocalypse: Postcolonialism and the New Testament* (Sheffield: Sheffield Phoenix, 2006), 90.

93. Otto, "Assyria and Judean Identity," 344.

94. So also Marvin A. Sweeney, *King Josiah of Judah: The Lost Messiah of Israel* (New York: Oxford University Press, 2001), 166–67.

95. Jeffrey Stackert, *A Prophet Like Moses: Prophecy, Law, and Israelite Religion* (New York: Oxford University Press, 2014), 32.

96. Philip R. Davies, "Josiah and the Law Book," in Lester L. Grabbe, ed., *Good Kings and Bad Kings,* LHBS 393 (London and New York: T & T Clark, 2005), 65–77, here 73.

97. Otto, "The History of the Legal-Religious Hermeneutics," 222.

98. So already Gustav Hölscher, "Komposition und Ursprung des Deuteronomiums," *ZAW* 40 (1922): 161–55; G. R. Berry, "The Code Found in the Temple," *JBL* 39 (1920): 44–51.

99. Juha Pakkala, "The Date of the Oldest Edition of Deuteronomy," *ZAW* 121 (2009): 388–401, here 392. He considers the law of the king in Deuteronomy 17 to be a later addition.

100. Nathan MacDonald, "Issues in the Dating of Deuteronomy: A Response to Juha Pakkala," *ZAW* 122 (2010): 431–35. Otto, "The History of the Legal-Religious Hermeneutics," 228, supposes that the setting was not part of *Urdeuteronomium,* but there is no indication that it was proclaimed by Josiah's own authority, rather than that of Moses.

101. Rainer Albertz, "Why a Reform Like Josiah's Must Have Happened," in Grabbe, *Good Kings and Bad Kings,* 27–46, contra Davies, "Josiah and the Law Book," 65–77.

102. Elizabeth Bloch-Smith, "Assyrians Abet Israelite Cultic Reforms: Sennacherib and the Centralization of the Israelite Cult," in J. David Schloen, ed., *Exploring the Long Durée: Essays in Honor of Lawrence E. Stager* (Winona Lake, IN: Eisenbrauns, 2009), 35–44.

103. J. Gordon McConville, "King and Messiah in Deuteronomy and the Deuteronomistic History," in John Day, ed., *King and Messiah in Israel and the Ancient Near East* (Sheffield: Sheffield Academic Press, 1998), 271–95, here 276; Gary N. Knoppers, "The Deuteronomist and the Deuteronomic Law of the King: A Reexamination of a Relationship," *ZAW* 108 (1996): 329–46, here 329.

104. Bernard M. Levinson, "The Reconceptualization of Kingship in Deuteronomy and the Deuteronomistic History's Reconceptualization of Torah," *VT* 51 (2001): 511–34, here 520–21.

105. Norbert Lohfink, "Distribution of the Functions of Power: The Laws Concerning Public Offices in Deuteronomy 16:18—18:22," in D. L. Christensen, ed., *A Song of Power and the Power of Song: Essays on the Book of Deuteronomy* (Winona Lake, IN: Eisenbrauns, 1993), 336–52.

106. Levinson, "The Reconceptualization of Kingship," 531.

107. Patricia Dutcher-Walls, "The Circumscription of the King: Deuteronomy 17:16–17 in Its Ancient Social Context," *JBL* 121 (2002): 601–16, here 615.

108. Davies, "Josiah and the Law Book," 74.

109. The argument that the law of the king requires a date after the collapse of the monarchy was made already by Lothar Perlitt, "Der Staatsgedanke im Deuteronomium," in Samuel E. Balentine and John Barton, eds., *Language, Theology, and the Bible: Essays in Honour of James Barr* (Oxford: Oxford University Press, 1994), 182–98. See also Römer, *The So-Called Deuteronomistic History,* 80.

110. Albertz, "Why a Reform like Josiah's Must Have Happened," 35. Shaphanide scribes were scribes associated with Shaphan, who figures prominently in the story of the book-finding in 2 Kings 22.

111. LeFebvre, *Collections, Codes, and Torah,* 61. Compare Levinson, "The Reconceptualization of Kingship in Deuteronomy," 523–26.

112. J. G. McConville, *Deuteronomy* (Leicester: Apollos, 2002), 33.

113. Dominik Markl, *Gottes Volk im Deuteronomium,* Beihefte zur Zeitschrift für Altorientalische und Biblische Rechtsgeschichte 18 (Wiesbaden: Harrassowitz, 2012), 301, 307, speaks of Deuteronomy as a constitutional theocracy, with God as king.

114. C.L. Crouch, *The Making of Israel: Cultural Diversity in the Southern Levant and the Formation of Ethnic Identity in Deuteronomy*, VTSup 162 (Leiden: Brill, 2014), 105–225.

115. A. Hastings, *The Construction of Nationhood: Ethnicity, Religion, and Nationalism* (Cambridge: Cambridge University Press, 1997), 18; K.L. Sparks, *Ethnicity and Identity in Ancient Israel: Prolegomena to the Study of Ethnic Sentiments and Their Expression in the Hebrew Bible* (Winona Lake, IN: Eisenbrauns, 1998), 260–61 and passim; Steven Grosby, *Biblical Ideas of Nationality: Ancient and Modern* (Winona Lake, IN: Eisenbrauns, 2002), 94–95; Anthony D. Smith, *The Nation in History* (Hanover, NH: The University Press of New England, 2000), 44–45; Mark Brett, " Nationalism and the Hebrew Bible," in John Rogerson, Margaret Davies, and M. Daniel Carroll R., eds., *The Bible in Ethics: The Second Sheffield Colloquium*, JSOTSup 207 (Sheffield: Sheffield Academic Press, 1995), 136–63, esp. 144–53.

116. Crouch, *The Making of Israel*, 109.

117. Deut 1:6, 35; 6:18, 23 etc. See Crouch, *The Making of Israel*, 91.

118. For the prevailing view, see Ernest Gellner, *Nations and Nationalism* (Oxford: Blackwell, 1983); Elie Kedourie, *Nationalism* (London: Hutchinson, 1963). On the similarity of Deuteronomy to later ideas of nationalism, see Stuart D.E. Weeks, "Biblical Literature and the Emergence of Ancient Jewish Nationalism," *BibInt* 10 (2002): 144–57.

119. Crouch, *The Making of Israel*, 109.

120. *Pace* Sparks, *Ethnicity and Identity*, 227, 234.

121. See John Barton and Francesca Stavrakopoulou, eds., *Religious Diversity in Ancient Israel and Judah* (London: Clark, 2010).

122. Otto, "The History of the Legal-Religious Hermeneutics," 228; Otto, *Das Gesetz des Mose* (Darmstadt: Wissenschaftliche Buchgesellschaft, 2007), 137–46.

123. Joel Baden, "The Deuteronomic Evidence for the Documentary Theory," in Dozeman, Schmid, and Schwartz, *The Pentateuch*, 327–44.

124. Markl, *Gottes Volk*, 88–125, cited from the English summary on p. 305.

125. Compare E. Theodore Mullen, Jr., *Narrative History and Ethnic Boundaries*, Semeia Studies (Atlanta: SBL, 1993), 58. The argument of Ernest W. Nicholson, *Deuteronomy and the Judaean Diaspora* (Oxford: Oxford University Press, 2014), for a diasporic Deuteronomy holds for the book in its final form, though not necessarily for *Urdeuteronomium*.

126. For a complex study of the redaction of Deuteronomy, see Otto, *Das Deuteronomium im Pentateuch und Hexateuch: Studien zur Literaturgeschichte von Pen-*

*tateuch und Hexateuch im Lichte des Deuteronomiumrahmens,* FAT 30 (Tübingen: Mohr Siebeck, 2000).

127. On the extent of the P source, see Baden, *The Composition of the Pentateuch,* 169–92.

128. Otto, "The History of the Legal-Religious Hermeneutics," 234.

129. See especially Leviticus 26–27.

130. Lori L. Rowlett, *Joshua and the Rhetoric of Violence: A New Historicist Analysis,* JSOTSup 226 (Sheffield: Sheffield Academic Press, 1996), 12–13.

131. Thomas Römer, "Conflicting Models of Identity and the Publication of the Torah in the Persian Period," in R. Albertz and J. Wöhrle, eds., *Between Cooperation and Hostility: Multiple Identities in Ancient Judaism and the Interaction with Foreign Powers,* JAJ Sup 11 (Göttingen: Vandenhoeck & Ruprecht, 2013), 33–51, here 45.

132. So already Julius Wellhausen, *Prolegomena to the History of Ancient Israel* (1885; repr., Atlanta: Scholars Press, 1994), 116. See further Saul M. Olyan, "An Eternal Covenant with Circumcision as Its Sign: How Useful a Criterion for Dating and Source Analysis?," in Dozeman, Schmid, and Schwartz, *The Pentateuch,* 347–58, esp. 347–48. Konrad Schmid, "Judean Identity and Ecumenicity: The Political Theology of the Priestly Document," in Oded Lipschits, Gary N. Knoppers, and Manfred Oeming, eds., *Judah and Judeans in the Achaemenid Period: Negotiating Identity in an International Context* (Winona Lake, IN: Eisenbrauns, 2011), 3–26, argues that the Priestly source posits an "Abrahamic circle" between the wider "world circle and the narrower Israelite circle," which seems to argue for an "Abrahamic ecumenicity" among Judeans, Israelites, Edomites, and Arabs.

133. See below, chapter 2.

134. Rainer Albertz, *A History of Israelite Religion in the Old Testament Period,* vol. 2, *From the Exile to the Maccabees,* OTL (Louisville, KY: Westminster John Knox, 1994), 468.

135. See Pierre Briant, *From Cyrus to Alexander: A History of the Persian Empire* (Winona Lake, IN: Eisenbrauns, 2002), 474; and below, chapter 2.

136. Ska, *Introduction,* 231.

137. Compare Joel S. Baden, *The Promise to the Patriarchs* (New York: Oxford University Press, 2013), on the treatment of the promises in the traditional sources; Benjamin D. Sommer, *Revelation and Authority: Sinai in Jewish Scripture and Tradition,* AYBRL (New Haven, CT: Yale University Press, 2015), 27–98 (on maximalist and minimalist approaches).

CHAPTER 2. TORAH IN THE PERSIAN PERIOD

1. Michael Satlow, *How the Bible Became Holy* (New Haven, CT: Yale University Press, 2014), 59.

2. David M. Carr, "The Rise of Torah," in Gary N. Knoppers and Bernard M. Levinson, *The Pentateuch as Torah: New Models for Understanding Its Promulgation and Acceptance* (Winona Lake, IN: Eisenbrauns, 2007), 39–56, here 50.

3. Carol L. Meyers and Eric M. Meyers, *Haggai: Zechariah 1–8*, AB 25B (New York: Doubleday, 1987), 77–78.

4. The classic study of priestly *torah* is J. Begrich, "Die priesterliche Torah," *ZAW* 66 (1936): 63–88.

5. Antonios Finitsis, *Visions and Eschatology: A Socio-Historical Analysis of Zechariah 1–6* (London and New York: T & T Clark, 2011), 125–36; John J. Collins, "The Eschatology of Zechariah," in Lester L. Grabbe and Robert D. Haak, eds., *Knowing the End from the Beginning: The Prophetic, the Apocalyptic, and Their Relationships* (London and New York: T & T Clark, 2003), 74–84.

6. Meyers and Meyers, *Haggai*, l—lxiii; David Petersen, *Haggai and Zechariah 1–8*, OTL (Philadelphia: Westminster, 1984), 110–24; Mark J. Boda, *Haggai, Zechariah*, NIV Application Commentary Series (Grand Rapids, MI: Zondervan, 2004), 38–41.

7. Meyers and Meyers, *Haggai*, 365–66, find an allusion to Deut 28:1 in Zech 6:15b ("This will happen if you diligently obey the voice of the Lord your God"), and suggest that Hag 1:12, where Zerubbabel and Joshua "obeyed the voice of the Lord their God," is also covenantal. In Haggai, however, the voice of God is clearly mediated by the prophets, not by a law book. Petersen, *Haggai and Zechariah 1–8*, argues that the voice of God is also mediated by the prophet in Zech 6:15.

8. Meyers and Meyers, *Haggai*, 283.

9. Ibid., 290–91.

10. Joachim Schaper, "Torah and Identity in the Persian Period," in Oded Lipschits, Gary N. Knoppers, and Manfred Oeming, eds., *Judah and the Judeans in the Achaemenid Period: Negotiating Identity in an International Context* (Winona Lake, IN: Eisenbrauns, 2011), 31.

11. H. Donner, "Jesaja lvi 1–7: Ein Abrogationsfall innerhalb des Kanons; Implikationen and Konsequenzen," in J. A. Emerton, ed., *Congress Volume Salamanca 1983*, VTSup 36 (Leiden: Brill, 1985), 81–95; Michael Fishbane, *Biblical Interpretation in Ancient Israel* (Oxford: Clarendon, 1985), 128; Joachim Schaper, "Rereading the Law: Inner-Biblical Exegesis of Divine Oracles in Ezekiel 44

and Isaiah 56," in B.M. Levinson and E. Otto, eds., *Recht und Ethik im Alten Testament*, Altes Testament und Moderne 13 (Münster: Lit Verlag, 2004), 125–44.

12. Schaper, "Torah and Identity," 30.

13. Christophe Nihan, "Ethnicity and Identity in Isaiah 56–66," in Lipschits, Knoppers, and Oeming, *Judah and the Judeans*, 75.

14. Fishbane, *Biblical Interpretation*, 128.

15. Saul Olyan, "'Sie sollen nicht in die Gemeinde des Herrn kommen: Aspekte gesellschaftlicher Inklusion und Exklusion in Dtn 23,4–9 und seine frühen Auslegungen," in Olyan, *Social Inequality in the World of the Text: The Significance of Ritual and Social Distinctions in the Hebrew Bible* (Göttingen: Vandenhoeck & Ruprecht, 2011), 172–85, here 179.

16. Joseph Blenkinsopp, *Isaiah 56–66*, AB 19B (New York: Doubleday, 2003), 135.

17. The archives that have been discovered from Babylonia (the Murashu and Al-Yahudu archives) deal mainly with business matters. They show that people with Yahwistic names engaged in business with their non-Jewish neighbors. In the case of the Al-Yahudu archive they show that Judean exiles lived together, at least in some cases, and had some community officials. These archives, however, shed no direct light on the religious beliefs and practices of the exiles. One assumes from the names that they worshiped Yahweh and identified as Judeans, but little more can be said about their identity. See Laurie E. Pearce and Cornelia Wunsch, *Documents of Judean Exiles and West Semites in Babylonia in the Collection of David Sofer* (Bethesda, MD: CDL, 2014); also Laurie E. Pearce, "New Evidence for Judeans in Babylonia," in Oded Lipschits and Manfred Oeming, eds., *Judah and the Judeans in the Persian Period* (Winona Lake, IN: Eisenbrauns, 2006), 399–411.

18. A.E. Cowley, *Aramaic Papyri of the Fifth Century B.C.* (Oxford: Clarendon, 1923) (henceforth *AP*); Bezalel Porten and Ada Yardeni, *Textbook of Aramaic Documents from Ancient Egypt*, 4 vols. (Jerusalem: Academon, 1986–99) (henceforth *TAD*); Bezalel Porten, *The Elephantine Papyri in English: Three Millennia of Cross-Cultural Continuity and Change* (Leiden: Brill, 1996).

19. *TAD* A 4.7:26–27.

20. *TAD* C 3:15.

21. *TAD* A 2.1:1; 2.4:1; 2.3:1.

22. Bezalel Porten, *Archives from Elephantine: The Life of an Ancient Jewish Military Colony* (Berkeley and Los Angeles: University of California Press, 1968), 156. On Anath-Yahu, see Karl van der Toorn, "Anat-Yahu, Some Other Deities, and the Jews of Elephantine," *Numen* 39 (1992): 80–101. A goddess Anath-Bethel

is known from the Succession Treaty of Esarhaddon. See also Bob Becking, "Die Gottheiten der Juden in Elephantine," in Manfred Oeming and Konrad Schmid, eds., *Der eine Gott und die Götter: Polytheismus und Monotheismus im antiken Israel* (Zurich: Theologischer Verlag, 2003), 203–26, esp. 219–25.

23. Reinhard G. Kratz, "The Legal Status of the Pentateuch between Elephantine and Qumran," in Knoppers and Levinson, *The Pentateuch as Torah*, 77–103, esp. 83–84.

24. Van der Toorn, "Anat-Yahu," 97. So also Manfred Weippert, "Synkretismus und Monotheismus: Religionsinterne Konfliktbewältigung im alten Israel," in Weippert, *Jahwe und die anderen Götter: Studien zur Religionsgeschicht des antiken Israel in ihrem syrisch-kanaanäischen Kontext*, FAT 18 (Tübingen: Mohr Siebeck, 1997), 1–24, esp. 15. For Judahite origins, see *AP* xv–xxviii; Paul-Eugène Dion, "La religion d'Éléphantine: Un reflet du Juda d'avant l'exil," in Ulrich Hübner and Ernst Axel Knauf, eds., *Kein Land für sich allein: Studien zum Kulturkontakt in Kanaan, Israel/Palästina und Ebirnâri für Manfred Weippert zum 65. Geburtstag*, OBO 186 (Freiburg: Universitätsverlag; Göttingen: Vandenhoeck & Ruprecht, 2002), 243–54, esp. 252–53.

25. André Lemaire, "Everyday Life according to the Ostraca from Elephantine," in Lipschitz, Knoppers, and Oeming, *Judah and the Judeans*, 365–73. On the religious life of the Judeans at Elephantine, see also Anke Joisten-Pruschke, *Das religiöse Leben der Juden von Elephantine in der Achämenidenzeit*, Göttinger Orientforschungen 3: Iranica Neue Folge 2 (Wiesbaden: Harrassowitz, 2008); Bob Becking, "Yehudite Identity in Elephantine," in Lipschitz, Knoppers, and Oeming, *Judah and the Judeans*, 403–19.

26. Dion, "La religion d'Elephantine," 249.

27. *AP* xiv.

28. *TAD* 1.54–55.

29. Porten, *Archives from Elephantine*, 139. For comparison of the missions of Nehemiah and Hananiah, see Reinhard G. Kratz, "Judean Ambassadors and the Making of Jewish Identity," in Lipschitz, Knoppers, and Oeming, *Judah and the Judeans*, 421–44.

30. *AP* 38:7–8; Porten, *Archives from Elephantine*, 280.

31. Porten, *Archives from Elephantine*, 132.

32. Kratz, "The Legal Status," 85.

33. Ernst Axel Knauf, "Elephantine und das vor-biblische Judentum," in Reinhard G. Kratz, ed., *Religion und Religionskontakte im Zeitalter der Achämeniden* (Gütersloh: Kaiser, 2002), 179–88, specifically 186. Cf. Porten, *The Elephantine Papyri in English*, 126.

34. *TAD* D 7.6:9–10; 7.24:5; Porten, *Archives from Elephantine*, 131–32; Kratz, "The Legal Status," 85. For another possible reference in an ostracon, see Lemaire, "Everyday Life," 370.

35. See Bob Becking, "Sabbath at Elephantine: A Short Episode in the Construction of Jewish Identity," in Becking, *Ezra, Nehemiah, and the Construction of Early Jewish Identity*, FAT 80 (Tübingen: Mohr Siebeck, 2011), 118–27.

36. *TAD* D 7.10:5; 7.12:9; 7.16:2; 7.35:7. See further Lutz Doering, *Schabbat: Sabbathalach und –praxis im antiken Judentum und Urchristentum*, TSAJ 78 (Tübingen: Mohr Siebeck, 1999), 23–42.

37. Kratz, "The Legal Status," 86. So also Doering, *Schabbat*, 42.

38. Julius Wellhausen, *Israelitische und jüdische Geschichte*, 10th ed. (Berlin: De Gruyter, 2004), 176–78, quoted in Kratz, "The Legal Status," 82.

39. So Bob Becking, "Yehudite Identity in Elephantine," in Becking, *Ezra, Nehemiah*, 128–42, concludes that "they seem to have been able to remain in their pre-biblical form of Yahwism" (142).

40. Kratz, "The Legal Status," 87.

41. Satlow, *How the Bible Became Holy*, 97–99.

42. *AP* 30–31; *TAD* A 4.7:68–71; Porten, *Archives from Elephantine*, 289.

43. *AP* 32; *TAD* A 4.9.

44. *AP* 33.

45. Lester L. Grabbe, *A History of the Jews and Judaism in the Second Temple Period*, vol. 1, *Yehud: A History of the Persian Province of Judah* (London and New York: Continuum, 2004), 324–31; Grabbe, *Ezra-Nehemiah* (London and New York: Continuum, 1998), 125–53.

46. See the balanced discussion of H. G. M. Williamson, *Ezra, Nehemiah*, WBC 16 (Waco, TX: Word, 1985), xl. On the problem of the relation between Ezra and Nehemiah, see now Anne Fitzpatrick McKinley, *Empire, Power, and Indigenous Elites: A Case Study of the Nehemiah Memoir*, JSJSup 169 (Leiden: Brill, 2015), 255–65.

47. For a survey of the debate, see Lester L. Grabbe, "The 'Persian Documents' in the Book of Ezra: Are They Authentic?," in Lipschits and Oeming, *Judah and the Judeans*, 531–70; Kyong-Jin Lee, *The Authority and Authorization of Torah in the Persian Period* (Leuven: Peeters, 2011), 214–35. The classic critique of the historical value of Ezra-Nehemiah was that of C. C. Torrey, *The Composition and Historical Value of Ezra-Nehemiah* (Giessen: Ricker, 1896); Torrey, *Ezra Studies* (Chicago: University of Chicago Press, 1910).

48. Jacob Wright, *Rebuilding Identity: The Nehemiah Memoir and Its Earliest Readers*, BZAW 348 (Berlin: De Gruyter, 2004), 90, refers to the "incredible amount of gold and silver for the maintenance of the temple."

49. Grabbe, *A History of the Jews and Judaism*, 77; Juha Pakkala, *Ezra the Scribe: The Development of Ezra 7–10 and Nehemia 8*, BZAW 347 (Berlin: De Gruyter, 2004), 47. Defenders of the authenticity of the decree argue that Ezra may have drafted it for Persian approval. So Williamson, *Ezra, Nehemiah*, 99, following Eduard Meyer, *Die Entstehung des Judenthums* (Halle: Niemeyer, 1896), 65.

50. Peter Frei and Klaus Koch, *Reichsidee und Reichsorganisation im Perserreich*, OBO 55 (Freiburg: Universitätsverlag, 1984); Frei, "Persian Imperial Authorization: A Summary," in James W. Watts, ed., *Persia and Torah: The Theory of Imperial Authorization of the Pentateuch*, SBLSymS 17 (Atlanta: SBL, 2001), 5–40. The latter volume contains a range of critical responses to Frei's theory. See also Lee, *The Authority and Authorization of Torah*; and Knoppers and Levinson, *The Pentateuch as Torah*, esp. the essay of Konrad Schmid, "The Persian Imperial Authorization as a Historical Problem," 23–38. Frei was not the first to propose some form of imperial authorization.

51. Wilhelm Spiegelberg, *Die sogenannte demotische Chronik des Pap. 215 der Bibliothèque nationale zu Paris, nebst den auf der Rückseite des Papyrus stehenden Texten* (Leipzig: Hinrichs, 1914), 31; English trans. in Amelie Kuhrt, *The Persian Empire* (London: Routledge, 2007), 1:125.

52. Spiegelberg also restored a reference to "the law of Pharaoh."

53. Frei, "Persian Imperial Authorization," 9. Frei is followed by Douglas A. Knight, *Law, Power, and Justice in Ancient Israel* (Louisville, KY: Westminster, 2011), 105–9.

54. Donald B. Redford, "The So-Called 'Codification' of Egyptian Law under Darius I," in Watts, *Persia and Torah*, 158.

55. Richard C. Steiner, "The *mbqr* at Qumran, the *episkopos* in the Athenian Empire, and the Meaning of *lbqr'* in Ezra 7:14: On the Relation of Ezra's Mission to the Persian Legal Project," *JBL* 120 (2001): 623–46; Knight, *Law, Power, and Justice*, 107–8.

56. Gary N. Knoppers, "An Achaemenid Imperial Authorization of Torah in Yehud?," in Watts, *Persia and Torah*, 115–34. For examples of Persian legislative action in Egypt and Asia Minor, see Lee, *The Authority and Authorization of Torah*, 31–154.

57. Frei, "Persian Imperial Authorization," 33. Note the clarification of Frei's thesis by Schmid, "The Persian Imperial Authorization," 27–33.

58. Joseph Blenkinsopp, "Was the Pentateuch the Civic and Religious Constitution of the Jewish Ethnos in the Persian Period?," in Watts, *Persia and Torah*, 41–62, esp. 45. On the understanding of law in Achaemenid Persia, see

Josef Wiesehöfer, "Law and Religion in Achaemenid Iran," in Anselm Hagedorn and Reinhard G. Kratz, eds., *Law and Religion in the Eastern Mediterranean: From Antiquity to Early Islam* (Oxford: Oxford University Press, 2013), 41–57.

59. See Lee, *The Authority and Authorization of Torah*, 213–53.

60. Watts, *Persia and Torah*, 3.

61. Lee, *The Authority and Authorization of Torah*, 249.

62. *TAD* 1.54–5; Lee, *The Authority and Authorization of Torah*, 72–82.

63. See Bob Becking, "The Idea of Torah in Ezra 7–10: A Functional Analysis," in Becking, *Ezra, Nehemiah*, 43–57, esp. 50–52.

64. Joseph Blenkinsopp, *Ezra-Nehemiah: A Commentary* (Philadelphia: Westminster, 1988), 151.

65. See the discussion by Pakkala, *Ezra the Scribe*, 284–90.

66. Blenkinsopp, *Ezra-Nehemiah*, 155.

67. Ibid.

68. Michael LeFebvre, *Collections, Codes, and Torah: The Re-Characterization of Israel's Written Law* (New York and London: T & T Clark, 2006), 103–31; Judson R. Shaver, *Torah and the Chronicler's History Work: An Inquiry into the Chronicler's References to Laws, Festivals, and Cultic Institutions in Relationship to Pentateuchal Legislation*, BJS 196 (Atlanta: Scholars Press, 1989), 100–103; Juha Pakkala, "The Quotations and References of the Pentateuchal Laws in Ezra-Nehemiah," in Hanne von Weissenberg, Juha Pakkala, and Karko Marttila, eds., *Changes in Scripture: Rewriting and Interpreting Authoritative Traditions in the Second Temple Period*, BZAW 419 (Berlin: De Gruyter, 2011), 193–221.

69. Schaper, "Torah and Identity in the Persian Period," 32.

70. Pakkala, "The Quotations and References," 214.

71. Fishbane, *Biblical Interpretation*, 107–34.

72. Lefebvre, *Collections, Codes, and Torah*, 108–9.

73. Fishbane, *Biblical Interpretation*, 111–12.

74. Ibid., 117.

75. Ibid., 108.

76. Lefebvre, *Collections, Codes, and Torah*, 129.

77. Ibid., 130–31.

78. So especially Cornelis Houtman, "Ezra and the Law: Observations on the Supposed Relation between Ezra and the Pentateuch," *OTS* 21 (1981): 91–115; Pakkala, "The Quotations and References," 217.

79. Schaper, "Torah and Identity in the Persian Period," 32.

80. L. Hänsel, "Studien zu 'Tora' in Esra-Nehemiah und Chronik" (PhD diss., Leipzig University, 1999), cited by Schaper, finds that this formula is only

used with reference to the Torah, and that the references in Chronicles, unlike those in Ezra-Nehemiah, correspond to the Torah as it is known to us.

81. Lefebvre, *Collections, Codes, and Torah*, 141.

82. Philip F. Esler, "Ezra-Nehemiah as a Narrative of (Re-Invented) Israelite Identity," *Biblical Interpretation* 11 (2003): 413–26; Katherine Southwood, *Ethnicity and the Mixed Marriage Crisis in Ezra 9–10: An Anthropological Approach* (Oxford: Oxford University Press, 2012); Donald P. Moffat, *Ezra's Social Drama: Identity Formation, Marriage, and Social Conflict in Ezra 9 and 10* (New York and London: Bloomsbury, 2013); and the essays in Christian Frevel, ed., *Intermarriage and Group Identity in the Second Temple Period* (London and New York: T & T Clark, 2011).

83. Saul M. Olyan, "Purity Ideology in Ezra-Nehemiah as a Tool to Reconstitute the Community," in Olyan, *Social Inequality in the World*, 159–72, here 159.

84. Ralf Rothenbusch, "The Question of Mixed Marriages: Between the Poles of Diaspora and Homeland; Observations in Ezra-Nehemiah," in Frevel, *Intermarriage and Group Identity*, 60–77, esp. 63; see also Rothenbusch, *"Abgesondert zur Tora Gottes hin": Ethnisch-religiöse Identitäten im Esra/Nehemiabuch* (Freiburg im Breisgau: Herder, 2012).

85. Daniel Smith-Christopher, *The Religion of the Landless: The Social Context of the Babylonian Exile* (Bloomington, IN: Meyer-Stone, 1989), 114.

86. Southwood, *Ethnicity and the Mixed Marriage Crisis*, 191–211.

87. Compare Peter R. Bedford, "Diaspora-Homeland Relations in Ezra-Nehemiah," *VT* 52 (2002): 147–65.

88. Christine Hayes, "Intermarriage and Impurity in Ancient Jewish Sources," *HTR* 92 (1999): 3–36.

89. Olyan, "Purity Ideology," 160, following Fishbane, *Biblical Interpretation*, 114–29.

90. Olyan, "Purity Ideology," 159.

91. D.L. Smith-Christopher, "Between Ezra and Isaiah: Exclusion, Transformation, and Inclusion of the 'Foreigner' in Post-Exilic Biblical Theology," in M.G. Brett, ed., *Ethnicity and the Bible*, BibInt 19 (Leiden: Brill, 1996) 117–44; compare Smith-Christopher, "The Mixed Marriage Crisis in Ezra 9–10 and Nehemiah 13: A Study of the Sociology of the Post-exilic Judean Community," in T.C. Eskenazi and K.H. Richards, eds., *Second Temple Studies 2* (Sheffield: JSOT, 1994), 243–65, esp. 257; Southwood, *Ethnicity and the Mixed Marriage Crisis*, 114–15.

92. See Fitzpatrick McKinley, *Empire, Power, and Indigenous Elites*, 230–38.

93. Lee, *The Authority and Authorization of Torah*, 246.

94. Satlow, *How the Bible Became Holy*, 79.

95. My use of the term "iconic" is different from, and less technical than, that of Karel van der Toorn, "The Iconic Book: Analogies between the Babylonian Cult of Images and the Veneration of the Torah," in van der Toorn, ed., *The Image and the Book: Iconic Cults, Aniconism, and the Rise of Book Religion in Israel and the Ancient Near East* (Leuven: Peeters, 1997), 229–48, who is concerned with display of physical objects in a cultic setting.

96. Compare Eckart Otto, *Das Gesetz des Moses* (Darmstadt: Wissenschaftliche Buchgesellschaft, 2007), 199: "Jude sei, wo immer er sich aufhalte, derjenige aus der Abraham-Linie, der die Tora Jahwes erfülle." Otto refers to this view as "Diaspora theology."

## CHAPTER 3. THE PERSISTENCE OF NON-MOSAIC JUDAISM

1. George Foot Moore, *Judaism in the First Centuries of the Christian Era* (Cambridge, MA: Harvard University Press, 1927–30; repr., New York: Schocken, 1971), 1:3.

2. Seth Schwartz, "How Many Judaisms Were There?" A Critique of Neusner and Smith on Definition and Mason and Boyarin on Categorization," *JAJ* 2 (2011): 208–38, here 210 n. 4. See already the critique of Moore by Frank C. Porter, review of *Judaism in the First Centuries of the Christian Era: The Age of the Tannaim* by G. F. Moore, *Journal of Religion* 8 (1928): 30–62.

3. E. P. Sanders, *Paul and Palestinian Judaism* (Philadelphia: Fortress, 1977), 60.

4. Ibid., 70. Tannaitic literature is literature related to the Mishnah, dating from the second or third century C.E.

5. Jacob Neusner, *The Way of Torah: An Introduction to Judaism*, 5th ed. (Belmont, CA: Wadsworth, 1992), 6.

6. Ibid., 8.

7. Jonathan Z. Smith, "Fences and Neighbors," in Smith, *Imagining Religion: From Babylon to Jonestown* (Chicago: University of Chicago Press, 1982), 14. This volume was published in a series edited by Jacob Neusner.

8. Smith, "Fences and Neighbors," 18. The contrast between Smith and Neusner is noted by Michael Satlow, "Accounting for 'Religions' in the Study of Religion," *JAAR* 74 (2006): 845.

9. Seth Schwartz, "How Many Judaisms," 221.

10. E. P. Sanders, *Judaism: Practice and Belief, 63 BCE–66 CE* (Philadelphia: Trinity Press International, 1992), 47–48.

11. Morton Smith, "The Dead Sea Sect in Relation to Ancient Judaism," *NTS* 7 (1960–61): 356.

12. James L. Crenshaw, *Old Testament Wisdom: An Introduction,* expanded ed. (Louisville, KY: Westminster John Knox, 1998), 21.

13. David M. Carr, "The Rise of Torah," in Gary N. Knoppers and Bernard M. Levinson, eds., *The Pentateuch as Torah: New Models for Understanding Its Promulgation and Acceptance* (Winona Lake, IN: Eisenbrauns, 2007), 43. See also Carr, *The Formation of the Hebrew Bible: A New Reconstruction* (New York: Oxford University Press, 2011), 403–31; Carr, *Writing on the Tablet of the Heart: Origins of Scripture and Literature* (New York: Oxford University Press, 2005), 111–73.

14. See my *Jewish Wisdom in the Hellenistic Age* (Louisville, KY: Westminster John Knox, 1997), 42–46.

15. Matthew J. Goff, *Discerning Wisdom: The Sapiential Literature of the Dead Sea Scrolls,* VTSup 116 (Leiden: Brill, 2007), 198–229.

16. Matthew J. Goff, *The Worldly and Heavenly Wisdom of 4QInstruction,* STDJ 50; (Leiden: Brill, 2003), 116–23; Lawrence H. Schiffman, "Halakhic Elements in the Sapiential Texts from Qumran," in John J. Collins, Gregory E. Sterling, and Ruth A. Clements, eds., *Sapiential Perspectives: Wisdom Literature in Light of the Dead Sea Scrolls,* STDJ 51 (Leiden: Brill, 2004), 89–100.

17. Bernd U. Schipper, "When Wisdom Is Not Enough! The Discourse on Wisdom and Torah and the Composition of the Book of Proverbs," in Bernd U. Schipper and D. Andrew Teeter, eds., *Wisdom and Torah,* JSJSup (Leiden: Brill 2013), 55–79, here 58. Compare already Michael Fishbane, "Torah and Tradition," in D.A. Knight, ed., *Tradition and Theology in the Old Testament* (Philadelphia: Fortress, 1977), 275–300, especially 284.

18. Schipper, "When Wisdom Is Not Enough!." 58–59.

19. Ibid., 60. Compare Schipper, *Hermeneutik der Tora: Studien zur Traditions-geschichte von Prov 2 und zur Komposition von Prov 1–9,* BZAW 432 (Berlin: de Gruyter, 2012), 297 (English summary); and compare also Scott L. Harris, *Proverbs 1–9: A Study of Inner-Biblical Interpretation* (Atlanta: Scholars Press, 1995).

20. Stuart Weeks, *Instruction and Imagery in Proverbs 1–9* (Oxford: Oxford University Press, 2007), 105.

21. Michael Fox, *Proverbs 1–9,* AB 18A (New York: Doubleday, 2000), 142–43.

22. Ibid., 79.

23. Moshe Weinfeld, *Deuteronomy and the Deuteronomic School* (Oxford: Oxford University Press, 1972; repr., Winona Lake, IN: Eisenbrauns, 1992), 244–81; Karin Finsterbusch, *Weisung für Israel: Studien zu religiösem Lehren und Lernen im Deuteronomium und in seinem Umfeld* (Tübingen: Mohr Siebeck, 2005).

24. As argued by Weeks, *Instruction and Imagery,* 104–5.

25. See Carolyn J. Sharp, *Irony and Meaning in the Hebrew Bible* (Bloomington, IN: Indiana University Press, 2009), 209–10; Thomas Krüger, *Qoheleth,* Hermeneia (Minneapolis: Fortress, 2004), 92. More generally, Krüger holds that "the main features of his view of the relationship of God and humankind seem, however, to be indebted to the essence of the Torah and more precisely to the so-called primal history in Genesis 1–11" (25).

26. Krüger, *Qoheleth,* 25; Bernard M. Levinson, *A More Perfect Torah: At the Intersection of Philology and Hermeneutics in Deuteronomy and the Temple Scroll,* Critical Studies in the Hebrew Bible 1 (Winona Lake, IN: Eisenbrauns, 2013), 54–61. Jennie Barbour, *The Story of Israel in the Book of Qohelet: Ecclesiastes as Cultural Memory* (Oxford: Oxford University Press, 2012), implausibly finds pervasive allusions to the history of Israel in Qoheleth.

27. Levinson, *A More Perfect Torah,* 56. Compare Thomas Krüger, "Die Rezeption der Tora aim Buch Kohelet," in Ludger Schwienhorst-Schönberger, ed., *Das Buch Kohelet: Studien zur Struktur, Geschichte, Rezeption und Theologie,* BZAW 254 (Berlin: De Gruyter, 1997), 303–25, reprinted in Krüger, *Kritische Weisheit: Studien zur weisheitlichen Traditionskritik im Alten Testament* (Zurich: Pano, 1997), 173–93 (quotation from p. 177).

28. Stuart Weeks, "'Fear God and Keep His Commandments': Could Qohelet Have Said This?," in Schipper and Teeter, *Wisdom and Torah,* 101–18.

29. *Pace* Sharp, *Irony and Meaning,* 196–220, who regards the epilogue as the true message of the book, and "Qoheleth" as an ironic persona. B. S. Childs, *Introduction to the Old Testament as Scripture* (Philadelphia: Fortress, 1981), 584, says that "the most obvious sign of canonical shaping appears in the epilogue."

30. Michael V. Fox, *A Time to Tear Down and a Time to Build Up: A Rereading Of Ecclesiastes* (Grand Rapids, MI: Eerdmans, 1999), 373–74.

31. This point is emphasized by Choon-Leong Seow, *Ecclesiastes,* AB 18C (New York: Doubleday, 1997), 395; Krüger, *Qoheleth,* 213.

32. Seow, *Ecclesiastes,* 395.

33. Weeks, "Fear God and Keep His Commandments," 112.

34. Gerald T. Sheppard, *Wisdom as a Hermeneutical Construct,* BZAW 151 (Berlin: De Gruyter, 1980), 127; Sheppard, "The Epilogue to Qoheleth as Theological Commentary," *CBQ* 39 (1977): 182–89.

35. Krüger, *Qoheleth,* 215.

36. Gabriele Boccaccini, *Beyond the Essene Hypothesis* (Grand Rapids, MI: Eerdmans, 1998), 12. For the antiquity of the earliest Enoch literature, see

already M.E. Stone, "The Book of Enoch and Judaism in the Third Century B.C.E.," *CBQ* 40 (1978): 479–92; Stone, *Scriptures, Sects, and Visions: A Profile of Judaism from Ezra to the Jewish Revolts* (Philadelphia: Fortress, 1980).

37. Boccaccini, *Beyond the Essene Hypothesis*. In this he builds on the work of his teacher, Paolo Sacchi, *Jewish Apocalyptic and Its History* (Sheffield: Sheffield Academic Press, 1997).

38. Gabriele Boccaccini, *Roots of Rabbinic Judaism: An Intellectual History from Ezekiel to Daniel* (Grand Rapids, MI: Eerdmans, 2002), 89, 99–103.

39. An independent formulation of "Enochic Judaism" as a paradigm of regularity and deviance can be found in David R. Jackson, *Enochic Judaism*, Library of Second Temple Studies 49 (London and New York: Continuum, 2004). Jackson distinguishes three "paradigm exemplars": the "Shemihazah exemplar," focusing on the union of angels with human women; the "Aza'el exemplar," focusing on improper revelation; and the "cosmic exemplar," focusing on the rebellion of angels who were in charge of cosmic phenomena related to the calendar.

40. See my essay "'Enochic Judaism' and the Sect of the Dead Sea Scrolls," in Gabriele Boccaccini and John J. Collins, eds., *The Early Enoch Literature*, JSJSup 121 (Leiden: Brill, 2007), 283–99; James C. VanderKam, "Mapping Second Temple Judaism," ibid., 1–20; VanderKam, "The Book of Enoch and the Dead Sea Scrolls," in Timothy H. Lim and John J. Collins, eds., *The Oxford Handbook of the Dead Sea Scrolls* (Oxford: Oxford University Press, 2010), 254–77.

41. See my essay "Pseudepigraphy and Group Formation in Second Temple Judaism," in Esther Chazon and Michael E. Stone, eds., *Pseudepigraphic Perspectives: The Apocrypha and Pseudepigrapha in Light of the Dead Sea Scrolls*, STDJ 31 (Leiden: Brill, 1999), 44–48.

42. See the review of the debate by Kelley Coblentz Bautch, *A Study of the Geography of 1 Enoch 17–19: 'No One Has Seen What I Have Seen,'* JSJSup 81 (Leiden: Brill, 2003), 289–99.

43. George W.E. Nickelsburg, "Enochic Wisdom: An Alternative to the Mosaic Torah?," in Jodi Magness and Seymour Gitin, eds., *Hesed Ve-Emet: Studies in Honor of Ernest S. Frerichs*, BJS 320 (Atlanta: Scholars Press, 1998), 123–32; Nickelsburg, *1 Enoch 1*, Hermeneia (Minneapolis: Fortress, 2001), 50–56.

44. E.P. Sanders, *Paul and Palestinian Judaism* (Philadelphia: Fortress, 1977), 346–62.

45. Mark Elliott, *The Survivors of Israel: A Reconsideration of the Theology of Pre-Christian Judaism* (Grand Rapids, MI: Eerdmans, 2000), 330–32, 529–33; Elliott, "Covenant and Cosmology in the *Book of the Watchers* and the Astro-

nomical Book," in Gabriele Boccaccini, ed., *The Origins of Enochic Judaism* = *Henoch* 24.1–2 (2002): 23–38.

46. See James C. VanderKam, "The Interpretation of Genesis in *1 Enoch*," in Peter W. Flint, ed., *The Bible at Qumran: Text, Shape, and Interpretation* (Grand Rapids, MI: Eerdmans, 2001), 129–48; VanderKam, "Biblical Interpretation in *1 Enoch* and *Jubilees*," in James H. Charlesworth and Craig A. Evans, eds., *The Pseudepigrapha and Early Biblical Interpretation*, JSPSup 14 (Sheffield: Sheffield Academic Press, 1993), 96–125; P. S. Alexander, "The Enochic Literature and the Bible: Intertextuality and Its Implications," in E. D. Herbert and E. Tov, eds., *The Bible as Book: The Hebrew Bible and the Judaean Desert Discoveries* (London: The British Library, 2002), 57–69.

47. J. T. Milik, *The Books of Enoch: Aramaic Fragments from Qumrân Cave Four* (Oxford: Clarendon, 1976), 31. Nickelsburg, *1 Enoch 1*, 176–77, shows that the Enochic text follows Genesis 6 quite closely.

48. Nickelsburg, *1 Enoch 1*, 30.

49. 1 Enoch 26–27; Nickelsburg, *1 Enoch 1*, 317–19.

50. Lars Hartman, *Asking for a Meaning: A Study of 1 Enoch 1–5*, CB NT series 12 (Lund: Gleerup, 1979).

51. Nickelsburg, *1 Enoch 1*, 165.

52. Helge S. Kvanvig, *Primeval History: Babylonian, Biblical, and Enochic; An Intertextual Reading*, JSJSup 149 (Leiden: Brill, 2011), 519–20.

53. James L. Kugel, *Traditions of the Bible* (Cambridge, MA: Harvard University Press, 1998), 180; compare Andreas Bedenbender, *Der Gott der Welt tritt auf den Sinai*, ANTZ 8 (Berlin: Institut Kirche und Judentum, 2000), 157–63.

54. On 1 Enoch 22, see M.-T. Wacker, *Weltordnung und Gericht: Studien zu 1 Henoch 22* (Würzburg: Echter, 1982). Coblentz Bautch, *A Study of the Geography*, 297, concludes that shared concerns about disobedience and illicit relationships do not necessarily demonstrate points of contact between these chapters and the Mosaic Torah.

55. Compare the reflections of VanderKam, "The Interpretation of Genesis in *1 Enoch*," 142–43. For reflections on the relation between Jubilees and 1 Enoch, see Gabriele Boccaccini and Giovanni Ibba, eds., *Enoch and the Mosaic Torah: The Evidence of Jubilees* (Grand Rapids, MI: Eerdmans, 2009). The argument of Paul Heger, *1 Enoch*—Complementary or Alternative to Mosaic Torah?," *JSJ* 41 (2010): 29–62, esp. 37–38, that Jubilees was admittedly written after Moses does not negate the significance of its retrojection of Mosaic law into the patriarchal period.

56. Nickelsburg, "Enochic Wisdom," 125.

57. Ibid., 129.

58. So again Heger, "*1 Enoch*"; Heger, *Challenges to Conventional Opinions on Qumran and Enoch Issues*, STDJ 100 (Leiden: Brill, 2012), 163–204.

59. Martha Himmelfarb, "Temple and Priests in the *Book of the Watchers*, the *Animal Apocalypse*, and the *Apocalypse of Weeks*," in Boccaccini and Collins, *The Early Enoch Literature*, 219–35, specifically 220.

60. Ibid., 230–31.

61. David Suter, "Fallen Angel, Fallen Priest: The Problem of Family Purity in *1 Enoch 6–16*," *HUCA* 50 (1979): 115–35; see also Suter, "Revisiting 'Fallen Angel, Fallen Priest,'" *Henoch* 24 (2002): 137–42.

62. Himmelfarb, "Temple and Priests," 223.

63. Ibid., 224. She bases this on the criticism of priestly marriages in Aramaic Levi and 4QMMT, which are very different documents.

64. Himmelfarb, "Temple and Priests," 222, 235. Cf. 1 Enoch 15:2–3.

65. We must allow for the possibility that the criticism of the Second Temple in the Animal Apocalypse was based on the events in the years leading up to the Maccabean revolt, rather than on long-standing issues.

66. Andreas Bedenbender, "The Place of the Torah in the Early Enoch Literature," in Boccaccini and Collins, *The Early Enoch Literature*, 65–79. See further Bedenbender, *Der Gott der Welt*, 208–11.

67. Bedenbender, *Der Gott der Welt*, 215.

68. See now the comprehensive commentary by George W. E. Nickelsburg and James C. VanderKam, *1 Enoch 2*, Hermeneia (Minneapolis: Fortress, 2012). They date the text around the turn of the era (pp. 62–63).

69. Nickelsburg and VanderKam, *1 Enoch 2*, 46–47

70. Michael V. Fox, *Character and Ideology in the Book of Esther* (Columbia: University of South Carolina, 1991; repr., Grand Rapids, MI: Eerdmans, 2001), 240. See Fox's discussion of the various attempts to find God in the book of Esther. He concludes: "If God is present in Esther he is certainly well-hidden" (241).

71. Jon D. Levenson, *Esther*, OTL (Louisville, KY: Westminster John Knox, 1997), 17.

72. Bernard W. Anderson, "The Place of the Book of Esther in the Christian Bible," *JR* 30 (1950): 40.

73. Timothy K. Beal, *Esther*, in Todd Linafelt, *Ruth*, and Timothy Beal, *Esther*, Berit Olam (Collegeville, MN: Liturgical Press, 1999), xx.

74. Arndt Meinhold, "Die Gattung der Josephgeschichte und des Estherbuches: Diasporanovelle I & II," *ZAW* 87 (1975): 306–24; 88 (1976): 79–93.

75. See my commentary *Daniel: A Commentary on the Book of Daniel,* Hermeneia (Minneapolis: Fortress, 1993), 265.

76. So Daniel Smith-Christopher, "Daniel," in NIB 7 (Nashville: Abingdon, 1996), 40–42.

77. R. H. Charles, *A Critical and Exegetical Comentary on the Book of Daniel* (Oxford: Clarendon, 1929), 129, speculated that Daniel was concerned that the food might have been sacrificed to idols.

78. Carol Newsom, *Daniel,* OTL (Louisville, KY: Westminster John Knox, 2014), 194.

79. See my essay "Nebuchadnezzar and the Kingdom of God: Deferred Eschatology in the Jewish Diaspora," in my book *Seers, Sibyls, and Sages in Hellenistic-Roman Judaism,* JSJSup 54 (Leiden: Brill, 1997), 131–37.

CHAPTER 4. TORAH AS NARRATIVE AND WISDOM

1. James A. Sanders, *Torah and Canon,* 2nd ed. (Eugene, OR: Cascade, 2005), 1–33. David Lambert, "How the 'Torah of Moses' Became Revelation: An Early Apocalyptic Theory of Pentateuchal Origins," *JSJ* 47 (2016): 22–54, points out that the narratives are not said to be revealed to Moses before the book of Jubilees in the second century B.C.E.

2. Thomas Römer, "Conflicting Models of Identity and the Publication of the Torah in the Persian Period," in R. Albertz and J. Wöhrle, eds., *Between Cooperation and Hostility: Multiple Identities in Ancient Judaism and the Interaction with Foreign Powers,* JAJ Sup 11 (Göttingen: Vandenhoeck & Ruprecht, 2013), 33–51, here 41. Compare Konrad Schmid, *The Old Testament: A Literary History* (Minneapolis: Fortress, 2012), 79–85; Schmid, *Genesis and the Moses Story: Israel's Dual Origins in the Hebrew Bible* (Winona Lake, IN: Eisenbrauns, 2010).

3. For a recent reconstruction of the formation of the Priestly strand, including the Holiness Code, see Christophe Nihan, *From Priestly Torah to Pentateuch: A Study of the Composition of the Book of Leviticus,* FAT 2/25 (Tübingen: Mohr Siebeck, 2007).

4. Römer, "Conflicting Models of Identity," 41.

5. Geza Vermes, *Scripture and Tradition in Judaism: Haggadic Studies,* SPB 4 (1961; Leiden: Brill, 1973), 67–126. See Philip S. Alexander, "Retelling the Old Testament," in D. A. Carson and H. G. M. Williamson, eds., *It is Written: Scripture Citing Scripture* (Cambridge: Cambridge University Press, 1988), 99–121; Moshe Bernstein, "'Rewritten Bible:' A Generic Category Which Has Outlived Its Usefulness?," *Textus* 22 (2005): 169–96; Sidnie White

Crawford, *Rewriting Scripture in Second Temple Times* (Grand Rapids, MI: Eerdmans, 2008).

6. See, e.g., Anders Klostergaard Petersen, "Rewritten Bible as a Borderline Phenomenon—Genre, Textual Strategy, or Canonical Anachronism?," in Anthony Hilhorst, Émile Puech, and Eibert Tigchelaar, eds., *Flores Florentino: Dead Sea Scrolls and Other Early Jewish Studies in Honour of Florentino García Martínez*, STDJ 122 (Leiden: Brill, 2007), 284–306. Jonathan G. Campbell, "'Rewritten Bible' and 'Parabiblical Texts': A Terminological and Ideological Critique," in Campbell et al., eds., *New Directions in Qumran Studies: Proceedings of the Bristol Colloquium on the Dead Sea Scrolls, 8–10 September 2003* (London: T & T Clark, 2005), 43–68, also objects to "rewritten scriptures." He suggests terminology along the lines of "scripture" and "parascripture."

7. So White Crawford, *Rewriting Scripture*, 14.

8. Molly M. Zahn, *Rethinking Rewritten Scripture: Composition and Exegesis in the 4QReworked Pentateuch Manuscripts*, STDJ 95 (Leiden: Brill, 2011).

9. See Alexander, "Retelling the Old Testament," 99–121; George J. Brooke, "Rewritten Bible," in L. H. Schiffman and J. C. VanderKam, eds., *The Encyclopedia of the Dead Sea Scrolls* (New York: Oxford University Press, 2000), 2:777–81; Brooke, "The Rewritten Law, Prophets, and Psalms: Issues for Understanding the Text of the Bible," in E. D. Herbert and Emanuel Tov, eds., *The Bible as Book: The Hebrew Bible and the Judaean Desert Discoveries* (London: British Library, 2002), 31–40; Bernstein, "'Rewritten Bible,'" 169–96; Antti Laato and Jacques van Ruiten, eds., *Rewritten Bible Reconsidered* (Winona Lake, IN: Eisenbrauns, 2008).

10. Alexander, "Retelling the Old Testament," 99–121, argues that the texts so classified by Vermes—Jubilees, the Genesis Apocryphon, the *Antiquities* of Josephus, and the *Biblical Antiquities* of Pseudo-Philo—do constitute a literary genre. These are all narrative texts, and do not include such compositions as the Temple Scroll.

11. Compare Brooke, "'Rewritten Bible,'" 780: "Rewritten Bible texts come in almost as many genres as can be found in the biblical books themselves."

12. See further John J. Collins, *Between Athens and Jerusalem: Jewish Identity in the Hellenistic Diaspora*, 2nd ed. (Grand Rapids, MI: Eerdmans, 2000), 29–63; Martin Goodman, "Jewish Literature Composed in Greek," in Geza Vermes, Fergus Millar, and Martin Goodman, eds., *The History of the Jewish People in the Age of Jesus Christ* (Edinburgh: Clark, 1986), 3.1:509–66.

13. See Timothy H. Lim, *The Formation of the Jewish Canon*, AYBRL (New Haven, CT: Yale University Press, 2013).

14. Robert Alter, *Canon and Authority: Modern Writing and the Authority of Scripture* (New Haven, CT: Yale University Press, 2000), 5.

15. Katell Berthelot and Daniel Stökl Ben Ezra, "Aramaica Qumranica: Introduction," in Berthelot and Stökl Ben Ezra, eds., *Aramaica Qumranica: Proceedings of the Conference on the Aramaic Texts from Qumran in Aix-en-Provence 30 June–2 July 2008*, STDJ 94 (Leiden: Brill, 2010), 1.

16. Ibid. On the visionary texts, see Andrew B. Perrin, *The Dynamics of Dream-Vision Revelation in the Aramaic Dead Sea Scrolls*, JAJSup (Göttingen: Vandenhoeck & Ruprecht, 2015).

17. Katell Berthelot, "References to Biblical Texts in the Aramaic Texts from Qumran," in Berthelot and Stökl Ben Ezra, *Aramaica Qumranica*, 183–98, here 183. Her article is devoted to the allusions in other books.

18. See Daniel A. Machiela, *The Dead Sea Genesis Apocryphon: A New Text and Translation with Introduction and Special Treatment of Columns 13–17*, STDJ 79 (Leiden: Brill, 2009).

19. Esther Eshel, "*Genesis Apocryphon*," in John J. Collins and Daniel C. Harlow, eds., *The Eerdmans Dictionary of Early Judaism* (Grand Rapids, MI: Eerdmans, 2010), 664–67.

20. The Arabic tradition is obviously much later. Early examples of *waṣf* style poetry can be found in the Song of Songs. See Marcia Falk, *Love Lyrics from the Bible: A Translation and Literary Study of the Song of Songs* (Sheffield: Almond, 1982), 80–87.

21. Moshe J. Bernstein, "The Genre(s) of the *Genesis Apocryphon*," in Berthelot and Stökl Ben Ezra, *Aramaica Qumranica*, 317–38.

22. He borrows the term "parabiblical" from White Crawford, *Rewriting Scripture*, 14. She does not place the Genesis Apocryphon in this category, but rather regards it as peripherally within the bounds of "rewritten scripture."

23. Bernstein, "The Genre(s) of the *Genesis Apocryphon*," 329. For an attempt to relate the techniques of the Apocryphon to those of the Targumim, see Thierry Legrand, "Exégèses targumiques et techniques de réécriture dans *L'Apocryphe de la Genèse* (1QAPGen AR)," in Berthelot and Stökl Ben Ezra, *Aramaica Qumranica*, 225–52. Compare M.J. Bernstein, "Re-arrangement, Anticipation, and Harmonization as Exegetical Features in the Genesis Apocryphon," *DSD* 3 (1996): 37–57. On the use of the Torah in the Genesis Apocryphon, see also Akio Moriya, "The Pentateuch Reflected in the Aramaic Documents of the Dead Sea Scrolls," in Akiyo Moriya and Gohei Hata, eds., *Pentateuchal Traditions in the Late Second Temple Period*, JSJSup 158 (Leiden: Brill, 2012), 201–12.

24. Machiela, *The Dead Sea Genesis Apocryphon*, 134.

25. Henryk Drawnel, *An Aramaic Wisdom Text from Qumran: A New Interpretation of the Levi Document*, JSJSup 86 (Leiden: Brill, 2004); Jonas C. Greenfield, Michael E. Stone, and Esther Eshel, *The Aramaic Levi Document: Edition, Translation, Commentary*, SVTP 19 (Leiden: Brill, 2004). The official publication of the Qumran fragments is by M.E. Stone and J.C. Greenfield, "Aramaic Levi Document," in George Brooke et al., *Qumran Cave 4, XVII: Parabiblical Texts*, pt. 3, DJD 22 (Oxford: Clarendon, 1996), 1–72.

26. Greenfield, Stone, and Eshel, *The Aramaic Levi Document*, 1–6.

27. Drawnel, *An Aramaic Wisdom Text*, 87; Greenfield, Stone, and Eshel, *The Aramaic Levi Document*, 27–28.

28. Drawnel, *An Aramaic Wisdom Text*, 88.

29. Bodleian MS. Drawnel, *An Aramaic Wisdom Text*, 118–21; Greenfield, Stone, and Eshel, *The Aramaic Levi Document*, 75.

30. R.A. Kugler, "Whose Scripture? Whose Community? Reflections on the Dead Sea Scrolls Then and Now, by Way of Aramaic Levi," *DSD* 15 (2008): 5–23, suggests that the Aramaic Levi Document underwent a sectarian redaction. I am not convinced that this was necessarily so.

31. James Kugel, "Which Is Older, *Jubilees* or the *Genesis Apocryphon?* An Exegetical Approach," in Adolfo D. Roitman, Lawrence H. Schiffman, and Shani Tzoref, eds., *The Dead Sea Scrolls and Contemporary Culture*, STDJ 93 (Leiden: Brill, 2011), 257–94. Kugel argues for the priority of Jubilees. Most scholars regard the Aramaic Levi Document as older, e.g., M.E. Stone, "Aramaic Levi Document," in Collins and Harlow, *The Eerdmans Dictionary of Early Judaism*, 362–64. Like Jubilees and 1 Enoch, the Aramaic Levi Document presupposes a 364-day calendar.

32. Drawnel, *An Aramaic Wisdom Text*, 89.

33. Ibid., 94.

34. E.J. Bickerman, "A Seleucid Proclamation Concerning the Temple in Jerusalem," in Bickerman, *Studies in Jewish and Christian History* (Leiden: Brill, 2011), 1:357–75, here 363.

35. Jon D. Levenson, "The Sources of Torah: Psalm 119 and the Modes of Revelation in Second Temple Judaism," in P.D. Miller et al., eds., *Ancient Israelite Religion: Essays in Honor of Frank Moore Cross* (Philadelphia: Fortress, 1987), 566.

36. Kent Aaron Reynolds, *Torah as Teacher: The Exemplary Torah Student in Psalm 119*, VTSup 137 (Leiden: Brill, 2010), 109–21; Karen Finsterbusch, "Yahweh's Torah and the Praying 'I' in Psalm 119," in Bernd U. Schipper and Andrew Teeter, eds., *Wisdom and Torah*, JSJSup (Leiden: Brill, 2013), 123–28.

37. Levenson, "The Sources of Torah," 565.

38. Reynolds, *Torah as Teacher*, 128, denies that it refers to unmediated revelation.

39. Reynolds, *Torah*, 183.

40. Anja Klein, "Half Way between Psalm 119 and Ben Sira: Wisdom and Torah in Psalm 19," in Schipper and Teeter, *Wisdom and Torah*, 148–49; compare Alexandra Grund, *"Die Himmel erzählen die Ehre Gottes": Psalm 19 im Kontext der nach-exilischen Toraweisheit*, WMANT 103 (Neukirchen-Vluyn: Neukirchener Verlag, 2004), 235–40.

41. Klein, "Half Way between Psalm 119 and Ben Sira," 149.

42. For the literature, see Benjamin G. Wright, "Torah and Sapiential Pedagogy in the Book of Ben Sira," in Schipper and Teeter, *Wisdom and Torah*, 157–86, esp. 157–58.

43. Klein, "Half Way between Psalm 119 and Ben Sira," 152–53. She also says that in Ben Sira the balance has shifted in favor of wisdom, but this seems hard to reconcile with the view that the law is the enactment of wisdom.

44. Wright, "Torah and Sapiential Pedagogy," 159.

45. Ibid., 169.

46. See Greg Schmidt Goering, *Wisdom's Root Revealed: Ben Sira and the Election of Israel*, JSJSup 139 (Leiden: Brill, 2009).

47. Wright, "Torah and Sapiential Pedagogy," 166.

48. The fullest and best introduction to the wisdom literature of the Scrolls is that of Matthew J. Goff, *Discerning Wisdom: The Sapiential Literature of the Dead Sea Scrolls*, VTSup 116 (Leiden: Brill, 2007).

49. Armin Lange, *Weisheit und Prädestination in den Textfunden von Qumran*, STDJ 18 (Leiden: Brill, 1995), 121–70, 195–32. Angela Kim Harkins, "The Community Hymns Classification: A Proposal for Further Differentiation," *DSD* 15 (2008): 121–54, suggests that the community hymns among the Hodayot may come from a nonsectarian context.

50. See, e.g., Lawrence H. Schiffman, "Halakic Elements in the Sapiential Texts from Qumran," in John J. Collins, Gregory E. Sterling, and Ruth A. Clements, eds., *Sapiential Perspectives: Wisdom Literature in Light of the Dead Sea Scrolls*, STDJ 51 (Leiden: Brill, 2004), 89–100.

51. John Strugnell and Daniel J. Harrington, *Qumran Cave 4, XXIV: Sapiential Texts*, pt. 2: *4QInstruction (Musar leMevin)*, DJD 34 (Oxford: Clarendon, 1999), 151–66. For more detailed analysis, see J.J. Collins, "In the Likeness of the Holy Ones: The Creation of Humankind in a Wisdom Text from Qumran," in D. W. Parry and E. Ulrich, eds., *The Provo International Conference on the Dead Sea Scrolls* (Leiden: Brill, 1999), 609–18; Collins, "The Interpretation of Genesis in

the Dead Sea Scrolls," in Moriya and Hata, *Pentateuchal Traditions in the Late Second Temple Period*, 156–75, esp. 166–73; M.J. Goff, *The Worldly and Heavenly Wisdom of 4Qinstruction*, STDJ 50 (Leiden: Brill, 2003), 83–126.

52. So Lange, *Weisheit und Prädestination*, 87; J. Frey, "Flesh and Spirit in the Palestinian Jewish Sapiential Tradition and in the Qumran Texts," in C. Hempel, A. Lange, and H. Lichtenberger, eds., *The Wisdom Texts from Qumran and the Development of Sapiential Thought*, BETL 159 (Leuven: Peeters, 2002), 367–404, esp. 393.

53. John J. Collins, *Apocalypticism in the Dead Sea Scrolls* (London: Routledge, 1997), 41–43; Collins, *The Dead Sea Scrolls: A Biography* (Princeton, NJ: Princeton University Press, 2013), 154–57; M. Philonenko, "La doctrine qoumrânienne de deux esprits," in G. Widengren, A. Hultgård, and M. Philonenko, *Apocalyptique iranienne et dualisme qoumrânien* (Paris: Maisonneuve, 1995), 163–211.

54. Goff, *Discerning Wisdom*, 198–29.

55. William Tooman, "Wisdom and Torah at Qumran," in Schipper and Teeter, *Wisdom and Torah*, 211, says that the Torah is the antecedent of these phrases, but in fact both wisdom and Torah are antecedents. See Elisa Uusimaki, "Turning Proverbs towards Torah: 4Q525 in the Context of Late Second Temple Wisdom Literature" (PhD diss., University of Helsinki, 2013), 244; Uusimaki's book is now published as STDJ 117 (Leiden: Brill, 2016).

56. Tooman, "Wisdom and Torah at Qumran," 212.

57. G.J. Brooke, "Biblical Interpretation in the Wisdom Texts from Qumran," in Hempel, Lange, and Lichtenberger, *The Wisdom Texts from Qumran*, 201–20, here 209.

58. Uusimaki, "Turning Proverbs," 247.

59. Carol Newsom, *The Self as Symbolic Space*, STDJ 52 (Leiden: Brill, 2004), 10–11.

60. Hindy Najman, "Torah and Tradition," in Collins and Harlow, *The Eerdmans Dictionary of Early Judaism*, 1316.

61. Goff, *Discerning Wisdom*, 122–45.

62. Tooman, "Wisdom and Torah at Qumran," 216.

63. Ibid.

64. Ibid.

65. See my essay "The Judaism of the Book of Tobit," in Géza G. Xeravits and József Zsengellér, *The Book of Tobit: Text, Tradition, and Theology*, JSJSup 98 (Leiden: Brill, 2005), 24–40. More complex redactional analyses have been proposed by Paul Deselaers, *Das Buch Tobit: Studien zu seiner Entstehung, Komposition und Theologie*, OBO 32 (Göttingen: Vandenhoeck & Ruprecht, 1982);

and Merten Rabenau, *Studien zum Buch Tobit*, BZAW 220 (Berlin: De Gruyter, 1994).

66. See Manfred Oeming, "Jewish Identity in the Eastern Diaspora," in Oded Lipschits, Gary N. Knoppers, and Manfred Oeming, eds., *Judah and the Judeans in the Achaemenid Period: Negotiating Identity in an International Context* (Winona Lake, IN: Eisenbrauns, 2011), 541–61, who speaks of "the harsh separation between Jews and non-Jews, especially with the central law of endogamy" (557).

67. See Joseph A. Fitzmyer, *Tobit*, CEJL (Berlin: De Gruyter, 2003), 234. The expression "according to the law of Moses" occurs in marriage documents from the Judean desert, in the early second century C.E.

68. See further J. Gamberoni, "Das 'Gesetz des Mose' im Buch Tobias," in G. Braulik, ed., *Studien zum Pentateuch: Walter Kornfeld zum 60. Geburtstag* (Freiburg: Herder, 1977), 227–42.

### CHAPTER 5. TORAH AS LAW

1. 1 Macc 2:45–46. See Eyal Regev, *The Hasmoneans: Ideology, Archaeology, Identity*, JAJSup 10 (Göttingen: Vandenhoeck & Ruprecht, 2013), 17.

2. *Ant.* 13.257–58; translated passages from this work by Josephus are taken from Josephus, *Jewish Antiquities. Books 12–14*, trans. Ralph Marcus, Loeb Classical Library (1933; repr., Cambridge, MA: Harvard University Press, 1976).

3. *Ant.* 13.318. Strabo (16.2.34), in contrast, portrays the incorporation of the Idumaeans and Itureans into Judea as voluntary. See the discussion by S.J.D. Cohen, *The Beginnings of Jewishness* (Berkeley: University of California Press, 1999), 112–13.

4. *Ant.* 13.397.

5. Cohen, *The Beginnings of Jewishness*, 136.

6. Ibid.

7. Compare Bob Becking, "Dimensions of Identity in 1 Macabees," in Becking, *Ezra, Nehemiah, and the Construction of Early Jewish Identity*, FAT 80 (Tübingen: Mohr Siebeck, 2011), 143–54: "The [First] Book of Maccabees not only lived by tradition, it also shaped tradition."

8. E.M. Meyers and M.A. Chancey, *Alexander to Constantine: Archaeology of the Land of the Bible*, AYBRL (New Haven, CT: Yale University Press, 2012), 34–35.

9. See Eric M. Meyers, "Sanders's 'Common Judaism' and the Common Judaism of Material Culture," in Fabian Udoh, with Susannah Heschel, Mark Chancey, and Gregory Tatum, eds., *Redefining First-Century Jewish and Christian Identities: Essays in Honor of Ed Parish Sanders* (Notre Dame, IN: University of

Notre Dame, 2008), 153–74, esp. 161–63, on the identification of plastered stepped pools as ritual baths. See also Stuart Miller, "Introduction: Ritual Baths and Ritual Purity, the Last Fifty Years," in Miller, *At the Intersection of Texts and Material Finds: Stepped Pools, Stone Vessels, and Ritual Purity among the Jews of Roman Galilee,* JAJSup 16 (Göttingen: Vandenhoeck & Ruprecht, 2015), 17–31. Miller cautions against the tendency to assume that pools of the Hasmonean period conformed to rabbinic norms.

10. Mark A. Chancey, "Stone Vessels," in John J. Collins and Daniel C. Harlow, eds., *The Eerdmans Dictionary of Early Judaism* (Grand Rapids, MI: Eerdmans, 2010), 1256.

11. Regev, *The Hasmoneans,* 17. See also Stuart S. Miller, "Stepped Pools, Stone Vessels, and Other Markers of 'Complex Common Judaism,'" *JSJ* 41 (2010): 214–43, esp. 222–23.

12. See especially Martha Himmelfarb, *A Kingdom of Priests: Ancestry and Merit in Ancient Judaism* (Philadelphia: University of Pennsylvania Press, 2005), 53–84 on Jubilees, and 92–98 on the Temple Scroll.

13. Sidnie White Crawford, *The Temple Scroll and Related Texts* (Sheffield: Sheffield Academic Press, 2000), 22.

14. Lawrence H. Schiffman, *Reclaiming the Dead Sea Scrolls: The History of Judaism, The Background of Christianity, The Lost Library of Qumran* (Philadelphia and Jerusalem: The Jewish Publication Society, 1994), 260; Schiffman, *The Courtyards of the House of the Lord: Studies on the Temple Scroll* (Leiden: Brill, 2008), xxvi.

15. Sidnie White Crawford, *Rewriting Scripture in Second Temple Times* (Grand Rapids, MI: Eerdmans, 2008), 39–59.

16. Lawrence H. Schiffman, "The *Temple Scroll* and the Halakhic Pseudepigrapha of the Second Temple Period," in Esther Chazon and Michael E. Stone, eds., *Pseudepigraphic Perspectives: The Apocrypha and Pseudepigrapha in Light of the Dead Sea Scrolls,* STDJ 31 (Leiden: Brill, 1999), 121–31.

17. Hindy Najman, *Seconding Sinai: The Development of Mosaic Discourse in Second Temple Judaism,* JSJSup 77 (Leiden: Brill, 2004), 68.

18. White Crawford, *Rewriting Scripture,* 87.

19. Hartmut Stegemann, *The Library of Qumran: On the Essenes, Qumran, John the Baptist, and Jesus* (Grand Rapids, MI: Eerdmans, 1998), 96.

20. White Crawford, *The Temple Scroll and Related Texts,* 12–16.

21. James H. Charlesworth, "*Temple Scroll*-Like Document (11Q21)," in Lawrence H. Schiffman, Andrew D. Gross, and Michael C. Rand, *Temple Scroll and Related Documents,* The Dead Sea Scrolls: Hebrew, Aramaic, and Greek Texts

with English Translations 7 (Tübingen: Mohr Siebeck; Louisville, KY: Westminster John Knox, 2011), 227.

22. Charlesworth, "*Temple Scroll* Source or Divergent Copy (4Q365a)," in Schiffman, Gross, and Rand, *Temple Scroll and Related Documents*, 235.

23. Charlesworth, "*Temple Scroll* Source or Earlier Edition (4Q524)," in Schiffman, Gross, and Rand, *Temple Scroll and Related Documents*, 247.

24. Émile Puech, *Qumrân Grotte 4, XVIII: Textes hébreux (4Q521-528, 4Q576-4Q579)*, DJD 25 (Oxford: Clarendon, 1998), 87.

25. So Lawrence H. Schiffman, "Temple Scroll, 11Q19 (11QTª)," in Schiffman, Gross, and Rand, *Temple Scroll and Related Documents*, 4.

26. Florentino García Martínez, "Temple Scroll," in Lawrence H. Schiffman and James C. VanderKam, eds., *Encyclopedia of the Dead Sea Scrolls* (New York: Oxford University Press, 2000), 2:931.

27. Ibid.

28. Schiffman, "Temple Scroll," 5.

29. See my discussion in *Beyond the Qumran Community: The Sectarian Movement of the Dead Sea Scrolls* (Grand Rapids, MI: Eerdmans, 2010), 88–121.

30. James C. VanderKam, *Textual and Historical Studies on the Book of Jubilees*, HSM 14 (Missoula, MT: Scholars Press, 1977), 207–85.

31. Fifteeen fragmentary Hebrew manuscripts of Jubilees are found in the Dead Sea Scrolls. See James C. VanderKam and J.T. Milik, "Jubilees," in H. Attridge et al., *Qumran Cave 4, VIII: Parabiblical Texts*, DJD 12 (Oxford Clarendon, 1994), 1–185.

32. G.W.E. Nickelsburg, "The Bible Rewritten and Expanded," in Michael E. Stone, ed., *Jewish Writings of the Second Temple Period*, CRINT 2/2 (Philadelphia: Fortress, 1984), 89–156, here 103.

33. Menahem Kister, "Concerning the History of the Essenes: A Study of the *Animal Apocalypse*, the *Book of Jubilees*, and the Damascus Covenant," *Tarbiz* 56 (1986): 1–18 (Heb.). Cf. Michael Segal, *The Book of Jubilees: Rewritten Bible, Redaction, Ideology, and Theology*, JSJSup 117 (Leiden: Brill, 2007), 35–41.

34. Doron Mendels, *The Land of Israel as a Political Concept in Hasmonean Literature* (Tübingen: Mohr Siebeck, 1987), 80.

35. See Robert Doran, "The Non-dating of Jubilees: *Jub* 34–38; 23:14–31 in Narrative Context," *JSJ* 20 (1989): 1–11.

36. Segal, *The Book of Jubilees*, 317–22; James L. Kugel, "The Interpolations in the Book of Jubilees," *RevQ* 24 (2009): 215–72; Kugel, *A Walk through Jubilees: Studies in the Book of Jubilees and the World of Its Creation*, JSJSup 156 (Leiden: Brill, 2012), 11–16. The unity of the composition is defended by James

C. VanderKam, "Moses Trumping Moses: Making the Book of *Jubilees*," in Sarianna Metso, Hindy Najman, and Eileen Schuller, *The Dead Sea Scrolls: Transmission of Traditions and Production of Texts*, STDJ 92 (Leiden: Brill, 2010), 25–44.

37. See James C. VanderKam, "The *Temple Scroll* and the Book of *Jubilees*," in George J. Brooke, ed., *Temple Scroll Studies*, JSPSup 7 (Sheffield: Sheffield Academic Press, 1989), 211–36; Lawrence H. Schiffman, "The Book of *Jubilees* and the *Temple Scroll*," in G. Boccaccini and G. Ibba, eds., *Enoch and the Mosaic Torah: The Evidence of Jubilees* (Grand Rapids, MI: Eerdmans, 2009), 99–115.

38. VanderKam, "Moses Trumping Moses," 25–44.

39. See my essay "The Genre of the Book of *Jubilees*," in Eric F. Mason, Kelley Coblentz Bautch, Angela Kim Harkins, and Daniel A. Machiela, eds., *A Teacher for All Generations: Essays in Honor of James C. VanderKam*, JSJSup 153/2 (Leiden: Brill, 2012), 737–55. On Jubilees as an apocalypse, see further Lambert, "How the 'Torah of Moses' Became Revelation: An Early Apocalyptic Theory of Pentateuchal Origins," *JSJ* 47 (2016): 42–47.

40. Hindy Najman, "Interpretation as Primordial Writing: *Jubilees* and Its Authority Conferring Strategies," in Najman, *Past Renewals: Interpretative Authority, Renewed Revelation, and the Quest for Perfection in Jewish Antiquity*, JSJSup 53 (Leiden: Brill, 2010), 39–71. This article was originally published in *JSJ* 30 (1999): 379–410. See also Martha Himmelfarb, "Torah, Testimony, and Heavenly Tablets: The Claim to Authority in the Book of *Jubilees*," in Benjamin G. Wright, ed., *A Multiform Heritage: Studies on Early Judaism and Christianity in Honor of Robert A. Kraft* (Atlanta: Scholars Press, 1999), 22–28. On the heavenly tablets, see Florentino García Martínez, "The Heavenly Tablets in the Book of *Jubilees*," in Matthias Albani, Jörg Frey, and Armin Lange, eds., *Studies in the Book of Jubilees* (Tübingen: Mohr Siebeck, 1997), 243–60.

41. VanderKam, "Moses Trumping Moses," 42.

42. Lambert, "How the 'Torah of Moses' Became Revelation," 33–35.

43. Himmelfarb, *A Kingdom of Priests*, 61–63, argues that Jubilees was especially drawn to the Holiness Code in Leviticus, while not distinguishing it from the rest of the Torah.

44. See Isaac W. Oliver, "Forming Jewish Identity by Formulating Legislation for Gentiles," *JAJ* 4 (2013): 105–32, esp. 108–15.

45. Segal, *The Book of Jubilees*, 317–19, argues that the halakic passages belong to a redactional layer.

46. Himmelfarb, *A Kingdom of Priests*, 66.

47. Himmelfarb, *A Kingdom of Priests*, 70, on the reasoning behind the claim that giving a daughter in marriage to a foreigner is equivalent to giving her to Molech.

48. Christine Hayes, *Gentile Impurities and Jewish Identities* (Oxford: Oxford University Press, 2002), 79.

49. Ibid., 75.

50. James Kugel, "The Holiness of Israel and the Land in Second Temple Times," in Michael V. Fox et al., eds., *Texts, Temples, and Traditions: A Tribute to Menahem Haran* (Winona Lake, IN: Eisenbrauns, 1996), 21–32, here 25.

51. See Eberhard Schwartz, *Identität durch Abgrenzung: Abgrenzungsprozesse im Israel im 2. vorchristlichen Jahrhundert und ihre traditionsgeschichtlichen Voraussetzungen; Zugleich ein Beitrag zur Erforschung des Jubiläenbuches* (Frankfurt am Main: Lang, 1982).

52. Himmelfarb, *A Kingdom of Priests*, 74–75. See also Matthew Thiessen, *Contesting Conversion: Genealogy, Circumcision, and Identity in Ancient Judaism and Christianity* (Oxford and New York: Oxford University Press, 2011), 67–86, on the insistence in Jubilees that circumcision be performed on the eighth day.

53. Hayes, *Gentile Impurities*, 79. She argues that Abraham is assimilated to Phinehas, since they are the only characters in the Bible of whom the phrase "it was reckoned to him as righteousness" is used (Gen 15:6; Ps 106:31).

54. See especially James C. VanderKam, "The Origins and Purposes of the Book of *Jubilees*," in Matthias Albani, Jörg Frey, and Armin Lange, eds., *Studies in the Book of Jubilees*, TSAJ 65 (Tübingen: Mohr Siebeck, 1997), 3–24.

55. Himmelfarb, *A Kingdom of Priests*, 80.

56. Ibid., 81.

57. See above, chapter 3.

58. E. P. Sanders, *Judaism: Practice and Belief, 63 BCE–66 CE* (Philadelphia: Trinity Press International, 1992), 47–48, following Morton Smith, "The Dead Sea Sect in Relation to Ancient Judaism," *NTS* 7 (1960–61): 347–60, esp. 356.

59. Meyers, "Sanders's 'Common Judaism' and the Common Judaism of Material Culture," 153–74; Jürgen Zangenberg, "Common Judaism and the Multidimensional Character of Material Culture," in Udoh et al., *Redefining First-Century Jewish and Christian Identities*, 175–93.

60. S. J. D. Cohen, "Common Judaism in Greek and Latin Authors," in Udoh et al., *Redefining First-Century Jewish and Christian Identities*, 69–87.

61. Joseph Sievers, "Josephus, First Maccabees, Sparta, the Three Haireseis—and Cicero," *JSJ* 32 (2001): 24–51. The passage in question is

paraphrasing 1 Maccabees 12, but omits the letter to Arius of Sparta. Sievers argues that this created a gap in a manuscript that had already been formatted, and that the passage on the sects was inserted to fill it. Cf. Hanan Eshel, *The Dead Sea Scrolls and the Hasmonean State* (Grand Rapids, MI: Eerdmans, 2008), 40.

62. Albert I. Baumgarten, *The Flourishing of Jewish Sects in the Maccabean Era: An Interpretation*, JSJSup 55 (Leiden: Brill, 1997), 20.

63. There is a parallel to this story in b.Qidd 66a, where the story is set in the reign of Alexander Jannaeus. See Emil Schuerer, *The History of the Jewish People in the Age of Jesus Christ (175 B.C.–A.D. 135)*, rev. and ed. Geza Vermes and Fergus Millar (Edinburgh: Clark, 1973), 1:213–14.

64. Martin Hengel and Roland Deines, "E. P. Sanders' 'Common Judaism', Jesus, and the Pharisees: Review article of *Jewish Law from Jesus to the Mishnah and Judaism: Practice and Belief* by E. P. Sanders," *JTS* 46 (1995): 1–70.

65. Zangenberg, "Common Judaism and the Character of Material Culture," esp. 178–79.

66. Elisha Qimron and John Strugnell, *Qumran Cave 4, V: Miqsat Ma'ase Ha-Torah*, DJD 10 (Oxford: Clarendon, 1994).

67. Jacob Sussmann, "The History of the Halakha and the Dead Sea Scrolls," in Qimron and Strugnell, *Miqsat Ma'ase Ha-Torah*, 179–200; L.H. Schiffman, "The Sadducean Origins of the Dead Sea Scrolls," in H. Shanks, ed., *Understanding the Dead Sea Scrolls* (New York: Random House, 1992), 35–49.

68. L.H. Schiffman, *The Halakhah at Qumran* (Leiden: Brill, 1975). On the interpretation of biblical law in the Scrolls, see further Moshe Bernstein, *Reading and Re-Reading Scripture at Qumran*, vol. 2, *Law, Pesher, and the History of Interpretation* (Leiden: Brill, 2013), 448–75.

69. Aharon Shemesh, *Halakhah in the Making: The Development of Jewish Law from Qumran to the Rabbis* (Berkeley: University of California Press, 2009) 42; Shemesh, "Halakhah between the Dead Sea Scrolls and Rabbinic Literature," in T.H. Lim and J.J. Collins, ed., *The Oxford Handbook of the Dead Sea Scrolls* (Oxford: Oxford University Press, 2010), 595–616, esp. 602.

70. Daniel R. Schwartz, "Law and Truth: On Qumran-Sadducean and Rabbinic Views of Law," in Devorah Dimant and Uriel Rappaport, eds., *The Dead Sea Scrolls: Forty Years of Research* (Leiden: Brill, 1992), 229–40.

71. Christine Hayes, "Legal Realism and the Fashioning of Sectarianism in Jewish Antiquity," in Sacha Stern, ed., *Sects and Sectarianism in Jewish Antiquity* (Leiden: Brill, 2011), 119–46, esp. 123–24.

72. Jeffrey L. Rubenstein, "Nominalism and Realism in Qumranic and Rabbinic Law: A Reassessment," *DSD* 6 (1999): 157–83; Vered Noam, "Ritual

Impurity in Tannaitic Literature: Two Opposing Perspectives," *JAJ* 1 (2010): 65–103.

73. Daniel R. Schwartz, *Judeans and Jews: Four Faces of Dichotomy in Ancient Jewish History* (Toronto: University of Toronto Press, 2014), 33.

74. Shemesh, "Halakhah between the Dead Sea Scrolls and Rabbinic Literature," 609.

75. Hayes, "Legal Realism," 121.

76. Michael O. Wise, "The Origins and History of the Teacher's Movement," in Lim and Collins, *The Oxford Handbook of the Dead Sea Scrolls*, 92–122, esp. 108–9. See my discussion in *Beyond the Qumran Community*, 116.

77. A.I. Baumgarten, "Seekers after Smooth Things," in Schiffman and VanderKam, *Encyclopedia of the Dead Sea Scrolls*, 2:857–59.

78. Jonathan Klawans, *Josephus and the Theologies of Ancient Judaism* (Oxford: Oxford University Press, 2012).

79. Morton Smith, "The Dead Sea Sect in Relation to Ancient Judaism," *NTS* 7 (1960): 347–60, here 360.

80. Naphtali Lewis, *The Documents from the Bar Kokhba Period in the Cave of Letters*, vol. 1, *Greek Papyri, with Aramaic and Nabatean Signatures and Subscriptions*, ed. Yigael Yadin and Jonas C. Greenfield (Jerusalem: Israel Exploration Society, 1989); Hannah M. Cotton and Ada Yardeni, *Aramaic, Hebrew, and Greek Documentary Texts from Naḥal Ḥever and Other Sites, with an Appendix Containing Alleged Qumran Texts (The Seiyal Collection II)*, DJD 27 (Oxford: Clarendon, 1997); Yigael Yadin, Jonas C. Greenfield, Ada Yardeni, and Baruch A. Levine, *The Documents from the Bar Kokhba Period in the Cave of Letters: Hebrew, Aramaic, and Nabatean-Aramaic Papyri* (Jerusalem: Israel Exploration Society, 2002).

81. Cotton and Yardeni, *Aramaic, Hebrew, and Greek Documentary Texts*, 154.

82. Ibid., 155; compare L.H. Schiffman, "Reflections on the Deeds of Sale from the Judaean Desert in Light of Rabbinic Literature," in Ranon Katzoff and David Schaps, eds., *Law in the Documents of the Judaean Desert* (Leiden: Brill, 2005), 185–203, here 186.

83. Hannah M. Cotton, "The Rabbis and the Documents," in Martin Goodman, ed., *Jews in a Graeco-Roman World* (Oxford: Clarendon, 1998), 167–79, here 174.

84. Jacobine G. Oudshoorn, *The Relationship between Roman and Local Law in the Babatha and Salome Komaise Archives: General Analysis and Three Case Studies on Law of Succession, Guardianship, and Marriage* (Leiden: Brill, 2007) 435.

85. See my essay "The Law in the Late Second Temple Period," in Pamela Barmash, ed., *The Oxford Handbook of Biblical Law* (Oxford: Oxford University Press, forthcoming).

## CHAPTER 6. TORAH AND APOCALYPTICISM

1. Wilhelm Bousset, *Die Religion des Judentums im neutestamentlichen Zeitalter* (Berlin: Reuther und Reichard, 1903).

2. For a critical case-by-case evaluation, see James R. Davila, *The Provenance of the Pseudepigrapha,* JSJSup 105 (Leiden: Brill, 2005).

3. So Felix Perles, *Bousset's "Religion des Judentums" im neutestamentlichen Zeitalter kritisch untersucht* (Berlin: Peiser, 1903), 22–23. See further Christian Wiese, *Challenging Colonial Discourse: Jewish Studies and Protestant Theology in Wilhelmine Germany* (Leiden: Brill, 2005), 159–215.

4. Wilhelm Bousset, *Volksfrömmigkeit und Schriftgelehrtentum: Antwort auf Herrn Perles' Kritik meiner "Religion des Judentums im N.T. Zeitalter"* (Berlin: Reuther und Reichard, 1903).

5. George Foot Moore, "Christian Writers on Judaism," *HTR* 14 (1921): 197–254, here 243.

6. On the formation of the editorial team, see Weston W. Fields, *The Dead Sea Scrolls: A Full History* (Leiden: Brill, 2009), 191–239.

7. Frank Moore Cross, *The Ancient Library of Qumran,* 3rd ed. (Sheffield: Sheffield Academic Press, 1995), 144.

8. Ibid., 145.

9. Neil Asher Silberman, *A Prophet from amongst You: The Life of Yigael Yadin; Soldier, Scholar, and Mythmaker of Modern Israel* (Reading, MA: Addison-Wesley, 1993), 304–11.

10. See Lawrence H. Schiffman, *Reclaiming the Dead Sea Scrolls* (Philadelphia: Jewish Publication Society, 1994), xvii–xviii. For the text, see Elisha Qimron and John Strugnell, *Qumran Cave 4, V: Miqsat Ma'ase Ha-Torah,* DJD 10 (Oxford: Oxford University Press, 1994).

11. E. P. Sanders, *Paul and Palestinian Judaism* (Philadelphia: Fortress, 1977).

12. Seth Schwartz, *Imperialism and Jewish Society, 200 B.C.E. to 640 C.E.* (Princeton, NJ: Princeton University Press, 2002), 78–82.

13. Eugene C. Ulrich, "The Text of Daniel in the Dead Sea Scrolls," in John J. Collins and Peter W. Flint, eds., *The Book of Daniel: Composition and Reception,* VTSup 83.2 (Leiden: Brill, 2001), 573–85.

14. Loren Stuckenbruck, "The Early Traditions Related to *1 Enoch* from the Dead Sea Scrolls: An Overview and Assessment," in Gabriele Boccaccini and John J. Collins, eds., *The Early Enoch Literature,* JSJSup 121 (Leiden, 2007), 41–63.

15. Gabriele Boccaccini, *Beyond the Essene Hypothesis: The Parting of the Ways between Qumran and Enochic Judaism* (Grand Rapids, MI: Eerdmans, 1998), 16.

16. See my essay "'Enochic Judaism' and the Sect of the Dead Sea Scrolls," in Boccaccini and Collins, *The Early Enoch Literature*, 283–99, reprinted in Collins, *Scriptures and Sectarianism*, WUNT 332 (Tübingen: Mohr Siebeck, 2014), 150–63.

17. John J. Collins, *Beyond the Qumran Community: The Sectarian Movement of the Dead Sea Scrolls* (Grand Rapids, MI: Eerdmans, 2010), 122–65.

18. Above, chapter 3.

19. See my essay "The Book of Daniel and the Dead Sea Scrolls," in Nora David, Armin Lange, Kristin De Troyer, and Shani Tzoreff, eds., *The Hebrew Bible in Light of the Dead Sea Scrolls*, FRLANT 239 (Göttingen: Vandenhoeck & Ruprecht, 2012), 203–17, reprinted in Collins, *Scriptures and Sectarianism*, 102–15.

20. David Flusser, "Apocalyptic Elements in the War Scroll," in Flusser, *Judaism in the Second Temple Period*, vol. 1, *Qumran and Apocalypticism* (Grand Rapids, MI: Eerdmans, 2007), 156. Compare Brian Schulz, *Conquering the World: The War Scroll (1QM) Reconsidered*, STDJ 76 (Leiden: Brill, 2009), 93–99.

21. See my essay "The Angelic Life," in Turid Karlsen Seim and Jorunn Økland, eds., *Metamorphoses: Resurrection, Body, and Transformative Practices in Early Christianity*, Ekstasis 1 (Berlin: De Gruyter, 2009), 291–310, reprinted in Collins, *Scriptures and Sectarianism*, 195–211.

22. Many of the apocalyptic writings in the Scrolls are in Aramaic. For an overview, see Andrew B. Perrin, *The Dynamics of Dream-Vision Revelation in the Aramaic Dead Sea Scrolls*, JAJSup 19 (Göttingen: Vandenhoeck & Ruprecht, 2015).

23. John J. Collins and Peter W. Flint, "243–245. 4QpsDaniel[a-c]," in George J. Brooke et al., *Qumran Cave 4, XVII*, DJD 22 (Oxford: Clarendon, 1996), 95–164.

24. Lorenzo DiTommaso, "4QPseudo-Daniel[a-b] (4Q243–244) and the Book of Daniel," *DSD* 12 (2005): 101–33.

25. Émile Puech, "246. 4QApocryphe de Daniel ar," in Brooke et al., *Qumran Cave 4, XVII*, 165–84; Adela Yarbro Collins and John J. Collins, *King and Messiah as Son of God* (Grand Rapids, MI: Eerdmans, 2008), 65–74.

26. Devorah Dimant, *Qumran Cave 4, XXI: Parabiblical Texts*, pt. 4: *Pseudo-Prophetic Texts* (Oxford: Clarendon, 2000); Dimant, "Hebrew Pseudepigrapha at Qumran," in Eibert Tigchelaar, ed., *Old Testament Pseudepigrapha and the Scriptures*, BETL 270 (Leuven: Peeters, 2015), 89–103; Matthew J. Neujahr, *Predicting the Past in the Ancient Near East*, Brown Judaic Studies 354 (Providence: Brown Judaic Studies, 2012), 163–80.

27. At one time the editor, Devorah Dimant, distinguished a third text, which she called Pseudo-Moses, exemplified in 4Q390, but she changed her mind in the official edition. B.H. Reynolds III, *Between Symbolism and Realism:*

*The Use of Symbolic and Non-Symbolic Language in Ancient Jewish Apocalypses, 333–63 B.C.E.*, JAJSup 8 (Göttingen: Vandenhoeck & Ruprecht, 2011), 268, has argued that 4Q390 is part of the Jeremianic text, but not integrated with the other fragments (compare Daniel 7–12, where the different textual units are formally distinct). C.J.P. Davis, "Torah-Performance and History in the Golah: Rewritten Bible or 'Re-Presentational' Authority in the Apocryphon of Jeremiah C," in P.W. Flint, J. Duhaime, and K.S. Baek, eds., *Celebrating the Dead Sea Scrolls: A Canadian Collection* (Leiden: Brill, 2012), 467–95, esp. 468–72, argues that 4Q390 represents a later reinterpretation of the Apocryphon. See now Davis, *The Cave 4 Apocryphon of Jeremiah and the Qumran Jeremianic Traditions: Prophetic Persona and Community Identity*, STDJ 111 (Leiden: Brill, 2014).

28. Lorenzo DiTommaso refers to this kind of historical overview as "apocalyptic historiography." DiTommaso, "The Development of Apocalyptic Historiography in Light of the Dead Sea Scrolls," in Flint, Duhaime, and Baek, *Celebrating the Dead Sea Scrolls*, 497–522.

29. See Reynolds, *Between Symbolism and Realism*, 268–72.

30. John Strugnell and Devorah Dimant, "4Q Second Ezekiel," *RevQ* 13 (1988): 45–56.

31. Loren T. Stuckenbruck, "Daniel and Early Enoch Traditions in the Dead Sea Scrolls," in Collins and Flint, *The Book of Daniel*, 368–86, esp. 378–85; Ryan E. Stokes, "The Throne Visions of Daniel 7, *1 Enoch* 14, and the Qumran Book of Giants (4Q530): An Analysis of Their Literary Relationship," *DSD* 15 (2008): 340–58; Jonathan Trotter, "The Tradition of the Throne Vision in the Second Temple Period: Daniel 7:9–10, *1 Enoch* 14:18–23, and the Book of Giants (4Q530)," *RevQ* 25 (1999): 451–66.

32. Émile Puech, *Qumrân Grotte 4, XXVII: Textes araméens; Deuxième partie: 4Q550–4Q575a, 4Q580–4Q587*, DJD 37 (Oxford: Clarendon, 2009), 57–90.

33. Reynolds, *Between Symbolism and Realism*, 200.

34. On the Aramaic literature from Qumran, see Katell Berthelot and Daniel Stoekl Ben Ezra, eds., *Aramaica Qumranica: Proceedings of the Conference on the Aramaic Texts from Qumran in Aix-en-Provence, 30 June–2 July 2008*, STDJ 94 (Leiden; Brill, 2010).

35. Christoph Berner, *Jahre, Jahrwochen und Jubiläen: Heptadische Geschichtskonzeptionen im antiken Judentum*, BZAW 363 (Berlin: De Gruyter, 2006), 429; Cana Werman, "Epochs and End-Time: The 490-Year Scheme in Second Temple Literature," *DSD* 13 (2006): 229–55. See the reflections of Eibert

Tigchelaar, "Classifications of the Collection of Dead Sea Scrolls and the Case of Apocryphon of Jeremiah C," *JSJ* 43 (2012): 519–50.

36. The parallels relate to specific sins and punishment, and the dominion of Belial.

37. Steven D. Fraade, "Interpretive Authority at Qumran," *JJS* 44 (1993): 46–69, here 49.

38. Samuel Byrskog, *Jesus the Only Teacher: Didactic Authority and Transmission in Ancient Israel, Ancient Judaism, and the Matthean Community*, ConBib, NT Series 24 (Stockholm: Almqvist & Wiksell, 1994), 151–52.

39. Charlotte Hempel, "The *Treatise on the Two Spirits* and the Literary History of the *Rule of the Community*," in Geza G. Xeravits, ed., *Dualism in Qumran* (London and New York: Clark, 2010), 102–20.

40. Hartmut Stegemann, *The Library of Qumran: On the Essenes, John the Baptist, and Jesus* (Grand Rapids, MI: Eerdmans, 1998), 110; Armin Lange, *Weisheit & Prädestination: Weisheitliche Urordnung & Prädestination in den Textfunden von Qumran*, STDJ 18 (Leiden: Brill, 1995), 127–28; Jörg Frey, "Different Patterns of Dualistic Thought in the Qumran Library," in Moshe Bernstein, Florentino García Martínez, and John Kampen, eds., *Legal Texts and Legal Issues* (Leiden: Brill, 1997), 289.

41. Prods Oktor Skjaervø, "Zoroastrian Dualism, with an Appendix on the Sources of Zoroastrianism," in Armin Lange, Eric M. Meyers, Bennie H. Reynolds III, and Randall Styers, eds., *Light against Darkness: Dualism in Ancient Mediterranean Religion and the Contemporary World*, JAJSup 2 (Göttingen: Vandenhoeck & Ruprecht, 2011), 55–91.

42. Plutarch, *Isis and Osiris* 47; J. Gwyn Griffiths, *Plutarch's De Iside et Osiride* (Cardiff: University of Wales Press, 1970), 46–47. On Plutarch's account, see Albert de Jong, *Traditions of the Magi: Zoroastrianism in Greek and Latin Literature* (Leiden: Brill, 1997), 157–204.

43. K. G. Kuhn, "Die Sektenschrift und die iranische Religion," *ZTK* 49 (1952): 296–316. See John J. Collins, *The Dead Sea Scrolls: A Biography* (Princeton, NJ: Princeton University Press, 2012), 154–57.

44. Albert de Jong, "Iranian Connections in the Dead Sea Scrolls," in Timothy H. Lim and John J. Collins, eds., *The Oxford Handbook of the Dead Sea Scrolls* (Oxford: Oxford University Press, 2010), 493–94.

45. Ibid., 492.

46. Émile Puech, *Qumrân Grotte 4, XXII: Textes araméens; Première partie: 4Q529–549*, DJD 31 (Oxford: Clarendon, 2001), 283–405; on the dating, see

pp. 285–87. Liora Goldman, "Dualism in the Visions of Amram," *RevQ* 95 (2010): 421–32.

47. Philip Alexander, "Predestination and Free Will in the Theology of the Dead Sea Scrolls," in John M.G. Barclay and Simon Gathercole, eds., *Divine and Human Agency in Paul and His Cultural Environment*, Library of New Testament Studies 335 (London and New York: Clark, 2006), 39–47. He points to 4Q502, the Songs of the Sabbath Sacrifice, and the physiognomic text, 4Q186.

48. 4Q266 (4QD$^a$).

49. As suggested by Jean Duhaime, "Dualistic Reworking in the Scrolls from Qumran," *CBQ* 49 (1987): 32–56.

50. See my essay "Covenant and Dualism in the Dead Sea Scrolls," in Collins, *Scriptures and Sectarianism*, 179–94.

51. Sanders, *Paul and Palestinian Judaism*, 17.

52. Ibid., 85.

53. Ibid., 237, citing Ephraim E. Urbach, *The Sages: Their Concepts and Beliefs* (Jerusalem: Magnes, 1975), 538–40.

54. On the ambiguity as to whether "Israel" in the Scrolls refers to empirical Israel or to Israel as it should be, see further my essay "The Construction of Israel in the Sectarian Rule Books," in Alan J. Avery-Peck, Jacob Neusner, and Bruce D. Chilton, eds., *Judaism in Late Antiquity*, pt. 5, *The Judaism of Qumran: A Systemic Reading of the Dead Sea Scrolls*, 1: *Theory of Israel* (Leiden: Brill, 2001), 25–42.

55. On the biblical and theological foundations, see Stephen Hultgren, *From the Damascus Covenant to the Covenant of the Community*, STDJ 66 (Leiden: Brill, 2007), 77–140.

56. See Yonder M. Gillihan, *Civic Ideology, Organization, and Law in the Rule Scrolls: A Comparative Study of the Covenanters' Sect and Contemporary Voluntary Associations in Political Context*, STDJ 97 (Leiden: Brill, 2012).

57. Philip Alexander, *The Mystical Texts: Songs of the Sabbath Sacrifice and Related Manuscripts*, Library of Second Temple Studies 61 (London and New York: Clark, 2006).

58. John J. Collins, *Apocalypticism in the Dead Sea Scrolls* (London: Routledge, 1997), 52–70.

59. Seth Schwartz, *Imperialism and Jewish Society*, 79.

60. Ibid., 78.

61. See my essay "Gentiles in the Dead Sea Scrolls," in David C. Sim and James S. McLaren, eds., *Attitudes to Gentiles in Ancient Judaism and Early Christianity* (London and New York: Clark, 2013), 46–61.

62. On the angelic identity of the holy ones, see my commentary in *Daniel: A Commentary on the Book of Daniel,* Hermeneia (Minneapolis: Fortress, 1993), 313–17.

63. Israel J. Yuval, "All Israel Have a Portion in the World to Come," in Fabian Udoh, with Susanna Heschel, Mark Chancey, and Gregory Tatum, eds., *Redefining First-Century Jewish and Christian Identities: Essays in Honor of Ed Parish Sanders* (Notre Dame, IN: University of Notre Dame, 2008), 170.

64. m. Sanhedrin 10.2.

65. The phrase "all Israel" elsewhere always designates ethnic Israel. See Joseph A. Fitzmyer, SJ, *Romans,* AB 33 (New York: Doubleday, 1992), 623.

66. Yuval, "All Israel Have a Portion in the World to Come," argues that this belief is a late, anti-Christian addition to the Mishnah.

67. For a general introduction to the Similitudes, see my book *The Apocalyptic Imagination,* 3rd ed. (Grand Rapids, MI: Eerdmans, 2016), 220–39.

68. See the essays in Gabriele Boccaccini, ed., *Enoch and the Messiah Son of Man: Revisiting the Book of Parables* (Grand Rapids, MI: Eerdmans, 2007).

69. Another example may be found in 2 Enoch, which is preserved in Slavonic and of uncertain provenance. It is usually thought to have been composed in Egypt in the late first century C.E. See my discussion in *The Apocalyptic Imagination,* 301–10.

70. See *The Apocalyptic Imagination,* 240–80.

71. See my essay "Enoch and Ezra," in Matthias Henze and Gabriele Boccaccini, eds., *Fourth Ezra and Second Baruch: Reconstruction after the Fall,* JSJSup 164 (Leiden: Brill, 2013), 83–97, reprinted in Collins, *Apocalypse, Prophecy, and Pseudepigraphy: Essays On Jewish Apocalyptic Literature* (Grand Rapids, MI: Eerdmans, 2015), 235–50.

72. On 4 Ezra as a debate, see Karina Martin Hogan, *Theologies in Conflict in 4 Ezra: Wisdom Debate and Apocalyptic Solution,* JSJSup 130 (Leiden: Brill, 2008).

73. See especially Michael E. Stone, "On Reading an Apocalypse," in John J. Collins and James H. Charlesworth, eds., *Mysteries and Revelations: Apocalyptic Studies since the Uppsala Colloquium,* JSPSup 9 (Sheffield: Sheffield Academic Press, 1991), 65–78; and more generally his classic *Fourth Ezra: A Commentary on the Book of Fourth Ezra,* Hermeneia (Minneapolis: Fortress, 1990).

74. On 4 Ezra's complex relationship to the scriptural tradition, see Hindy Najman, *Losing the Temple and Recovering the Future: An Analysis of 4 Ezra* (Cambridge: Cambridge University Press, 2014), 69–93.

75. See Karina Martin Hogan, "The Meanings of *tôrah* in 4 Ezra," *JSJ* 38 (2007): 53–52.

76. The best recent discussion is that of Matthias Henze, *Jewish Apocalypticism in Late First-Century Israel,* TSAJ 142 (Tübingen: Mohr Siebeck, 2011).

77. Henze, *Jewish Apocalypticism,* 103; see also pp. 206–27.

## CHAPTER 7. THE LAW IN THE DIASPORA

1. See above, the introduction, note 62. Menahem Stern, *Greek and Latin Authors on Jews and Judaism,* vol. 1, *From Herodotus to Plutarch* (Jerusalem: The Israel Academy of Sciences and Humanities, 1976), 20–35. The account is preserved by Diodorus, *Bibliotheca Historica* 40.3. The authenticity of the attribution has been questioned by Daniel R. Schwartz, "Diodorus Siculus 40.3—Hecataeus or Pseudo-Hecataeus?," in M. Mor, A. Oppenheimer, J. Pastor, and D. R. Schwartz, eds., *Jews and Gentiles in the Holy Land in the Days of the Second Temple, the Mishnah, and Talmud: A Collection of Articles* (Jerusalem: Yad Ben-Zvi, 2003), 181–97, but I do not find the objections persuasive.

2. Stern, *Greek and Latin Authors,* 1:21.

3. On Hecataeus, see P. M. Fraser, *Ptolemaic Alexandria* (Oxford: Clarendon, 1972), 1:496–504; G. E. Sterling, *Historiography and Self-Definition: Josephos, Luke, Acts, and Apologetic Historiography* (Leiden: Brill, 1992), 59–91; B. Bar-Kochva, *Pseudo-Hecataeus "On the Jews": Legitimizing the Jewish Diaspora* (Berkeley: University of California Press, 1998), 7–43.

4. Diodorus 40.3.2; Stern, *Greek and Latin Authors,* 1:27.

5. Diodorus 40.3.4; Stern, *Greek and Latin Authors,* 1:28.

6. E. S. Gruen, *Heritage and Hellenism: The Reinvention of Jewish Tradition* (Berkeley: University of California Press, 1998), 52.

7. Diodorus 40.3.6; Stern, *Greek and Latin Authors,* 1:28.

8. For recent discussions, see Stewart Moore, *Jewish Ethnic Identity and Relations in Hellenistic Egypt: With Walls of Iron,* JSJSup 171 (Leiden: Brill, 2015), 210–13; Benjamin G. Wright III, *The Letter of Aristeas: "Aristeas to Philocrates" or "On the Translation of the Law of the Jews,"* CEJL (Berlin: De Gruyter, 2015), 21–30.

9. E.g., Gruen, *Heritage and Hellenism,* 208–9.

10. Tessa Rajak, *Translation and Survival: The Greek Bible of the Ancient Jewish Diaspora* (Oxford: Oxford University Press, 2009), 38–43.

11. Demetrius frag. 6 (*Strom.* 1.141.8); C. R. Holladay, *Fragments from Hellenistic Jewish Authors,* vol. 1, *Historians* (Chico, CA: Scholars Press, 1983), 78–79.

12. See my book *Between Athens and Jerusalem: Jewish Identity in the Hellenistic Diaspora,* 2nd ed. (Grand Rapids, MI: Eerdmans, 2000); Gruen, *Heritage and Hellenism;* Michael Tuval, *From Jerusalem Priest to Roman Jew: Of Josephus and the*

*Paradigms of Ancient Judaism,* WUNT 2/357 (Tübingen: Mohr Siebeck, 2013), 41–78.

13. See Collins, *Between Athens and Jerusalem,* 155–85 ("The Common Ethic").

14. Translations of the *Sibylline Oracles* are from J.J. Collins, "The *Sibylline Oracles,*" in J.H. Charlesworth, ed., *Old Testament Pseudepigrapha,* vol. 1, *Apocalyptic Literature and Testaments* (Garden City, NY: Doubleday, 1983), 317–472.

15. For text and commentary, see P.W. van der Horst, *The Sentences of Pseudo-Phocylides* (Leiden: Brill, 1978); Walter T. Wilson, *The Sentences of Pseudo-Phocylides,* CEJL (Berlin: De Gruyter, 2005).

16. K.-W. Niebuhr, *Gesetz und Paränese: Katechismusartige Weisungreihen in der frühjüdischen Literatur,* WUNT 2/28 (Tübingen: Mohr Siebeck, 1987), 6–72, esp. 31–72; Gregory E. Sterling, "Universalizing the Particular: Natural Law in Second Temple Ethics," *Studia Philonica Annual* 15 (2003): 64–80, esp. 65–73.

17. D.L. Balch, "Household Codes," in D.E. Aune, ed., *The New Testament and Graeco-Roman Literature* (Atlanta: Scholars Press, 1988), 25–30; Balch, "Household Codes," *ABD,* 3:328–29.

18. *Hypothetica* 7.6.

19. Deut 22:6.

20. On Buzyges, see L. Schmidt, *Die Ethik der alten Griechen* (Berlin: Hertz, 1882), 2:278–79; H. Bolkenstein, *Wohltätigkeit and Armenpflege im vorchristlichen Altertum* (Utrecht: Oosthoek, 1939), 69–70.

21. Gregory E. Sterling, "Was There a Common Ethic in Second Temple Judaism," in J.J. Collins, G.E. Sterling, and R.A. Clements, eds., *Sapiential Perspectives: Wisdom Literature in Light of the Dead Sea Scrolls,* STDJ 51 (Leiden: Brill, 2004), 171–94, here 183.

22. See the synopsis by Sterling, "Universalizing the Particular," 69–70.

23. Philo, *Migr.* 89–93.

24. See the commentary by Wright, *The Letter of Aristeas,* 246–313.

25. See my essay "Joseph and Aseneth: Jewish or Christian?," in *Jewish Cult and Hellenistic Culture,* JSJSup 100 (Leiden: Brill, 2005), 112–27.

26. *Pace* J.M.G. Barclay, *Jews in the Mediterranean Diaspora from Alexander to Trajan (323 BCE–117 CE)* (Edinburgh: Clark, 1996), 204–16, who classifies it as an example of "cultural antagonism."

27. See further my essay "The Transformation of Aseneth," in Anne Hege Grung, Marianne Bjelland Kartzow, and Anna Rebecca Solevåg, eds., *Bodies, Borders, Believers: Ancient Texts and Present Conversations; Essays in Honor of Turid Karlsen Seim on her 70th Birthday* (Eugene, OR: Pickwick, 2015), 93–108.

28. See my essay "A Symbol of Otherness: Circumcision and Salvation in the First Century," in *Seers, Sibyls, and Sages in Hellenistic-Roman Judaism,* JSJSup 54 (Leiden: Brill, 1997), 211–35.

29. Juvenal, *Satires* 14.96–106; Stern, *Greek and Latin Authors* 2:102–3.

30. *Ag. Ap.* 2.282.

31. *Opif.* 3. See Hindy Najman, "A Written Copy of the Law of Nature: An Unthinkable Paradox?," *Studia Philonica Annual* 15 (2003): 54–63, here 59.

32. Barclay, *Jews in the Mediterranean Diaspora*, 218–25.

33. *Mos.* 2.44. See Alan Mendelson, *Philo's Jewish Identity,* BJS 161 (Atlanta: Scholars Press, 1988), 128–32.

34. See Moore, *Jewish Ethnic Identity*, 258–59.

35. Philo, *Mos.* 2.216. Cf. *Legat.* 312; *Spec.* 2.62–63, no. 168.

36. So Najman, "A Written Copy of the Law of Nature," 57. Compare the tension between universalist and particularist perspectives in the Wisdom of Solomon, and my essay "Natural Theology and Biblical Tradition: The Case of Hellenistic Judaism," *CBQ* 60 (1998): 1–15. See also Gregory E. Sterling, "'A Law to Themselves': Limited Universalism in Philo and Paul," *ZNW* 107 (2016): 30–47.

37. *Ag. Ap.* 2.199. Cf. *J.W.* 1.161 on the Essenes.

38. 4Q270 7 i 12–13.

39. *Spec.* 2.62–63 (282). Cf. *Mos.* 2.216 (168); Klaus Berger, *Die Gesetzesauslegung Jesu,* WMANT 40 (Neukirchen-Vluyn: Neukirchener Verlag, 1972), 137–76.

40. Najman, "A Written Copy of the Law of Nature," 62.

41. V. Tcherikover, "Prolegomena," in Victor A. Tcherikover and Alexander Fuks, eds., *Corpus Papyrorum Judaicarum* (Cambridge, MA: Harvard University Press, 1957), 1:5.

42. Ibid., 6.

43. Josephus, *Ant.* 12.3.3 (138–44). See the introduction in this book.

44. Tcherikover, "Prolegomena," 7.

45. Ibid.

46. A. Kasher, *The Jews in Hellenistic and Roman Egypt: The Struggle for Equal Rights* (Tübingen: Mohr Siebeck, 1985), 4.

47. J. Mélèze Modrzejewski, *The Jews of Egypt. From Rameses II to Emperor Hadrian,* trans. Robert Cornman (Princeton, NJ: Princeton University Press, 1997), 107–15; cf. Rajak, *Translation and Survival*, 84.

48. Modrzejewski, *The Jews of Egypt*, 108; *CPJ* I 19.

49. Modrzejewski, *The Jews of Egypt*, 112.

50. So Tcherikover and Fuks, *CPJ* I 128, n. 2.

51. *CPJ* I 20. See Moore, *Jewish Ethnic Identity*, 95.

52. James S. Cowey and Klaus Maresch, *Urkunden des Politeuma der Juden von Herakleopolis (144/3–133/2 v. Chr.) (P. Polit Iud.)*, Abhandlungen der Nordrhein-Westfälischen Akademie der Wissenschaften; Papyrological Coloniensia 29 (Wiesbaden: Westdeutscher Verlag, 2001).

53. Constantine Zuckerman, "Hellenistic *politeumata* and the Jews: A Reconsideration," *SCI* 8–9 (1985–88), 171–85.

54. Dorothy J. Thompson Crawford, "The Idumeans of Memphis and the Ptolemaic *politeumata*," in *Atti del XVII congresso internazionale di papirologia* (Naples: Centro Internazionale per lo Studio dei Papiri Ercolanesi, 1984), 3:1069–75.

55. Gerd Lüderitz, "What Is the Politeuma?," in Jan Willem van Henten and Pieter Willem van der Horst, eds., *Studies in Early Jewish Epigraphy* (Leiden: Brill, 1994), 183–225.

56. Lüderitz, "What Is the Politeuma?," 185.

57. Ibid., 185, 215. The *politeuma* in Berenike in Cyrenaica seems to have had some administrative authority.

58. Cowey and Maresch, *Urkunden*, 7, 12, 21.

59. K. Maresch and J. M. S. Cowey, "'A Recurrent Inclination to Isolate the Case of the Jews from Their Ptolemaic Environment'? Eine Antwort auf Sylvie Honigman," *SCI* 22 (2003): 307–10, here 307.

60. Aryeh Kasher, review of *Urkunden des Politeuma der Juden von Herakleopolis (144/3–133/2 v. Chr.) (P. Polit. Iud.)*, *JQR* 93 (2002): 257–68.

61. Sylvie Honigman, "The Jewish *Politeuma* at Heracleopolis," *SCI* 21 (2002): 251–66, here 265.

62. Robert A. Kugler, "Dorotheos Petitions for the Return of Philippa (*P.Polit.Jud.* 7): A Case Study in the Jews and Their Law in Ptolemaic Egypt," in Traianos Gagos, ed., *Proceedings of the Twenty-Fifth International Congress of Papyrology, Ann Arbor 2007* (Ann Arbor: University of Michigan Press, 2010), 387–96; Kugler, "Uncovering a New Dimension of Early Judean Interpretation of the Greek Torah: Ptolemaic Law Interpreted by Its Own Rhetoric," in Hanne von Weissenberg, Juha Pakkala, and Marko Marttila, eds., *Changes in Scripture: Rewriting and Interpreting Authoritative Traditions in the Second Temple Period*, BZAW 419 (Berlin: De Gruyter, 2011), 165–75; Kugler, "Dispelling an Illusion of Otherness? Juridical Practice in the Heracleopolis Papyri," in Daniel C. Harlow, Karina Martin Hogan, Matthew Goff, and Joel S. Kaminsky, eds., *The "Other" in Second Temple Judaism: Essays in Honor of John J. Collins* (Grand Rapids, MI: William B. Eerdmans, 2011), 457–70; Kugler, "Peton Contests Paying Double Rent

on Farmland (*P.Heid.Inv.* G 5100): A Slice of Judean Experience in the Second Century B.C.E. Herakleopolite Nome," in Eric F. Mason, Kelley Coblentz Bautch, Angela Kim Harkins, and Daniel A. Machiela, eds., *A Teacher for All Generations: Essays in Honor of James C. VanderKam* (Leiden: Brill, 2012), 2:537–51; Kugler, "Uncovering Echoes of LXX Legal Norms in Hellenistic Egyptian Documentary Papyri: The Case of the Second-Century Herakleopolite Nome," in Melvin K. H. Peters, ed., *XIV Congress of the IOSCS, Helsinki, 2010*, SBL Series 59 (Atlanta: Society of Biblical Literature, 2013), 142–53; Kugler, "Delineating the Particulars of Dispute Settlement among the Jews of Second Century BCE Herakleopolis: A Glimpse of Jewish Life in Hellenistic Egypt" (paper presented in Jerusalem in December 2014). I am grateful to Robert Kugler for providing me with copies of the first and last of these articles.

63. Kugler, "Dispelling the Illusion of Otherness?," 459.

64. Ibid., 461.

65. Ibid., 464.

66. Ibid., 461.

67. Kugler, "Uncovering Echoes of LXX Legal Norms," 147.

68. Cowey and Maresch, *Urkunden*, 26; cf. Honigman, "The Jewish *Politeuma*," 261.

69. Cowey and Maresch, *Urkunden*, 123; Honigman, "The Jewish *Politeuma*," 261.

70. See the critique of Kugler's arguments by Moore, *Jewish Ethnic Identity*, 82–86.

71. See Kugler, "Dorotheos Petitions for the Return of Philippa."

72. Kugler, "Dispelling an Illusion of Otherness," 465.

73. See the comments of Moore, *Jewish Ethnic Identity*, 83.

74. Kugler, "Peton Contests Paying Double Rent."

75. Kugler, "Uncovering a New Dimension of Early Judean Interpretation," 170.

76. Ibid., 173.

77. Kugler, "Uncovering Echoes of LXX Legal Norms," discusses nine texts.

78. Kugler, "Delineating the Particulars of Dispute Settlement." He discusses *P. Polit. Iud.* 2 as an example.

79. Moore, *Jewish Ethnic Identity*, 85.

80. E.g., Bernard S. Jackson, *Wisdom-Laws: A Study of the Mishpatim of Exodus 21:1–22:16* (Oxford: Oxford University Press, 2006).

81. Tcherikover, "Prolegomena," 36.

82. Ibid.

83. Modrzejewski, *The Jews of Egypt*, 119.

84. Tcherikover, "Prolegomena," 36; Modrejewski, *The Jews of Egypt*, 119.

85. The centrality of the Torah for diaspora Jews is emphasized by Tuval, *From Jerusalem Priest*, 11.

86. Seth Schwartz, *Imperialism and Jewish Society, 200 B.C.E. to 640 C.E.* (Princeton, NJ: Princeton University Press, 2001), 68.

87. The following discussion is adapted from my essay "The Transformation of Aseneth."

88. The text exists in short and long recensions. Most, but not all, scholars regard the short recension as secondary. Neither recension can be held to preserve the original text.

89. See Ross S. Kraemer, *When Aseneth Met Joseph: A Late Antique Tale of the Biblical Patriarch and His Egyptian Wife Reconsidered* (New York: Oxford University Press, 1998), 225.

90. P. Battifol, "Le livre de la prière d'Aseneth," in Battifol, *Studia patristica: Études d'ancienne littérature chrétienne* (Paris: Leroux, 1889–90), 1–115.

91. Kraemer, *When Aseneth Met Joseph*, 245–85; Rivka Nir, *Joseph and Aseneth: A Christian Book* (Sheffield: Sheffield Phoenix, 2012).

92. See my essay "Joseph and Aseneth: Jewish or Christian?," *JSP* 14 (2005): 97–112, reprinted in Collins, *Jewish Cult and Hellenistic Culture*, JSJSup 100 (Leiden: Brill, 2005), 112–27. James R. Davila, *The Provenance of the Pseudepigrapha*, JSJSup 105 (Leiden: Brill, 2005), 190–95, is indecisive.

93. See Jürgen Zangenberg, "Joseph und Aseneths Ägypten: Oder: Von der Domestikation einer 'gefährlichen' Kultur," in Eckart Reinmuth, ed., *Joseph und Aseneth* (Tübingen: Mohr Siebeck, 2009), 159–86.

94. Collins, "Joseph and Aseneth: Jewish or Christian?"

95. Kraemer, *When Aseneth Met Joseph*, 20.

96. L.M. Wills, *The Jewish Novel in the Ancient World* (Ithaca, NY: Cornell University Press, 1995), 170–84; Catherine Hezser, "'Joseph and Aseneth' in the Context of Ancient Greek Novels," *Frankfurter judäistische Beiträge* 24 (1997): 1–40; Sara R. Johnson, *Historical Fictions and Hellenistic Jewish Identity: Third Maccabees in Its Cultural Context* (Berkeley: University of California Press, 2004), 108–20.

97. Barclay, *Jews in the Mediterranean Diaspora*, 204–16.

98. See George Brooke, "Joseph, Aseneth, and Lévi-Strauss," in G.J. Brooke and J.-D. Kaestli, eds., *Narrativity in Biblical and Related Texts* (Leuven: Peeters, 2000), 185–200.

99. Randall Chesnutt, *From Death to Life: Conversion in "Joseph and Aseneth,"* JSPSup 16 (Sheffield: Sheffield Academic Press, 1995), 128–37; Dieter Sänger, *Antikes Judentum und die Mysterien: Religionsgeschichtliche Untersuchungen zu Joseph und Aseneth,* WUNT 2/5 (Tübingen: Mohr Siebeck, 1980), 167–74.

100. Chesnutt, "Perceptions of Oil in Early Judaism and the Meal Formula in Joseph and Aseneth," *JSP* 14 (2005): 113–32, here 113.

101. Philo, *Virt.* 102; Shaye J.D. Cohen, *The Beginnings of Jewishness: Boundaries, Varieties, Uncertainties* (Berkeley: University of California Press, 1999), 157.

102. See the thorough discussion by Chesnutt, *From Death to Life,* 152–84.

103. See Collins, *Between Athens and Jerusalem,* 235, and the literature there cited. Also Edith M. Humphreys, "On Bees and Best Guesses: The Problem of Sitz im Leben from Internal Evidence, as Illusrated by Joseph and Aseneth," *Currents in Research: Biblical Studies* 7 (1999): 223–36; and Anathea Portier-Young, "Sweet Mercy Metropolis: Interpreting Aseneth's Honeycomb," *JSP* 14 (2005): 133–57. Portier-Young argues that the honey symbolizes mercy.

104. On the role of angelomorphism in the story, see especially George J. Brooke, "Men and Women as Angels in Joseph and Aseneth," *JSP* 14 (2005): 159–77.

105. Portier-Young, "Sweet Mercy Metropolis," 135–38.

106. On the theme of nonretaliation in Hellenistic Jewish sources, see G.M. Zerbe, *Non-Retaliation in Early Jewish and New Testament Texts: Ethical Themes in Social Contexts,* JSPSup 13 (Sheffield: Sheffield Academic Press, 1993).

107. The ethnic character of that to which Aseneth converts is emphasized by Barclay, *Jews in the Mediterranean Diaspora,* 213–14.

108. Gruen, *Heritage and Hellenism,* 96.

109. See especially Gideon Bohak, *Joseph and Aseneth and the Jewish Temple in Heliopolis,* SBLEJL 10 (Atlanta: Scholars Press, 1996). He summarizes the history of the Oniad temple on pp. 19–40.

110. So also Noah Hacham, "Joseph and Aseneth: Loyalty, Traitors, Antiquity, and Diaspora Identity," *JSP* 22 (2012): 63–67.

CHAPTER 8. PAUL, TORAH, AND JEWISH IDENTITY

1. Philipp Vielhauer, "Zum 'Paulinismus' der Apostelgeschichte," *EvT* 10 (1950–51): 1–15; English translation, "On the 'Paulinism' of Acts," *Perkins School of Theology Journal* 17 (1963): 5–17, reprinted in L.E. Keck and J.L. Martyn, eds., *Studies in Luke-Acts: Essays Presented in Honor of Paul Schubert* (Nashville: Abing-

don, 1966), 33–50. See the comments of Joseph A. Fitzmyer, *The Acts of the Apostles,* AB 31 (New York: Doubleday, 1998), 145–47.

2. Krister Stendahl, *Paul among Jews and Gentiles* (Philadelphia: Fortress, 1977), especially the essays "Paul among Jews and Gentiles" (1–77) and "Paul and the Introspective Conscience of the West" (78–96). Others before Stendahl had raised similar objections to the traditional view of Paul. See the survey of scholarship in Frank Thielman, *From Plight to Solution: A Jewish Framework for Understanding Paul's View of the Law in Galatians and Romans,* NTSup 61 (Leiden: Brill, 1989), 1–27, esp. 45, on the work of George Foot Moore.

3. E.P. Sanders, *Paul and Palestinian Judaism: A Comparison of Patterns of Religion* (Philadelphia: Fortress, 1977).

4. See, e.g., Sanders, *Paul and Palestinian Judaism,* 180.

5. Sanders, *Paul and Palestinian Judaism,* 552.

6. James D.G. Dunn, "The New Perspective on Paul," *Bulletin of the John Rylands Library* 65 (1983): 95–122, reprinted, with an "additional note," in Dunn, *Jesus, Paul, and the Law: Studies in Mark and Galatians* (Louisville, KY: Westminster John Knox, 1990), 183–214.

7. Dunn, "The New Perspective on Paul," 100–101.

8. Ibid., 102.

9. Dunn, *Jesus, Paul, and the Law,* 211.

10. The point that Paul objected to Jewish particularism was already made by E.P. Sanders, *Paul, the Law, and the Jewish People* (Philadelphia: Fortress, 1983), 47: "It is the notion of Jewish privilege and the idea of election that he attacks."

11. N.T. Wright, *What Saint Paul Really Said: Was Paul of Tarsus the Real Founder of Christianity?* (Grand Rapids, MI: Eerdmans, 1997), 84, 87.

12. Lloyd Gaston, *Paul and the Torah* (Vancouver: University of British Columbia Press, 1987).

13. John G. Gager, *The Origins of Anti-Semitism: Attitudes towards Judaism in Pagan and Christian Antiquity* (New York: Oxford University Press, 1983), esp. 200–201; Gager, *Reinventing Paul* (New York: Oxford University Press, 2000). The position of Stanley K. Stowers, *A Rereading of Romans: Justice, Jews, and Gentiles* (New Haven, CT: Yale University Press, 1994) is more nuanced. See the discussion in Gager, *Reinventing Paul,* 59–60.

14. Gager, *Reinventing Paul,* 59.

15. Ibid., 60.

16. Matthew Thiessen, *Contesting Conversion: Genealogy, Circumcision, and Identity in Ancient Judaism and Christianity* (New York: Oxford University Press,

2011), 147; Thiessen, *Paul and the Gentile Problem* (New York: Oxford, 2016). See also Christine Hayes, *What's Divine about Divine Law? Early Perspectives* (Princeton, NJ: Princeton University Press, 2015), 143–48.

17. Thiessen, *Contesting Conversion*, 13.

18. Magnus Zetterholm, "Paul and the Missing Messiah," in Zetterholm, ed., *The Messiah in Early Judaism and Christianity* (Minneapolis: Fortress, 2007), 47; Zetterholm, "Jews, Christians, and Gentiles: Rethinking the Categorization within the Early Christian Movement," in Kathy Ehrensperger and Brian J. Tucker, eds., *Reading Paul in Context: Explorations in Identity Formation*, LNTS (formerly JSNTS) 428 (London and New York: T. & T. Clark International, 2010), 242–54, here 250. In contrast, Mekilta de R. Ishmael (Bahodesh 1) says of the Torah that everyone wishing to accept it could come and accept it.

19. Hayes, *What's Divine about Divine Law?* 149.

20. Mark D. Nanos and Magnus Zetterholm, eds., *Paul within Judaism: Restoring the First-Century Context to the Apostle* (Minneapolis: Fortress, 2015). See Zetterholm, "Paul within Judaism: The State of the Questions," ibid., 31–51.

21. Daniel Boyarin, *A Radical Jew: Paul and the Politics of Identity* (Berkeley: University of California Press, 1994).

22. Joshua Garroway, *Paul's Gentile-Jews: Neither Jew nor Gentile but Both* (New York: Palgrave MacMillan, 2012), 3.

23. Neil Elliott, *Liberating Paul: The Justice of God and the Politics of the Apostle* (Maryknoll, NY: Orbis, 1994); Elliott, *The Arrogance of the Nations: Reading Romans in the Shadow of Empire* (Minneapolis: Fortress, 2008).

24. See Michael P. Theophilos, "The Portrayal of Gentiles in Jewish Apocalyptic Literature," in David C. Sim and James S. McLaren, eds., *Attitudes to Gentiles in Ancient Judaism and Early Christianity*, Library of New Testament Studies 499 (London: Bloomsbury, 2013), 72–91.

25. See Terence L. Donaldson, *Judaism and the Gentiles: Patterns of Jewish Universalism (to 135 CE)* (Waco, TX: Baylor University Press, 2007), 499–505.

26. Compare Gal 2:11–14, where he upbraids Peter for hypocrisy, for desisting from eating with Gentiles when some people came from James; and his discussion of meat sacrificed to idols in 1 Corinthians 8.

27. *Pace* Mark Nanos, "The Myth of the 'Law-Free' Paul Standing between Christians and Jews," *Studies in Christian-Jewish Relations* 4:1–21. http://ejournals.bc.edu/ojs/index.php/scjr/article/view/1511/1364; Nanos, "Paul's Relationship to Torah in Light of His Strategy 'to Become Everything to Everyone' (1 Corinthians 9:19–23)," in Didier Pollefeyt and Reimund Bieringer, eds., *Paul and*

*Judaism: Crosscurrents in Pauline Exegesis and the Study of Jewish-Christian Relations* (London: Clark, 2012), 106–40. Nanos affirms that Paul was Torah observant.

28. Garroway, *Paul's Gentile-Jews,* 59–60, makes the extraordinary claim that "Paul does not discard the importance of genital circumcision in favor of the spiritual circumcision of the heart. On the contrary, Paul believes that the mark of circumcision—even genital circumcision—remains the definitive indicator of inclusion in the Abrahamic covenant; he simply maintains that baptism into Christ, and not a knife, becomes the mode by which one becomes genitally circumcised." He goes on to qualify: "Of course Paul does not think that baptism into Christ alters the physiological constitution of believers manifestly. Baptism did not remove the foreskins from his male charges." But in that case, what baptism accomplished was not genital circumcision, and the initial statement is only a verbal sleight of hand.

29. See Joseph A. Fitzmyer, *First Corinthians,* AYB 32 (New Haven, CT: Yale University Press, 2008), 308.

30. Sanders, *Paul, the Law, and the Jewish People,* 95. Cf. Heikki Räisänen, "Paul's Theological Difficulties with the Law," in E. A. Livingstone, ed., *Studia Biblica 1978,* vol. 3, *Papers on Paul and Other New Testament Authors,* JSNTSup 3 (Sheffield: JSNT, 1980), 301–20, here 312: "Paul obliged his Gentile converts to lead a decent life according to normal Jewish standards.

31. Sanders, *Paul, the Law, and the Jewish People,* 97.

32. J. D. G. Dunn, *Romans 1–8,* Word Bible Commentary 38a (Dallas: Word, 1988), 186–87. Compare Boyarin, *A Radical Jew,* 55.

33. See Donaldson, *Judaism and the Gentiles.*

34. See my book *Between Athens and Jerusalem: Jewish Identity in the Hellenistic Diaspora,* 2nd ed. (Grand Rapids, MI: Eerdmans, 2000), 155–85.

35. On the *Letter of Aristeas,* see now Benjamin G. Wright, *Aristeas to Philocrates, or On the Translation of the Law of the Jews,* CEJL 8 (Berlin: De Gruyter, 2015), 246–313; Stewart Moore, *Jewish Ethnic Identity and Relations in Hellenistic Egypt,* JSJSup 171 (Leiden: Brill, 2015), 204–54.

36. Donaldson, *Judaism and the Gentiles,* 499–505. Paula Fredriksen, "Judaism, the Circumcision of the Gentiles, and Apocalyptic Hope: Another Look at Galatians 1 and 2," *JTS* 42 (1991): 532–64, suggests that Paul's expectations for the Gentiles conformed to this hope. See now the nuanced discussion by Karin B. Neutel, *A Cosmopolitan Ideal: Paul's Declaration "Neither Jew nor Greek, Neither Slave nor Free, nor Male and Female" in the Context of First-Century Thought,* LNTS 513 (London: Bloomsbury, 2015), 92–104, who recognizes the importance of

Jewish eschatological traditions but argues that they do not provide a complete explanation of Paul's position.

37. Donaldson, *Judaism and the Gentiles,* 471.

38. Compare Philo, *Mos.* 1.35: almost every other people values the laws of the Jews.

39. See my essay "A Symbol of Otherness: Circumcision and Salvation in the First Century," in Collins, *Seers, Sibyls, and Sages in Hellenistic-Roman Judaism,* JSJSup 54 (Leiden: Brill, 1997), 211–35, esp. 226–28.

40. On the relevance of the Adiabene story to the Pauline dispute, as portrayed in Acts 15, see Daniel R. Schwartz, "God, Gentiles, and Jewish Law: On Acts 15 and Josephus' Adiabene Narrative," in Hubert Cancik, Hermann Lichtenberger, and Peter Schäfer, eds., *Geschichte—Tradition—Reflexion: Festschrift für Martin Hengel zum 70. Geburtstag* (Tübingen: Mohr Siebeck, 1996), 1:263–82. Mark D. Nanos, "The Question of Conceptualization: Qualifying Paul's Position on Circumcision in Dialogue with Josephus's Advisors to King Izates," in Nanos and Zetterholm, *Paul within Judaism,* 105–52, emphasizes that circumcision was the decisive step in becoming a Jew.

41. The symbolic understanding of circumcision as circumcision of the heart is found already in the Torah and the prophets: Lev 26:41; Deut 10:16, 30:6; Jer 4:4, 9:25; Ezek 44:7, 9. Cf. also 1QS 5:5.

42. Philo, *Spec.* 1.4–7.

43. See the overview and assessment by Gregory E. Sterling, "Was There a Common Ethic in Second Temple Judaism?," in John J. Collins, Gregory E. Sterling, and Ruth A. Clements, eds., *Sapiential Perspectives: Wisdom Literature in Light of the Dead Sea Scrolls,* STDJ 51 (Leiden: Brill, 2004), 171–94, especially his comments on the difference in basic orientation between diasporic and Hellenistic Judaism (p. 184).

44. Thielman, *From Plight to Solution,* 52.

45. Rom 3:20, 28; 4:2, 6; 9:12, 32; 11:16.

46. See above, chapter 5. The Hebrew word *ma'asim,* "works" or "deeds," is also found in CD 5:5–6 and 4Q174 iii 7. See Jacqueline C. R. de Roo, *Works of the Law at Qumran and in Paul* (Sheffield: Sheffield Phoenix, 2007), 4–25. In the first case the reference is to the deeds of David. In the second, it is not clear whether the reference is to works of the Law or works of praise.

47. 4QMMT C 26–32, trans. Michael Wise, Martin Abegg, Jr., and Edward Cook, *The Dead Sea Scrolls: A New Translation* (San Francisco: Harper San Francisco, 1996), 365, slightly adapted.

48. Martin Abegg, "Paul, 'Works of the Law,' and MMT," *BAR*, November/December 1994, 52–55, 82, argues that Paul was disputing not with mainstream Judaism but with the sectarians, but the usage was not necessarily peculiar to the sect known from the Scrolls.

49. See N. T. Wright, "4QMMT and Paul: Justification, 'Works,' and Eschatology," in Aang-Won (Aaron) Son, ed., *History and Exegesis: New Testament Essays in Honor of Dr. E. Earle Ellis for His 80th Birthday* (New York and London: T. & T. Clark, 2006), 104–32, here 110.

50. James D. G. Dunn, "4QMMT and Galatians," *NTS* 43 (1997): 147–53, here 151.

51. Michael Bachmann, "4QMMT und Galaterbrief, *m'sy htwrh*, und ERGA NOMOU," *ZNW* 89 (1998): 91–113, here 98. Wright, "4QMMT and Paul," 110, argues that Paul was not opposing halakah, understood as the detailed post-biblical elaboration of biblical law, but rather the insistence on basic biblical commandments such as circumcision. It is doubtful, however, whether biblical commandments can be separated from halakah, as the interpretation of biblical commandments was the underlying issue in a text like 4QMMT.

52. Compare the distinction between ritual and moral impurity formulated by Jonathan Klawans, *Impurity and Sin in Ancient Judaism* (New York: Oxford, 2000), 21–42, granted that this distinction is never explicit in the ancient texts.

53. See Jörg Frey, "Paul's Jewish Identity," in Jörg Frey, Daniel R. Schwartz, and Stephanie Gripentrog, eds., *Jewish Identity in the Greco-Roman World,* AGJU 71 (Leiden: Brill, 2007), 285–321, esp. 315–21.

54. Neither, I would argue, was it due to his encounter with the cosmopolitan ideals of the Hellenistic-Roman world adduced by Neutel, *A Cosmopolitan Ideal,* although these too may have informed his thinking to some degree.

55. On the idea of participating in Christ's resurrection, see Frederick S. Tappenden, *Resurrection in Paul: Cognition, Metaphor, and Transformation,* Early Christianity and Its Literature 19 (Atlanta: SBL, 2016), 203–68.

56. On the disputed meaning of this expression, see Joseph A. Fitzmyer, *Romans,* AB 33 (New York: Doubleday, 1992), 584–85; Robert Badenas, *Christ the End of the Law: Romans 10,4 in Pauline Perspective.* JSNTSup 10 (Sheffield: JSOT, 1985).

57. Thielman, *From Plight to Solution,* 126; see his full critique of Gaston and Gager, pp. 123–32. Also Garroway, *Paul's Gentile-Jews,* 78–79.

58. Boyarin, *A Radical Jew,* 42.

59. Hayes, *What's Divine about Divine Law?* 161.

60. Neil Elliott, "The Question of Politics: Paul as a Diaspora Jew under Roman Rule," in Nannos and Zetterholm, *Paul within Judaism*, 203–43, argues that Paul's revelation can be understood in the context of Jewish apocalypticism (see pp. 217–22): "There is nothing 'essentially' Christian about a Pharisee experiencing a visionary ascent to heaven and seeing the resurrected Jesus there" (p. 222). But the fact that such a vision is intelligible in a Jewish context does not lessen its transforming effect on Paul.

61. So Alex P. Jassen, *Mediating the Divine: Prophecy and Revelation in the Dead Sea Scrolls and Second Temple Judaism*, STDJ 68 (Leiden: Brill, 2007), 160, followed by Calvin J. Roetzel, "Paul and Nomos in the Messianic Age," in Ehrensperger and Tucker, *Reading Paul in Context*, 113–27, here 117–18. W. D. Davies, *Torah in the Messianic Age and/or Age to Come*, SBLMS 7 (Philadelphia: Society of Biblical Literature, 1952), had argued that the Torah would continue to be observed in the age to come, although possibly modified by the messiah.

62. I take the faith in question to be the faithfulness of Christ, rather than belief in him. See Richard B. Hays, *The Faith of Jesus Christ: The Narrative Substructure of Galatians 3:1–4:11*, 2nd ed. (Grand Rapids, MI: Eerdmans, 2002), 175; Stephen L. Young, "Paul's Ethnic Discourse on 'Faith': Christ's Faithfulness and Gentile Access to the Judean God in Romans 3:21–5:1," *HTR* 108 (2015): 30–51. Note, however, Hays's caution that "*pistis* is not a univocal concept for Paul" (*The Faith of Jesus Christ*, 174), and that Paul also calls for faith/trust in Christ.

63. See Donaldson, *Judaism and the Gentiles*; see also Donaldson, "Paul within Judaism: A Critical Evaluation from a 'New Perspective' Perspective," in Nanos and Zetterholm, *Paul within Judaism*, 277–301, esp. 284–85.

64. This point is emphasized by Garroway, *Paul's Gentile-Jews*, 2.

65. Hans Dieter Betz, *Galatians: A Commentary on Paul's Letters to the Churches in Galatia*, Hermeneia (Philadelphia: Fortress, 1979), 190.

66. Boyarin, *A Radical Jew*, 52. Neutel, *A Cosmopolitan Ideal*, 72–143, also emphasizes Greco-Roman ideas of the unity of all humanity.

67. Caroline Johnson Hodge, "Olive Trees and Ethnicities: Judeans and Gentiles in Rom. 11. 17–24," in Jürgen Zangenberg and Michael Labahn, eds., *Christians as a Religious Minority in a Multicultural City: Modes of Interaction and Identity Formation in Early Imperial Rome*, JSNTSup 243 (London and New York: T. & T. Clark, 2004), 77–89.

68. Ibid., 84.

69. The expression comes from Jonathan Hall, *Ethnic Identity in Greek Antiquity* (Cambridge: Cambridge University Press, 1997), 47–51.

70. So Dorians, Ionians, and Achaeans are all said to be descendants of Hellen.

71. See also William S. Campbell, *Paul and the Creation of Christian Identity*, LNTS (formerly JSNTS) 322 (London and New York: T. & T. Clark International, 2006), 61–67.

72. See further Johnson Hodge, *If Sons, Then Heirs: A Study of Kinship and Ethnicity in the Letters of Paul* (Oxford: Oxford University Press, 2007), 79–80.

73. Garroway, *Paul's Gentile-Jews*, 5.

74. Ibid., 59–60.

75. Ibid., 132: "reckoned genital circumcision."

76. Garroway, *Paul's Gentile-Jews*, 140.

77. Ibid., 151.

78. On the "double talk," or vacillation between old and new meanings, inherent in the process of redefinition, see Garroway, *Paul's Gentile-Jews*, 63.

79. Garroway, *Paul's Gentile-Jews*, 2.

80. Dunn, *Romans*, 1:128.

81. Garroway, *Paul's Gentile-Jews*, 95.

82. Campbell, *Paul and the Creation of Christian Identity*, 94, claims that "so far from opposing Jewish identity in Romans, Paul seeks to make space to allow it to continue indefinitely (and not simply to be temporarily tolerated)."

83. Philo uses the term *Ioudaios* twenty times in the *Exposition of the Law*, but never in the *Allegorical Commentary*, where he uses the term *Israel*. He uses *Israel* twice in the *Exposition*. See Ellen Birnbaum, *The Place of Judaism in Philo's Thought: Israel, Jews, and Proselytes*, BJS 290 (Atlanta: Scholars Press, 1986), 43–49. Birnbaum suggests that the difference in terminology is due to different audiences.

84. Garroway, *Paul's Gentile-Jews*, 144.

85. Boyarin, *A Radical Jew*, 151.

86. Ibid.

87. Ibid., 124–25. In contrast, Garroway's claim that Paul sees Gentile believers as descended from Abraham according to the flesh rests on tenuous exegesis of a difficult passage in Rom 4:1. Garroway, *Paul's Gentile-Jews*, 101–9.

88. John M. G. Barclay, "'Neither Jew nor Greek': Multiculturalism and the New Perspective on Paul," in Mark G. Brett, ed., *Ethnicity and the Bible* (Leiden: Brill, 1996), 197–214, here 210.

89. Arthur J. Droge, *Homer or Moses? Early Christian Interpretations of the History of Culture* (Tübingen: Mohr Siebeck, 1989), 196, referring to such writers as Aristides, the anonymous author of the Epistle to Diognetus, and Eusebius; Denise Kimber Buell, *Why This New Race? Ethnic Reasoning in Early Christianity* (New York: Columbia University Press, 2005).

90. Anthony D. Smith, *The Ethnic Origins of Nations* (Oxford: Blackwell, 1986), 35.

91. Frank M. Snowden, Jr., *Before Color Prejudice: The Ancient View of Blacks* (Cambridge, MA: Harvard University Press, 1983), 99. See further Buell, *Why This New Race?* 1.

92. Frances Young, "Greek Apologists of the Second Century," in Mark Edwards, Martin Goodman, and Simon Price, eds., *Apologetics in the Roman Empire* (New York: Oxford University Press, 1999), 103.

93. Buell, *Why This New Race?* 63, following Droge, *Homer or Moses?*

94. See Stanley K. Stowers, "Does Pauline Christianity Resemble a Hellenistic Philosophy?," in Troels Engberg-Pedersen, ed., *Paul beyond the Judaism/Hellenism Divide* (Louisville, KY: Westminster John Knox, 2001), 81–102; John M.G. Barclay, "Matching Theory and Practice: Josephus's Constitutional Ideal and Paul's Strategy in Corinth," ibid., 139–63.

95. Boyarin, *A Radical Jew*, 228.

### EPILOGUE

1. C.L. Crouch, *The Making of Israel*, VTSup 162 (Leiden: Brill, 2014), 109. See also above, chapter 1, note 116.

2. 2 Bar 85:3; trans. Matthias Henze, in Michael E. Stone and Mattathias Henze, *4Ezra and 2 Baruch: Translations, Introductions, and Notes* (Minneapolis: Fortress, 2013), 140.

# BIBLIOGRAPHY

Abegg, Martin, Jr. "Paul, 'Works of the Law,' and MMT." *BAR*, November/ December 1994, 52–55, 82.

Achenbach, Reinhard. "The Story of the Revelation at the Mountain of God." In Eckart Otto and J. LeRoux, eds., *A Critical Study of the Pentateuch: An Encounter between Europe and Africa*, 126–52. Altes Testament und Moderne 20. Münster: Lit Verlag, 2005.

Ackerman, Susan. *Under Every Green Tree: Popular Religion in Sixth-Century Judah*. Harvard Semitic Monographs 46. Atlanta: Scholars Press, 1992.

Albertz, Rainer. *A History of Israelite Religion in the Old Testament Period*. 2 vols. Old Testament Library. Louisville, KY: Westminster John Knox, 1994.

———. "Why a Reform like Josiah's Must Have Happened." In Grabbe, *Good Kings and Bad Kings*, 27–46.

———. "Zur Theologisierung des Rechts im Alten Israel." In Rainer Albertz, ed., *Religion und Gesellschaft: Studien zu ihrer Wechselbeziehung in den Kulturen des Antiken Orients*, 115–32. Alter Orient und Altes Testament 248. Münster: Ugarit Verlag, 1997.

Alexander, Philip S. "The Enochic Literature and the Bible: Intertextuality and Its Implications." In E. D. Herbert and E. Tov, eds., *The Bible as Book: The Hebrew Bible and the Judaean Desert Discoveries*, 57–69. London: The British Library, 2002.

———. *The Mystical Texts: Songs of the Sabbath Sacrifice and Related Manuscripts*. Library of Second Temple Studies 61. London and New York: Clark, 2006.

————. "Predestination and Free Will in the Theology of the Dead Sea Scrolls." In John M.G. Barclay and Simon Gathercole, eds., *Divine and Human Agency in Paul and His Cultural Environment,* 39–47. Library of New Testament Studies 335. London and New York: Clark, 2006.

————. "Retelling the Old Testament." In D.A. Carson and H.G.M. Williamson, eds., *It is Written: Scripture Citing Scripture,* 99–121. Cambridge: Cambridge University Press, 1988.

Alter, Robert. *Canon and Authority: Modern Writing and the Authority of Scripture.* New Haven, CT: Yale University Press, 2000.

Anderson, Benedict. *Imagined Communities. Reflections on the Origin and Spread of Nationalism.* London: Verso, 1983.

Anderson, Bernard W. "The Place of the Book of Esther in the Christian Bible." *JR* 30 (1950): 32–43.

Assmann, Jan. *Herrschaft und Heil: Politische Theologie in Ägypten, Israel und Europa.* Munich and Vienna: Hanser, 2000.

Bachmann, Michael. "4QMMT und Galaterbrief, *m'sy ḥtwrh,* und ERGA NOMOU." *ZNW* 89 (1998): 91–113.

Baden, Joel. *The Composition of the Pentateuch: Renewing the Documentary Hypothesis.* Anchor Yale Bible Reference Library. New Haven, CT: Yale University Press, 2012.

————. "The Deuteronomic Evidence for the Documentary Theory." In Dozeman, Schmid, and Schwartz, *The Pentateuch,* 327–44.

————. *The Promise to the Patriarchs.* New York: Oxford University Press, 2013.

Badenas, Robert. *Christ the End of the Law: Romans 10,4 in Pauline Perspective.* Journal for the Study of the New Testament Supplements 10. Sheffield: JSOT, 1985.

Baker, Cynthia. "A 'Jew' by Any Other Name?" *JAJ* 2 (2011): 153–80.

Balch, David L. "Household Codes." *Anchor Bible Dictionary,* 3:328–29.

————. "Household Codes." In D.E. Aune, ed., *The New Testament and Graeco-Roman Literature,* 25–30. Atlanta: Scholars Press, 1988.

Barbour, Jennie. *The Story of Israel in the Book of Qohelet: Ecclesiastes as Cultural Memory.* Oxford: Oxford University Press, 2012.

Barclay, John M.G. *Flavius Josephus, Against Apion: Translation and Commentary.* Leiden: Brill, 2007.

————. *Jews in the Mediterranean Diaspora from Alexander to Trajan (323 BCE–117 CE).* Edinburgh: Clark, 1996.

———. "Matching Theory and Practice: Josephus's Constitutional Ideal and Paul's Strategy in Corinth." In Engberg-Pedersen, *Paul beyond the Judaism/Hellenism Divide*, 139–63.

———. "'Neither Jew nor Greek': Multiculturalism and the New Perspective on Paul." In Mark G. Brett, ed., *Ethnicity and the Bible*, 197–214. Leiden: Brill, 1996.

Bar-Kochva, Bezalel. *Pseudo-Hecataeus "On the Jews": Legitimizing the Jewish Diaspora.* Berkeley: University of California Press, 1998.

Barrick, W. Boyd. *The King and the Cemeteries: Toward a New Understanding of Josiah's Reform.* Vetus Testamentum Supplements 88. Leiden: Brill, 2002.

Barth, Fredrik. *Ethnic Groups and Boundaries.* Boston: Little, Brown and Co., 1969.

———. "Ethnic Groups and Boundaries." In Hutchinson and Smith, *Ethnicity*, 75–83.

Barton, John, and Francesca Stavrakopoulou, eds. *Religious Diversity in Ancient Israel and Judah.* London: Clark, 2010.

Batnitzky, Leora. *How Judaism Became a Religion: An Introduction to Modern Jewish Thought.* Princeton, NJ: Princeton University Press, 2011.

Battifol, P. "Le livre de la prière d'Aseneth." In P. Battifol, *Studia patristica: Études d'ancienne littérature chrétienne*, 1–115. Paris: Leroux, 1889–90.

Baumgarten, Albert I. *The Flourishing of Jewish Sects in the Maccabean Era: An Interpretation.* JSJSup 55. Leiden: Brill, 1997.

———. "Seekers after Smooth Things." In L. H. Schiffman and J. C. VanderKam, eds., *Encyclopedia of the Dead Sea Scrolls*, 2:857–59. New York: Oxford University Press, 2000.

Beal, Timothy K. *Esther.* Berit Olam. Collegeville, MN: Liturgical Press, 1999.

Becking, Bob. "Die Gottheiten der Juden in Elephantine." In Manfred Oeming and Konrad Schmid, eds., *Der eine Gott und die Götter: Polytheismus und Monotheismus im antiken Israel*, 203–26. Zurich: Theologischer Verlag, 2003.

———. *Ezra, Nehemiah, and the Construction of Early Jewish Identity.* Forschungen zum Alten Testament 80. Tübingen: Mohr Siebeck, 2011.

———. "Yehudite Identity in Elephantine." In Lipschitz, Knoppers, and Oeming, *Judah and the Judeans in the Achaemenid Period*, 403–19.

Bedenbender, Andreas. *Der Gott der Welt tritt auf den Sinai.* Arbeiten zur neutestamentlichen Theologie und Zeitgeschichte 8. Berlin: Institut Kirche und Judentum, 2000.

————. "The Place of the Torah in the Early Enoch Literature." In Boccaccini and Collins, *The Early Enoch Literature*, 65–79.

Bedford, Peter R. "Diaspora-Homeland Relations in Ezra-Nehemiah." *VT* 52 (2002): 147–65.

Begrich, J. "Die priesterliche Torah." *ZAW* 66 (1936): 63–88.

Berger, Klaus. *Die Gesetzesauslegung Jesu*. Wissenschaftliche Monographien zum Alten und Neuen Testament 40. Neukirchen-Vluyn: Neukirchener Verlag, 1972,

Berman, Joshua. "The History of Legal Theory and the Study of Biblical Law." *CBQ* 76 (2014): 19–39.

Berner, Christoph. *Jahre, Jahrwochen und Jubiläen: Heptadische Geschichtskonzeptionen im antiken Judentum*. Beihefte zur Zeitschrift für die alttestamentliche Wissenschaft 363. Berlin: De Gruyter, 2006.

Bernstein, Moshe. "The Genre(s) of the *Genesis Apocryphon*." In Berthelot and Stökl Ben Ezra, *Aramaica Qumranica*, 317–38.

————. *Reading and Re-Reading Scripture at Qumran*. Vol. 2, *Law, Pesher, and the History of Interpretation*. Leiden: Brill, 2013.

————. "Re-arrangement, Anticipation, and Harmonization as Exegetical Features in the Genesis Apocryphon." *DSD* 3 (1996): 37–57.

————. "'Rewritten Bible': A Generic Category Which Has Outlived Its Usefulness?" *Textus* 22 (2005): 169–96.

Berry, G. R. "The Code Found in the Temple." *JBL* 39 (1920): 44–51.

Berthelot, Katell. "References to Biblical Texts in the Aramaic Texts from Qumran." In Berthelot and Stökl Ben Ezra, *Aramaica Qumranica*, 183–98.

Berthelot, Katell, and Daniel Stökl Ben Ezra. "Aramaica Qumranica: Introduction." In Berthelot and Stökl Ben Ezra, *Aramaica Qumranica: Proceedings of the Conference on the Aramaic Texts from Qumran in Aix-en-Provence 30 June–2 July 2008*, 1–12. Studies on the Texts of the Desert of Judah 94. Leiden: Brill, 2010.

Betz, Hans Dieter. *Galatians: A Commentary on Paul's Letter to the Churches in Galatia*. Hermeneia. Philadelphia: Fortress, 1979.

Bhabha, Homi K. *The Location of Culture*. London: Routledge, 1994.

Bickerman, Elias J. *Studies on Jewish and Christian History*. 2 vols. Leiden: Brill, 2011.

Birnbaum, Ellen. *The Place of Judaism in Philo's Thought: Israel, Jews, and Proselytes*. Brown Judaic Studies 290. Atlanta: Scholars Press, 1986.

Blenkinsopp, Joseph. *Ezra-Nehemiah: A Commentary*. Philadelphia: Westminster, 1988.

————. *Isaiah 56–66*. Anchor Bible 19B. New York: Doubleday, 2003.

————. *Judaism: The First Phase; The Place of Ezra and Nehemiah in the Origins of Judaism.* Grand Rapids, MI: Eerdmans, 2009.

————. "Was the Pentateuch the Civic and Religious Constitution of the Jewish Ethnos in the Persian Period?" In Watts, *Persia and Torah*, 41–62.

Bloch-Smith, Elizabeth. "Assyrians Abet Israelite Cultic Reforms: Sennacherib and the Centralization of the Israelite Cult." In J. David Schloen, ed., *Exploring the Long Durée: Essays in Honor of Lawrence E. Stager*, 35–44. Winona Lake, IN: Eisenbrauns, 2009.

Blum, Erhard. "The Decalogue and the Composition History of the Pentateuch." In Dozeman, Schmid, and Schwartz, *The Pentateuch*, 289–301.

————. "Israël à la montagne de Dieu: Remarques sur Ex 19–24. 32–34 et sur le contexte littéraire et historique de sa composition." In Albert de Pury, ed., *Le Pentateuque en question*, 271–95. Le Monde de la Bible 19. Geneva: Labor et Fides, 1989.

Boccaccini, Gabriele. *Beyond the Essene Hypothesis.* Grand Rapids, MI: Eerdmans, 1998.

————, ed. *Enoch and the Messiah Son of Man: Revisiting the Book of Parables.* Grand Rapids, MI: Eerdmans, 2007.

————, ed. *The Origins of Enochic Judaism, Proceedings of the First Enoch Seminar, University of Michigan, Sesto Fiorentino, Italy, June 19–23, 2001 = Henoch* 24.1–2 (2002).

————. *Roots of Rabbinic Judaism: An Intellectual History from Ezekiel to Daniel.* Grand Rapids, MI: Eerdmans, 2002.

Boccaccini, Gabriele, and John J. Collins, eds. *The Early Enoch Literature.* JSJSup 121. Leiden: Brill, 2007.

Boccaccini, Gabriele, and Giovanni Ibba, eds. *Enoch and the Mosaic Torah: The Evidence of Jubilees.* Grand Rapids, MI: Eerdmans, 2009.

Boda, Mark. *Haggai, Zechariah.* NIV Application Commentary Series. Grand Rapids, MI: Zondervan, 2004.

Bohak, Gideon. *Joseph and Aseneth and the Jewish Temple in Heliopolis.* Society of Biblical Literature, Early Judaism and Its Literature 10. Atlanta: Scholars Press, 1996.

Bolkenstein, H. *Wohltätigkeit and Armenpflege im vorchristlichen Altertum.* Utrecht: Oosthoek, 1939.

Bousset, Wilhelm. *Die Religion des Judentums im neutestamentlichen Zeitalter.* Berlin: Reuther und Reichard, 1903.

————. *Volksfrömmigkeit und Schriftgelehrtentum: Antwort auf Herrn Perles' Kritik meiner "Religion des Judentums im N.T. Zeitalter."* Berlin: Reuther und Reichard, 1903.

Boyarin, Daniel. *A Radical Jew: Paul and the Politics of Identity*. Berkeley: University of California Press, 1994.

———. "Rethinking Jewish Christianity: An Argument for Dismantling a Dubious Category (to Which Is Appended a Correction of My *Border Lines*)." *JQR* 99 (2009): 7–36.

Brett, Mark G., ed. *Ethnicity and the Bible*. Biblical Interpretation 19. Leiden: Brill, 1996.

———. "Nationalism and the Hebrew Bible." In John Rogerson, Margaret Davies, and M. Daniel Carroll R., eds., *The Bible in Ethics: The Second Sheffield Colloquium*, 136–63. Journal for the Study of the Old Testament Supplements 207. Sheffield: Sheffield Academic Press, 1995.

Briant, Pierre. *From Cyrus to Alexander: A History of the Persian Empire*. Winona Lake, IN: Eisenbrauns, 2002.

Brooke, George J. "Biblical Interpretation in the Wisdom Texts from Qumran." In C. Hempel, A. Lange, and H. Lichtenberger, eds., *The Wisdom Texts from Qumran and the Development of Sapiential Thought*, 201–20. Bibliotheca Ephemeridum Theologicarum Lovaniensium 159. Leuven: Peeters, 2002.

———. "Joseph, Aseneth, and Lévi-Strauss." In G. J. Brooke and J.-D. Kaestli, eds., *Narrativity in Biblical and Related Texts*, 185–200. Leuven: Peeters, 2000.

———. "Men and Women as Angels in Joseph and Aseneth." *JSP* 14 (2005): 159–77.

———. "Rewritten Bible." In L. H. Schiffman and J. C. VanderKam, eds., *The Encyclopedia of the Dead Sea Scrolls*, 2:777–81. New York: Oxford University Press, 2000.

———. "The Rewritten Law, Prophets, and Psalms: Issues for Understanding the Text of the Bible." In E. D. Herbert and Emanuel Tov, eds., *The Bible as Book: The Hebrew Bible and the Judaean Desert Discoveries*, 31–40. London: British Library, 2002.

Brooke, George J., et al. *Qumran Cave 4, XVII*. Discoveries in the Judean Desert 22. Oxford: Clarendon, 1996.

Buell, Denise Kimber. *Why This New Race? Ethnic Reasoning in Early Christianity*. New York: Columbia University Press, 2005.

Byrskog, Samuel. *Jesus the Only Teacher: Didactic Authority and Transmission in Ancient Israel, Ancient Judaism, and the Matthean Community*. Coniectanea Biblica, NT Series 24. Stockholm: Almqvist & Wiksell, 1994.

Calhoun, Craig. "Nationalism and Ethnicity." *Annual Review of Sociology* 19 (1993): 211–39.

Campbell, Antony F., and Mark A. O'Brien, *Sources of the Pentateuch: Texts, Introductions, Annotations.* Minneapolis: Fortress, 1993.

Campbell, Jonathan G. "'Rewritten Bible' and 'Parabiblical Texts': A Terminological and Ideological Critique." In Jonathan Campbell et al., eds., *New Directions in Qumran Studies: Proceedings of the Bristol Colloquium on the Dead Sea Scrolls, 8–10 September 2003,* 43–68. London: T & T Clark, 2005.

Campbell, William S. *Paul and the Creation of Christian Identity.* Library of New Testament Studies (formerly Journal for the Study of the New Testament Supplements) 322. London and New York: T & T Clark International, 2006.

Carr, David M. *The Formation of the Hebrew Bible: A New Reconstruction.* Oxford: Oxford University Press, 2011.

———. "The Rise of Torah." In Knoppers and Levinson, *The Pentateuch as Torah,* 39–56.

———. *Writing on the Tablet of the Heart: The Origins of Scripture and Literature.* Oxford and New York: Oxford University Press, 2005.

Charles, Robert Henry. *A Critical and Exegetical Comentary on the Book of Daniel.* Oxford: Clarendon, 1929.

Charlesworth, James H., ed. *Old Testament Pseudepigrapha.* Vol. 1, *Apocalyptic Literature and Testaments.* Garden City, NY: Doubleday, 1983.

———. "*Temple Scroll*-Like Document (11Q21)." In Schiffman, Gross, and Rand, *Temple Scroll and Related Documents,* 227.

———. "*Temple Scroll* Source or Divergent Copy (4Q365a)." In Schiffman, Gross, and Rand, *Temple Scroll and Related Documents,* 235.

———. "*Temple Scroll* Source or Earlier Edition (4Q524)." In Schiffman, Gross, and Rand, *Temple Scroll and Related Documents,* 247.

Chesnutt, Randall S. *From Death to Life: Conversion in "Joseph and Aseneth."* Journal for the Study of the Pseudepigrapha Supplements 16. Sheffield: Sheffield Academic Press, 1995.

Childs, Brevard S. *Introduction to the Old Testament as Scripture.* Philadelphia: Fortress, 1981.

Coblentz Bautch, Kelley. *A Study of the Geography of 1 Enoch 17–19: "No One Has Seen What I Have Seen."* Journal for the Study of Judaism 81. Leiden: Brill, 2003.

Cogan, Mordechai, and Hayim Tadmor. *II Kings.* AB 11. New York: Doubleday, 1988.

Cohen, Abner P. *Two-Dimensional Man: An Essay on Power and Symbolism in Complex Society.* London: Routledge & Kegan Paul, 1974.

———, ed. *Urban Ethnicity.* London: Tavistock, 1974.

Cohen, Shaye J. D. *The Beginnings of Jewishness: Boundaries, Varieties, Uncertainties.* Berkeley: University of California Press, 1999.

———. "Common Judaism in Greek and Latin Authors." In Udoh et al., *Redefining First-Century Jewish and Christian Identities,* 69–87.

Collins, John J. "The Angelic Life." In Turid Karlsen Seim and Jorunn Økland, eds., *Metamorphoses: Resurrection, Body, and Transformative Practices in Early Christianity,* 291–310. Ekstasis 1. Berlin: De Gruyter, 2009. Reprinted in Collins, *Scriptures and Sectarianism,* 195–211.

———. *Apocalypse, Prophecy, and Pseudepigraphy: Essays on Jewish Apocalyptic Literature.* Grand Rapids, MI: Eerdmans, 2015.

———. *The Apocalyptic Imagination.* 3rd ed. Grand Rapids, MI: Eerdmans, 2016.

———. *Apocalypticism in the Dead Sea Scrolls.* London: Routledge, 1997.

———. *Between Athens and Jerusalem: Jewish Identity in the Hellenistic Diaspora.* 2nd ed. Grand Rapids, MI: Eerdmans, 2000.

———. *Beyond the Qumran Community: The Sectarian Movement of the Dead Sea Scrolls.* Grand Rapids, MI: Eerdmans, 2010.

———. "The Book of Daniel and the Dead Sea Scrolls." In Nora David, Armin Lange, Kristin De Troyer, and Shani Tzoreff, eds., *The Hebrew Bible in Light of the Dead Sea Scrolls,* 203–17. Forschungen zur Religion und Literatur des Alten und Neuen Testaments 239. Göttingen: Vandenhoeck & Ruprecht, 2012. Reprinted in Collins, *Scriptures and Sectarianism,* 102–15.

———. "The Construction of Israel in the Sectarian Rule Books." In Alan J. Avery-Peck, Jacob Neusner, and Bruce D. Chilton, eds., *Judaism in Late Antiquity,* pt. 5, *The Judaism of Qumran: A Systemic Reading of the Dead Sea Scrolls,* 1: *Theory of Israel,* 25–42. Leiden: Brill, 2001.

———. *Daniel: A Commentary on the Book of Daniel.* Hermeneia. Minneapolis: Fortress, 1993.

———. *The Dead Sea Scrolls: A Biography.* Princeton, NJ: Princeton University Press, 2013.

———. "Enoch and Ezra." In Matthias Henze and Gabriele Boccaccini, eds., *Fourth Ezra and Second Baruch: Reconstruction after the Fall,* 83–97. Journal for the Study of Judaism Supplements 164. Leiden: Brill, 2013. Reprinted in Collins, *Apocalypse, Prophecy, and Pseudepigraphy,* 235–50.

———. "'Enochic Judaism' and the Sect of the Dead Sea Scrolls." In Boccaccini and Collins, *The Early Enoch Literature,* 283–99. Reprinted in Collins, *Scriptures and Sectarianism,* 150–63.

———. "The Eschatology of Zechariah." In Lester L. Grabbe and Robert D. Haak, eds., *Knowing the End from the Beginning: The Prophetic, the Apocalyptic and Their Relationships*, 74–84. London and New York: T & T Clark, 2003.

———. "The Genre of the Book of *Jubilees*." In Eric F. Mason, Kelley Coblentz Bautch, Angela Kim Harkins, and Daniel A. Machiela, eds., *A Teacher for All Generations: Essays in Honor of James C. VanderKam*, 737–55. Journal for the Study of Judaism Supplements 153/2. Leiden: Brill, 2012.

———. "Gentiles in the Dead Sea Scrolls." In David C. Sim and James S. McLaren, eds., *Attitudes to Gentiles in Ancient Judaism and Early Christianity*, 46–61. London and New York: Clark, 2013.

———. "The Interpretation of Genesis in the Dead Sea Scrolls." In Moriya and Hata, *Pentateuchal Traditions in the Late Second Temple Period*, 156–75.

———. "In the Likeness of the Holy Ones: The Creation of Humankind in a Wisdom Text from Qumran." In D. W. Parry and E. Ulrich, eds., *The Provo International Conference on the Dead Sea Scrolls*, 609–18. Leiden: Brill, 1999.

———. *Jewish Cult and Hellenistic Culture*. Journal for the Study of Judaism Supplements 100. Leiden: Brill, 2005.

———. *Jewish Wisdom in the Hellenistic Age*. Louisville, KY: Westminster John Knox, 1997.

———. "The Judaism of the Book of Tobit." In Géza G. Xeravits and József Zsengellér, *The Book of Tobit: Text, Tradition, and Theology*, 24–40. Journal for the Study of Judaism Supplements 98. Leiden: Brill, 2005.

———. "The Law in the Late Second Temple Period." In Pamela Barmash, ed., *The Oxford Handbook of Biblical Law*. Oxford: Oxford University Press, forthcoming.

———. "Pseudepigraphy and Group Formation in Second Temple Judaism." In Esther Chazon and Michael E. Stone, eds., *Pseudepigraphic Perspectives: The Apocrypha and Pseudepigrapha in Light of the Dead Sea Scrolls*, 43–58. Studies in the Texts of the Desert of Judah 31. Leiden: Brill, 1999.

———. *Scriptures and Sectarianism*. Wissenschaftliche Untersuchungen zum Neuen Testament 332. Tübingen: Mohr Siebeck, 2014.

———. *Seers, Sibyls, and Sages in Hellenistic-Roman Judaism*. Journal for the Study of Judaism Supplements 54. Leiden: Brill, 1997.

———. "The Sibylline Oracles." In Charlesworth, *Old Testament Pseudepigrapha*, 1:317–472.

———. "Temple or Taxes? What Sparked the Maccabean Revolt?" In J.J. Collins and J.G. Manning, eds., *Revolt and Resistance in the Ancient Classical World and the Near East: In the Crucible of Empire*, 189–201. Leiden: Brill, 2016.

———. "The Transformation of Aseneth." In Anne Hege Grung, Marianne Bjelland Kartzow, and Anna Rebecca Solevåg, eds., *Bodies, Borders, Believers: Ancient Texts and Present Conversations; Essays in Honor of Turid Karlsen Seim on Her 70th Birthday*, 93–108. Eugene, OR: Pickwick, 2015.

Collins, John J., and Peter W. Flint. "243–245. 4QpsDaniel$^{a-c}$." In Brooke et al., *Qumran Cave 4, XVII*, 95–164.

———, eds. *The Book of Daniel: Composition and Reception*. VTSup 83. Leiden: Brill, 2001.

Collins, John J., and Daniel C. Harlow, eds. *The Eerdmans Dictionary of Early Judaism*. Grand Rapids, MI: Eerdmans, 2010.

Cotton, Hannah M. "The Rabbis and the Documents." In Martin Goodman, ed., *Jews in a Graeco-Roman World*, 167–79. Oxford: Clarendon, 1998.

Cotton, Hannah M., and Ada Yardeni. *Aramaic, Hebrew, and Greek Documentary Texts from Naḥal Ḥever and Other Sites, with an Appendix Containing Alleged Qumran Texts (The Seiyal Collection II)*. Discoveries in the Judean Desert 27. Oxford: Clarendon, 1997.

Cowey, James S., and Klaus Maresch. *Urkunden des Politeuma der Juden von Herakleopolis (144/3–133/2 v. Chr.) (P. Polit Iud.)*. Abhandlungen der Nordrhein-Westfälischen Akademie der Wissenschaften. Papyrologica Coloniensia 29. Wiesbaden: Westdeutscher Verlag, 2001.

Cowley, A.E. *Aramaic Papyri of the Fifth Century B.C.* Oxford: Clarendon, 1923.

Crenshaw, James L. *Old Testament Wisdom: An Introduction*. Expanded ed. Louisville, KY: Westminster John Knox, 1998.

Cross, Frank Moore. *The Ancient Library of Qumran*. 3rd ed. Sheffield: Sheffield Academic Press, 1995. Original publication: Garden City, NY: Doubleday, 1958.

———. *Canaanite Myth and Hebrew Epic*. Cambridge, MA: Harvard University Press, 1973.

Crouch, C.L. *Israel and the Assyrians: Deuteronomy, the Succession Treaty of Esarhaddon, and the Nature of Subversion*. SBL Ancient Near East Monographs 8. Atlanta: SBL, 2014.

———. *The Making of Israel: Cultural Diversity in the Southern Levant and the Formation of Ethnic Identity in Deuteronomy*. Vetus Testamentum Supplements 162. Leiden: Brill, 2014.

Crüsemann, Frank. "Das Bundesbuch: Historischer Ort und institutioneller Hintergrund." In J.A. Emerton, ed., *Congress Volume: Jerusalem 1986*, 27–41. Vetus Testamentum Supplements 40. Leiden: Brill, 1988.

Davies, Philip R. "Josiah and the Law Book." In Grabbe, *Good Kings and Bad Kings*, 65–77.

Davies, W.D. *Torah in the Messianic Age and/or Age to Come*. Society of Biblical Literature Monograph Series 7. Philadelphia: SBL, 1952.

Davila, James R. *The Provenance of the Pseudepigrapha*. Journal for the Study of Judaism Supplements 105. Leiden: Brill, 2005.

Davis, C.J.P. *The Cave 4 Apocryphon of Jeremiah and the Qumran Jeremianic Traditions: Prophetic Persona and Community Identity*. Studies in the Texts of the Desert of Judah 111. Leiden: Brill, 2014.

———. "Torah-Performance and History in the Golah: Rewritten Bible or 'Re-Presentational' Authority in the Apocryphon of Jeremiah C." In Flint, Duhaime, and Baek, *Celebrating the Dead Sea Scrolls*, 467–95.

Deselaers, Paul. *Das Buch Tobit: Studien zu seiner Entstehung, Komposition und Theologie*. Orbis Biblicus et Orientalis 32. Göttingen: Vandenhoeck & Ruprecht, 1982.

Deutsch, Karl. *Nationalism and Its Alternatives*. New York: Knopf, 1969.

Dever, William G. *Did God Have a Wife?* Grand Rapids, MI: Eerdmans, 2005.

———. "The Silence of the Text: An Archaeological Commentary on 2 Kings 23." In Michael D. Coogan, J. Cheryl Exum, and Lawrence E. Stager, eds., *Scripture and Other Artifacts: Essays on the Bible and Archaeology in Honor of Philip J. King*, 143–68. Louisville, KY: Westminster John Knox, 1994.

———. *Who Were the Early Israelites and Where Did They Come From?* Grand Rapids, MI: Eerdmans, 2003.

Diebner, B.-J., and C. Nauerth. "Die Inventio des *seper hatorah* in 2 Kön 22: Struktur, Intention und Funktion von Auffindungslegenden." *DBAT* 18 (1984): 95–118.

Dimant, Devorah. "Hebrew Pseudepigrapha at Qumran." In Eibert Tigchelaar, ed., *Old Testament Pseudepigrapha and the Scriptures*, 89–103. Bibliotheca Ephemeridum Theologicarum Lovaniensium 270. Leuven: Peeters, 2015.

———. *Qumran Cave 4, XXI: Parabiblical Texts*. Pt. 4: *Pseudo-Prophetic Texts*. Discoveries in the Judean Desert 30. Oxford: Clarendon, 2000.

Dion, Paul-Eugène. "La religion d'Éléphantine: Un reflet du Juda d'avant l'exil." In Ulrich Hübner and Ernst Axel Knauf, eds., *Kein Land für sich allein: Studien zum Kulturkontakt in Kanaan, Israel/Palästina und Ebirnâri für Manfred Weippert zum 65. Geburtstag*, 243–54. Orbis Biblicus et Orientalis 186. Freiburg: Universitätsverlag; Göttingen: Vandenhoeck & Ruprecht, 2002.

DiTommaso, Lorenzo. "4QPseudo-Daniel[a-b] (4Q243–244) and the Book of Daniel." *DSD* 12 (2005): 101–33.

Doering, Lutz. *Schabbat: Sabbathalacha und –praxis im antiken Judentum und Urchristentum.* Texte und Studien zum Antiken Judentum 78. Tübingen: Mohr Siebeck, 1999.

Donaldson, Terence L. *Judaism and the Gentiles: Patterns of Jewish Universalism (to 135 CE).* Waco, TX: Baylor University Press, 2007.

———. "Paul within Judaism: A Critical Evaluation from a 'New Perspective' Perspective." In Nanos and Zetterholm, eds., *Paul within Judaism,* 277–301.

Donner, Hubert. "Jesaja lvi 1–7: Ein Abrogationsfall innerhalb des Kanons; Implikationen and Konsequenzen." In J.A. Emerton, ed., *Congress Volume Salamanca 1983,* 81–95. Vetus Testamentum Supplements 36. Leiden: Brill, 1985.

Doran, Robert. *2 Maccabees.* Hermeneia. Minneapolis: Fortress, 2012.

———. "The Non-dating of *Jubilees: Jub* 34–38. 23:14–31 in Narrative Context." *JSJ* 20 (1989): 1–11.

———. "The Persecution of Judeans by Antiochus IV Epiphanes: The Significance of 'Ancestral Laws.'" In Daniel C. Harlow, Karina Martin Hogan, Matthew Goff, and Joel Kaminsky, eds., *The "Other" in Second Temple Judaism,* 423–33. Grand Rapids, MI: Eerdmans, 2011.

Dozeman, Thomas B. *Exodus.* Eerdmans Critical Commentary. Grand Rapids, MI: Eerdmans, 2009.

Dozeman, Thomas B., Konrad Schmid, and Baruch J. Schwartz, eds. *The Pentateuch: International Perspectives on Current Research.* Tübingen: Mohr Siebeck, 2011.

Drawnel, Henryk. *An Aramaic Wisdom Text from Qumran: A New Interpretation of the Levi Document.* Journal for the Study of Judaism 86. Leiden: Brill, 2004.

Driver, S.R. *Introduction to the Literature of the Old Testament.* Edinburgh: Clark, 1891.

Droge, Arthur J. *Homer or Moses? Early Christian Interpretations of the History of Culture.* Tübingen: Mohr Siebeck, 1989.

Duhaime, Jean. "Dualistic Reworking in the Scrolls from Qumran." *CBQ* 49 (1987) 32–56.

Dunn, James D.G. "4QMMT and Galatians." *NTS* 43 (1997): 147–53.

———. *Jesus, Paul, and the Law: Studies in Mark and Galatians.* Louisville, KY: Westminster John Knox, 1990.

———. "The New Perspective on Paul." *Bulletin of the John Rylands Library* 65 (1983): 95–122. Reprinted, with an "additional note," in Dunn, *Jesus, Paul, and the Law,* 183–214.

————. *Romans 1–8*. Word Bible Commentary 38a. Dallas: Word, 1988.

Dutcher-Walls, Patricia. "The Circumscription of the King: Deuteronomy 17:16–17 in Its Ancient Social Context." *JBL* 121 (2002): 601–16.

Edelman, Diana. "Ethnicity and Early Israel." In Brett, *Ethnicity and the Bible*, 25–55.

Ehrensperger, Kathy, and Brian J. Tucker, eds. *Reading Paul in Context: Explorations in Identity Formation*. Library of New Testament Studies (formerly Journal for the Study of the New Testament Supplements) 428. London and New York: T & T Clark International, 2010.

Elliott, Mark. "Covenant and Cosmology in the *Book of the Watchers* and the Astronomical Book." In Boccaccini, *The Origins of Enochic Judaism*, 23–38.

————. *The Survivors of Israel: A Reconsideration of the Theology of Pre-Christian Judaism*. Grand Rapids, MI: Eerdmans, 2000.

Elliott, Neil. *The Arrogance of the Nations: Reading Romans in the Shadow of Empire*. Minneapolis: Fortress, 2008.

————. *Liberating Paul: The Justice of God and the Politics of the Apostle*. Maryknoll, NY: Orbis, 1994.

————. "The Question of Politics: Paul as a Diaspora Jew under Roman Rule." In Nanos and Zetterholm, eds., *Paul within Judaism*, 303–43.

Engberg-Pedersen, Troels, ed. *Paul beyond the Judaism/Hellenism Divide*. Louisville, KY: Westminster John Knox, 2001.

Eshel, Esther. "*Genesis Apocryphon.*" In Collins and Harlow, *The Eerdmans Dictionary of Early Judaism*, 664–67.

Eshel, Hanan. *The Dead Sea Scrolls and the Hasmonean State*. Grand Rapids, MI: Eerdmans, 2008.

Esler, Philip F. "Ezra-Nehemiah as a Narrative of (Re-Invented) Israelite Identity." *Biblical Interpretation* 11 (2003): 413–26.

————. "Judean Ethnic Identity in Josephus' *Against Apion*." In Zuleika Rodgers, with Margaret Daly-Denton and Anne Fitzpatrick McKinley, eds., *A Wandering Galilean: Essays in Honour of Seán Freyne*, 73–91. Journal for the Study of Judaism Supplements 132. Leiden: Brill, 2009.

Eynikel, Erik. *The Reform of King Josiah and the Composition of the Deuteronomistic History*. OTS 33. Leiden: Brill, 1996.

Faber, Richard, and Renate Schlesier, eds. *Die Restauration der Götter: Antike Religionen und Neo-Paganismus*. Würzburg: Königshausen und Neumann, 1986.

Fales, F. M. "After Ta'yinat: The New Status of Esarhaddon's *adê* for Assyrian History." *Revue d'Assyriologie* 106 (2012): 133–58.

Falk, Marcia. *Love Lyrics from the Bible: A Translation and Literary Study of the Song of Songs*. Sheffield: Almond, 1982.

Fields, Weston W. *The Dead Sea Scrolls: A Full History*. Leiden: Brill, 2009.

Finitsis, Antonios. *Visions and Eschatology: A Socio-Historical Analysis of Zechariah 1–6*. London and New York: T & T Clark, 2011.

Finsterbusch, Karin. *Weisung für Israel: Studien zu religiösem Lehren und Lernen im Deuteronomium und in seinem Umfeld*. Tübingen: Mohr Siebeck, 2005.

——. "Yahweh's Torah and the Praying 'I' in Psalm 119." In Schipper and Teeter, *Wisdom and Torah*, 123–28.

Fishbane, Michael. *Biblical Interpretation in Ancient Israel*. Oxford: Clarendon, 1985.

——. "Torah and Tradition." In D. A. Knight, ed., *Tradition and Theology in the Old Testament*, 275–300. Philadelphia: Fortress, 1977.

Fitzmyer, Joseph A., SJ. *The Acts of the Apostles*. AB 31. New York: Doubleday, 1998.

——. *First Corinthians*. Anchor Yale Bible 32. New Haven, CT: Yale University Press, 2008.

——. *Romans*. Anchor Bible 33. New York: Doubleday, 1992.

——. *Tobit*. Commentaries on Early Jewish Literature. Berlin: De Gruyter 2003.

Fitzpatrick McKinley, Anne. *Empire, Power, and Indigenous Elites: A Case Study of the Nehemiah Memoir*. Journal for the Study of Judaism Supplements 169. Leiden: Brill, 2015.

Flint, P. W., J. Duhaime, and K. S. Baek, eds. *Celebrating the Dead Sea Scrolls: A Canadian Collection*. Leiden: Brill, 2012.

Flusser, David. *Judaism in the Second Temple Period*. Vol. 1, *Qumran and Apocalypticism*. Grand Rapids, MI: Eerdmans, 2007.

Fox, Michael V. *Character and Ideology in the Book of Esther*. Columbia: University of South Carolina Press, 1991; reprint, Grand Rapids: Eerdmans, 2001.

——. *A Time to Tear Down and A Time to Build Up: A Rereading Of Ecclesiastes*. Grand Rapids, MI: Eerdmans 1999.

Fraade, Steven D. "Interpretive Authority at Qumran." *JJS* 44 (1993): 46–69.

Fraser, P. M. *Ptolemaic Alexandria*. Oxford: Clarendon, 1972.

Frei, Peter. "Persian Imperial Authorization: A Summary." In Watts, *Persia and Torah*, 5–40.

Frei, Peter, and Klaus Koch. *Reichsidee und Reichsorganisation im Perserreich*. Orbis Biblicus et Orientalis 55. Freiburg: Universitätsverlag, 1984.

Frevel, Christian, ed. *Intermarriage and Group Identity in the Second Temple Period*. New York and London: T & T Clark, 2011.

Frey, Jörg. "Different Patterns of Dualistic Thought in the Qumran Library." In Moshe Bernstein, Florentino García Martínez, and John Kampen, eds., *Legal Texts and Legal Issues,* 275–335. Leiden: Brill, 1997.

———. "Flesh and Spirit in the Palestinian Jewish Sapiential Tradition and in the Qumran Texts." In C. Hempel, A. Lange, and H. Lichtenberger, eds., *The Wisdom Texts from Qumran and the Development of Sapiential Thought,* 367–404. Bibliotheca Ephemeridum Theologicarum Lovaniensium 159. Leuven: Peeters, 2002.

———. "Paul's Jewish Identity." In Frey, Schwartz, and Gripentrog, *Jewish Identity in the Greco-Roman World,* 285–321.

Frey, Jörg, Daniel R. Schwartz, and Stephanie Gripentrog, eds. *Jewish Identity in the Greco-Roman World.* Ancient Judaism and Early Christianity 71. Leiden: Brill, 2007.

Friedriksen, Paula. "Judaism, the Circumcision of the Gentiles, and Apocalyptic Hope: Another Look at Galatians 1 and 2." *JTS* 42 (1991): 532–64.

Fuks, Alexander. *The Ancestral Constitution: Four Studies in Athenian Party Politics at the End of the Fifth Century B.C.* London: Routledge and Kegan Paul, 1953.

Gager, John G. *Moses in Greco-Roman Paganism.* Society of Biblical Literature Monograph Series 16. Nashville: Abingdon, 1972.

———. *The Origins of Anti-Semitism: Attitudes towards Judaism in Pagan and Christian Antiquity.* New York: Oxford University Press, 1983.

———. *Reinventing Paul.* New York: Oxford University Press, 2000.

Gamberoni, J. "Das 'Gesetz des Mose' im Buch Tobias." In G. Braulik, ed., *Studien zum Pentateuch: Walter Kornfeld zum 60. Geburtstag,* 227–42. Freiburg: Herder, 1977.

García Martínez, Florentino. "The Heavenly Tablets in the Book of *Jubilees.*" In Matthias Albani, Jörg Frey, and Armin Lange, eds., *Studies in the Book of Jubilees,* 243–60. Tübingen: Mohr Siebeck, 1997.

———. "Temple Scroll." In L. H. Schiffman and J. C. VanderKam, eds., *Encyclopedia of the Dead Sea Scrolls,* 2:927–33. New York: Oxford University Press, 2000.

Garroway, Joshua D. *Paul's Gentile-Jews: Neither Jew nor Gentile, but Both.* New York: Palgrave Macmillan, 2012.

Gaston, Lloyd. *Paul and the Torah.* Vancouver: University of British Columbia Press, 1987.

Geertz, Clifford. *The Interpretation of Cultures.* New York: Basic Books, 1973.

Gellner, Ernest. *Nations and Nationalism.* Oxford: Blackwell, 1983.

Gesundheit, Shimon. *Three Times a Year: Studies on Festival Legislation in the Pentateuch.* Forschungen zum Alten Testament 82. Tübingen: Mohr Siebeck, 2012.

Gillihan, Yonder M. *Civic Ideology, Organization, and Law in the Rule Scrolls: A Comparative Study of the Covenanters' Sect and Contemporary Voluntary Associations in Political Context.* Studies on the Texts of the Judean Desert 97. Leiden: Brill, 2012.

Goering, Greg Schmidt. *Wisdom's Root Revealed: Ben Sira and the Election of Israel.* Journal for the Study of Judaism Supplements 139. Leiden: Brill, 2009.

Goff, Matthew J. *Discerning Wisdom: The Sapiential Literature of the Dead Sea Scrolls.* Vetus Testamentum Supplements 116. Leiden: Brill, 2007.

———. *The Worldly and Heavenly Wisdom of 4QInstruction.* Studies on the Texts of the Judean Desert 50. Leiden: Brill, 2003.

Goldman, Liora. "Dualism in the Visions of Amram." *RevQ* 95 (2010): 421–32.

Goodblatt, David. *Elements of Ancient Jewish Nationalism.* Cambridge: Cambridge University Press, 2006.

Goodman, Martin. "Jewish Literature Composed in Greek." In Geza Vermes, Fergus Millar, and Martin Goodman, eds., *The History of the Jewish People in the Age of Jesus Christ,* 3.1:509–66. Edinburgh: Clark, 1986.

Grabbe, Lester L. *Ezra-Nehemiah.* London and New York: Continuum, 1998.

———, ed. *Good Kings and Bad Kings.* Library of Hebrew Bible Studies 2005. London and New York: T & T Clark, 2005.

———. *A History of the Jews and Judaism in the Second Temple Period.* Vol. 1, *Yehud: A History of the Persian Province of Judah.* London and New York: Continuum, 2004.

———. "The 'Persian Documents' in the Book of Ezra: Are They Authentic?" In Lipschitz and Oeming, *Judah and the Judeans in the Persian Period,* 531–70.

Greenfield, Jonas C. *The Aramaic Levi Document: Edition, Translation, Commentary.* Studia in Veteris Testamenti Pseudepigrapha 19. Leiden: Brill, 2004.

Grene, David, trans. *Herodotus, The History.* Chicago and London: University of Chicago Press, 1987.

Griffiths, J. Gwyn. *Plutarch's De Iside et Osiride.* Cardiff: University of Wales Press, 1970.

Grosby, Steven. *Biblical Ideas of Nationality: Ancient and Modern.* Winona Lake, IN: Eisenbrauns, 2002.

Gross, Walter, ed. *Jeremia und die "deuteronomistische Bewegung'"* BBB 98. Weinheim: Beltz Athenäeum, 1995.

Gruen, Erich. *Heritage and Hellenism: The Reinvention of Jewish Tradition*. Cambridge, MA: Harvard University Press, 1998.

Grund, Alexandra. *"Die Himmel erzählen die Ehre Gottes": Psalm 19 im Kontext der nach-exilischen Toraweisheit*. Wissenschaftliche Monographien zum Alten und Neuen Testament 103. Neukirchen-Vluyn: Neukirchener Verlag, 2004.

Hacham, Noah. "Joseph and Aseneth: Loyalty, Traitors, Antiquity, and Diaspora Identity." *JSP* 22 (2012): 63–67.

Hagedorn, Anselm C., and Reinhard G. Kratz, eds. *Law and Religion in the Eastern Mediterranean: From Antiquity to Islam*. Oxford: Oxford University Press, 2013.

Hall, Jonathan M. *Ethnic Identity in Greek Antiquity*. Cambridge: Cambridge University Press, 1997.

——. *Hellenicity: Between Ethnicity and Culture*. Chicago: University of Chicago Press, 2002.

Hänsel, L. "Studien zu 'Tora' in Esra-Nehemiah und Chronik." PhD diss., Leipzig University, 1999.

Hardmeier, Christoph. "König Joschija in der Klimax des DtrG (2Reg 22f.) und das vordtr Dokument einer Kultreform am Residenzort (23,4–15*)." In Rüdiger Lux, ed., *Erzählte Geschichte: Beiträge zur narrativen Kultur im alten Israel*, 81–145. Neukirchen-Vluyn: Neukirchener Verlag, 2000.

Harris, Scott. *Proverbs 1–9: A Study of Inner-Biblical Interpretation*. Atlanta: Scholars Press, 1995.

Hartman, Lars. *Asking for a Meaning: A Study of 1Enoch 1–5*. Coniectanea Biblica, NT Series 12. Lund: Gleerup, 1979.

Hastings, A. *The Construction of Nationhood: Ethnicity, Religion, and Nationalism*. Cambridge: Cambridge University Press, 1997.

Hayes, Christine. *Gentile Impurities and Jewish Identities*. Oxford: Oxford University Press, 2002.

——. "Intermarriage and Impurity in Ancient Jewish Sources." *HTR* 92 (1999): 3–36.

——. "Legal Realism and the Fashioning of Sectarianism in Jewish Antiquity." In Sacha Stern, ed., *Sects and Sectarianism in Jewish Antiquity*, 119–46. Leiden: Brill, 2011.

——. *What's Divine about Divine Law? Early Perspectives*. Princeton, NJ: Princeton University Press, 2015.

Hays, Richard D. *The Faith of Jesus Christ: The Narrative Substructure of Galatians 3:1–4:11*. 2nd ed. Grand Rapids, MI: Eerdmans, 2002.

Heger, Paul. "*1 Enoch*—Complementary or Alternative to Mosaic Torah?" *JSJ* 41 (2010): 29–62.

———. *Challenges to Conventional Opinions on Qumran and Enoch Issues.* Studies on the Texts of the Desert of Judah 100. Leiden: Brill, 2012.

Hempel, Charlotte. "The *Treatise on the Two Spirits* and the Literary History of the *Rule of the Community.*" In Xeravits, ed., *Dualism in Qumran,* 102–20.

Hengel, Martin. *Judaism and Hellenism.* 2 vols. Philadelphia: Fortress, 1974.

Hengel, Martin, and Roland Deines. "E.P. Sanders' 'Common Judaism', Jesus, and the Pharisees: Review of *Jewish Law from Jesus to the Mishnah and Judaism; Practice and Belief* by E.P. Sanders." *JTS* 46 (1995): 1–70.

Henze, Matthias. *Jewish Apocalypticism in Late First-Century Israel.* Texte und Studien zum Antiken Judentum 142. Tübingen: Mohr Siebeck, 2011.

Herzog, Ze'ev. "The Date of the Temple at Arad: Reassessment of the Stratigraphy and the Implications for the History of Religion in Judah." In Amihai Mazar, ed., *Studies in the Archaeology of the Iron Age in Israel and Jordan,* 156–78. Journal for the Study of the Old Testament Supplements 331. Sheffield: Sheffield Academic Press, 2001.

Hezser, Catherine. "'Joseph and Aseneth' in the Context of Ancient Greek Novels." *Frankfurter judäistische Beiträge* 24 (1997): 1–40.

Himmelfarb, Martha. *A Kingdom of Priests: Ancestry and Merit in Ancient Judaism.* Philadelphia: University of Pennsylvania Press, 2005.

———. "Temple and Priests in the *Book of the Watchers,* the *Animal Apocalypse,* and the *Apocalypse of Weeks.*" In Boccaccini and Collins, *The Early Enoch Literature,* 219–35.

———. "Torah, Testimony, and Heavenly Tablets: The Claim to Authority in the Book of Jubilees." In Benjamin G. Wright, ed., *A Multiform Heritage: Studies on Early Judaism and Christianity in Honor of Robert A. Kraft,* 22–28. Atlanta: Scholars Press, 1999.

Hodge, Caroline Johnson. *If Sons, Then Heirs: A Study of Kinship and Ethnicity in the Letters of Paul.* Oxford: Oxford University Press, 2007.

———. "Olive Trees and Ethnicities: Judeans and Gentiles in Rom. 11.17–24." In Jürgen Zangenberg and Michael Labahn, eds., *Christians as a Religious Minority in a Multicultural City: Modes of Interaction and Identity Formation in Early Imperial Rome,* 77–89. Journal for the Study of the New Testament Supplements 243. London and New York: T & T Clark, 2004.

Hoffmann, H.-D. *Reform und Reformen: Untersuchungen zu einem Grundthema der deuteronomistischen Geschichtsschreibung.* Abhandlungen zur Theologie des Alten und Neuen Testaments 66. Zurich: Theologischer Verlag, 1980.

Hogan, Karina Martin. "The Meanings of *tôrah* in 4 Ezra." *JSJ* 38 (2007): 530–52.

———. *Theologies in Conflict in 4 Ezra: Wisdom Debate and Apocalyptic Solution.* Journal for the Study of Judaism Supplements 130. Leiden: Brill, 2008.

Holladay, Carl M. *Fragments from Hellenistic Jewish Authors.* Vol. 1, *Historians.* Chico, CA: Scholars Press, 1983.

———. *Fragments from Hellenistic Jewish Authors.* Vol. 3, *Aristobulus.* Atlanta: SBL, 1995.

Hölscher, Gustav. "Komposition und Ursprung des Deuteronomiums." *ZAW* 40 (1922): 161–255.

Honigman, Sylvie. "The Jewish *Politeuma* at Heracleopolis." *SCI* 21 (2002): 251–66.

———. *Tales of High Priests and Taxes: The Books of the Maccabees and the Judean Rebellion against Antiochus IV.* Oakland: University of California Press, 2014.

Horst, P. W. van der. *The Sentences of Pseudo-Phocylides.* Leiden: Brill, 1978.

Houtman, Cornelis. "Ezra and the Law: Observations on the Supposed Relation between Ezra and the Pentateuch." *OTS* 21 (1981): 91–115.

Hultgren, Stephen. *From the Damascus Covenant to the Covenant of the Community.* Studies on the Texts of the Desert of Judah 66. Leiden: Brill, 2007.

Humphreys, Edith M. "On Bees and Best Guesses: The Problem of Sitz im Leben from Internal Evidence, as Illusrated by Joseph and Aseneth." *Currents in Research: Biblical Studies* 7 (1999): 223–36.

Hutchinson, John, and Anthony D. Smith, eds. *Ethnicity.* Oxford: Oxford University Press, 1996.

Jackson, Bernard S. *Studies in the Semiotics of Biblical Law.* Journal for the Study of the Old Testament Supplements 314. Sheffield: Sheffield Academic Press, 2000.

———. *Wisdom-Laws: A Study of the Mishpatim of Exodus 21:1–22:16.* Oxford: Oxford University Press, 2006.

Jackson, David. *Enochic Judaism.* Library of Second Temple Studies 49. London and New York: Continuum, 2004.

Japhet, Sarah. "Law and 'the Law' in Ezra-Nehemiah." In *The Proceedings of the Ninth World Congress of Jewish Studies,* 99–115. Jerusalem: Magnes, 1988.

Jassen, Alex P. *Mediating the Divine: Prophecy and Revelation in the Dead Sea Scrolls and Second Temple Judaism.* Studies on the Texts of the Desert of Judah 68. Leiden: Brill, 2007.

Johnson, Sara R. *Historical Fictions and Hellenistic Jewish Identity: Third Maccabees in Its Cultural Context.* Berkeley: University of California Press, 2004.

Joisten-Pruschke, Anke. *Das religiöse Leben der Juden von Elephantine in der Achämenidenzeit*. Göttinger Orientforschungen 3: Iranica Neue Folge 2. Wiesbaden: Harrassowitz, 2008.

Jong, Albert de. "Iranian Connections in the Dead Sea Scrolls." In Timothy H. Lim and John J. Collins, eds., *The Oxford Handbook of the Dead Sea Scrolls*, 493–94. Oxford: Oxford University Press, 2010.

———. *Traditions of the Magi: Zoroastrianism in Greek and Latin Literature*. Leiden: Brill, 1997.

Kasher, Aryeh. *The Jews in Hellenistic and Roman Egypt: The Struggle for Equal Rights*. Tübingen: Mohr Siebeck, 1985.

———. Review of *Urkunden des Politeuma der Juden von Herakleopolis (144/3–133/2 v. Chr.) (P. Polit. Iud.)*. *JQR* 93 (2002): 257–68.

Kedourie, Elie. *Nationalism*. London: Hutchinson, 1963.

Killebrew, Ann E. *Biblical Peoples and Ethnicity: An Archaeological Study of Egyptians, Canaanites, Philistines, and Early Israel, 1300–1100 B.C.E.* SBL Archaeology and Biblical Studies 9. Atlanta: SBL, 2005.

Kim Harkins, Angela. "The Community Hymns Classification: A Proposal for Further Differentiation." *DSD* 15 (2008): 121–54.

Kippenberg, Hans G. "Die jüdischen Überlieferungen als *patroi nomoi*." In Richard Faber and Renate Schlesier, eds., *Die Restauration der Götter: Antike Religionen und Neo-Paganismus*, 45–60. Würzburg: Königshausen und Neumann, 1986.

Kister, Menahem. "Concerning the History of the Essenes: A Study of the *Animal Apocalypse*, the Book of *Jubilees*, and the Damascus Covenant." *Tarbiz* 56 (1986): 1–18 (Heb.).

Kitchen, Kenneth A., and Paul J. N. Lawrence. *Treaty, Law, and Covenant in the Ancient Near East*. 3 vols. Wiesbaden: Harrassowitz, 2012.

Klawans, Jonathan. *Impurity and Sin in Ancient Judaism*. New York: Oxford University Press, 2000.

———. *Josephus and the Theologies of Ancient Judaism*. Oxford: Oxford University Press, 2012.

Klein, Anja. "Half Way between Psalm 119 and Ben Sira: Wisdom and Torah in Psalm 19." In Schipper and Teeter, *Wisdom and Torah*, 148–49.

Klein, Ralph. *1 Chronicles*. Hermeneia. Minneapolis: Fortress, 2006.

———. *2 Chronicles*. Hermeneia. Minneapolis: Fortress, 2012.

─el Ernst. "Elephantine und das vor-biblische Judentum." In Rein-
        ┌z, ed., *Religion und Religionskontakte im Zeitalter der Achämeniden*,
          ˙ · Kaiser, 2002.

Knight, Douglas A. *Law, Power, and Justice in Ancient Israel.* Louisville, KY: Westminster John Knox, 2011.

———. "Village Law and the Book of the Covenant." In Saul M. Olyan and Robert C. Culley, eds., *"A Wise and Discerning Mind": Essays in Honor of Burke O. Long,* 163–79. Brown Judaic Studies 235. Providence, RI: Brown Judaic Studies, 2000.

Knoppers, Gary N. "An Achaemenid Imperial Authorization of Torah in Yehud?" In Watts, *Persia and Torah,* 115–34.

———. "The Deuteronomist and the Deuteronomic Law of the King: A Reexamination of a Relationship." *ZAW* 108 (1996): 329–46.

Knoppers, Gary N., and Bernard M. Levinson, eds. *The Pentateuch as Torah: New Models for Understanding Its Promulgation and Acceptance.* Winona Lake, IN: Eisenbrauns, 2007.

Koch, C. *Vertrag, Treueid und Bund: Studien zur Rezeption des altorientalischen Vertragsrechts im Deuteronomium und zur Ausbildung der Bundestheologie im alten Testament.* Beihefte zur Zeitschrift für die alttestamentliche Wissenschaft 383. Berlin: De Gruyter, 2008.

Kraemer, Ross S. *When Aseneth Met Joseph: A Late Antique Tale of the Biblical Patriarch and His Egyptian Wife Reconsidered.* New York: Oxford University Press, 1998.

Kratz, Reinhard G. *The Composition of the Narrative Books of the Old Testament.* London: Clark, 2005.

———. "Judean Ambassadors and the Making of Jewish Identity." In Lipschitz, Knoppers, and Oeming, *Judah and the Judeans in the Achaemenid Period,* 421–44.

———. "The Legal Status of the Pentateuch between Elephantine and Qumran." In Knoppers and Levinson, *The Pentateuch as Torah,* 77–103.

———. "'The Peg in the Wall': Cultic Centralization Revisited." In Hagedorn and Kratz, *Law and Religion in the Eastern Mediterranean,* 251–85.

Krüger, Thomas. "Die Rezeption der Tora im Buch Kohelet." In Ludger Schwienhorst-Schönberger, ed., *Das Buch Kohelet: Studien zur Struktur, Geschichte, Rezeption und Theologie,* 303–25. Beihefte zur Zeitschrift für die alttestamentliche Wissenschaft 254. Berlin: De Gruyter, 1997.

———. *Kritische Weisheit: Studien zur weisheitlichen Traditionskritik im Alten Testament.* Zurich: Pano, 1997.

———. *Qoheleth.* Hermeneia. Minneapolis: Fortress, 2004.

Kugel, James L. "The Holiness of Israel and the Land in Second Temple Times." In Michael V. Fox et al., eds., *Texts, Temples, and Traditions: A Tribute to Menahem Haran,* 21–32. Winona Lake, IN: Eisenbrauns, 1996.

———. "The Interpolations in the Book of *Jubilees*." *RevQ* 24 (2009): 215–72.

———. *Traditions of the Bible*. Cambridge, MA: Harvard, 1998.

———. *A Walk through Jubilees: Studies in the Book of Jubilees and the World of Its Creation.* Journal for the Study of Judaism Supplements 156. Leiden: Brill, 2012.

———. "Which Is Older, *Jubilees* or the *Genesis Apocryphon?* An Exegetical Approach." In Adolfo D. Roitman, Lawrence H. Schiffman, and Shani Tzoref, eds., *The Dead Sea Scrolls and Contemporary Culture*, 257–94. Studies on the Texts of the Desert of Judah 93. Leiden: Brill, 2011.

Kugler, Robert A. "Delineating the Particulars of Dispute Settlement among the Jews of Second Century BCE Herakleopolis: A Glimpse of Jewish Life in Hellenistic Egypt." Paper delivered in Jerusalem, December 2014.

———. "Dispelling an Illusion of Otherness? Juridical Practice in the Heracleopolis Papyri." In Daniel C. Harlow, Karina Martin Hogan, Matthew Goff, and Joel S. Kaminsky, eds., *The "Other" in Second Temple Judaism: Essays in Honor of John J. Collins*, 457–70. Grand Rapids, MI: William B. Eerdmans, 2011.

———. "Dorotheos Petitions for the Return of Philippa (*P.Polit.Jud.* 7): A Case Study in the Jews and Their Law in Ptolemaic Egypt." In Traianos Gagos, ed., *Proceedings of the Twenty-Fifth International Congress of Papyrology, Ann Arbor 2007*, 387–96. Ann Arbor: University of Michigan Press, 2010.

———. "Peton Contests Paying Double Rent on Farmland (*P.Heid.Inv.* G 5100): A Slice of Judean Experience in the Second Century B.C.E. Herakleopolite Nome." In Eric F. Mason, Kelley Coblentz Bautch, Angela Kim Harkins, and Daniel A. Machiela, eds., *A Teacher for All Generations: Essays in Honor of James C. VanderKam*, 2:537–51. Leiden: Brill, 2012.

———. "Uncovering Echoes of LXX Legal Norms in Hellenistic Egyptian Documentary Papyri: The Case of the Second-Century Herakleopolite Nome." In Melvin K.H. Peters, ed., *XIV Congress of the IOSCS, Helsinki, 2010*, 142–53. SBL Series 59. Atlanta: Society of Biblical Literature, 2013.

———. "Uncovering a New Dimension of Early Judean Interpretation of the Greek Torah: Ptolemaic Law Interpreted by Its Own Rhetoric." In Hanne von Weissenberg, Juha Pakkala, and Marko Marttila, eds., *Changes in Scripture: Rewriting and Interpreting Authoritative Traditions in the Second Temple Period*, 165–75. Beihefte zur Zeitschrift für die alttestamentliche Wissenschaft 419. Berlin: De Gruyter, 2011.

———. "Whose Scripture? Whose Community? Reflections on the Dead Sea Scrolls Then and Now, by Way of Aramaic Levi." *DSD* 15 (2008): 5–23.

Kuhn, K.G. "Die Sektenschrift und die iranische Religion." *ZTK* 49 (1952): 296–316.

Kuhrt, Amelie. *The Persian Empire.* 2 vols. London: Routledge, 2007.

Kvanvig, Helge S. *Primeval History: Babylonian, Biblical, and Enochic; An Intertextual Reading.* Journal for the Study of Judaism Supplements 149. Leiden: Brill, 2011.

Laato, Antti, and Jacques van Ruiten, eds. *Rewritten Bible Reconsidered.* Winona Lake, IN: Eisenbrauns, 2008.

Lambert, David. "How the 'Torah of Moses' Became Revelation: An Early Apocalyptic Theory of Pentateuchal Origins." *JSJ* 47 (2016): 22–54.

Lange, Armin. *Weisheit und Prädestination in den Textfunden von Qumran.* Studies on the Texts of the Desert of Judah 18. Leiden: Brill, 1995.

Lange, Armin, Eric M. Meyers, Bennie H. Reynolds III, and Randall Styers, eds. *Light against Darkness: Dualism in Ancient Mediterranean Religion and the Contemporary World.* Journal of Ancient Judaism Supplements 2. Göttingen: Vandenhoeck & Ruprecht, 2011.

Lee, Kyong-Jin. *The Authority and Authorization of Torah in the Persian Period.* Leuven: Peeters, 2011.

LeFebvre, Michael. *Collections, Codes, and Torah: The Re-characterization of Israel's Written Law.* New York and London: Clark, 2006.

Legrand, Thierry. "Exégèses targumiques et techniques de réécriture dans *L'Apocryphe de la Genèse* (1QAPGen AR)." In Berthelot and Stökl Ben Ezra, *Aramaica Qumranica*, 225–52.

Lemaire, André. "Everyday Life according to the Ostraca from Elephantine." In Lipschitz, Knoppers, and Oeming, *Judah and the Judeans in the Achaemenid Period*, 365–73.

Levenson, Jon D. *Esther.* Old Testament Library. Louisville, KY: Westminster John Knox, 1997.

———. "The Sources of Torah: Psalm 119 and the Modes of Revelation in Second Temple Judaism." In P. D. Miller et al., eds., *Ancient Israelite Religion: Essays in Honor of Frank Moore Cross,* 559–74. Philadelphia: Fortress, 1987.

Levin, Christoph. "Joschija im deuteronomistischen Geschichtswerk." *ZAW* 96 (1984): 351–71.

Levine, Lee I., and Daniel R. Schwartz, eds. *Jewish Identities in Antiquity: Studies in Memory of Menahem Stern.* Texte und Studien zum Antiken Judentum 130. Tübingen: Mohr Siebeck, 2009.

Levinson, Bernard M. *Deuteronomy and the Hermeneutics of Legal Innovation.* Oxford and New York: Oxford University Press, 1997.

———. "Is the Covenant Code an Exilic Composition?" In John Day, ed., *In Search of Pre-Exilic Israel,* 272–325. London and New York: T & T Clark, 2004.

———. *A More Perfect Torah: At the Intersection of Philology and Hermeneutics in Deuteronomy and the Temple Scroll.* Critical Studies in the Hebrew Bible 1. Winona Lake, IN: Eisenbrauns, 2013.

———. "The Reconceptualization of Kingship in Deuteronomy and the Deuteronomistic History's Reconceptualization of Torah." *VT* 51 (2001): 511–34.

Levinson, Bernard, and Jeffrey Stackert, "Between the Covenant Code and Esarhaddon's Succession Treaty: Deuteronomy 13 and the Composition of Deuteronomy." *JAJ* 3 (2012): 123–40.

Lewis, Naphtali. *The Documents from the Bar Kokhba Period in the Cave of Letters.* Vol. 1, *Greek Papyri, with Aramaic and Nabatean Signatures and Subscriptions,* ed. Yigael Yadin and Jonas C. Greenfield. Jerusalem: Israel Exploration Society, 1989.

Lim, Timothy H. *The Formation of the Jewish Canon.* AYBRL. New Haven, CT: Yale University Press, 2013.

Lim, Timothy H., and John J. Collins, eds. *The Oxford Handbook of the Dead Sea Scrolls.* Oxford: Oxford University Press, 2010.

Linafelt, Todd. *Ruth.* Berit Olam. Collegeville, MN: Liturgical Press, 1999.

Lipschitz, Oded, and Manfred Oeming, eds. *Judah and the Judeans in the Persian Period.* Winona Lake, IN: Eisenbrauns, 2006.

Lipschitz, Oded, Gary N. Knoppers, and Manfred Oeming, eds. *Judah and the Judeans in the Achaemenid Period: Negotiating Identity in an International Context.* Winona Lake, IN: Eisenbrauns, 2011.

Lohfink, Norbert. "The Cult Reform of Josiah of Judah: 2 Kings 22–23 as a Source for the History of Israelite Religion." In Patrick D. Miller, Paul D. Hanson, and S. Dean McBride, eds., *Ancient Israelite Religion: Essays in Honor of Frank Moore Cross,* 459–75. Philadelphia: Fortress, 1987.

———. "Distribution of the Functions of Power: The Laws Concerning Public Offices in Deuteronomy 16:18—18:22." In D.L. Christensen, ed., *A Song of Power and the Power of Song: Essays on the Book of Deuteronomy,* 336–52. Winona Lake, IN: Eisenbrauns, 1993.

Long, Burke O. *2 Kings.* Forms of Old Testament Literature 10. Grand Rapids, MI: Eerdmans, 1991.

Lowery, R.H. *The Reforming Kings: Cults and Society in First Temple Judah.* JSOTSup 120. Sheffield: Sheffield Academic Press, 1991.

Lüderitz, Gerd. "What Is the Politeuma?" In Jan Willem van Henten and Pieter Willem van der Horst, eds., *Studies in Early Jewish Epigraphy,* 183–225. Leiden: Brill, 1994.

Ma, John. *Antiochus III and the Cities of Western Asia Minor.* Oxford: Oxford University Press, 2000.

MacDonald, Nathan. *Deuteronomy and the Meaning of "Monotheism."* Forschungen zum Alten Testament 2/1. Tübingen: Mohr Siebeck, 2003.

———. "Issues in the Dating of Deuteronomy: A Response to Juha Pakkala." *ZAW* 122 (2010): 431–35.

Machiela, Daniel A. *The Dead Sea Genesis Apocryphon: A New Text and Translation with Introduction and Special Treatment of Columns 13–17.* Studies on the Texts of the Desert of Judah 79. Leiden: Brill, 2009.

Maresch, K., and J.M.S. Cowey. "'A Recurrent Inclination to Isolate the Case of the Jews from their Ptolemaic Environment'? Eine Antwort auf Sylvie Honigman." *SCI* 22 (2003): 307–10.

Markl, Dominik, SJ. *Gottes Volk im Deuteronomium.* Beihefte zur Zeitschrift für altorientalische und biblische Rechtsgeschichte 18. Wiesbaden: Harrassowitz, 2012.

———. "No Future without Moses: The Disastrous End of 2 Kings 22–25 and the Chance of the Moab Covenant (Deuteronomy 29–30)." *JBL* 133 (2014): 711–28.

———. "The Ten Words Revealed and Revised." In Dominik Markl, SJ, ed., *The Decalogue and Its Cultural Influence.* Hebrew Bible Monographs 58. Sheffield: Sheffield Phoenix, 2013.

Mason, Steve. "Ancient Jews or Judeans? Different Questions, Different Answers." *Marginalia,* August 26, 2014.

———. "Jews, Judaeans, Judaizing, Judaism: Problems of Categorization in Ancient History." *JSJ* 38 (2007): 457–512.

McConville, J. Gordon. *Deuteronomy.* Leicester: Apollos, 2002.

———. "King and Messiah in Deuteronomy and the Deuteronomistic History." In John Day, ed., *King and Messiah in Israel and the Ancient Near East,* 271–95. Sheffield: Sheffield Academic Press, 1998.

Meinhold, Arndt. "Die Gattung der Josephgeschichte und des Estherbuches: Diasporanovelle I & II." *ZAW* 87 (1975): 306–24; 88 (1976): 79–93.

Mendels, Doron. *The Land of Israel as a Political Concept in Hasmonean Literature.* Tübingen: Mohr Siebeck, 1987.

———. *The Rise and Fall of Jewish Nationalism.* Anchor Bible Reference Library. New York: Doubleday, 1992; 2nd ed., Grand Rapids, MI: Eerdmans, 1997.

Mendelson, Alan. *Philo's Jewish Identity.* Brown Judaic Studies 161. Atlanta: Scholars Press, 1988.

Meyer, Eduard. *Die Entstehung des Judenthums.* Halle: Niemeyer, 1896.

Meyers, Carol L., and Eric M. Meyers, *Haggai; Zechariah 1–8.* Anchor Bible 25B. New York: Doubleday 1987.

Meyers, E. M., and M. A. Chancey. *Alexander to Constantine: Archaeology of the Land of the Bible.* Anchor Yale Reference Library. New Haven, CT: Yale University Press, 2012.

Meyers, Eric M. "Sanders's 'Common Judaism' and the Common Judaism of Material Culture." In Fabian Udoh, with Susannah Heschel, Mark Chancey, and Gregory Tatum, eds., *Redefining First-Century Jewish and Christian Identities: Essays in Honor of Ed Parish Sanders,* 153–74. Notre Dame, IN: University of Notre Dame, 2008.

Milik, J. T. *The Books of Enoch: Aramaic Fragments from Qumrân Cave Four.* Oxford: Clarendon, 1976.

Miller, Stuart S. "Introduction: Ritual Baths and Ritual Purity, the Last Fifty Years." In Stuart S. Miller, *At the Intersection of Texts and Material Finds: Stepped Pools, Stone Vessels, and Ritual Purity among the Jews of Roman Galilee,* 17–31. Journal of Ancient Judaism Supplements 16. Göttingen: Vandenhoeck & Ruprecht, 2015.

———. "Stepped Pools, Stone Vessels, and Other Markers of 'Complex Common Judaism.'" *JSJ* 41 (2010): 214–43.

Mittag, Peter Franz. *Antiochus IV. Epiphanes: Eine politische Biographie.* Klio: Beiträge zur Alten Geschichte, Beihefte, N.F. 11. Berlin: Akademie, 2006.

Modrzejewski, J. Mélèze. *The Jews of Egypt: From Rameses II to Emperor Hadrian.* Translated by Robert Cornman. Princeton, NJ: Princeton University Press, 1997.

Moffat, Donald P. *Ezra's Social Drama: Identity Formation, Marriage, and Social Conflict in Ezra 9 and 10.* New York and London: Bloomsbury, 2013.

Monroe, Lauren S. *Josiah's Reform and the Dynamics of Defilement: Israelite Rites of Violence and the Making of a Biblical Text.* New York: Oxford University Press, 2011.

Moore, George Foot. "Christian Writers on Judaism." *HTR* 14 (1921): 197–254.

———. *Judaism in the First Centuries of the Christian Era.* 3 vols. Cambridge, MA: Harvard University Press, 1927–30; reprint, New York: Schocken, 1971.

Moore, Stephen. *Empire and Apocalypse: Postcolonialism and the New Testament.* Sheffield: Sheffield Phoenix, 2006.

Moore, Stewart A. *Jewish Ethnic Identity and Relations in Hellenistic Egypt: With Walls of Iron?* Journal for the Study of Judaism Supplements 171. Leiden: Brill, 2015.

Moran, W. L. "The Ancient Near Eastern Background of the Love of God in Deuteronomy." *CBQ* 25 (1963): 77–87.

Moriya, Akiyo. "The Pentateuch Reflected in the Aramaic Documents of the Dead Sea Scrolls." In Moriya and Hata, *Pentateuchal Traditions in the Late Second Temple Period,* 201–12.

Moriya, Akiyo, and Gohei Hata, eds. *Pentateuchal Traditions in the Late Second Temple Period.* Journal for the Study of Judaism Supplements 158. Leiden: Brill, 2012.

Mullen, E. Theodore, Jr. *Narrative History and Ethnic Boundaries.* Semeia Studies. Atlanta: SBL, 1993.

Na'aman, Nadav. "The Abandonment of Cult Places in the Kingdoms of Israel and Judah as Acts of Cult Reform." *UF* 34 (2002): 585–602.

Najman, Hindy. "Interpretation as Primordial Writing: *Jubilees* and Its Authority Conferring Strategies." In Hindy Najman, *Past Renewals: Interpretative Authority, Renewed Revelation, and the Quest for Perfection in Jewish Antiquity,* 39–71. Journal for the Study of Judaism Supplements 53. Leiden: Brill, 2010. Originally published in *JSJ* 30 (1999): 379–410.

———. *Losing the Temple and Recovering the Future: An Analysis of 4 Ezra.* Cambridge: Cambridge University Press, 2014.

———. *Seconding Sinai: The Development of Mosaic Discourse in Second Temple Judaism.* Journal for the Study of Judaism Supplements 77. Leiden: Brill, 2004.

———. "Torah and Tradition." In Collins and Harlow, *The Eerdmans Dictionary of Early Judaism,* 1316–17.

———. "A Written Copy of the Law of Nature: An Unthinkable Paradox?" *The Studia Philonica Annual* 15 (2003): 54–63.

Nanos, Mark D. "The Myth of the 'Law-Free' Paul Standing between Christians and Jews." *Studies in Christian-Jewish Relations* 4:1–21. http://ejournals.bc.edu/ojs/index.php/scjr/article/view/1511/1364.

———. "Paul's Relationship to Torah in Light of His Strategy 'to Become Everything to Everyone' (1 Corinthians 9:19–23)." In Pollefeyt and Bieringer, *Paul and Judaism,* 106–40.

———. "The Question of Conceptualization: Qualifying Paul's Position on Circumcision in Dialogue with Josephus's Advisors to King Izates." In Nanos and Zetterholm, *Paul within Judaism,* 105–52.

Nanos, Mark D., and Magnus Zetterholm, eds. *Paul within Judaism: Restoring the First-Century Context to the Apostle.* Minneapolis: Fortress, 2015.

Nelson, Richard D. *Deuteronomy.* Old Testament Library. Louisville, KY: Westminster John Knox, 2002.

Nestle, Eberhard. "Miscellen." *ZAW* 22 (1902): 170–72.

Nestor, Dermot A. *Cognitive Perspectives on Israelite Identity*. London and New York: T & T Clark International, 2010.

Neujahr, Matthew. *Predicting the Past in the Ancient Near East*. Brown Judaic Studies 354. Providence: Brown Judaic Studies, 2012.

Neusner, Jacob. *The Way of Torah: An Introduction to Judaism*. 5th ed. Belmont, CA: Wadsworth, 1992.

Neutel, Karin B. *A Cosmopolitan Ideal: Paul's Declaration "Neither Jew nor Greek, Neither Slave nor Free, nor Male and Female" in the Context of First-Century Thought*. Library of New Testament Studies 513. London: Bloomsbury, 2015.

Newsom, Carol A. *Daniel*. OTL. Louisville, KY: Westminster John Knox, 2014.

———. *The Self as Symbolic Space*. Studies on the Texts of the Desert of Judah 52. Leiden: Brill, 2004.

Nicholson, Ernest. *Deuteronomy and the Judaean Diaspora*. Oxford: Oxford University Press, 2014.

———. *The Pentateuch in the Twentieth Century: The Legacy of Julius Wellhausen*. Oxford: Clarendon, 1998.

Nickelsburg, George W. E. *1 Enoch 1*. Hermeneia. Minneapolis: Fortress, 2001.

———. "The Bible Rewritten and Expanded." In Michael E. Stone, ed., *Jewish Writings of the Second Temple Period*, 89–156. Compendia Rerum Iudaicarum ad Novum Testamentum 2/2. Philadelphia: Fortress, 1984.

———. "Enochic Wisdom: An Alternative to the Mosaic Torah?" In Jodi Magness and Seymour Gitin, eds., *Ḥesed ve-emet: Studies in Honor of Ernest S. Frerichs*, 123–32. Brown Judaic Studies 320. Atlanta: Scholars Press, 1998.

Nickelsburg, George W. E., and James C. VanderKam. *1 Enoch 2*. Hermeneia. Minneapolis: Fortress, 2012.

Niebuhr, K.-W. *Gesetz und Paränese: Katechismusartige Weisungreihen in der frühjüdischen Literatur*. Wissenschaftliche Untersuchungen zum Neuen Testament 2/28. Tübingen: Mohr Siebeck, 1987.

Niehr, Herbert. "Die Reform des Joschija: Methodische, historische und religionsgeschichtliche Aspekte." In Gross, *Jeremia und die "deuteronomistische Bewegung,"* 33–55.

Nihan, Christoph. "Ethnicity and Identity in Isaiah 56–66." In Lipschitz, Knoppers, and Oeming, *Judah and the Judeans in the Achaemenid Period*, 67–104.

———. *From Priestly Torah to Pentateuch: A Study of the Composition of the Book of Leviticus*. Forschungen zum Alten Testament 2/25. Tübingen: Mohr Siebeck, 2007.

Nir, Rivka. *Joseph and Aseneth: A Christian Book*. Sheffield: Sheffield Phoenix, 2012.

Noam, Vered. "Ritual Impurity in Tannaitic Literature: Two Opposing Perspectives." *JAJ* 1 (2010): 65–103.

Nock, Arthur Darby. *Conversion: The Old and the New in Religion from Alexander the Great to Augustine of Hippo*. Oxford: Clarendon, 1933; reprint, Baltimore: Johns Hopkins University Press, 1988.

Nongbri, Brent. *Before Religion: A History of a Modern Concept*. New Haven, CT: Yale University Press, 2013.

Noth, Martin. *A History of Pentateuchal Traditions*. Englewood Cliffs, NJ: Prentice-Hall, 1972.

Oeming, Manfred. "Jewish Identity in the Eastern Diaspora." In Lipschitz, Knoppers, and Oeming, *Judah and the Judeans in the Achaemenid Period*, 541–61.

Oestreicher, Theodor. "Das deuteronomische Grundgesetz." *Beiträge zur Förderung christlicher Theologie* 27.4 (1923): 37–58.

Oliver, Isaac. "Forming Jewish Identity by Formulating Legislation for Gentiles." *JAJ* 4 (2013): 105–32.

Olyan, Saul M. "An Eternal Covenant with Circumcision as Its Sign: How Useful a Criterion for Dating and Source Analysis?" In Dozeman, Schmid, and Schwartz, *The Pentateuch*, 347–58.

———. "Purity Ideology in Ezra-Nehemiah as a Tool to Reconstitute the Community." In Olyan, *Social Inequality in the World of the Text*, 159–72.

———. "'Sie sollen nicht in die Gemeinde des Herrn kommen': Aspekte gesellschaftlicher Inklusion und Exklusion in Dtn 23,4–9 und seine frühen Auslegungen." In Olyan, *Social Inequality in the World of the Text*, 172–85.

———. *Social Inequality in the World of the Text: The Significance of Ritual and Social Distinctions in the Hebrew Bible*. Göttingen: Vandenhoeck & Ruprecht, 2011.

Östborn, Gunnar. *Tora in the Old Testament*. Lund: Ohlsson, 1945.

Otto, Eckart. "Aspects of Legal Reforms and Reformulations in Ancient Cuneiform and Israelite Law." In Bernard M. Levinson, ed., *Theory and Method in Biblical and Cuneiform Law: Revision, Interpolation, and Development*, 160–96. Journal for the Study of the Old Testament Supplements 181. Sheffield: JSOT, 1994.

———. "Assyria and Judean Identity: Beyond the *Religionsgeschichtliche Schule*." In David S. Vanderhooft and Abraham Winitzer, eds., *Literature as Politics, Politics as Literature: Essays in Honor of Peter Machinist*, 339–47. Winona Lake, IN: Eisenbrauns, 2013.

———. *Das Deuteronomium: Politische Theologie und Rechtsreform in Juda und Assyrien*. Beihefte zur Zeitschrift für die alttestamentliche Wissenschaft 284. Berlin: De Gruyter, 1999.

———. "Das Deuteronomium als Archimedischer Punkt der Pentateuchkritik: Auf dem Wege zu einer Neubegründung der De Wette'schen Hypothese." In M. Vervenne and J. Lust, eds., *Deuteronomy and Deuteronomic Literature: Festschrift C. H. W. Brekelmans*, 321–39. Bibliotheca Ephemeridum Theologicarum Lovaniensium 133. Leuven: Peeters, 1997.

———. *Das Deuteronomium im Pentateuch und Hexateuch: Studien zur Literaturgeschichte von Pentateuch und Hexateuch im Lichte des Deuteronomiumrahmens.* Forschungen zum Alten Testament 30. Tübingen: Mohr Siebeck, 2000.

———. *Das Gesetz des Mose.* Darmstadt: Wissenschaftliche Buchgesellschaft, 2007.

———. "Die Ursprünge der Bundestheologie im Alten Testament und im Alten Orient." *Zeitschrift für altorientalische und biblische Rechtsgeschichte* 4 (1998): 1–84.

———. "The History of the Legal-Religious Hermeneutics of the Book of Deuteronomy from the Assyrian to the Hellenistic Period." In Hagedorn and Kratz, *Law and Religion in the Eastern Mediterranean*, 211–50.

———. "The Pre-Exilic Deuteronomy as a Revision of the Covenant Code." In Eckart Otto, *Kontinuum und Proprium: Studien zur Sozial- und Rechtsgeschichte des Alten Orients und des Alten Testaments,* 112–22. Wiesbaden: Harrassowitz, 1996.

———. "Recht/Rechtswesen im Alten Orient und im Alten Testament." In *Theologische Realenzyklopädie*, 28:197–210. Berlin: De Gruyter, 1997.

———. "Vom Bundesbuch zum Deuteronomium: Die deuteronomische Redaktion in Dtn 12–26." In Georg Braulik, Walter Gross, and Sean McEvenue, eds., *Biblische Theologie und gesellschaftlicher Wandel: Für Norbert Lohfink,* 260–78. Freiburg: Herder, 1993.

Oudshoorn, Jacobine G. *The Relationship between Roman and Local Law in the Babatha and Salome Komaise Archives: General Analysis and Three Case Studies on Law of Succession, Guardianship, and Marriage.* Leiden: Brill, 2007.

Pakkala, Juha. "The Date of the Oldest Edition of Deuteronomy." *ZAW* 121 (2009): 388–401.

———. "Der literar- und religionsgeschichtliche Ort von Deuteronomium 13." In M. Witte, K. Schmid, D. Prechel, and J. C. Gertz, eds., *Die deuteronomistischen Geschichtswerke: Redactions- und religionsgeschichtliche Perspektiven zur "Deuteronomismus"-Diskussion in Tora und Vorderen Propheten,* 239–48. Beihefte zur Zeitschrift für die alttestamentliche Wissenschaft 365. Berlin: De Gruyter, 2006.

———. *Ezra the Scribe: The Development of Ezra 7–10 and Nehemia 8*. Beihefte zur Zeitschrift für die alttestamentliche Wissenschaft 347. Berlin: De Gruyter, 2004.

———. "The Quotations and References of the Pentateuchal Laws in Ezra-Nehemiah." In Hanne von Weissenberg, Juha Pakkala, and Karko Marttila, eds., *Changes in Scripture: Rewriting and Interpreting Authoritative Traditions in the Second Temple Period*, 193–221. Beihefte zur Zeitschrift für die alttestamentliche Wissenschaft 419. Berlin: De Gruyter, 2011.

Parpola, Simo, and K. Watanabe. *Neo-Assyrian Treaties and Loyalty Oaths*. Helsinki: Helsinki University Press, 1988.

Pearce, Laurie. "New Evidence for Judeans in Babylonia." In Lipschitz and Oeming, *Judah and the Judeans in the Persian Period*, 399–411. Winona Lake, IN: Eisenbrauns, 2006.

Pearce, Laurie, and Cornelia Wunsch. *Documents of Judean Exiles and West Semites in Babylonia in the Collection of David Sofer*. Bethesda, MD: CDL, 2014.

Perles, Felix. *Bousset's "Religion des Judentums" im neutestamentlichen Zeitalter kritisch untersucht*. Berlin: Peiser, 1903.

Perlitt, Lothar. "Der Staatsgedanke im Deuteronomium." In Samuel E. Balentine and John Barton, eds., *Language, Theology, and the Bible: Essays in Honour of James Barr*, 182–98. Oxford: Oxford University Press, 1994.

Perrin, Andrew B. *The Dynamics of Dream-Vision Revelation in the Aramaic Dead Sea Scrolls*. Journal of Ancient Judaism Supplements Göttingen: Vandenhoeck & Ruprecht, 2015.

Petersen, Anders Klostergaard. "Rewritten Bible as a Borderline Phenomenon—Genre, Textual Strategy, or Canonical Anachronism?" In Anthony Hilhorst, Émile Puech, and Eibert Tigchelaar, eds., *Flores Florentino: Dead Sea Scrolls and Other Early Jewish Studies in Honour of Florentino García Martínez*, 284–306. Studies on the Texts of the Desert of Judah 122. Leiden: Brill, 2007.

Petersen, David. *Haggai and Zechariah 1–8*. Old Testament Library. Philadelphia: Westminster, 1984.

Philonenko, M. "La doctrine qoumrânienne de deux esprits." In G. Widengren, A. Hultgård, and M. Philonenko, *Apocalyptique iranienne et dualisme qoumrânien*, 163–211. Paris: Maisonneuve, 1995.

Pietsch, Michael. *Die Kultreform Josias*. Forschungen zum Alten Testament 86. Tübingen: Mohr Siebeck, 2013.

Pollefeyt, Didier, and Reimund Bieringer, eds. *Paul and Judaism: Crosscurrents in Pauline Exegesis and the Study of Jewish-Christian Relations*. London: Clark, 2012.

Porten, Bezalel. *Archives from Elephantine: The Life of an Ancient Jewish Military Colony.* Berkeley and Los Angeles: University of California Press, 1968.

———. *The Elephantine Papyri in English: Three Millennia of Cross-Cultural Continuity and Change.* Leiden: Brill, 1996.

Porten, Bezalel, and Ada Yardeni. *Textbook of Aramaic Documents from Ancient Egypt.* 4 vols. Jerusalem: Academon, 1986–99.

Porter, Frank C. Review of *Judaism in the First Centuries of the Christian Era: The Age of the Tannaim* by G. F. Moore. *Journal of Religion* 8 (1928): 30–62.

Portier-Young, Anathea. *Apocalypse against Empire: Theologies of Resistance in Early Judaism.* Grand Rapids, MI: Eerdmans, 2010.

———. "Sweet Mercy Metropolis: Interpreting Aseneth's Honeycomb." *JSP* 14 (2005): 133–57.

Puech, Émile. "246. 4QApocryphe de Daniel ar." In Brooke et al., *Qumran Cave 4, XVII,* 165–84.

———. *Qumrân Grotte 4, XVIII: Textes hébreux (4Q 521-528, 4Q 576-4Q 579).* Discoveries in the Judean Desert 25. Oxford: Clarendon, 1998.

———. *Qumrân Grotte 4, XXII: Textes araméens; Première partie: 4Q 529–549.* Discoveries in the Judean Desert 31. Oxford: Clarendon, 2001.

———. *Qumrân Grotte 4, XXVII: Textes araméens; Deuxième partie: 4Q 550–4Q 575a, 4Q 580–4Q 587.* Discoveries in the Judea Desert 37. Oxford: Clarendon, 2009.

Qimron, Elisha, and John Strugnell. *Qumran Cave 4, V: Miqsat Ma'ase Ha-Torah.* Discoveries in the Judean Desert 10. Oxford: Clarendon, 1994.

Rabenau, Merten. *Studien zum Buch Tobit.* Beihefte zur Zeitschrift für die alttestamentliche Wissenschaft 220. Berlin: De Gruyter, 1994.

Rad, Gerhard von. "The Form-Critical Problem of the Hexateuch." In Gerhard von Rad, *The Form-Critical Problem of the Hexateuch and Other Essays,* 1–78. Edinburgh: Clark, 1965.

Räisänen, Heikki. "Paul's Theological Difficulties with the Law." In E. A. Livingstone, ed., *Studia Biblica 1978,* vol. 3, *Papers on Paul and Other New Testament Authors,* 301–20. Journal for the Study of the New Testament 3. Sheffield: JSNT, 1980.

Rajak, Tessa. *Translation and Survival: The Greek Bible of the Ancient Jewish Diaspora.* Oxford: Oxford University Press, 2009.

Redford, Donald. "The So-Called 'Codification' of Egyptian Law under Darius I." In Watts, *Persia and Torah,* 135–59.

Regev, Eyal. *The Hasmoneans: Ideology, Archaeology, Identity.* Journal of Ancient Judaism Supplements 10. Göttingen: Vanenhoeck & Ruprecht, 2013.

Reinhartz, Adele. "The Vanishing Jews of Antiquity." *Marginalia,* June 24, 2014.

Reinmuth, Eckart, ed. *Joseph und Aseneth.* Tübingen: Mohr Siebeck, 2009.

Reynolds, Bennie H., III. *Between Symbolism and Realism: The Use of Symbolic and Non-Symbolic Language in Ancient Jewish Apocalypses, 333–63 B.C.E.* Journal for the Study of Judaism 8. Göttingen: Vandenhoeck & Ruprecht, 2011.

Reynolds, Kent Aaron. *Torah as Teacher: The Exemplary Torah Student in Psalm 119.* Vetus Testamentum Supplements 137. Leiden: Brill, 2010.

Roetzel, Calvin J. "Paul and Nomos in the Messianic Age." In Ehrensperger and Tucker, *Reading Paul in Context,* 113–27.

Römer, Thomas. "Conflicting Models of Identity and the Publication of the Torah in the Persian Period." In R. Albertz and J. Wöhrle, eds., *Between Cooperation and Hostility: Multiple Identities in Ancient Judaism and the Interaction with Foreign Powers,* 33–51. Journal of Ancient Judaism Supplements 11. Göttingen: Vandenhoeck & Ruprecht, 2013.

———. *The So-Called Deuteronomistic History: A Sociological, Historical, and Literary Introduction.* London and New York: T & T Clark, 2007.

Roo, Jacqueline C. R. de. *Works of the Law at Qumran and in Paul.* Sheffield: Sheffield Phoenix, 2007.

Roth, Martha. *Law Collections from Mesopotamia and Asia Minor.* 2nd ed. SBL Writings from the Ancient World 6. Atlanta: Scholars Press, 1997.

Rothenbusch, Ralf. *"Abgesondert zur Tora Gottes hin": Ethnisch-religiöse Identitäten im Esra/Nehemiabuch.* Freiburg im Breisgau: Herder, 2012.

———. "The Question of Mixed Marriages: Between the Poles of Diaspora and Homeland; Observations in Ezra-Nehemiah." In Frevel, *Intermarriage and Group Identity in the Second Temple Period,* 60–77.

Rowlett, Lori L. *Joshua and the Rhetoric of Violence: A New Historicist Analysis.* Journal for the Study of the Old Testament Supplements 226. Sheffield: Sheffield Academic Press, 1996.

Rubenstein, Jeffrey L. "Nominalism and Realism in Qumranic and Rabbinic Law: A Reassessment." *DSD* 6 (1999): 157–83.

Sacchi, Paolo. *Jewish Apocalyptic and Its History.* Sheffield: Sheffield Academic Press, 1997.

Sanders, E. P. *Judaism: Practice and Belief, 63 BCE–66 CE.* Philadelphia: Trinity Press International, 1992.

———. *Paul, the Law, and the Jewish People.* Philadelphia: Fortress, 1983.

———. *Paul and Palestinian Judaism.* Philadelphia: Fortress, 1977.

Sanders, James A. *Torah and Canon.* 2nd ed. Eugene, OR: Cascade, 2005.

Sänger, Dieter. *Antikes Judentum und die Mysterien: Religionsgeschichtliche Untersuchungen zu Joseph und Aseneth*. Wissenschaftliche Untersuchungen zum Neuen Testament 2/5. Tübingen: Mohr Siebeck, 1980.

Satlow, Michael. "Defining Judaism: Accounting for 'Religions' in the Study of Religion." *JAAR* 74 (2006): 837–60.

———. *How the Bible Became Holy*. New Haven, CT: Yale University Press, 2014.

———. "Jew or Judean?" In Caroline Johnson Hodge, Saul M. Olyan, and Daniel Ullucci, eds., *One Who Sows Bountifully: Essays in Honor of Stanley K. Stowers*, 165–74. Brown Judaic Studies 356. Providence: Brown Judaic Studies, 2013.

Schaper, Joachim. "Rereading the Law: Inner-Biblical Exegesis of Divine Oracles in Ezekiel 44 and Isaiah 56." In B. M. Levinson and E. Otto, eds., *Recht und Ethik im Alten Testament*, 125–44. Altes Testament und Moderne 13. Münster: Lit Verlag, 2004.

———. "Torah and Identity in the Persian Period." In Lipschitz, Knoppers, and Oeming, *Judah and the Judeans in the Achaemenid Period*, 27–38.

Schiffman, Lawrence H. "The Book of *Jubilees* and the *Temple Scroll*." In Boccaccini and Ibba, *Enoch and the Mosaic Torah*, 99–115.

———. *The Courtyards of the House of the Lord: Studies on the Temple Scroll*. Leiden: Brill, 2008.

———. *The Halakhah at Qumran*. Leiden: Brill, 1975.

———. "Halakhic Elements in the Sapiential Texts from Qumran." In John J. Collins, Gregory E. Sterling, and Ruth A. Clements, eds., *Sapiential Perspectives: Wisdom Literature in Light of the Dead Sea Scrolls*, 89–100. Studies on the Texts of the Desert of Judah 51. Leiden: Brill, 2004.

———. *Reclaiming the Dead Sea Scrolls: The History of Judaism, the Background of Christianity, the Lost Library of Qumran*. Philadelphia and Jerusalem: The Jewish Publication Society, 1994.

———. "Reflections on the Deeds of Sale from the Judaean Desert in Light of Rabbinic Literature." In Ranon Katzoff and David Schaps, eds., *Law in the Documents of the Judaean Desert*, 185–203. Leiden: Brill, 2005.

———. "The Sadducean Origins of the Dead Sea Scrolls." In H. Shanks, ed., *Understanding the Dead Sea Scrolls*, 35–49. New York: Random House, 1992.

———. "The *Temple Scroll* and the Halakhic Pseudepigrapha of the Second Temple Period." In Esther Chazon and Michael E. Stone, eds., *Pseudepigraphic Perspectives: The Apocrypha and Pseudepigrapha in Light of the Dead Sea Scrolls*, 121–31. Studies on the Texts of the Desert of Judah 31. Leiden: Brill, 1999.

Schiffman, Lawrence H., Andrew D. Gross, and Michael C. Rand, *Temple Scroll and Related Documents.* The Dead Sea Scrolls: Hebrew, Aramaic, and Greek Texts with English Translations 7. Tübingen: Mohr Siebeck/Louisville, KY: Westminster John Knox, 2011.

Schipper, Bernd U. *Hermeneutik der Tora: Studien zur Traditionsgeschichte von Prov 2 und zur Komposition von Prov 1–9.* Beihefte zur Zeitschrift für die alttestamentliche Wissenschaft 432. Berlin: De Gruyter, 2012.

———. "When Wisdom Is Not Enough! The Discourse on Wisdom and Torah and the Composition of the Book of Proverbs." In Schipper and Teeter, *Wisdom and Torah*, 55–79.

Schipper, Bernd U., and D. Andrew Teeter, eds. *Wisdom and Torah.* Journal for the Study of Judaism Supplements 163. Leiden: Brill 2013.

Schmid, Konrad. *Genesis and the Moses Story: Israel's Dual Origins in the Hebrew Bible.* Winona Lake, IN: Eisenbrauns, 2010.

———. "Judean Identity and Ecumenicity: The Political Theology of the Priestly Document." In Lipschitz, Knoppers, and Oeming, *Judah and Judeans in the Achaemenid Period,* 3–26.

———. *The Old Testament: A Literary History.* Minneapolis: Fortress, 2012.

———. "The Persian Imperial Authorization as a Historical Problem." In Knoppers and Levinson, *The Pentateuch as Torah,* 23–38.

Schmidt, L. *Die Ethik der alten Griechen.* 2 vols. Berlin: Hertz, 1882.

Schröder, Bernd. *Die "väterlichen Gesetze": Flavius Josephus als Vermittler von Halachah an Griechen und Römer.* Tübingen: Mohr Siebeck, 1996.

Schuerer, Emil. *The History of the Jewish People in the Age of Jesus Christ (175 B.C. – A.D. 135).* Rev. and ed. Geza Vermes and Fergus Millar. Vol. 1. Edinburgh: Clark, 1973.

Schulz, Brian. *Conquering the World: The War Scroll (1QM) Reconsidered.* Studies on the Texts of the Desert of Judah 76. Leiden: Brill, 2009.

Schwartz, Daniel R. *2 Maccabees.* Commentaries on Early Jewish Literature. Berlin: De Gruyter, 2008.

———. "Diodorus Siculus 40.3—Hecataeus or Pseudo-Hecataeus?" In M. Mor, A. Oppenheimer, J. Pastor, and D. R. Schwartz, eds., *Jews and Gentiles in the Holy Land in the Days of the Second Temple, the Mishnah and Talmud: A Collection of Articles,* 181–97. Jerusalem: Yad Ben-Zvi, 2003.

———. "God, Gentiles, and Jewish Law: On Acts 15 and Josephus' Adiabene Narrative." In Hubert Cancik, Hermann Lichtenberger, and Peter Schäfer, eds., *Geschichte—Tradition—Reflexion: Festschrift für Martin Hengel zum 70. Geburtstag,* 1:263–82. Tübingen: Mohr Siebeck, 1996.

———. "'Judaean' or 'Jew'? How Should We Translate *ioudaios* in Josephus?" In Jörg Frey, Daniel R. Schwartz, and Stephanie Gripentrog, eds., *Jewish Identity in the Greco-Roman World*, 3–27. Ancient Judaism and Early Christianity 71. Leiden: Brill, 2007.

———. "Judeans, Jews, and Their Neighbors: Jewish Identity in the Second Temple Period." In Rainer Albertz and Jakob Wöhrle, eds., *Between Cooperation and Hostility: Multiple Identities in Ancient Judaism and the Interaction with Foreign Powers*, 13–31. Journal of Ancient Judaism Supplements 11. Göttingen: Vandenhoeck & Ruprecht, 2013.

———. *Judeans and Jews: Four Faces of Dichotomy in Ancient Jewish History*. Toronto: University of Toronto Press, 2014.

———. "Law and Truth: On Qumran-Sadducean and Rabbinic Views of Law." In Devorah Dimant and Uriel Rappaport, eds., *The Dead Sea Scrolls: Forty Years of Research*, 229–40. Leiden: Brill, 1992.

Schwartz, Eberhard. *Identität durch Abgrenzung: Abgrenzungsprozesse im Israel im 2. vorchristlichen Jahrhundert und ihre traditionsgeschichtlichen Voraussetzungen; zugleich ein Beitrag zur Erforschung des Jubiläenbuches*. Frankfurt am Main: Lang, 1982.

Schwartz, Seth. "How Many Judaisms Were There? A Critique of Neusner and Smith on Definition and Mason and Boyarin on Categorization." *JAJ* 2 (2011): 208–38.

———. *Imperialism and Jewish Society, 200 B.C.E. to 640 C.E.* Princeton, NJ: Princeton University Press, 2002.

Segal, Michael. *The Book of Jubilees: Rewritten Bible, Redaction, Ideology, and Theology*. Journal for the Study of Judaism Supplements 117. Leiden: Brill, 2007.

Seow, Choon-Leong. *Ecclesiastes*. Anchor Bible 18C. New York: Doubleday, 1997.

Seters, John van. *A Law Book for the Diaspora: Revision in the Study of the Covenant Code*. Oxford and New York: Oxford University Press, 2003.

Sharp, Carolyn J. *Irony and Meaning in the Hebrew Bible*. Bloomington: Indiana University Press, 2009.

Shaver, Judson R. *Torah and the Chronicler's History Work: An Inquiry into the Chronicler's References to Laws, Festivals, and Cultic Institutions in Relationship to Pentateuchal Legislation*. Brown Judaic Studies 196. Atlanta: Scholars Press, 1989.

Shemesh, Aharon. "Halakhah between the Dead Sea Scrolls and Rabbinic Literature." In Lim and Collins, *The Oxford Handbook of the Dead Sea Scrolls*, 595–616.

————. *Halakhah in the Making: The Development of Jewish Law from Qumran to the Rabbis.* Berkeley: University of California Press, 2009.

Sheppard, Gerald T. "The Epilogue to Qoheleth as Theological Commentary." *CBQ* 39 (1977): 182–89.

————. *Wisdom as a Hermeneutical Construct.* Beihefte zur Zeitschrift für die alttestamentliche Wissenschaft 151. Berlin: De Gruyter, 1980.

Shils, Edward. "Primordial, Personal, Sacred, and Civil Ties: Some Particular Observations on the Relationships of Sociological Research and Theory." *British Journal of Sociology* 8 (1957): 130–45.

Sievers, Joseph. "Josephus, First Maccabees, Sparta, the Three Haireseis— and Cicero." *JSJ* 32 (2001): 24–51.

Silberman, Neil Asher. *A Prophet from amongst You: The Life of Yigael Yadin; Soldier, Scholar, and Mythmaker of Modern Israel.* Reading, MA: Addison-Wesley, 1993.

Ska, Jean-Louis. *Introduction to Reading the Pentateuch.* Winona Lake, IN: Eisenbrauns, 2006.

————. "The Law of Israel in the Old Testament." In Jean-Louis Ska, *The Exegesis of the Pentateuch: Exegetical Studies and Basic Questions*, 196–220. Forschungen zum Alten Testament 66. Tübingen: Mohr Siebeck, 2009.

Skjaervø, Prods Oktor. "Zoroastrian Dualism, with an Appendix on the Sources of Zoroastrianism." In Lange et al., *Light against Darkness*, 55–91.

Smith, Anthony D. *The Ethnic Origins of Nations.* Oxford: Blackwell, 1986.

————. *The Nation in History.* Hanover, NH: The University Press of New England, 2000.

Smith, Jonathan Z. "Fences and Neighbors." In Jonathan Z. Smith, *Imagining Religion: From Babylon to Jonestown.* Chicago: University of Chicago Press, 1982.

Smith, Morton. "The Dead Sea Sect in Relation to Ancient Judaism." *NTS* 7 (1960–61): 347–60.

Smith-Christopher, Daniel. "Between Ezra and Isaiah: Exclusion, Transformation, and Inclusion of the 'Foreigner' in Post-Exilic Biblical Theology." In M.G. Brett, ed., *Ethnicity and the Bible*, 117–44. Biblical Interpretation Series 19. Leiden: Brill, 1996.

————. "Daniel." In *New Interpreter's Bible*, 7:19–194. Nashville: Abingdon, 1996.

————. "The Mixed Marriage Crisis in Ezra 9–10 and Nehemiah 13: A Study of the Sociology of the Post-exilic Judean Community." In T.C. Eskenazi and K.H. Richards, eds., *Second Temple Studies 2*, 243–65. Sheffield: JSOT, 1994.

————. *The Religion of the Landless: The Social Context of the Babylonian Exile.* Bloomington, IN: Meyer-Stone, 1989.

Snowden, Frank M., Jr. *Before Color Prejudice: The Ancient View of Blacks.* Cambridge, MA: Harvard University Press, 1983.

Sommer, Benjamin D. *Revelation and Authority: Sinai in Jewish Scripture and Tradition.* Anchor Yale Bible Reference Library. New Haven, CT: Yale University Press, 2015.

Southwood, Katherine E. *Ethnicity and the Mixed Marriage Crisis in Ezra 9–10: An Anthropological Approach.* Oxford: Oxford University Press, 2012.

Sparks, Kenton L. *Ethnicity and Identity in Ancient Israel: Prolegomena to the Study of Ethnic Sentiments and Their Expression in the Hebrew Bible.* Winona Lake, IN: Eisenbrauns, 1998.

Speyer, Wolfgang. *Bücherfunde in der Glaubenswerbung der Antike: Mit einem Ausblick auf Mittelalter und Neuzeit.* Hypomnemata 24. Göttingen: Vandenhoeck & Ruprecht, 1970.

Spiegelberg, Wilhelm. *Die sogenannte demotische Chronik des Pap. 215 der Bibliothèque nationale zu Paris, nebst den auf der Rückseite des Papyrus stehenden Texten.* Leipzig: Hinrichs, 1914.

Stackert, Jeffrey. *A Prophet like Moses: Prophecy, Law, and Israelite Religion.* New York: Oxford University Press, 2014.

Stegemann, Hartmut. *The Library of Qumran: On the Essenes, Qumran, John the Baptist, and Jesus.* Grand Rapids, MI: Eerdmans, 1998.

Steiner, Richard C. "The *mbqr* at Qumran, the *episkopos* in the Athenian Empire, and the Meaning of *lbqr'* in Ezra 7:14: On the Relation of Ezra's Mission to the Persian Legal Project." *JBL* 120 (2001): 623–46.

Stendahl, Krister. *Paul among Jews and Gentiles.* Philadelphia: Fortress, 1977.

Sterling, Gregory E. *Historiography and Self-Definition: Josephos, Luke, Acts, and Apologetic Historiography.* Leiden: Brill, 1992.

————. "Universalizing the Particular: Natural Law in Second Temple Ethics." *Studia Philonica Annual* 15 (2003): 64–80.

————. "Was There a Common Ethic in Second Temple Judaism." In J.J. Collins, G.E. Sterling, and R.A. Clements, eds., *Sapiential Perspectives: Wisdom Literature in Light of the Dead Sea Scrolls,* 171–94. Studies on the Texts of the Desert of Judah 51. Leiden: Brill, 2004.

Stern, Menahem. *Greek and Latin Authors on Jews and Judaism.* 2 vols. Jerusalem: The Israel Academy of Sciences and Humanities, 1974.

Steymans, H. U. *Deuteronomium 28 und die adê zur Thronfolgeregelung Asarhaddons: Segen und Fluch im Alten Orient und in Israel.* Orbis Biblicus et Orientalis

145. Freiburg: Universitätsverlag; Göttingen: Vandenhoeck & Ruprecht, 1995.

Stokes, Ryan E. "The Throne Visions of Daniel 7, *1 Enoch* 14, and the Qumran Book of Giants (4Q530): An Analysis of Their Literary Relationship." *DSD* 15 (2008): 340–58.

Stone, Michael E. "Aramaic Levi Document." In Collins and Harlow, *The Eerdmans Dictionary of Early Judaism*, 362–64.

———. "The Book of Enoch and Judaism in the Third Century B.C.E." *CBQ* 40 (1978): 479–92.

———. *Fourth Ezra: A Commentary on the Book of Fourth Ezra*. Hermeneia. Minneapolis: Fortress, 1990.

———. "On Reading an Apocalypse." In John J. Collins and James H. Charlesworth, eds., *Mysteries and Revelations: Apocalyptic Studies since the Uppsala Colloquium*, 65–78. Journal for the Study of the Pseudepigrapha Supplements 9. Sheffield: Sheffield Academic Press, 1991.

———. *Scriptures, Sects, and Visions: A Profile of Judaism from Ezra to the Jewish Revolts*. Philadelphia: Fortress, 1980.

Stone, M.E., and J.C. Greenfield. "Aramaic Levi Document." In Brooke et al., *Qumran Cave 4, XVII: Parabiblical Texts*, pt. 3, 1–72.

Stowers, Stanley K. "Does Pauline Christianity Resemble a Hellenistic Philosophy?" In Engberg-Pedersen, *Paul beyond the Judaism/Hellenism Divide*, 81–102.

———. *A Rereading of Romans: Justice, Jews, and Gentiles*. New Haven, CT: Yale University Press, 1994.

Strugnell, John, and Devorah Dimant. "4Q Second Ezekiel." *RevQ* 13 (1988): 45–56.

Strugnell, John, and Daniel J. Harrington. *Qumran Cave 4, XXIV: Sapiential Texts*, pt. 2: *4QInstruction (Mûsār leMēvîn)*. Discoveries in the Judean Desert 34. Oxford: Clarendon, 1999.

Stuckenbruck, Loren. "Daniel and Early Enoch Traditions in the Dead Sea Scrolls." In Collins and Flint, *The Book of Daniel*, 368–86.

———. "The Early Traditions Related to *1 Enoch* from the Dead Sea Scrolls: An Overview and Assessment." In Boccaccini and Collins, *The Early Enoch Literature*, 41–63.

Sussmann, Jacob. "The History of the Halakha and the Dead Sea Scrolls." In Qimron and Strugnell, *Miqṣat Ma'ase Ha-Torah*, 179–200.

Suter, David W. "Fallen Angel, Fallen Priest: The Problem of Family Purity in *1 Enoch* 6–16." *HUCA* 50 (1979): 115–35.

————. "Revisiting 'Fallen Angel, Fallen Priest.'" *Henoch* 24 (2002): 137–42.

Sweeney, Marvin. *King Josiah of Judah: The Lost Messiah of Israel.* New York: Oxford University Press, 2001.

Tappenden, Frederick S. *Resurrection in Paul: Cognition, Metaphor, and Transformation.* Early Christianity and Its Literature 19. Atlanta: SBL, 2016.

Tcherikover, Victor. *Hellenistic Civilization and the Jews.* Peabody, MA: Hendrickson, 1999. Original publication: Philadelphia: Jewish Publication Society, 1959.

Tcherikover, Victor, and Alexander Fuks, eds. *Corpus Papyrorum Judaicarum.* Vol. 1. Cambridge, MA: Harvard University Press, 1957.

Thackeray, H. St. John, trans. *Josephus,* vol. 1, *The Life; Against Apion.* Loeb Classical Library. 1926. Reprint, Cambridge, MA: Harvard University Press, 1976.

Theophilos, Michael P. "The Portrayal of Gentiles in Jewish Apocalyptic Literature." In David C. Sim and James S. McLaren, eds., *Attitudes to Gentiles in Ancient Judaism and Early Christianity,* 72–91. Library of New Testament Studies 499. London: Bloomsbury, 2013.

Thielman, Frank. *From Plight to Solution: A Jewish Framework for Understanding Paul's View of the Law in Galatians and Romans.* Novum Testamentum Supplements 61. Leiden: Brill, 1989.

Thiessen, Matthew. *Contesting Conversion: Genealogy, Circumcision, and Identity in Ancient Judaism and Christianity.* Oxford and New York: Oxford University Press, 2011.

————. *Paul and the Gentile Problem.* New York: Oxford University Press, 2016.

Thompson Crawford, Dorothy J. "The Idumeans of Memphis and the Ptolemaic *politeumata.*" In *Atti del XVII congresso internazionale di papirologia,* 3:1069–75. Naples: Centro Internazionale per lo Studio dei Papiri Ercolanesi, 1984.

Tigchelaar, Eibert. "Classifications of the Collection of Dead Sea Scrolls and the Case of Apocryphon of Jeremiah C." *JSJ* 43 (2012): 519–50.

Tooman, William. "Wisdom and Torah at Qumran." In Schipper and Teeter, *Wisdom and Torah,* 203–32.

Toorn, Karel van der. "Anat-Yahu, Some Other Deities, and the Jews of Elephantine." *Numen* 39 (1992): 80–101.

————. "The Iconic Book: Analogies between the Babylonian Cult of Images and the Veneration of the Torah." In Karel van der Toorn, ed., *The Image and the Book: Iconic Cults, Aniconism, and the Rise of Book Religion in Israel and the Ancient Near East,* 229–48. Leuven: Peeters, 1997.

Torrey, C.C. *The Composition and Historical Value of Ezra-Nehemiah.* Giessen: Ricker, 1896.

————. *Ezra Studies*. Chicago: University of Chicago Press, 1910.

Trotter, Jonathan. "The Tradition of the Throne Vision in the Second Temple Period: Daniel 7:9–10, *1 Enoch* 14:18–23, and the Book of Giants (4Q530)." *RevQ* 25 (1999): 451–66.

Tuval, Michael. *From Jerusalem Priest to Roman Jew: Of Josephus and the Paradigms of Ancient Judaism*. Wissenschaftliche Untersuchungen zum Neuen Testament 2/357. Tübingen: Mohr Siebeck, 2013.

Udoh, Fabian, with Susannah Heschel, Mark Chancey, and Gregory Tatum, eds. *Redefining First-Century Jewish and Christian Identities: Essays in Honor of Ed Parish Sanders*. Notre Dame, IN: University of Notre Dame, 2008.

Uehlinger, Christoph. "Gab es eine joschijanische Kultreform? Pladoyer für ein begründetes Minimum." In Gross, *Jeremia und die "deuteronomistische Bewegung,"* 57–89.

————. "Was There a Cult Reform under King Josiah? The Case for a Well-Grounded Minimum." In Grabbe, *Good Kings and Bad Kings*, 279–316. London and New York: T & T Clark, 2005.

Ulrich, Eugene C. "The Text of Daniel in the Dead Sea Scrolls." In Collins and Flint, *The Book of Daniel*, 573–85. Vetus Testament Supplements 83.2. Leiden: Brill, 2001.

Urbach, Ephraim E. *The Sages: Their Concepts and Beliefs*. Jerusalem: Magnes, 1975.

Uusimaki, Elisa. "Turning Proverbs towards Torah: 4Q525 in the Context of Late Second Temple Wisdom Literature." PhD diss., University of Helsinki, 2013 = *Turning Proverbs towards Torah: An Analysis of 4Q525*. Studies on the Texts of the Desert of Judah 117. Leiden: Brill, 2016.

VanderKam, James C. "Biblical Interpretation in *1 Enoch* and *Jubilees*." In James H. Charlesworth and Craig A. Evans, eds., *The Pseudepigrapha and Early Biblical Interpretation*, 96–125. Journal for the Study of the Pseudepigrapha 14. Sheffield: Sheffield Academic Press, 1993.

————. "The Book of Enoch and the Dead Sea Scrolls." In Lim and Collins, *The Oxford Handbook of the Dead Sea Scrolls*, 254–77.

————. "The Interpretation of Genesis in *1 Enoch*." In Peter W. Flint, ed., *The Bible at Qumran: Text, Shape, and Interpretation*, 129–48. Grand Rapids, MI: Eerdmans, 2001.

————. "Mapping Second Temple Judaism." In Boccaccini and Collins, *The Early Enoch Literature*, 1–20.

————. "Moses Trumping Moses: Making the Book of *Jubilees*." In Sarianna Metso, Hindy Najman, and Eileen Schuller, *The Dead Sea Scrolls: Transmission of Traditions and Production of Texts,* 25–44. Studies on the Texts of the Desert of Judah 92. Leiden: Brill, 2010.

———. "The Origins and Purposes of the Book of *Jubilees.*" In Matthias Albani, Jörg Frey, and Armin Lange, eds., *Studies in the Book of Jubilees,* 3–24. Texte und Studien zum Antiken Judentum 65. Tübingen: Mohr Siebeck, 1997.

———. "The *Temple Scroll* and the Book of *Jubilees.*" In George J. Brooke, ed., *Temple Scroll Studies,* 211–36. Journal for the Study of the Pseudepigrapha 7. Sheffield: Sheffield Academic Press, 1989.

———. *Textual and Historical Studies on the Book of Jubilees.* HSM 14. Missoula, MT: Scholars Press, 1977.

VanderKam, James C., and J. T. Milik. "*Jubilees.*" In H. Attridge et al., *Qumran Cave 4, VIII: Parabiblical Texts,* 1–185. Discoveries in the Judean Desert 12. Oxford: Clarendon, 1994.

Vermes, Geza. *Scripture and Tradition in Judaism: Haggadic Studies.* Studia Postbiblica 4. 1961. Leiden: Brill, 1973.

Vielhauer, Philipp. "Zum 'Paulinismus' der Apostelgeschichte." *EvT* 10 (1950–51): 1–15. English translation: "On the 'Paulinism' of Acts." *Perkins School of Theology Journal* 17 (1963): 5–17. Reprinted in L.E. Keck and J.L. Martyn, eds., *Studies in Luke-Acts: Essays Presented in Honor of Paul Schubert,* 33–50. Nashville: Abingdon, 1966.

Vos, George De, and L. Romanucci-Ross, eds. *Ethnic Identity: Creation, Conflict, and Accommodation.* 3rd ed. Walnut Creek, CA, and London: Altamira, 1995.

Wacker, M.-T. *Weltordnung und Gericht: Studien zu 1 Henoch 22.* Würzburg: Echter, 1982.

Watts, James W., ed. *Persia and Torah: The Theory of Imperial Authorization of the Pentateuch.* SBL Symposium Series 17. Atlanta: SBL, 2001.

Weber, Max. *Economy and Society: An Outline of Interpretive Sociology.* Berkeley: University of California Press, 1978.

Weeks, Stuart E. "Biblical Literature and the Emergence of Ancient Jewish Nationalism." *BibInt* 10 (2002): 144–57.

———. "'Fear God and Keep His Commandments': Could Qohelet Have Said This?" In Schipper and Teeter, *Wisdom and Torah,* 101–18.

———. *Instruction and Imagery in Proverbs 1–9.* Oxford: Oxford University Press, 2007.

Weinfeld, Moshe. *Deuteronomy 1–11.* Anchor Bible 5. New York: Doubleday, 1991.

———. *Deuteronomy and the Deuteronomic School.* Oxford: Oxford University Press, 1972; reprint, Winona Lake, IN: Eisenbrauns, 1992.

Weippert, Manfred. "Synkretismus und Monotheismus: Religionsinterne Konfliktbewältigung im alten Israel." In Manfred Weippert, *Jahwe und die anderen Götter: Studien zur Religionsgeschicht des antiken Israel in ihrem syrisch-kanaanäischen Kontext*, 1–24. Forschungen zum Alten Testament 18. Tübingen: Mohr Siebeck, 1997.

Wellhausen, Julius. *Israelitische und jüdische Geschichte*. 10th ed. Berlin: De Gruyter, 2004.

———. *Prolegomena to the History of Ancient Israel*. 1885. Reprint, Atlanta: Scholars Press, 1994.

Werman, Cana. "Epochs and End-Time: The 490-Year Scheme in Second Temple Literature." *DSD* 13 (2006): 229–55.

Wette, W. M. L. de. "Dissertatio critico-exegetica, qua Deuteronomium a prioribus Pentateuchi libris diversum, alius cuiusdam auctoris opus esse monstratur." PhD diss., University of Jena, 1805.

White Crawford, Sidnie. *Rewriting Scripture in Second Temple Times*. Grand Rapids, MI: Eerdmans, 2008.

———. *The Temple Scroll and Related Texts*. Sheffield: Sheffield Academic Press, 2000.

Wiese, Christian. *Challenging Colonial Discourse: Jewish Studies and Protestant Theology in Wilhelmine Germany*. Leiden: Brill, 2005.

Wiesehöfer, Josef. "Law and Religion in Achaemenid Iran." In Hagedorn and Kratz, *Law and Religion in the Eastern Mediterranean*, 41–57.

Williamson, H. G. M. *Ezra, Nehemiah*. WBC 16. Waco, TX: Word, 1985.

Wills, L. M. *The Jewish Novel in the Ancient World*. Ithaca, NY: Cornell University Press, 1995.

Wilson, Walter T. *The Sentences of Pseudo-Phocylides*. Commentaries on Early Jewish Literature. Berlin: De Gruyter, 2005.

Wise, Michael O. "The Origins and History of the Teacher's Movement." In Lim and Collins, *The Oxford Handbook of the Dead Sea Scrolls*, 92–122.

Wise, Michael O., Martin Abegg, Jr., and Edward Cook. *The Dead Sea Scrolls: A New Translation*. San Francisco: Harper San Francisco, 1996.

Wiseman, D. J. "The Vassal Treaties of Esarhaddon." *Iraq* 20 (1958): 1–99.

Wright, Benjamin G. *The Letter of Aristeas: "Aristeas to Philocrates" or "On the Translation of the Law of the Jews."* Commentaries on Early Jewish Literature. Berlin: De Gruyter, 2015.

———. "Torah and Sapiential Pedagogy in the Book of Ben Sira." In Schipper and Teeter, *Wisdom and Torah*, 157–86.

Wright, David P. *Inventing God's Law: How the Covenant Code of the Bible Used and Revised the Laws of Hammurabi.* Oxford and New York: Oxford University Press, 2009.

Wright, Jacob. *Rebuilding Identity: The Nehemiah Memoir and Its Earliest Readers.* Beihefte zur Zeitschrift für die alttestamentliche Wissenschaft 348. Berlin: De Gruyter, 2004.

Wright, N. T. "4QMMT and Paul: Justification, 'Works,' and Eschatology." In Aang-Won (Aaron) Son, ed., *History and Exegesis: New Testament Essays in Honor of Dr. E. Earle Ellis for His 80th Birthday*, 104–32. New York and London: T & T Clark, 2006.

———. *What Saint Paul Really Said: Was Paul of Tarsus the Real Founder of Christianity?* Grand Rapids, MI: Eerdmans, 1997.

Xeravits, Geza. *Dualism in Qumran.* London and New York: Clark, 2010.

Yadin, Yigael, Jonas C. Greenfield, Ada Yardeni, and Baruch A. Levine. *The Documents from the Bar Kokhba Period in the Cave of Letters: Hebrew, Aramaic, and Nabatean-Aramaic Papyri.* Jerusalem: Israel Exploration Society, 2002.

Yarbro Collins, Adela, and John J. Collins. *King and Messiah as Son of God.* Grand Rapids, MI: Eerdmans, 2008.

Young, Frances. "Greek Apologists of the Second Century." In Mark Edwards, Martin Goodman, and Simon Price, eds., *Apologetics in the Roman Empire,* 81–104. New York: Oxford University Press, 1999.

Young, Stephen L. "Paul's Ethnic Discourse on 'Faith': Christ's Faithfulness and Gentile Access to the Judean God in Romans 3:21–5:1." *HTR* 108 (2015): 30–51.

Yuval, Israel. "All Israel Have a Portion in the World to Come." In Udoh et al., *Redefining First-Century Jewish and Christian Identities,* 114–38.

Zahn, Molly M. *Rethinking Rewritten Scripture: Composition and Exegesis in the 4Q Reworked Pentateuch Manuscripts.* Studies on the Texts of the Desert of Judah 95. Leiden: Brill, 2011.

Zangenberg, Jürgen, "Common Judaism and the Multidimensional Character of Material Culture." In Udoh et al., *Redefining First-Century Jewish and Christian Identities,* 175–93.

———. "Joseph und Aseneths Ägypten: Oder: Von der Domestikation einer 'gefährlichen' Kultur." In Reinmuth, *Joseph und Aseneth,* 159–86.

Zerbe, Gordon M. *Non-Retaliation in Early Jewish and New Testament Texts: Ethical Themes in Social Contexts.* Journal for the Study of the Pseudepigrapha 13. Sheffield: Sheffield Academic Press, 1993.

Zetterholm, Magnus. "Jews, Christians, and Gentiles: Rethinking the Categorization within the Early Christian Movement." In Ehrensperger and Tucker, *Reading Paul in Context*, 242–54.

———, ed. *The Messiah in Early Judaism and Christianity.* Minneapolis: Fortress, 2007.

———. "Paul within Judaism: The State of the Questions." In Nanos and Zetterholm, *Paul within Judaism,* 31–51.

Zuckerman, Constantine. "Hellenistic *politeumata* and the Jews: A Reconsideration." *SCI* 8–9 (1985–88): 171–85.

# INDEX OF SCRIPTURE AND OTHER
# ANCIENT SOURCES

# INDEX OF MODERN AUTHORS

# Lehigh

- start w/ Religion — teaching and research

> List Theory → Burke
> Music Diss →
> - Tying texts
> - Arch,
> - cog science

1st year sem.

Workshop — How to use using comics + films in the classroom

Seminar — origin of Religion

5 × $^{\$}_{5}$ = Museum of the Bible

- Why Religion Matters for Today's Climate

→ What is Rel really about
→ Origins of

Ess: Fantasy to Reality
    Intermedia... int.
    ... 
    - Backgrounds to xxy + Egy ...
    - Politics                    drod...
    = Tech + ...
    - Adam + the              Pirate
                              world
  People ... ... to super
     present

~ import stars + ... 
     ... in bible


    2d Temple
  Shepal med. ... 
- Is a criticism of ... a
       critique of heroes
- ...
  - heroes
  - ... ... - call of
     (de of ...         witches

CPSIA information can be obtained
at www.ICGtesting.com
Printed in the USA
LVOW03s0206210218
567336LV00002B/6/P